THE EARTHSCAN READER IN

Business
and the
Environment

To Mum, Dad and Ruth – with love and thanks
Richard Starkey, March 1996

For Chris
Richard Welford, March 1996

THE EARTHSCAN READER IN

Business
and the
Environment

EDITED BY

RICHARD WELFORD and
RICHARD STARKEY

EARTHSCAN

Earthscan Publications Ltd, London

In February 1995 Shell, with the permission of the UK government, announced its plans to dump Brent Spar – an oil installation thought to be loaded with toxic and radioactive sludge – in the North Atlantic. Shell's actions caused public outrage and a consumer boycott, and Greenpeace set up an operation to take over and occupy the rig in order to prevent the dumping.

Eventually, Shell bowed to public pressure and halted the dumping operation. The company is now seeking alternative disposal methods, and Brent Spar is currently in temporary storage in a Norwegian fjord.

The cover illustration for this book shows Brent Spar in the North Sea in June 1995. The supply boat *Torbas* is showering the rig with a water cannon, while a helicopter comes in with provisions for the two Greenpeace activists on board.

First published in the UK 1996 by
Earthscan Publications Limited

Copyright © Richard Welford, 1996

A catalogue record for this book is available from the British Library

ISBN: 1 85383 301 0 Paperback   1 85383 315 0 Hardback

Figures, typesetting and page design by PCS Mapping & DTP, Newcastle upon Tyne

Printed and bound by Biddles Ltd, Guildford and Kings Lynn

Cover design by Andrew Corbett

For a full list of publications please contact:

Earthscan Publications Limited
120 Pentonville Road
London N1 9JN
Tel: (0171) 278 0433
Fax: (0171) 278 1142
E-mail: sales@earthscan.co.uk

Earthscan is an editorially independent subsidiary of Kogan Page Limited and publishes in association with the WWF-UK and the International Institute for Environment and Development.

The environmental crisis is an outward manifestation of a crisis of mind and spirit. There could be no greater misconception of its meaning than to believe it is concerned only with endangered wildlife, human-made ugliness and pollution. These are part of it, but more importantly, the crisis is concerned with the kind of creatures we are and what we must become in order to survive.

Lynton T Caldwell
From *Living in the Environment*, by G Tyler Miller
(Wadsworth: Belmont, California, 1992)

Contents

PART I
PERSPECTIVES ON BUSINESS AND THE ENVIRONMENT

PART II
BUSINESS STRATEGY AND THE ENVIRONMENT

PART III
RESEARCH, DEVELOPMENT AND TECHNOLOGY

PART IV
TECHNIQUES FOR ENVIRONMENTAL IMPROVEMENT

PART V
BUSINESS AND THE ECONOMY

List of Illustrations

FIGURES

TABLES

Preface

There can be little doubt that humankind, and indeed the whole planet, is facing a severe environmental crisis, aspects of which include such problems as global warming, acid rain, ozone depletion, loss of biodiversity, topsoil erosion, tropical deforestation, desertification and groundwater depletion and pollution. This book examines the part that business has played in bringing about this crisis and examines the various ways in which it can help to protect the environment in the future.

What part has business played? It is business that produces the goods and services that meet so many of our needs, wants and desires, and it is this process of production that is responsible for much of the environmental degradation that has occurred and continues to take place. This is not to say that business is solely responsible for the damage that has occurred. (Governments must take some share of the responsibility, for it is governments that set the rules by which business plays the economic game and it is these sets of economic and legal rules that have allowed environmental degradation to occur. Some would also argue that as consumers we must share some of the responsibility in that we have consented to consume goods and services that have been produced by processes that are environmentally damaging.) However, the intimate connection between production and the health of the environment does mean that business has an important role to play in preventing further environmental damage.

From an environmental point of view, what production does is to turn resources into wastes. Every quantity of resources that enters the economic process must eventually emerge as the same quantity of waste. Of course, much of the resource input will go to make a product (this is the whole point of the exercise!) and so initially only a proportion of the resource input will emerge as waste. But when the product is used up, or wears out, it too re-enters the environment. Similarly, the energy used in production must eventually end up as waste heat. There is simply no escaping the fact that what goes into the economic process must come out of it and therefore the more resources are used, the more wastes need to be assimilated. Resource depletion and pollution are essentially the same problem, two sides of the same coin.

Obviously, current modes of production are having a severely damaging impact on the global environment and we believe that this impact must be reduced to a level which is environmentally sustainable. Sustainable development, which, since the Rio Earth Summit, in 1992, has been internationally accepted as the ultimate goal of environmental policy, requires the maintaining of global life-support systems or, more specifically, maintaining environmental sink capacities to assimilate wastes and maintaining environmental source capacities to generate raw materials. Sustainable production would therefore be production where the throughput of materials and energy was reduced to a level where the regenerative and assimilative capacities of environmental sources and sinks were maintained. This will have to be achieved in the face of an ever increasing global population (a population expected to at least double before it stabilizes) which will mean an increasing demand for goods and services. Achieving sustainable production under these circumstances is the enormous challenge we now face.

So what needs to be achieved is clear. This book is a contribution to the discussion about *how* it can be achieved, specifically the part that business can play in bringing about a sustainable future. It is not a text which simply describes what is going on in the field of corporate environmental management but one which attempts to build up a picture of the challenges facing business. Although traditional approaches to environmental management are considered within many of the contributions, most, if not all, of the authors recognize that these alone will not deliver sustainability. Throughout the text most of the contributors consider not only what needs to be done in the short term, but also outline some of the strategies which we need to consider in the medium to long term as we search for a more sustainable way of doing business. For some, this requires a complete re-evaluation of the way we do business and a challenge to many of the dominant ideologies which exist in the corporate world. Some contributors suggest that we should expect business to take a lead while others argue forcefully that business cannot achieve everything on its own and that there needs to be a new partnership between business, local and national governments, and individuals and pressure groups. A clear message emerges from the articles in this Reader: change will have to be fundamental.

All the articles included in this Reader have been chosen because they represent important contributions to the various debates and discussions that are taking place within the field of business and the environment. Indeed, this is the first book to bring together the work of leading experts in this field. A wide-ranging consultation process was undertaken as the first step in choosing the articles that appear in this Reader. A large Editorial Advisory Team, composed of recognized experts in the field of business and the environment (listed in the next section), were asked to suggest articles that would be suitable for the Reader and it was from the large and varied list that resulted that the final articles were chosen. Without the help of the Advisory Team we would not have been able to produce a book of such high quality and we sincerely thank the team members for their time and efforts.

The book is divided into five parts with small introductions raising key issues at the beginning of each. In Part I Paul Hawken and James Robertson outline rather different perspectives on business and the environment. They agree that the challenge facing us is huge, although their separate agendas for change are somewhat different. Hawken argues that business must see itself within the larger environment and be instrumental in taking a lead because no other institution other than business is really powerful enough to foster the necessary changes. Robertson puts his emphasis on the role of independent citizens and independent people's movements who must map out the route to a more sustainable future. The main message for us is that business does need to work co-operatively and effectively with a whole range of institutions and individuals if we are to move towards a sustainable future.

Part II considers how business strategies can and must integrate environment management. In a debate about how a link between competitiveness and environmentalism can lead the now ubiquitous win-win outcome, many contributors identify the important elements in that strategic approach. There is some disagreement about where the emphasis should lie, but authors such as Edward and Jean Stead remind us that we must develop a proper strategic vision. Their fundamental vision of sustainability starts with a vision of the firm and what it will become. Colin Hutchinson also reminds us of the very important human dimension in any strategic approach. He argues that the scale and the nature of the environmental challenge facing any organization requires a holistic approach where all staff at all levels are involved.

In Part III we look at the important issue of research, development and technology. In the introduction to this section Kenneth Green and Ian Miles remind us that technology is the result of social processes and that technology comprises not only things, but also the knowledge of how they work and the skills required to make them work effectively. The contributions begin with a critique of clean technology which is seen as much more than the simple technological fix solutions which we so often see in industry. Other chapters go on to call for new technological concepts and the need for a more vigorous pursuit of environmentally conscious basic research. David Fleming's contribution returns to the issue of technological fix where he argues that we simply cannot put all our trust in a technological solution to our problems. He suggests that social and cultural changes will be more crucial.

Part IV considers some specific techniques for environmental improvement. We could have filled the whole book with contributions in this area, but have deliberately chosen to focus on techniques which can push us beyond the more narrowly defined corporate environmental management and towards sustainable development. Rob Gray argues that we, as citizens, have a right to a detailed account of corporate environmental performance and explores ways in which the sustainability, or otherwise, of a company can be measured. Rolf Marstrander sees industry as a leader, co-operating with all stakeholders, establishing new social insights, new tools for decision-making, training systems and techniques for organizational development and a greater understanding of environmental issues. Richard Welford argues for a systems-based approach which puts more emphasis on auditing for sustainability and life-cycle assessment of products. But all contributors agree that we need to see a new, more fundamental approach and a commitment within every firm to go through radical change in its corporate culture.

In Part V we explore the linkages between business and the economy in which it operates. The relationship between business and government is of particular importance and the articles that have been chosen in this section look at business interaction with various levels of government. Anthony Ikwue and Jim Skea look at the part played by business in the formulation of the European Union's carbon/energy tax proposals and discuss what this tells us about business attitudes to the new models of policy-making being advocated by the EU. Michael Jacobs looks at the 'jobs versus environment' debate and concludes that environmental policies (both national and EU) do not, in general, destroy jobs and that many environmental measures are likely to be job-creating. Finally, Roger Levett examines the efforts being made at local government level to 'green' the local economy and shows that the approaches taken have brought real benefits to both businesses and the environment. He argues that a great deal more needs to be done at a national government level to allow business and local government to go further in their efforts.

After reading the contributions in this book we hope that the reader will be better aware of the complex issues facing business and have a view about the strategies, technologies and techniques which we need to develop in order to do business in a way which is consistent with sustainable development. The consistent message is that we must do more and that only a real commitment to change will enable us to act effectively. We must have a clear vision about the future and about how to do business within a more sustainable economy. We might not know precisely what sustainable development actually looks like in a business context, but the various contributions in this Reader do map out a clear path down which we should tread. That journey has started, but we have not got very far yet. We hope that this book will contribute to that journey.

This book would not have been possible without the help and support of a great many people. In addition to the individual contributors and the Editorial Advisory Team, we would particularly like to thank Kenneth Green for his commitment in helping us with Part III. Special thanks go to Carmel Milner who provided the much needed secretarial support to this project. Sue Hayward provided patient advice on all computing matters during the editing of this book which was much appreciated. Thanks also to all those who undertook the onerous task of checking the manuscript: Sangeeta Bhargava, Gordon Black, Michael Brophy, Eleanor Davies, Tina Goy, Amanda Knowles, Graym McMillan, Joe Milner, Leigh Morland, Alan Netherwood, Fiona Ryan, Charles Starkey, Dan Vale and William Young. And finally thanks to Jonathan Sinclair Wilson, Andrew Young, Jo O'Driscoll and Rowan Davies for their support during the preparation of this Reader.

Richard Welford
Richard Starkey

Editorial Advisory Team

Biographical Information on Authors

Roland Clift is Professor of Environmental Technology and Director of the Centre for Environmental Strategy at the University of Surrey. The many posts he holds include Chairman of the Engineering and Physical Sciences Committee of the Biotechnology and Biological Sciences Research Council (BBSRC) and he is a member of the Management Committee of the DTI/DoE Environmental Best Practice Programme. He is one of the few UK academics who are developing the life-cycle assessment of products known as 'cradle-to-grave analysis' and in the 1994 New Year's Honours he was awarded an OBE for his services to science and technology.

David Fleming is an economist, a consultant in environmental policy for government and business, and a consultant in corporate strategy for the financial services industry. He writes and lectures on environmental policy issues, specializing in the 'low output economy' – the economic and social stabilization issues arising in the event of a long-term failure of economic growth.

Rob Gray is Matthew Professor of Accounting and Information Systems in the Department of Accountancy and Business Finance at the University of Dundee. He is a qualified Chartered Accountant, Editor of the journal *Social and Environmental Accounting*, Director of the Centre for Social and Environmental Accounting Research at the University of Dundee and author/co-author of over 100 books, monographs and articles. His books include *Corporate Social Reporting: accounting and accountability* (1987), *The Greening of Accountancy* (1990) and *Accounting for the Environment* (1993).

Kenneth Green is a senior lecturer in technology and innovation management at the Manchester School of Management. He has a long-established interest in how industry responds to market, regulatory and public pressures by innovating: that is, by developing new products and processes. Currently, he leads a research group on business strategies for 'greening' technological innovation looking at what firms are doing to develop cleaner production methods and how firms' purchasing policies are influential in greening their suppliers. He is an active member of the international 'Greening of Industry Network'.

Paul Hawken has been described as America's leading green entrepreneur. He has put his principles into practice with the companies he has co-founded: Erewhon Foods, the first natural-foods wholesaler in the USA, and Smith & Hawken, a mail-order company selling cooking and garden products. His *Growing a Business* (1987) has been published in 28 languages and a television series based on the book has been broadcast in 115 countries. His most recent book *The Ecology of Commerce* was published in 1993. In 1995 he was named by the Utne Reader magazine as one of '100 Visionaries Who Could Change Our Lives'.

Colin Hutchinson is an Environmental Strategy Consultant and former Chairman of Sheppard Moscow Ltd, consultants in organization development. He is a Trustee of Global Action Plan (UK) and a member of the Council of AMED – the Developers' Network. He is author of *Vitality & Renewal: A Manager's Guide to the 21st Century* (1995) Adamantine Press.

Anthony Ikwue is a Research Fellow in the Programme on Environmental Policy and Regulation at the Science Policy Research Unit (SPRU), University of Sussex. He has previously worked at Loughborough University developing marketing and running short courses for environmental professionals and at Warren Springs Laboratories where he was involved in project management, research and development and environmental consultancy.

Michael Jacobs is an economist and Research Fellow at the Centre for the Study of Environmental Change, Lancaster University. He was formerly Managing Director of CAG Consultants, where he worked on environmental auditing and management and sustainable development policy with local authorities, government agencies and NGOs. He is author of *The Green Economy: Environment, Sustainable Development and the Politics of the Future* (Pluto Press, 1991).

Roger Levett has worked for CAG Consultants since 1992 and has been Environment Team Leader since 1994. He has led a number of the projects on the implementation of sustainable development for clients including the Department of the Environment, the European Commission, the OECD, the Countryside Commission and Natural Heritage, and a large number of local authorities. Roger helped to develop the Eco-Management and Audit Scheme for UK local government, researched and wrote *Greening Economic Development* for the Local Government Management Board (LGMB) and was also the main author of the LGMB's *Framework for Local Sustainability* and *Local Agenda 21 Principles and Process*.

Anita Longley graduated from the University of Wales, Cardiff, with a degree in Applied Biology. In 1988 she joined the Science and Engineering Research Council (SERC) as a scientific administrator and developed the Clean Technology Initiative. In 1992 she won a Churchill Fellowship and spent two months in Eastern Europe lecturing on Clean Technology. Anita is now responsible for the Process Industries Sector within the Engineering and Physical Sciences Research Council's (EPSRC) Innovative Manufacturing Initiative

Rolf Marstrander is Senior Vice President of Hydro Aluminium a.s., with responsibility for technology and ecology. His previous posts include Senior Vice President of Norsk Hydro a.s., Director and General Manager of the Norwegian State Pollution Control Authority, and Assistant Director of the Norwegian Scientific and Industrial Research Council.

Ian Miles is Director of Policy Research in Engineering, Science and Technology (PREST) at the Victoria University of Manchester. He moved there in 1990 after a long sojourn at the Science Policy Research Unit (SPRU) at the University of Sussex. His work has focused on innovation studies, especially with respect to the 'service economy' and social aspects of information technology and recently on issues surrounding 'clean technology'. His publications include *The Shape of Things to Come* (A Cawson, L Haddon and I Miles, 1995), *Development Technology and Flexibility: Brazil Faces the Industrial Divide* (J C Ferraz, H J Rush and I Miles, 1992) and *Mapping and Measuring the Information Economy* (I Miles with others, 1990).

Michael Porter is the C Roland Christensen Professor of Business Administration at the Harvard Business School and a leading authority on competitive strategy and international competitiveness. He is the author of 14 books, including *Competitive Strategy: Techniques for Analyzing Industries and Competitors* (1980 – now in its 45th printing), *Competitive Advantage: Creating and Sustaining Superior Performance* (1985) and *The Competitive Advantage of Nations* (1990). Professor Porter has served as an adviser on competitive strategy to many leading US and international companies. He has also served as an adviser to the US government, being appointed by President Reagan in 1983 to the President's Commission on Industrial Competitiveness.

James Robertson has worked in Whitehall (the Cabinet Office) and the City (directing inter-bank research), and as a parliamentary adviser (on public expenditure control), and now writes and speaks on the transition to people-centred, ecologically sustainable development. He is a trustee of the New Economics Foundation and is a Visiting Fellow (1995–96) at the Green College Centre for Environmental Understanding and Policy in Oxford. His books include *The Sane Alternative, Future Work* and *Future Wealth*.

Jim Skea is British Gas/Economic and Social Research Council (ESRC) Professorial Fellow in Clean Technologies, and Leader of the Programme on Environmental Policy and Regulation at the Science Policy Research Unit (SPRU) at the University of Sussex. He has taken a particular interest in the development of the acid rain issue in Europe and has co-authored a book on the subject, *Acid Rain*, published by Belhaven Press. He is a convening lead author for the second assessment of the Intergovernmental Panel on Climate Change (IPCC) and Director of the ESRC Global Environmental Change programme.

Richard Starkey is a research fellow in the Centre for Corporate Environmental Management (CCEM) at the University of Huddersfield. He has recently completed work on environmental management system standards and on corporate environmental reporting. Richard has previously worked in the Sustainable Development Research Unit at Friends of the Earth.

Edward and **Jean Garner Stead** are both Professors of Management at East Tennessee State University. Previously, they have served on the faculty of Western Illinois University and Ed has also served on the faculties of the University of Alabama and the University of Louisiana. They have been involved in environmental management research for over 15 years and are widely recognized and published in this field. Their 1992 book, *Management for a Small Planet: Strategic Decision Making and the Environment*, was a recipient of *Choice* magazine's 1992 Outstanding Academic Book Award. It is currently in its fourth printing and will be published in an expanded second edition in 1996.

Claas van der Linde is a member of the faculty at the St Gallen Graduate School of Economics in Switzerland, where he has been an Associate at the Research Institute of International Management (FIM) since October 1992. He specializes on issues of competitiveness and competition at the international and regional level. His current research focuses on the relationship between environmental regulation and international competitiveness. Dr van der Linde has researched and developed competitive strategies for cities, regions and entire countries. In 1992–93 he advised the government of a small European country on developing a comprehensive strategy to enhance its competitiveness. Currently he is advising a German state government on issues such as industrial cluster development and removing hurdles to competition.

Noah Walley was a consultant at McKinsey & Company from 1990 to 1994 where, as well as serving clients in the telecommunications and healthcare industries, he helped to launch the firm's environmental practice. Currently he works for Desai Capital Management, a venture capital firm in New York. Mr Walley has an MA from Oxford University in Modern History and a JD from Stanford Law School.

Richard Welford is Professor of Business Economics at the University of Huddersfield and is Director of the Centre for Corporate Environmental Management, a research unit based in the University's School of Business. He has published widely in the field of environmental management and his books include *Environmental Management and Business Strategy* (1993) and *Environmental Strategy and Sustainable Development* (1995). Richard is also a director of ERP Environment, a publishing company which produces a number of environmental journals, including *Business Strategy and the Environment, European Environment, Eco-Management and Auditing* and *Sustainable Development*.

Bradley Whitehead is a principal in the Cleveland office of McKinsey & Company and a leader of the firm's environmental practice. He has worked with clients throughout the Americas, Asia and Europe on a wide variety of environmental issues as they relate to business strategy. He has written and spoken widely on the subject of value-based environmental management and environmental partnerships. In addition to his corporate client base, Brad has worked with a number of environmental organizations and government institutions.

Part I

Perspectives on Business and the Environment

Introduction

Richard Welford

In its early stages, the environmental debate in industry was largely one of rhetoric rather than action. More recently, businesses have recognized the need to improve their environmental performance, but we have still not seen any radical shift in business practices which are capable of bringing about a lasting reversal of trends towards environmental destruction. While it is difficult for industry to refute the general need for environmental protection, their response has often been sporadic, initially adopting bolt-on strategies aimed at fine-tuning their environmental performance and, more latterly, developing management systems to achieve continual environmental improvement. There is clearly a need to continue to develop practical solutions and management techniques to meet the environmental challenge. However, it must be recognized that those solutions mean re-evaluating the very basis on which we do business.

Traditionally, the view of the corporate world has been based on the idea that the investments and innovations of industry drive economic growth and satisfy the demands of the consumer. However, in doing so, be it because of the resources that they consume, the processes that they apply or the products that they manufacture, business activity has become a major contributor to environmental destruction. Many reformists argued that we need to find new technologies and to develop more efficient methods of production. But more fundamentally we need to recognize that growth can no longer be a sole objective which stands alone and pays no heed to its environmental consequences now and into the future. Growth is only justifiable if it is associated with development which in itself needs to concentrate more directly on its environmental consequences. We know that the technological solution is insufficient in itself and we cannot assume that science and technology will cure the wrongs of the past and provide a new growth path. There is a need for a change in attitudes towards both consumption and production. Moreover, there is a need to look closely at the ethics of business and to discover new forms of industrial organization and culture which, while existing in a broad free market framework with due regulation, promote sustainable development in the future.

The first two chapters of this Reader begin to address many of these issues. In 'A Teasing Irony' by Paul Hawken, the conflicts between environmental improvement and the wish to 'maintain business as usual' are explored. Hawken argues that we are on the verge of a transformation which could make business unrecognizable in the future. But business must recognize that it is the problem and must be part of the solution. To date, however, business has often thwarted any constructive changes in our relationship with the environment because it is not properly designed to adapt to the situation we face. The internationalization of business, in particular, has produced a dominant culture that believes that all resource and social inequalities can be resolved through invention, finance and growth. Moreover, the free market has done little to address environmental degradation.

Hawken's message is nevertheless not one of despair. He argues that if business can take on a new language, a new role and a new way of seeing itself within the larger environment, then it can discover the remedies and undertake the transformations necessary to reverse worldwide environmental damage. Individuals and governments will also have roles to play in such a transformation. However, Hawken concludes by arguing that perhaps no other institution other than business is really powerful enough to foster the necessary changes.

James Robertson's contribution to the debate in 'Shaping the Post-Modern Economy: Can Business Play a Creative Part?' is more sceptical about business being able to lead the way into a greener, more people-centred, more holistic future. He argues that conventional approaches to economic development are flawed and that the process of transformation will be a very complicated one. Moreover, few business leaders and thinkers really understand the scale of the challenge they face.

Robertson points towards power structures and dominant value systems as being the major impediment to achieving a sustainable future. But, like Hawken, his message is not necessarily one of despair. However, his solution is different. Rather than seeing business as the main driving force, his emphasis is on independent citizens and independent people's movements who must map out the route to a new tomorrow.

These first two contributions point to very similar impediments to environmental improvement and make us think about the scale of the challenge which lies ahead. However, their solutions and perspectives are rather different and it is left to you, the reader, to think carefully about the structures and cultures which are at the root of both the problem and the solution.

A Teasing Irony

Paul Hawken

I have come to believe that we in America and in the rest of the industrialized West do not know what business really is, or, therefore, what it can become. Perhaps this is a strange remark, given that free-market capitalism is now largely unchallenged as the economic and social credo of just about every society on earth, but I believe it's correct. Despite our management schools, despite the thousands of books written about business, despite the legions of economists who tinker with the trimtabs of the $21 trillion world economy, despite and maybe because of the victory of free-market capitalism over socialism worldwide, our understanding of business – what makes for healthy commerce, what the role of such commerce should be within society as a whole – is stuck at a primitive level.

The ultimate purpose of business is not, or should not be, simply to make money. Nor is it merely a system of making and selling things. The promise of business is to increase the general well-being of humankind through service, a creative invention and ethical philosophy. Making money is, on its own terms, totally meaningless, an insufficient pursuit for the complex and decaying world we live in. We have reached an unsettling and portentous turning point in industrial civilization. It is emblematic that the second animal ever to be 'patented' is a mouse with no immune system that will be used to research diseases of the future and that mothers' milk would be banned by the food safety laws of industrialized nations if it were sold as a packaged good. What's in the milk besides milk and what's suppressing our immune system is literally industry – its by-products, wastes and toxins. Facts like this lead to an inevitable conclusion: businesspeople must either dedicate themselves to transforming commerce to a restorative undertaking, or march society to the undertaker.

I believe business is on the verge of such a transformation, a change brought on by social and biological forces that can no longer be ignored or put aside, a change so thorough and sweeping that in the decades to come business will be unrecognizable when compared to the commercial institutions of today. We have the capacity and ability to create a remarkably different economy, one that can restore ecosystems and protect the environment while bringing forth innovation, prosperity, meaningful work and true security. As long as we continue to ignore the evolutionary thrust and potential of the existing economy, the world of commerce will continue to be in a state of disorder and constant restructuring. This is not because the worldwide recession has been so deep and long, but because there is a widening gap between the rapid rate at which society and the natural world are decaying and the agonizingly slow rate at which business is effecting any truly fundamental change.

This turbulent, transformative period we now face might be thought of as a system shedding its skin; it signals the first attempts by commerce to adapt to a new era. Many people in business, the media and politics do not perceive this evolutionary step, while others who do understand, fight it. Standing in the way of change are corporations who want to continue worldwide deforestation and build coal-fired power plants, who see the storage or dumping of billions of tons of waste as a plausible strategy for the future, who imagine a world of industrial farms sustained by chemical feed-stocks. They can slow the process down, make it more difficult, but they will not stop it. Like a sunset effect, the glories of the industrial economy may mask the fact that it is poised at a declining horizon of options and possibilities. Just as internal contradictions brought down the Marxist and Socialist economies, so do a different set of social and biological forces signal our own possible demise. Those forces can no longer be ignored or put aside.

That the title *The Ecology of Commerce* [from which this chapter is taken] reads today as an oxymoron speaks to the gap between how the earth lives and how we now conduct our commercial lives. We don't usually think of ecology and commerce as compatible subjects. While much of our current environmental policy seeks a 'balance' between the needs of business and the needs of the environment, common sense says there is only one critical balance and one set of needs: the dynamic, ever-changing interplay of the forces of life. The restorative economy envisioned and described in this book respects this fact. It unites ecology and commerce into one sustainable act of production and distribution that mimics and enhances natural processes. It proposes a newborn literacy of enterprise that acknowledges that we are all here together, at once, at the service of and at the mercy of nature, each other and our daily acts.

A hundred years ago, or even 50 years ago, it did not seem urgent that we understand the relationship between business and a healthy environment, because natural resources seemed unlimited. But on the verge of a new millennium we know that we have decimated 97 per cent of the ancient forests in North America; every day our farmers and ranchers draw out 20 billion more gallons of water from the ground than are replaced by rainfall; the Ogalala Aquifer, an underground river beneath the Great Plains, larger than any body of fresh water on earth, will dry up within 30 to 40 years at present rates of extraction; globally, we lose 25 billion tons of fertile topsoil every year, the equivalent of all the wheatfields in Australia. These critical losses are occurring while the world population is increasing at the rate of 90 million people per year. Quite simply, our business practices are destroying life on earth. Given current corporate practices, not one wildlife reserve, wilderness, or indigenous culture will survive the global market economy. We know that every natural system on the planet is disintegrating. The land, water, air and sea have been functionally transformed from life-supporting systems into repositories for waste. There is no polite way to say that business is destroying the world.

Having served on the boards of several environmental organizations, I thought I understood the nature and extent of the problems we face. But as I prepared to write this chapter, I reviewed much of the new literature in the field and discovered that the more I researched the issues, the more disquieting I found the information. The rate and extent of environmental degradation is far in excess of anything I had previously imagined. The situation was like the textbook illusion in which the viewer is presented with a jumble of halftone dots that reveals the image of Abraham Lincoln only when seen from a distance. Each of the sources I worked with was one such dot, not meaningless in itself, but only a part of the picture. The problem we face is far greater than anything portrayed by the media. I came to understand well the despair of one epidemiologist who, after reviewing the work in her field and convening a conference to examine the effects of chlorinated compounds on embryonic development, went into a clinical depression for six months. The revelations of that conference were worse than any single participant could have anticipated: the immune system of every unborn child in the world will soon be adversely and irrevocably affected by the persistent toxins in our food, air and water.

A subtler but similarly disquieting development was reported by the *New York Times* (1992) in an article entitled 'The Silence of the Frogs'. At an international conference on herpetology (the study of amphibians and reptiles), while 1,300 participants gave hundreds of official papers on specialized subjects, none had focused on the total picture. Pieced together informally in the hallways and in the lunch lines at the conference was the fact that frogs are disappearing from the face of the earth at an inexplicably rapid rate. Even more disturbing was the conclusion that these populations are crashing not merely in regions where there are known industrial toxins, but also in pristine wilderness areas where there is abundant food and no known sources of pollution. The implications of such a die-off go beyond frogs. The human endocrine system is remarkably similar to that of fish, birds and wildlife; it is, from an evolutionary point of view, an ancient system. If endocrine and immune systems are failing and breaking down at lower levels of the animal kingdom, we may be similarly vulnerable. The reason we may not yet be experiencing the same types of breakdown seen in other species is because we gestate and breed comparatively rather slowly. On complex biological levels such as ours, bad news travels unhurriedly, but it eventually arrives. In other words, something unusual and inauspicious may be occurring globally at all levels of biological development: a fundamental decline that we are only beginning to comprehend and that our efforts at 'environmentalism' have failed to address.

From this perspective, recycling aluminium cans in the company cafeteria and ceremonial tree plantings are about as effective as bailing out the *Titanic* with teaspoons. While recycling and tree planting are good and necessary ideas, they are woefully inadequate. How can business itself survive a continued pattern of worldwide degradation in living systems? What is the logic of extracting diminishing resources in order to create capital to finance more consumption and demand on those same diminishing resources? How do we imagine our future when our commercial systems conflict with everything nature teaches us?

Constructive changes in our relationship to the environment have thus far been thwarted primarily because business is not properly designed to adapt to the situation we face. Business is the practice of the possible: highly developed and intelligent in many respects, it is, however, not a science. In many ways business economics makes itself up as it progresses, and essentially lacks any guiding principles to relate it to such fundamental and critical concepts as evolution, biological diversity, carrying capacity and the health of the commons. Business is designed to break through limits, not to respect them, especially when the limits posed by ecological constraints are not always as glaring as dead rivers or human birth defects, but are often expressed in small, refined relationships and details.

The past one hundred years have seen waves of enterprise sweep across the world, discovering, mining, extracting, and processing eons' worth of stored wealth and resources. This flood of commerce has enriched capital cities, ruling families, powerful governments and corporate élites. It has, therefore, quite naturally produced a dominant commercial culture that believes all resource and social inequities can be resolved through development, invention, high finance and growth – always growth. For centuries, business has been able to claim that it is the organizational key to 'unlocking the hidden wealth of creation for distribution to the masses'. By and large, that has been true. But now, rather than distributing the wealth of the present, we are stealing the wealth of the future to enrich a society that seems none the less deeply troubled about its 'good fortune'. While democratic capitalism still emanates an abundant and optimistic vision of humankind and its potential, it also retains the means to negate this vision in ways that are as harmful as any war.

It is lamentable to extinguish a species by predation and killing, whether the perceived gain is leather, feather, pelt or horn. But how will we explain that the disappearance of songbirds, frogs, fireflies, wildflowers and the hundreds of thousands of other species that will become extinct in our lifetime had no justification other than ignorance and denial? How will we explain to our children that we knew they would be born with compromised immune systems, but we did nothing? When will the business world look honestly at itself and ask whether it isn't time to change?

Having expropriated resources from the natural world in order to fuel a rather transient period of materialistic freedom, we must now restore no small measure of those resources and accept the limits and discipline inherent in that relationship. Until business does this, it will continue to be maladaptive and predatory. In order for free-market capitalism to transform itself in the century to come, it must fully acknowledge that the brilliant monuments of its triumph cast the darkest of shadows. Whatever possibilities business once represented, whatever dreams and glories corporate success once offered, the time has come to acknowledge that business as we know it is over. Over because it failed in one critical and thoughtless way: it did not honour the myriad forms of life that secure and connect its own breath and skin and heart to the breath and skin and heart of our earth.

Although the essential nature of commerce has not altered since the very first exchange of coin for corn, the power and impact of corporate capitalism have increased so dramatically as to dwarf all previous forms of international power. No empire – Greek, Roman, Byzantine, British or any other – has had the reach of the modern global corporation, which glides easily across borders, cultures and governments in search of markets, sales, assets and profits. This institutional concentration of human energy and creativity is unparalleled in history.

But if capitalism has pillaged, it has also delivered the goods, and in quantities that could not have been imagined just two generations ago. Providing that abundance is one of the central goals of doing business, and those who believe in capitalism believe that goal must be facilitated at every opportunity. Government is key to this strategy.

The Conservative view of free-market capitalism asserts that nothing should be allowed to hinder commerce. Sacrifices might be called for here and there, but in the end, the environment, the poor, the Third World will all benefit as business more fully realizes its potential. In the new world order of the post-Communist age, free-market capitalism promises to be the secular saviour, echoing theologian Michael Novak's homage: 'No system has so revolutionized ordinary expectations of human life – lengthened the life-span, made the elimination of poverty and famine thinkable, enlarged the range of human choice – as democratic capitalism.' This view of business was fervently embraced by the recent Republican adminis-trations, who found in Novak's words an unimpeachable affirmation of many of their programmes of deregulation.

Invoking the sanctity of the free market to prove that present business practices are sound and constructive, and using it to rebut every charge of ecological malfeasance is, at its heart, dishonest. Historically, we have given industry great latitude for its miscalculations because there was no science sufficiently developed to inform society of industrialism's effects. One hundred years ago, industrial cities were coated with grime and cut off from the sun by permanent palls of smoke; the citizens were beset by disease; the very conditions under which workers toiled and died were inhumane and exploitative. These conditions had their analogue in the industrial processes of waste and despolia-tion, and were the direct costs of the Industrial Revolution. It took many decades before an appreciation of the social and environmental damage spread beyond a small circle of Marxists and muckrakers to society as a whole. Today, business-people readily concede the abuses of the early days of this revolution, but they do not wholly and genuinely acknowledge the more threatening abuses perpetuated by current practices. Troubling untruths lie uneasily within a colossal economic system that denies what we all know while it continues to degrade our world, our society and our bodies. Business economists can explain in detail the workings of the modern corporation, its complex interrelation with financial markets, how its holdings might be valued on a discounted cash-flow basis, or the dynamics of global competitive advantages. These pronouncements and equations promise hope but they cannot explain – much less justify – the accelerating extinction of species, the deterioration of human health, the stress and anguish of the modern worker, and the loss of our air, water and forests. In short, they cannot explain the consequences of their actions.

Why, then, do we accept the excuses? Why do we hand business a blank cheque and exempt enterprise from the responsibility for maintaining social values? One reason might be that, like the conferees, we have only a piecemeal view of events. We have no hallways to congregate in and so accumulate the overall image of cumulative destruction. Furthermore, their actions are defended – I daresay have to be defended – because most of us are dependent upon them for our livelihood. Even a declining General Motors still employs nearly 600,000 people. A supermarket chain such as American Stores employs 200,000 or more. The 400 companies profiled in *Everybody's Business Almanac* employ or support one-fourth of the US population. The largest 1,000 companies in America account for over 60 per cent of the GNP, leaving the balance to 11 million small businesses. The average large business is 16,500 times larger than the average small business. And since much of the population is now employed by these large corporations, they naturally see their interest as being linked to the success and growth of their employers. Such fealty resembles the allegiance that sustained feudal baronies: the vassal serfs believed that the lord who exploited them was better than the uncertainty of no lord at all. But in the competitive world of modern commerce, loyalty to the system prevents an objective examination of how market capitalism can also work against those who serve it.

Tinkering with the system will not bring species back to life, profit-sharing schemes do not restore our wetlands, donating money for a new production of *Don Giovanni* will not purify our water, nor will printing annual reports on recycled paper save us. The dilemma that confronts business is the contradiction that a commercial system that works well, by its own definitions, violates the greater and more profound ethic of biology. Succeeding in business today is like winning a battle and then discovering that the war was unjust. Of course, the discovery that a loyalty which has served so well can betray so badly is a troubling concept for any culture.

From my observations, most people involved with commerce who are also educated about environmental issues care deeply about commerce's effects. At the same time, such people feel anxious about their jobs, the economy and the future in general. The environment becomes just one more thing to worry about. It looms in the future at a time when we are beset with many other, more immediate, concerns. It is like being a single parent when the dog has run away, the children are fighting, the dinner is burning, the babysitter hasn't shown up, we are late for the PTA meeting, and have just spilled gravy on the carpet when someone doing a survey knocks at the door and wants to know how we feel about the proposed landfill at the edge of town. Although the landfill will affect our lives in the future, we are afflicted with pressing problems today. Similarly, when environmental issues are presented to businesspeople as one more cost and one more regulation, 'doing the right thing' becomes burdensome and intrusive. And the way our economy is organized today, businesspeople are right: doing the right thing might indeed put them out of business.

We should not be surprised, then, that there is a deep-seated unwillingness to face the necessary reconstruction of our commercial institutions so that they function on behalf of our lives. Business believes that if it does not continue to grow and instead cuts back and retreats, it will destroy itself. Ecologists believe that if business continues its unabated expansion, it will destroy the world around it. This book will discuss a third way, a path that restores the natural communities on earth but uses many of the historically effective organizational and market techniques of free enterprise.

The act of doing business carries with it ethical import, so, given the dominance of business in our time, we must ask the question: 'how do we want our principal economic organism to conduct its commerce?' Is it to be as a marauder, high on the food chain, pinning its prey with ease? If business is based on the notion that it can call upon nature without constraint to submit to the objectives of commerce, it will destroy the foundation on which rests the society it has pledged to serve. Though 'nothing seems foul to those that win', the cultures that have been previously harmed and the lands we have forfeited must now be reincorporated into the body economic. Business must judge its goals and behaviour, not from inherited definitions of the corporate culture, but from the perspective of the world and society beyond its self-referential borders.

If business is prepared to re-examine its underlying assumptions and listen to ecologists, botanists, toxicologists, zoologists, wildlife management experts, endocrinologists, indigenous cultures and victims of industrial processes, without the selective filter of its internal rationale and biases, it will not only fulfil its own agenda of contributing to society by providing products, jobs and prosperity, but will also initiate a new era of ecological commerce, more promising and ultimately more fulfilling than the industrial age that preceded it.

While business teaches us effective forms of human organization, environmental science reveals that those forms do not necessarily preserve the natural resources that are the basis of our well-being. While business teaches how to gain financial wealth, ecological understanding demonstrates that wealth to be ultimately illusory unless it is based on the principles and cyclical processes of nature. The dialogue reconciling these dichotomies will be the fundamental basis for economic transformation.

In order for this dialogue to succeed, business needs a new language, a new role, a new way of seeing itself within the larger environment. Business parlance is a specific, rarefied and, for most of us, borrowed language. It is useful when it describes the mechanics of commerce, but fails when we try to connect it with biology, society, or feeling, yet this specialized dialect has established itself as the planetary lingua franca. In the language and accounting of classical economics, resources do not technically exist until they are drilled, extracted, pumped or cut; in biological accounting, the principle is reversed. Business language reduces living transactions to costs and exchange value. From this semantic strait emerges the talk of trade-offs and compromises between growth and conservation, jobs and ecology, society and biodiversity, American competitiveness and resource pricing.

The language of commerce sounds specific, but in fact it is not explicit enough. If Hawaiians had 138 different ways to describe falling rain, we can assume that rain had a profound importance in their lives. Business, on the other hand, only has two words for profit – gross and net. The extraordinarily complex manner in which a company recovers profit is reduced to a single numerically neat and precise concept. It makes no distinctions as to how the profit was made. It does not factor in whether people or places were exploited, resources depleted, communities enhanced, lives lost, or whether the entire executive suite was in such turmoil as to require stress consultants and outplacement services for the victims. In other words, business does not discern whether the profit is one of quality or mere quantity.

It is understandable that a more meticulous language has not developed in this area because, until relatively recently in history, business has not been central to how societies and cultures defined themselves. In fact, its hegemony is still debated, especially by politicians who cling to the outdated vanity that government is in control. While governments still retain the power to wage war, defend territory and issue currency, they can do little to create wealth except to work with business. Given that power, the modern corporation needs to expand and widen its vocabulary to become more environmentally accurate and culturally enduring. Without this new vocabulary, capitalism will become the commercial equivalent of the Holy Roman Empire: an amorphous global-corporate state taking what it needs and forcing smaller governments into financial subjugation, since no governing body can retain political legitimacy without money, credits, investment and the sanction of the international business community. Biologically speaking, such unbalanced dominance will precipitate the demise of global capitalism, just as it brought down Rome.

Free-market purists believe that their system works so perfectly that even without an overarching vision, the marketplace will attain the best social and environmental outcome. The restorative economy is organized in a profoundly different way. It does not depend upon a transformed human nature, but it does require that people accept that business is an ethical act and attempt to extend to commerce the interwoven, complex and efficient models of natural systems. Current commercial practices are guided by the promise that we can stay the way we are, live the way we have, think the thoughts of old, and do business unburdened by real connections to cycles, climate, earth or nature. Restorative economics challenges each of these assumptions.

The economics of restoration is the opposite of industrialization. Industrial economics separated production processes from land values, the land from people and, ultimately, economic values from personal values. In an industrial, extractive economy, businesses are created to make money. Their financing and ability to grow are determined by their capacity to produce money. In a restorative economy, viability is determined by the ability to integrate with or replicate cyclical systems in its means of production and distribution. The restorative economy would invert many fundamentals of the present system. In such an economy there is the prospect that restoring the environment and making money would be the same process. As in nature, business and restoration should be part of a seamless web. Environmental protection should not be carried out at the behest of charity, altruism or legislative fiats. As long as it is done so, it will remain a decorous subordinate to finance, growth and technology.

Business has three basic issues to face – what it takes, what it makes and what it wastes – and the three are intimately connected. First, business takes too much from the environment and does so in a harmful way; second, the products it makes require excessive amounts of energy, toxins and pollutants; and finally, the method of manufacture and the very products themselves produce extraordinary waste and cause harm to present and future generations of all species, including humans.

The solution for all three dilemmas is three fundamental principles that govern nature. First, waste equals food. In nature, detritus is constantly recycled to nourish other systems with a minimum of energy and inputs. We call ourselves consumers but the problem is that we do not consume. Each person in America produces twice his weight per day in household, hazardous and industrial waste, and an additional half-ton per week when gaseous wastes such as carbon dioxide are included. An ecological model of commerce would imply that all waste has value to other modes of production so that everything is either reclaimed, reused or recycled. Second, nature runs off current solar income. The only input into the closed system of the earth is the sun. Last, nature depends on diversity, thrives on differences and perishes in the imbalance of uniformity. Healthy systems are highly varied and specific to time and place. Nature is not mass produced.

Many industries are now trying to resource their raw materials to take into account sustainability, methods of extraction, means of processing, and impact on local cultures and ecosystems. For example, Herman Miller, the Knoll Group and Wal-Mart have all committed themselves to paying higher prices for sustainably produced timber. They join many thousands of businesses, most much smaller, in recognizing their responsibility to initiate an ecological commerce. They should not have to pay more for raw materials that are produced in a sustainable manner. They should pay less. It should be possible to secure sustainably produced raw materials without the extraordinary expense and effort that is required today. Preserving life should be the natural result of commerce, not the exception.

In order to accomplish this, we need to rethink our markets entirely, asking ourselves how it is that products which harm and destroy life can be sold more cheaply than those that don't. Markets, so extremely effective at setting prices, are not currently equipped to recognize the true costs of producing goods. Because of this, business has two contradictory forces operating upon it: the need to achieve the lowest price in order to thrive if not survive in the marketplace, and the increasingly urgent social demand that it internalize the expense of acting more responsibly towards the environment.

Without doubt, the single most damaging aspect of the present economic system is that the expense of destroying the earth is largely absent from the prices set in the marketplace. A vital and key piece of information is therefore missing in all levels of the economy. This omission extends the dominance of industrialism beyond its useful life and prevents a restorative economy from emerging.

Despite that disadvantage, the restorative economy is beginning to prosper. In the United States alone, an estimated 70,000 companies are already committed to some form of environmental commerce that competes with businesses that are not willing to adapt. The impulse to enhance the economic viability of life on earth *through* the recognition and preservation of all living systems is one that is becoming increasingly central to religion, science, medicine, literature, the arts and women. It should be the dominant theme of generations to come.

Because the restorative economy inverts ingrained beliefs about how business functions, it may precipitate unusual changes in the economy. As will be discussed in later chapters, the restorative economy will be one in which some businesses get smaller but hire more people, where money can be made by selling the absence of a product or service, as is the case where public utilities sell efficiency rather than additional power, and where profits increase when productivity is lowered. Corporations can compete to conserve and increase resources rather than deplete them. Complex and onerous regulations will be replaced by motivating standards.

Author Ivan Illich (1974) has pointed out that the average American is involved with his or her car – working in order to buy it, actually driving it, getting it repaired, and so on – for 1600 hours a year. This means when all car mileage in a given year is divided by the time spent supporting the vehicle, the average car owner is travelling at an average speed of five miles per hour. To attain the speed of a bicycle, we are devastating our cities, air, lungs and lives, while bringing on the threat of global warming. It is the restorative, not the industrial, economy that can and will address such aberrations. Restorative entrepreneurs may not be as mediagenic as Wall Street tycoons because their companies will be smaller, quieter and less glamorous. However, it is the former which challenge the economic superstitions and fantasies that determine our concept of what a business should be.

A business works best when it has a positive vision, good morale, definite standards and high goals. Such an organization is receptive to ideas that reinforce corporate growth as it is currently defined, but may be hostile to ideas that are critical of the basic system. After all, a successful business is in effect an advertisement that so much is working, that so many people have done a good job. This intolerance of seemingly irrelevant advice and information allows a company to concentrate single-mindedly on carving out market niches, but it also creates a yawning chasm between business economics and good ecology. If corporations were to take worldwide environmental degradation as seriously as they take demographic changes in consumer tastes, they would discover that the remedies for their depredation are more profound and transformative than the measures currently proposed by a few businesses, or even by many of the large environmental organizations. Perhaps that is why they have not delved more deeply.

On the other hand, it is important to understand that we consumers are accessories before and after the fact. We create businesses just as much as businesses create our wants. We have been enthralled by the opportunities, wealth, image and power offered by business success. We like our comfortable lifestyles if we have them and want them if we don't. Business has intrinsic flaws, but they are created and reinforced by our own desires. Essayist and farmer Wendell Berry (1992) writes:

> 'However destructive may be the policies of the government and the methods and products of the corporation, the root of the problem is always to be found in private life. We must learn to see that every problem that concerns us ... always leads straight to the question of how we live. The world is being destroyed – no doubt about it – by the greed of the rich and powerful. It is also being destroyed by popular demand. There are not enough rich and powerful people to consume the whole world; for that, the rich and powerful need the help of countless ordinary people.'

The restorative economy comes down to this: we need to imagine a prosperous commercial culture that is so intelligently designed and constructed that it mimics nature at every step, a symbiosis of company and customer and ecology. This book, then, is ultimately about redesigning our commercial systems so that they work for owners, employees, customers and life on earth without requiring a complete transformation of humankind. Much has been written linking our environmental crises to everything from patriarchal values to a spiritual malaise that has accompanied industrial riches. But this is counter-productive. Science teaches us that everything is interdependent: the respiration of the blossom of a lily in the backwaters of the Rio Negro in the Amazon basin affects the weather in New York. At the same time, if we are to be effective in our lives, we have to find workable techniques and programmes that can be put into practice soon, tools for change that are easily grasped and understood, and that conform naturally to the landscape of human nature.

If this scenario sounds dreamy and Arcadian it is because we assume that economic forces only exploit and destroy. *The Ecology of Commerce* [from which this chapter is taken] will try to demonstrate that while this has been largely true up until now, and will continue to be true for some time in the future, this behaviour is not the inherent nature of business, nor the inevitable outcome of a free-market system. It is merely the result of the present commercial system's design and use. The human matures from a state of grasping ego gratification to some degree of ethical awareness. Our species is not perfect, but is certainly not depraved either. Like individuals, societies also mature, albeit more slowly and haltingly. America ended institutionalized slavery, for example, but is only now beginning to address its many forms of racism. I believe our economic system can also mature in a similar fashion.

In *The Merchant of Prato*, Iris Origo's recent account of a fourteenth-century

Tuscan merchant, Francisco di Marco Datini, we recognize in Datini all the anxiety, fear, and daily vicissitudes of a contemporary. Datini was worried about his investments, taxes, and penalties. As his successes grew, so, too, did his insecurity. He devoted increasing amounts of his riches to acts of piety, from penance to munificent acts for the church, but largess could not alleviate Datini's guilt and maniconia (the stress of constant worry and doubt). Datini sounds like every modern businessperson who, approaching death, ponders not the deals that got away, but the humanity and society forsaken in the rush to profit.

Annie Dillard recounts a story with a similar moral in *Pilgrim at Tinker Creek*. A 19th-century French physician, having perfected the first procedure to remove cataracts safely, travelled throughout his country restoring sight to people blinded from birth. He witnessed two distinct reactions when people saw the world for the first time: some were appalled at the squalor and ugliness (one person blinded himself in order to forget what he had seen and return to what he imagined the world to be); the greater number were overwhelmed by the beauty, vastness and colours of the world, their senses flooded with the newness and variety of a creation that had heretofore lacked its most beautiful dimension.

We who are in business today are like these fortunate French men and women. Scientists, naturalists, essayists and poets are offering us vision, a means with which to see and understand the splendour and sacredness of life. They help us understand that we, as Whitman wrote, 'are nature, long have we been absent, but now we return'. Will we tear out our eyes, ignore what we are being shown, and continue commercial practices that demean the earth and hasten that day when everything we hold precious has been destroyed? Will we die burdened with Datini's many regrets, or will we exult and exclaim, grateful for the possibilities, the newness, the knowledge offered us to transform our world and our relationship to it?

Many believe that it is too late, that at this moment in our history we cannot be redeemed through existing institutions. It is true that in our lifetime we cannot restore felled ancient forests, vanished wetlands, ghostly strip mines, or the ruined lives of toxic waste victims. Contemporary events support Oliver Goldsmith's longstanding declaration, 'Honour sinks where commerce long prevails.' It takes a serious leap of faith to imagine a transformed *Fortune 500*, a restorative sustainable economy that will offer full employment, more security, better education, less fear, more stability and a higher quality of life. But I believe this will happen because prior forms of economic behaviour no longer produce the desired results. Even though the GNP of the United States grew considerably during the 1980s, three-fourths of the gain in pre-tax income went to the richest 1 per cent. The majority of Americans had less money and lower incomes than they did when the decade began. Primarily, what growth in the 1980s produced was higher levels of apprehension, violence, dislocation, and environmental degradation.

Gordon Sherman, the founder of Midas Muffler, once wrote (1986):

> *There is a teasing irony: we spend our lives evading our own redemption. And this is naturally so because something in us knows that to be fully human we must experience pain and loss. Therefore, we are at ceaseless effort to elude this high cost, whatever the price, until at last it overtakes us. And then in spite of ourselves we do realize our humanity. We are put in worthier possession of our souls. Then we look back and know that even our grief contained our blessing.*

Ironically, business contains our blessing. It must, because no other institution in the modern world is powerful enough to foster the necessary changes. Perhaps during the many battles between environmentalists and businesspeople we have been asking the wrong question all these years. As generally proposed, the question is, 'How do we save the environment?' As ridiculous as it may first sound to both sides, the question may be, 'How do we save business?'

Business is the problem and it must be a part of the solution. Its power is more crucial than ever if we are to organize and efficiently meet the world's needs. This book [*The Ecology of Commerce*] contains quite a few horror stories perpetrated by large, respected, well-managed businesses. I do not cite them to demonize corporations, but to lay the foundation and basis of understanding that will allow us to re-create these companies. Commerce can be one of the most creative endeavours available to us, but it is not worthy of business to be the convenient and complicit bedfellow to a culture divorced from nature. While commerce at its worst sometimes appears to be a shambles of defilement compared to the beauty and complexity of the natural world, the ideas and much of the technology required for the redesign of our businesses and the restoration of the world are already in hand. What is wanting is collective will.

REFERENCES

Berry, W (1992) 'Conservation is Good Work' *The Amicus Journal* Winter 1992, p 33

Illich, I (1974) *Energy and Equity* Calder and Boyars, London

Sherman, G (1986) 'Commencement Address' California School of Professional Psychology

2

Shaping the Post-Modern Economy: Can Business Play a Creative Part?

James Robertson

FACING UP TO THE FUTURE

Human history has evolved from one age to another. Each successive age has had its own closely interrelated set of characteristics. These have included the way people lived their lives, the social institutions which organized and influenced them, the technologies they used, and their dominant consciousness or world view – including their values and theories, and their understanding of themselves, one another, nature, and the supernatural or divine. So we Europeans can look back to: a prehistoric era; ancient societies like Greece and Rome; a medieval age, from, say, AD1000 to 1500; and the modern period, starting in about AD1500 with people like Columbus and Machiavelli and Copernicus, and peaking at the time of the Enlightenment rather more than 200 years ago.

This modern era is now coming to an end. As we reach the final years of the present millennium we are entering a new phase of human history. The new post-modern, post-European patterns of life and thought will reflect the emergence of a pluralistic one-world human community in which people will relate in new post-modern ways to themselves, to one another, to nature, and to what they sense is behind all those and provides the framework and context for them.

Many people today – including most people in business, government, science, the professions and academe – conditioned as they are by the scientific world view of the modern age, think of the future as something independent of themselves. Their interest in the future, if they have one, is to forecast it, adapt to it, and survive and succeed in it however it turns out. Business planning and forecasting is a typical example.

That approach is not fully human. The emerging post-modern perception is that we humans help to create the future, each one of us, whether we like it or not, whether consciously or by default. We cannot escape our share of responsibility for choosing or failing to choose between possible futures and for helping one of them to come about. In Francis Bacon's words, 'it is given only to God and angels to be lookers on in this theatre of man's life'. In other words, we are ourselves part of the process of transforming the old era that is now dying into the new one that is to be born. We have to choose what part we shall try to play in this historic transition.

Big business and big finance, like big government, have been characteristic of the modern age. Orientated towards money values as a pseudo-objective norm, they have reduced to monocultural uniformity much of the multicultural richness that existed in the world before them and will blossom again in the future. Twenty years' working for them, followed by twenty years as an independent home-based person, have made me conscious of how big a gap there is between the organizational and career values still prevalent in those industrial-age institutions and the evolving values and perceptions of people outside them. I now experience quite a severe culture shock when I find myself discussing matters that affect the human condition and its future with a roomful consisting almost entirely of middle-aged men in business suits.

Some of my friends believe that business can lead the way into a greener, more people-centred, more holistic, post-modern future. I am doubtful. I sense that big business, big finance and big government – in the forms in which we now know them – are aspects of a past which will soon be on the defensive, in retreat. But this does not mean they are now unimportant. Quite the reverse. The way they respond to that situation will help to determine whether the transition to the post-modern period of world history will be moderately smooth or whether it will involve worldwide collapse and chaos.

In this contribution, then, I discuss the challenge confronting business. I describe how awareness has grown through the 1980s and 1990s of the need to change direction to a new path of human progress. From that point of view, conventional economic development and thought are flawed by a number of damaging faults. New principles are emerging, which will be relevant to every aspect of post-modern economic life and thought. The shift to this new path of progress will involve a complex process of transformation, in which many different kinds of people will have many different parts to play. I end by asking whether it is realistic to expect big business to play a creative part and, if not, what conclusion we should draw.

A CHANGE OF DIRECTION

The Need for a New Direction

There are now rather more than 5 billion people in the world. Well over 1 billion, more than ever before, live in absolute poverty. And the activities of today's population are threatening – in many cases already destroying – the planet's ecosystems. According to demographic projections, world population will rise to 10 billion, or perhaps 15 billion, before it stabilizes some time in the next century. That implies a doubling or trebling of our present ecological impact, even with little development in the poor countries of the majority world. Meanwhile, the rich minority (about 1 billion people) are consuming and polluting 10 to 20 times as much per capita as the 'less developed' majority (about 4 billion). And today's vision of 'development' and economic growth, relentlessly propagated worldwide by governments, rich-country businesses, mainstream economists and the media, offers all humans on earth the prospect of rising to present rich-country levels. If that prospect were ever achieved, it would multiply today's ecological impacts many more times over – and that would be catastrophic.

New Approaches

As this became increasingly apparent through the 1980s, pressure grew for new approaches to environment and development, integrating environmental conservation with the kind of development that would emphasize the eradication of poverty. At the official level, the World Commission on Environment and Development (the Brundtland Commission) published its report, *Our Common Future*, in 1987.[1] There followed five years of worldwide preparations for the United Nations Conference on Environment and Development (UNCED), or 'Earth Summit', which was held in Rio de Janeiro in June 1992.

Governments, multinational businesses and scientific organizations have been heavily involved throughout. Their approach has been to modify, rather than radically reorientate, the conventional direction of development based on free-market capitalism and conventional economic growth. This 'establishment' approach failed to achieve agreement at Rio between the governments of the rich North and those of the poor South on the measures needed to switch the world to a new, sustainable path of development. As a result, the official Rio conference is widely judged to have failed to rise to the challenge it was held to meet, although the very fact of its being held at all marked a much-needed new recognition of the seriousness of the problems facing humankind.

At the unofficial level, a growing grassroots concern for more equitable and sustainable development has surfaced in the last few years in a new worldwide coalition of non-governmental organizations (NGOs) and citizens' and people's movements. This rapidly growing network of informal links between environmental and development pressure groups (such as the World Wide Fund for Nature and Christian Aid) in the rich North, environmental and other citizens' groups in the former Socialist economies, and alternative development, environmental and social justice movements in the South, brought thousands of people from all parts of the world to the Global Forum which was held in Rio in parallel with the official UNCED. To quote one participant: 'Being present with perhaps 10,000 individuals in a common quest for sanity on earth was a strangely uplifting experience.'

As part of this wider movement for change, a new economics movement has emerged. The Other Economic Summit (TOES) and the New Economics Foundation in Britain and similar groups in many other countries are now focusing specifically on the changes needed in economic ways of life, economic institutions and practices, and economic understanding and theorizing.

Supporters of the new economics movement believe a more radical economic reorientation is necessary than business and governments yet understand. They do not believe that sustainable development can be achieved by conventional free-market economics any more than by the planned economies of the former Soviet bloc. They see the collapse of Communism and the decline of Socialism not as 'the end of history' but as the first stage in a larger global transition that will also involve the transformation of conventional capitalism.

---

1 The World Commission on Environment and Development (Brundtland Commission) Report (1987) *Our Common Future*, Oxford University Press, Oxford

The Significance of 1992

The UNCED Earth Summit was the first time in history that representatives of all the peoples of the world met to discuss 'our common future'. That it coincided with Columbus' 500th anniversary year underlined its historical significance. It prompted many people to reflect on the outcomes of 500 years of Euro-American expansion and world domination, and the shape of the new, post-European period of history that may now be beginning.

What was needed as the outcome of UNCED was that the various charters, conventions, treaties and declarations reached should add up to a global compact on the following lines:

- The rich countries would commit themselves to a new path of progress, concentrating on improving their people's quality of life, while reducing their per capita ecological impact to a level sustainable by an eventual world population of, say, 10 billion people. This might eventually involve, for example, a cut of four-fifths in present per capita fossil-fuel energy consumption.
- The 'less developed' (and also the formerly Socialist) countries would accept that they can never attain today's rich-world per capita levels of material throughput, pollution and waste. They, too, would commit themselves to a new, post-Euro-American, people-centred, ecologically sustainable path of development, including population-stabilization policies and an enhanced development role for women.
- In their own self-interest, the rich countries would commit themselves to effective technical and financial support for sustainable development elsewhere in the world, recognizing that ecological damage there affects global ecosystems on which their own future depends.
- They would also recognize their huge development debt to the 'less developed' countries, arising from the damage done by the rich countries, both to the global environment and to other peoples over the last few hundred years. They would agree to write off the outstanding Third World financial debts as part of the new global compact for sustainable development.
- Finally, agreement would be reached on restructuring the United Nations as a system of one-world governance which would, for example:
  - Include regular annual procedures for negotiating, monitoring and reporting progress on national and global policies for equitable and sustainable development.
  - Bring world economic institutions – notably the IMF, the World Bank and GATT – within that policy framework, under the democratic supervision of the UN Assembly acting on behalf of the one-world human community.

The UNCED conference in Rio did not come anywhere near reaching agreement on these lines. This reinforced already existing doubts about the willingness and capacity of the business-dominated Western world to provide world leadership. Reaching some such agreement is the first challenge the peoples of the world still face, as we confront our common future.

CONVENTIONAL ECONOMIC DEVELOPMENT AND THOUGHT

Origins of the Modern Economic World View

The key features of today's conventional economic outlook originated with the founding fathers of secular, modern European thought. Following the European breakout (by Columbus and others) of 500 years ago and the subsequent breakdown of the medieval Christian world view, it took some time – nearly 300 years – for the modern European world view to crystallize in its place. Among the thinkers in that intervening period who helped to shape it were René Descartes, Francis Bacon, Isaac Newton and Thomas Hobbes. Theirs were among the ideas on which Adam Smith built when, as part of the 'Enlightenment' of the eighteenth century, he systematized the modern approach to economic life and thought.

Descartes' division of reality into the two categories, *res cogitans* and *res extensa* (thinking matter and extended matter), led to the concentration of knowledge and science on those aspects of human experience and understanding which are material and measurable and outside ourselves. His analytical method also encouraged us to split those aspects of reality into separate fields, so that now our conventional way of understanding wealth and the processes of creating wealth – the province of economics and business – is divorced from our understanding of other important things such as health, wisdom and the divine – which belong to the quite separate professional and academic disciplines of medicine, philosophy and theology.

Bacon encouraged knowledge and science to focus on harnessing and exploiting the resources of nature. He told us to torture nature in order to learn her secrets, so that we could use her for 'the relief of the inconveniences of man's estate'. Hence another key feature of modern economic and business progress.

Newton led science to interpret reality in the form of mechanistic, mathematically structured, value-free systems, in no need of ethical or divine intervention to keep them going. Thus, science now teaches us to understand the workings of the universe in terms of numbers and to assume that neither the universe itself nor any of its component parts are guided by purposes or moral choices. Conventional economics follows suit. The belated, marginal addition of 'business ethics' to the business curriculum only underlines the limited attention given by business to ethical considerations.

What most people remember about Hobbes is his argument that, since in fact, regardless of theory, moral and divine law do not effectively control human behaviour, people must submit to control by an earthly sovereign, otherwise their lives are bound to be 'solitary, poor, nasty, brutish and short'. Hobbes' significance for modern economic thinking, however, is that, like Machiavelli, he taught his successors to see human society not as it ought to be but as it actually appeared to be – a competitive struggle for power. For many people, success in economic life now means being more successful than other people – or at least keeping up with the Jones. And the mainspring of business activity is the competition to succeed, or at least survive, in national and international markets.

Adam Smith followed Descartes in excluding from his economic analysis the less tangible aspects of human experience and activity, such as those we now call 'participation', 'self-fulfilment' and 'self-development'. He followed Bacon in accepting that economic life was about exploiting the resources of nature for human advancement. He followed Hobbes in interpreting economic life as a competitive struggle for power over other people, and, in particular, over other people's labour and its products. He followed Newton in explaining economic life as a value-free system, governed by its own impersonal laws. Although Smith himself, as a moral philosopher, may have regarded the 'invisible hand' of supply and demand as providential, his successors have taken it to mean that neither God nor ethics have a part to play in economic life. If everyone pursues his or her own self-interest, the economic system will work in the interest of all: 'It is not from the benevolence of the butcher, the brewer or the baker that we expect our dinner, but from their regard to their own interest.'

Smith also took it for granted that economic life revolves around money – prices, wages, profits, rents, etc. The growing importance of numerical data in modern science had been paralleled by the growing importance of monetary values in modern economic life. On the supremacy of quantitative data in modern scientific knowledge, Lord Kelvin later explained:

> *When you can measure what you are speaking of and express it in numbers, you know that on which you are discoursing, but when you cannot measure it and express it in numbers, your knowledge is of a very meagre and unsatisfactory kind.*

As with knowledge, so with value. Money puts numbers on value, and conventional economic understanding regards as very meagre and unsatisfactory the value of goods, services and work (such as what used to be called 'women's work'), which are not paid for with money. In conventional economic analysis, if you cannot count the money value of something, it does not count. There is no place for qualitative considerations in economic valuation and no such thing as intrinsic value. Business, as we know it today, lives and dies by the value of money.

Damaging Features of Conventional Economic Development

That brief historical background explains some of the damaging features of conventional economic progress and business success, including the prevailing direction of technological development and the degree of economic dependence on military technologies and military production that the world is saddled with today.

1. Conventional economic progress has systematically extended dominance/dependency relationships. It has deprived people and local communities of the capacity for self-reliance. It has made them dependent on powerful people and organizations, and impersonal economic factors over which they can have no control. For example, the enclosures in countries like Britain drove the 'common people' off the land, deprived them of their self-reliant subsistence livelihoods and made them dependent on paid labour. The same pattern is repeated in countries like Brazil and Indonesia today, where the tribal people are driven out of the forests to make way for logging or ranching, and the peasants are driven off their lands to make way for large dams. Many of us certainly now enjoy greater material comfort than our ancestors, but at the cost of having become dependent on remote

employers to provide us with work, on remote businesses and other organizations to provide us with the means of daily life, on a remote bureaucratic state to provide us with welfare and security, and on the remote impersonal forces of national and international financial markets to decide whether we shall keep our houses and our jobs.

2. The conventional path of economic progress and business success is ecologically damaging. This needs no further elaboration. Almost everyone is now aware of the part played by business activities in promoting global warming, holes in the ozone layer, acid rain, pollution of air and water, deforestation, soil erosion and desertification, overfishing, and other such threats to human well-being and survival.

3. The conventional modern understanding is that economic life should be treated as if it were amoral and value-free. 'Don't confuse ethics with economics' is one of the first lessons economics students have to learn. Unfortunately, nature abhors a vacuum, and, in practice, the ethical vacuum in modern economic life has been filled with the values of power and ambition, competition and greed, envy and fear. So the conventional 'free market' within nations and between nations means that the rich minority inevitably get richer while an increasing number of people get poorer and more dependent. Community and family life are damaged by the increasing mobility of labour and capital which national and global free-market competition demands. Business contributes importantly to 'progress' of this kind.

4. Modern economic life and understanding have been too much preoccupied with money and monetary calculation. The dominating role of money in modern life, and the dominating role of financial institutions and occupations in modern society, reflect an overemphasis on quantitative as opposed to qualitative values. Money worship has become a religion for many people in industrialized countries, and to many of those it brings disillusion and dissatisfaction – widespread diseases of affluence, spiritual poverty and misery.

5. Following Adam Smith's focus on the wealth of nations, modern economic understanding and organization still put the nation state at the centre. Conventional economic policy is still too much concerned with competition between nations, and not enough with the wealth of people or the earth, or of the household or the local community. The international economic game of winners and losers increases the potential for international conflict and war – a factor in the increasing militarization of many societies – just as the national economic game of winners and losers sharpens internal sectional conflict.

6. Closely related to each of the earlier points, modern economic life and thought – business civilization – are heavily biased towards masculine rather than feminine drives and values.

These damaging features of the conventional modern approach to economic life are of a fundamental nature. They cannot be rectified by minor modifications, only by a fundamental reorientation based on a different set of principles.

THE NEW ECONOMICS

Principles

The following principles underlie the thinking of the new economics movement about the new direction for economic progress and the new basis for economic understanding that are now needed:

1. The new direction should positively *enable and empower* communities and nations, especially those in today's majority world, to take control over their economic lives. It should positively foster a high degree of co-operative and community self-reliance.
2. It should positively *conserve* the earth and all its resources. If for no other reason, human survival and self-interest now requires this. But increasing numbers of people also feel that the new direction of economic progress should not be narrowly anthropocentric. It should not attach overriding importance to the interests of humankind.
3. It should positively *encourage ethical choice* in economic life and the reintroduction of ethical values into economic understanding.
4. It should *emphasize qualitative as well as quantitative values* in economic life, valuing unpaid as well as paid activities and recognizing that many important things cannot be bought and sold, and understanding that many important decisions, public as well as personal, cannot be based on monetary calculations of costs and benefits.
5. It should recognize that we are now a one-world human community, for which we need to evolve fair trading arrangements as part of a decentralizing, multi-level, one-world economy that will be enabling for people, conserving for the earth, and respectful of cultural and religious pluralism.
6. It should recognize that, both for its own sake and because it will make an essential contribution to the five points above, the new direction of economic progress must *emphasize feminine values and the key role of women* in economic life, and the importance of a new masculine/feminine balance.

Application of the Principles

People in the new economics movement are working to apply these principles to every aspect of economic life and thought, including the following:

*   the ways people live;
*   the activities of the household;
*   local economies (for example, city economies);
*   national economies and national economic policies;
*   supranational economic developments – for example in Europe;
*   the global economy, including international trade;
*   businesses and other organizations;
*   money: taxes, incomes, currency, credit, debt, etc;
*   work;

- technology and industry;
- energy;
- food and agriculture;
- transport, housing and planning;
- rights of future generations;
- methods of economic measurement and analysis.

To give a few illustrative examples, increasing attention is now being paid in a number of countries to:

- The desirability and feasibility of replacing existing taxes on incomes with new taxes on energy.
- The proposal that all citizens should receive an unconditional basic income from the community, which would reduce their dependence on getting a job and liberate them to work in other ways.
- The scope for enlarging the part played in the economy by co-operatives, community businesses and other 'third sector' enterprises.
- The scope for revising company mission statements and professional codes of conduct to incorporate value statements.

THE PROCESS OF CHANGE AND TRANSFORMATION

Within the new economics movement there are differences of emphasis on how the change of direction will come about. But the following would carry broad agreement.

Negative factors, as well as positive action, will play their part. Particular industrial disasters like Chernobyl, the *Exxon Valdez* and Bhopal will continue to reinforce a more general awareness that things are going wrong – such as the growing risk of skin cancer from holes in the ozone layer, the growing congestion and pollution caused by road traffic or the growing damage caused by an international financial system that has been allowed to run out of control. Pressure for greater personal accountability on the part of business and financial leaders will increase. Awareness that we cannot long continue on our present path will continue to spread. The prospect of breakdown will loom larger. The need for change will continue to be highlighted by environmental and developmental NGOs and pressure groups.

When it comes to positive action, to create the breakthrough to the new path, the possibilities are almost unlimited. There are pieces of the action for everyone. The following are some examples:

1. *Lifestyle changes.* These include many kinds of personal action, many quite small and humble, to change one's own patterns of living, eating, spending, saving, working, travelling, leisure and household management.
2. *Economic, social and political changes.* This kind of action can take many forms. It is about changing social institutions (like the tax system) and organizational procedures (like the publication of relevant statistics) so that they legitimize ethical values and influence people's behaviour for better rather than worse. It includes seeking to change the organization for which one works from

within, supporting outside pressure group action – for example, for environmental conservation – taking part in active politics, using one's money power (one's saving and investing) in one way rather than another, taking part in many other forms of non-violent direct action, communicating the need for particular changes, and so on. Again, individual involvement is supported and reinforced by a growing number of NGOs, facilitating organizations and pressure groups across a very wide range of action.

3. *New technology development.* This kind of action is about developing and spreading the use of technologies that are enabling and conserving, such as soft energy technologies. There is an important role here for inventors and innovators, scientists and engineers, industrialists and business people, politicians and government officials, as well as for citizen purchasers, investors and voters. Appropriate technology organizations are already pioneering in many countries.

4. *New economics thinking and research.* There is action here both within the economics profession and outside it:
   – Economists can work, as increasing numbers are doing, to include in economic analyses the values and costs (as of natural resources) which conventional economists have hitherto ignored.
   – Meanwhile, non-economists (and economists, too, for that matter) can help to put conventional economics in its proper place, realizing that many really important decisions have to be based on more than a calculation of money values, and that other forms of knowledge and experience are just as relevant to the way we conduct our economic lives.

5. *The ecology of change.* These various ways of acting are mutually reinforcing. Each occupies its own niche in the ecology of change. There are limits to what each person can undertake, and different souls have different roles. But we can all try to understand the larger picture, while acting on our own part of it. 'Think globally, act locally' is a phrase often used to suggest the action philosophy of the new economics, though, as many are now aware, we have to act globally too.

CAN BUSINESS MEET THE CHALLENGE?

Few business leaders and thinkers yet appear to understand the scale of the challenge they face. They have learned to talk about 'sustainable development', but they behave as if what has to be sustained is the onward stampede of the Gadarene swine. They have not yet recognized that conventional economic progress – which encourages an eventual world population of 10 or 15 billion people to seek the high-consumption, high-pollution lifestyles of today's rich countries – is hopelessly unsustainable. Few have yet begun to grasp the massive scale of the economic conversion that this demands. They appear to see the challenge for business as basically the same as before: to adapt to changing demands – of customers; investors; workers; affected communities; local, national and international government agencies; voters; pressure groups, etc. And their goal still seems to be to achieve the same kind of corporate success as now.

Take green consumerism. This is now promoted as a marketing ploy, a straightforward means to conventional business and financial success. On a longer view, however, the green consumer will be seen to have been a red herring, a distraction from the need to reduce consumption altogether.

But could the big business of today, given the constant pressure to maximize shareholder profits in predatory, impersonal, international financial markets, expect to survive if it took the path of reduced consumption, reduced production, reduced throughput and reduced turnover for which a sustainable future calls? Is it reasonable to expect business to take initiatives to solve the problem of environmental sustainability or other important problems, such as worldwide poverty, unemployment and ill health? Would it be realistic to expect today's financial institutions to take the lead in developing national and international financial systems which actually serve the well-being of the billions of people whose lives they now damage and destroy?

The answer, I fear, is 'No'. If business and financial leaders consider these really important problems at all, they have to put them to one side as someone else's responsibility. To accept responsibility for them would mean redefining business goals and business success and evolving a new, more holistic, less instrumental corporate culture. Business leaders cannot be expected to do that. Their overriding priority must be to survive and succeed in today's corporate jungle. Moreover, having risen in the corporate culture that exists today – money-maximizing, value-free, careerist – they are themselves too deeply conditioned to today's business values and horizons.

I fear, therefore, that it is only prudent for us, as people and citizens, to suspect that our business and financial (and political) leaders may be floundering in uncharted seas, like the Communist leaders in Eastern Europe in 1989, without the capacity to confront the historic challenge of their time, even if they were able to recognize it. It is only realistic to accept that people pursuing career success and survival in business and finance, and in politics and government, find it virtually impossible to escape from the power structures and dominant value systems which enclose them, that they cannot step out of line if they want to stay in the game.

This is not a counsel of despair. It is a guide to practical action. We must recognize that only independent citizens and independent people's movements are free to map out the route to a new tomorrow and lead the way along it, that business and financial leaders will not be able to initiate the necessary changes, and that only if we compel them to follow our lead will they be able to take the right course. If we recognize that, we can then act to ensure not only that the post-modern economy serves the needs of people and the earth, but also that the transition to it will be smoother and less chaotic than it would otherwise be.

Part II

Business Strategy and the Environment

Introduction

Richard Welford

Corporate strategy has been driven by different forces in the past, from production pressures, personnel pressures and more lately from information pressures. This decade as well as the next shows clear signs of corporate strategy being driven by environmental pressures. Major changes in corporate strategy are clearly visible due to increased environmental concerns from stakeholders and the belief that being 'green' pays through cost reduction and market entry. In the 1970s, environmental management was regarded by companies with little enthusiasm. More recently, companies have begun to regard environmental management as a strategic tool for gaining competitive advantage. This usually implies incorporating environmental management into the overall business strategy. However, the most important aspects of that business strategy are open to considerable debate. In this part of the book many of those debates are aired and various authors make an attempt to describe a strategic vision for the future.

In 'America's Green Strategy', Michael Porter points out that apparent conflicts between economic competitiveness and environmental management are a false dichotomy, stemming from too narrow a view of the sources of prosperity and a static view of competition. Perhaps surprisingly he suggests that strict environmental regulations do not inevitably hinder competitiveness and that a concentration on environmental technology can lead to competitive advantage. However, the type of win-win strategies typified in the view of commentators such as Porter are seen as unrealistic by Noah Walley and Bradley Whitehead in 'It's Not Easy Being Green'. They argue that concentrating on enhancing the efficiency and effectiveness of environmental spending may not have the rhetorical appeal of win-win talk but, in the long run, will be far more effective.

Walley and Whitehead argue that environmental issues can be broken down into three broad categories: strategic, operational and technical, each requiring a distinctive managerial approach. But the overriding message is that it is a hard-headed approach based on business experience and a concentration on shareholder value (rather than compliance, emissions or costs) which will bring about sustainability in the future. Such a position is hardly likely to go unchallenged, but it will also have its supporters. In 'The Challenge of Going Green' various commentators put forward their own views on the win-win debate.

Joan Bavaria's view is that Walley and Whitehead's arguments ignore the ability of managers to think creatively. She suggests that companies must challenge their reason for being or their core competencies, and questions, for example, whether an oil company is in the oil business long term or in the fuel business, or in the energy business. Daniel Esty builds on the Porter hypothesis by arguing that the ability to innovate and develop new technologies is a greater determinant of economic success than traditional factors of comparative advantage. Further, it is argued that government must bear responsibility for establishing regulatory conditions that promote economic creativity and efficient business responses to environmental demands. Kurt Fischer and Johan Schot argue that we need to go further than simply concentrating on shareholder value and that new relationships with employees, environmental groups, customers and the public at large are needed to widen the scope of accountability.

In 'Green and Competitive: Ending the Stalemate', Michael Porter and Claas van der Linde argue that tensions exist between environmental regulation and competitiveness only if we take a static view of business. In the world of dynamic competition companies find innovative solutions to environmental pressures from stakeholders. Moreover, the authors argue that regulation can actually provide the push which encourages the innovations leading to new profitable opportunities. Regulation can also be justified on the grounds of information provision, education and the need for the ubiquitous level playing-field.

Porter and van der Linde go on to argue that the process of globalization makes traditional notions of comparative advantage obsolete. We need to turn our attentions to the use of resources which add value to the consumer, increasing competitiveness and facilitating environmental improvement through innovation. There is therefore a need for a paradigm shift which recognizes that environmental improvement is good business.

In 'Strategic Management for a Small Planet', Edward and Jean Stead present an appealing approach based on the development of a proper strategic vision. Their vision of sustainability starts with a vision of the firm and what it will become. Strategic management is then about moulding the firm's core values into actions. They argue that sustainability must be a core value because it supports a strategic vision of firms surviving over the long term by integrating their need to earn an economic profit with their responsibility to protect the environment. Economic success and the health of the ecosystem are therefore inextricably linked. Their conclusion revolves around a need for a new concentration on high-quality products where environmental damage would simply be seen as a quality defect.

In his article on 'Corporate Strategy and the Environment', Colin Hutchinson puts much greater emphasis than many other authors on the human dimension. He argues that the scale and the nature of the environmental challenge facing any organization is such that it becomes apparent sooner or later that the strategic approach can only be developed successfully if staff at all levels are involved. Therefore, to achieve a sustainable business, opportunities should be provided to enable people from top management to the shop floor to come to terms with their changing responsibilities. Hutchinson also argues strongly that many organizations are going to find that the implications of moving towards a sustainable future will only be possible if the issue of culture change is tackled as part of the business strategy.

3

America's Green Strategy

Michael Porter

Do strict environmental standards make American industry less competitive in international markets? Many observers answer 'Yes'. Richard Darman, director of the Office of Management and Budget, has quipped that 'Americans did not fight and win the wars of the 20th century to make the world safe for green vegetables'.

The conflict between environmental protection and economic competitiveness is a false dichotomy. It stems from a narrow view of the sources of prosperity and a static view of competition. Strict environmental regulations do not inevitably hinder competitive advantage against foreign rivals; indeed, they often enhance it. Tough standards trigger innovation and upgrading. In my book *The Competitive Advantage of Nations* (Porter, 1990), I found that the nations with the most rigorous requirements often lead in exports of affected products.

Although the US once clearly led in setting standards, that position has been slipping away. Until the passage of the Clean Air Act in 1990, itself the result of 12 years of foot-dragging, Congress had passed little environmental legislation since the mid-1970s. Today the US remains the only industrialized country without a policy on carbon dioxide, and our leadership in setting environmental standards has been lost in many areas. Even Japan, a nation many think of as relatively unconcerned about the environment, has moved ahead of the US in important fields. Japan's NO_x emission standards for vehicles are significantly more stringent than those in the US and Europe: its stationary SO_x and NO_x standards are set in terms of rigorous daily (versus yearly) average hourly emissions.

As other nations have pushed ahead, US trade has suffered. Germany has had perhaps the world's tightest regulations in stationary air-pollution control, and German companies appear to hold a wide lead in patenting, and exporting, air-pollution and other environmental technologies. As much as 70 per cent of the air pollution-control equipment sold in the US today is produced by foreign companies. Britain is another case in point. As its environmental standards have lagged, Britain's ratio of exports to imports in environmental technology has fallen from 8:1 to 1:1 over the past decade.

In contrast, the US leads in those areas in which its regulations have been the strictest, such as pesticides and the remediation of environmental damage. Such leads should be treasured and extended. Environmental protection is a universal need, an area of growing expenditure in all the major national economies

($50 billion a year in Europe alone) and a major export industry. Without competitive technology, America will not only forsake a growth industry, but more and more of our own environmental spending will go to imports.

Even in the broader economy, strict environmental codes may actually foster competitiveness. Exacting standards seem at first blush to raise costs and make firms less competitive, particularly if competitors are from nations with fewer regulations. This may be true if everything stays the same, except that expensive pollution-control equipment is added.

But everything will not stay the same. Properly constructed regulatory standards, which aim at outcomes and not methods, will encourage companies to re-engineer their technology. The result in many cases is a process that not only pollutes less but lowers costs or improves quality. Processes will be modified to decrease the use of scarce or toxic resources and to recycle wasted by-products. The 3M Company, for example, estimates that its 'Pollution Prevention Pays' programme has saved $482 million since 1975, while eliminating more than 500,000 tons of waste and pollutants, and has saved another $650 million by conserving energy.

Strict product regulations can also prod companies into innovating to produce less polluting or more resource-efficient products that will be highly valued internationally. As a result of the US proposed phase-out of chlorofluorocarbons (CFCs), for example, Du Pont and other American firms are pioneers in finding substitutes.

This is not to say that all companies will be happy about tough regulations: increased short-term costs and the need to redesign products and processes are unsettling at the least. The aversion to tough standards will be particularly strong in industries that feel threatened by international competition, as is too often the case in America today. The car industry, for example, has been fighting mandates to improve fuel efficiency, even though meeting them could stimulate innovations that made products more competitive.

The strongest proof that environmental protection does not hamper competitiveness is the economic performance of nations with the strictest laws. Both Germany and Japan have tough regulations, and both countries continue to surpass the US in GNP growth rates and rates of productivity growth. Japan has become a world leader in developing pollution-control equipment and cleaner, more efficient processes. It is noteworthy that in America many of the sectors subject to the greatest environmental costs have improved their international trade performance, among them chemicals, plastics, synthetics, fabrics and paints.

Turning environmental concern into competitive advantage demands that we establish the right kind of regulations. They must stress pollution prevention rather than merely abatement or clean-up. They must not constrain the technology used to achieve them, or innovation will be stifled. And standards must be sensitive to the costs involved and use market incentives to contain them.

Because US environmental regulations have traditionally violated these principles, the substantial amount we spend on protecting the environment has not yielded the benefits it could have. In the 1970s, for example, ambient air-quality standards encouraged tall smokestacks, some as high as 800 feet, which exported pollution somewhere else instead of reducing it. Even today, most standards are met with end-of-pipe technology, where equipment is simply added to the end of a process.

The resurgence of concern for the environment, then, should be viewed not with alarm but as an important step in regaining America's pre-eminence in environmental technology. The Environmental Protection Agency must see its mandate as stimulating investment and innovation, not just setting limits.

In companies, the 'Chicken Little' mind-set that regulation inevitably leads to costs and an adversarial posture towards regulators must be discarded. Environmental protection can benefit America's competitiveness if we simply approach it properly.

REFERENCES

Porter, M (1990) *The Competitive Advantage of Nations* Macmillan, London

4

It's Not Easy Being Green

Noah Walley and Bradley Whitehead

For years, the goals of business and the environment seemed hopelessly irreconcilable. According to common wisdom, what helped one would almost certainly harm the other. Yet nearly a decade of 'green' initiatives in the world's corporations has given rise to a more optimistic mind-set which promises the ultimate reconciliation of environmental and economic concerns. In this new world, both business and the environment can win. Being green is no longer a cost of doing business; it is a catalyst for constant innovation, new market opportunity and wealth creation.

Everyone from American vice president Al Gore to Harvard Business School Professor Michael Porter has sung the praises of being green. In fact, Gore argues, making environmental improvements is often the best way to increase a company's efficiency and, therefore, profitability. Gore and other proponents of this new popular wisdom cite an increasing number of projects that benefit the environment and create financial value. As an example of such a 'win-win' project, Gore points to 3M's 'Pollution Prevention Pays' programme, a group of over 3,000 mainly employee-generated projects, which have reduced 3M's emissions by over 1 billion pounds since 1975 while saving the company approximately $500 million.

Questioning today's win-win rhetoric is akin to arguing against motherhood and apple pie. After all, the idea that environmental initiatives will systematically increase profitability has tremendous appeal. Unfortunately, this popular idea is also unrealistic. Responding to environmental challenges has always been a costly and complicated proposition for managers. In fact, environmental costs at most companies are sky-rocketing, with little economic payback in sight.

In industries such as petroleum and chemicals, which are already plagued with overcapacity, fierce competition and declining margins, a company's ability to respond to environmental challenges in a cost-efficient manner may well determine its viability. A major North American chemical company, for example, was enjoying an internal rate of return of 55 per cent on employee-generated environmental initiatives similar to the win-win opportunities Gore cites. But when those impressive returns were added to the internal rate of return on *all* corporate environmental projects, the return dropped to a negative 16 per cent.

We do not argue that win-win situations do not exist; in fact, they do, but they are very rare and will likely be overshadowed by the total cost of a company's environmental programme. Win-win opportunities become insignificant in the face of the enormous environmental expenditures that will never generate a positive financial return.

Texaco, for example, plans to invest $1.5 billion per year over a five-year period on environmental compliance and emission reductions for a total investment of over $7 billion, an amount three times the book value of the company and twice its asset base. In other words, the company plans to double its asset base on projects expected to provide little, if any, revenues. Can anyone argue convincingly that an investment of this magnitude will yield a positive financial return to shareholders? We doubt it.

We must question the current euphoric environmental rhetoric by asking if win-win solutions should be the foundation of a company's environmental strategy. At the risk of arguing against motherhood (and mother earth), we must answer 'No'. Ambitious environmental goals have real economic costs. As a society, we may rightly choose those goals despite their costs, but we must do so knowingly, and we must not kid ourselves. Talk is cheap; environmental efforts are not.

But just because environmental managers should not continue to search exclusively for win-win solutions does not mean that they should return to their old ways of fighting, ignoring and hamstringing any and all environmental regulatory efforts. On the contrary, being conscious of shareholder value while protecting the environment requires, among other things, a deep understanding of the environmental and strategic consequences of business decisions, collaboration with environmental groups and regulators, involvement in shaping legislation (and even avoiding the need for it), and a sincere commitment to cleaning up and preventing pollution. The challenge for managers today is knowing how to pick the shots that will have the greatest impact. To achieve truly sustainable environmental solutions, managers must concentrate on finding smarter and finer trade-offs between business and environmental concerns, acknowledging that, in almost all cases, it is impossible to get something for nothing.

Concentrating on enhancing the efficiency and effectiveness of environmental spending may not have the rhetorical appeal of the current win-win talk, but in the long run, such an approach will be far more effective. Consider DuPont, which has the equivalent of a 35 per cent of its share price invested in capital and operating expenditures related to protecting the environment. Rather than searching for elusive, but virtuous, win-win situations, DuPont can protect shareholder value more successfully by finding ways to improve its long-term environmental efficiency. A 15 per cent improvement in efficiency, for instance, could yield nearly $3 per share.

Other companies in pollution-intensive industries would see similar results from efforts to improve environmental efficiency. We estimate that between one-quarter and one-half of an industry's market value is vulnerable to increased environmental costs. And while it is difficult to know how much value will *actually* be destroyed by the increased cost of environmental compliance, it is clear that managers face a daunting task. The recently reauthorized Clean Air Act, for example, is expected to cost US petroleum refiners $37 billion, over $6 billion more than the book value of the entire industry. And stories like that will likely multiply. McKinsey & Company's 1991 worldwide survey of several hundred executives, *The Corporate Response to the Environmental Challenge*, shows that top managers expect environmental expenditures to double as a percentage of sales over the next decade.

Given that scenario, companies should seek to minimize the destruction of shareholder value that is likely to be caused by environmental costs rather than attempt to create value through environmental enhancements. Indeed, the current win-win rhetoric is not just misleading; it is dangerous. In an area like the environment, which requires long-term commitment and co-operation, untempered idealism is a luxury. By focusing on the laudable but illusory goal of win-win solutions, corporations and policymakers are setting themselves up for a fall with shareholders and the public at large. Both constituencies will become cynical, disappointed and unco-operative when the true costs of being green come to light. Companies are already beginning to question their public commitment to the environment, especially since such costly obligations often come at a time when many companies are undergoing dramatic expense with regard to restructurings and layoffs.

EVOLVING ERAS OF ENVIRONMENTAL MANAGEMENT

The history of the complex relationship between business and the environment illuminates the appeal as well as the considerable danger of the win-win approach. As Professors Kurt Fischer and Johan Schot outline in their introduction to *Environmental Strategies for Industry*, the current approach to environmental management developed in two eras over two decades, beginning in the early 1970s.

In the first era, which lasted from roughly 1970 to 1985, companies faced with new regulations of high technical specificity did little more than comply with the regulations and often fought or stymied them. Fischer and Schot accurately describe this phase as one of 'resistant adaptation'. During this period, companies were generally unwilling to internalize environmental issues, a reluctance that was reflected in the delegation of environmental protection to local facilities, a widespread failure to create environmental performance-measurement systems, and a refusal to view environmental issues as realities that needed to be incorporated into business strategy.

During the mid to late 1980s, a shift in the regulatory context and the maturing of the environmental movement created an incentive for managers to look beyond the narrow, predominantly technical approach. With regulations focused more on ultimate environmental results and less on the mechanics of compliance, managers began to exercise greater discretion in their environmental response. For the first time, environmental strategy became possible.

Fischer and Schot call this second phase 'embracing environmental issues without innovating'. Because corporate response in the first era was minimal and grudging, companies were able to make easy, but often very significant, improvements in the second era. Between 1989 and 1991, for example, Texaco achieved a 40 per cent reduction in its combined air, water and solid-waste streams and a 58 per cent reduction in its toxic emissions through pollution-control equipment, tighter monitoring and control systems, and the introduction of an improved waste-reduction process. Similarly, between 1988 and 1992, Georgia-Pacific secured a 65 per cent reduction in dioxins and a 34 per cent decrease in chloroform emissions by relying on substitute chemicals, upgraded equipment and improved process controls.

The emergence of the win-win mind-set is a direct result of the extraordinary success that companies achieved in reducing pollution in this second era. Many of the reduction programmes made good financial sense, while few required truly fundamental changes in production processes or product designs. Anxious to demonstrate their commitment to environmental progress, companies were quick to tout their successes. Even informed observers easily came to the conclusion that continued environmental action could more than pay for itself

WHY WIN-WIN WON'T WORK

In the Foreword to the new edition of *Earth in the Balance*, Vice President Al Gore writes, 'We can prosper by leading the environmental revolution and producing for the world marketplace the new products and technologies that foster economic progress without environmental destruction.' While Gore focuses primarily on the government's role, he clearly believes that many win-win opportunities exist for corporations and that trade-offs can largely be avoided through smart decision-making and technical innovation.

In his brief but influential article in *Scientific American* (see Chapter 3), Michael Porter echoes Gore's view, arguing that the perceived conflict between environmental protection and economic competitiveness is, in fact, a false dichotomy:

> *Strict environmental regulations do not inevitably hinder competitive advantage against foreign rivals; indeed, they often enhance it. Properly constructed regulatory standards, which aim at outcomes and not methods, will encourage companies to re-engineer their technology. The result in many cases is a process that not only pollutes less but lowers costs or improves quality.*

In Gore and Porter's world, managers might redesign a product so that it uses fewer environmentally harmful or resource-depleting raw materials. If successful, that effort could also result in significant cuts in direct manufacturing costs and inventory savings and appeal to consumers' growing desire for environmentally friendly products.

That argument, with its rabbit-out-of-the-hat solutions to many environmental and economic ills, is certainly appealing. Who wouldn't be enamoured of an approach that promises that a renewed concern for the environment will revive the country's economic and competitive outlook? Gore's book and Porter's persuasive arguments have unleashed, or at least reinforced, a school of thought that denies the necessity of trade-offs and encourages companies to pursue prosperity through green initiatives.

Yet while Gore and Porter give an inspirational rallying cry, they offer little specific guidance to managers. Porter writes mainly about how a country can gain competitive advantage through strict environmental policies, not about how individual companies might actually seek to gain competitive advantage by becoming green. But that hasn't stopped environmentalists from seizing on Porter's argument and urging businesses to capture the many opportunities to help the environment that await them.

Win-win rhetoric already pervades popular opinion. An April 1993 Times Mirror-Roper poll shows that over two-thirds of Americans do not believe the country must choose between environmental protection and economic development. Yet those who extrapolate a specific strategy for industry from Porter's argument are wrongly assuming that the recent spate of easy environmental wins can be carried on indefinitely. While tough environmental standards may yield significant positive results for the economy as a whole, individual companies will actually be battling with increasingly complex environmental problems at a much higher cost than ever before.

For example, one large chemical company, anxious to capitalize on its early successes, committed itself to a programme to reduce emissions of hazardous wastes. The company soon found that it was starving other important projects, like plant upgrades, and that roughly two-thirds of its capital budget went to environmental spending. Perhaps even more alarming, nearly 80 per cent of plant engineers' time was being consumed by environmental projects. Managers at this company are just beginning to understand that all their relatively easy environmental problems have already been solved and that the economic forces at work in the industry are making it increasingly difficult to find win-win solutions. The company is now exploring ways to achieve greater efficiency and perhaps even to reduce some of its commitments to the environment.

As environmental challenges become more complex and costs continue to skyrocket, win-win solutions will become increasingly scarce. Environmental costs have stubbornly continued to outpace both inflation and economic growth for the past two decades. Between 1972 and 1992, for instance, total annualized environmental protection costs for the United States tripled as a percentage of gross domestic product (GDP) from 0.88 per cent to 2.39 per cent, with a further increase to 2.47 per cent, or around $200 billion, projected by the year 2000. In pollution-intensive sectors like oil and gas, the problem is much worse. Compound annual growth in environmental expenditures for a selection of oil and gas companies between 1987 and 1990 was 12.9 per cent, compared with only 7.3 per cent for employee benefits (including health care) and 2.7 per cent for direct labour charges.

Costs are destined to increase even more, especially since the increase in regulations shows no signs of abating. One crude but indicative proxy is that the number of federal environmental acts in force has risen from 5 in 1972 to over 40 today, a spate of legislative activity that has been responsible for a twelvefold increase in the number of pages of federal environmental regulation over the same period. By 1992, Title 40 of the Federal Code contained over 12,000 pages of regulations, and several pieces of environmental legislation, such as the Clean Water Act and the Resources Conservation and Recovery Act, are currently on the congressional docket.

Even without additional regulations, however, progressively tighter standards within current regulations will push corporate environmental spending higher. For example, nitrogen oxides standards (which cover a major air pollutant that often comes from the coal burned to generate electricity) were originally set by the Clean Air Act at a limit of 0.5 pounds per million British Thermal Units (BTUs) for electric utilities. This standard was subsequently superseded by many states with tighter limits, culminating in a 0.2 pounds per million BTUs standard to be achieved by 1999, which will result in a tenfold cost increase. While it may be possible to respond creatively to each new environmental regulation or enforcement, the burden on corporations is tremendous.

Moreover, within industries, the burden falls unevenly among companies. In the top ten companies in the oil industry, reported environmental expenditures vary from 5.1 per cent to 1.3 per cent of sales over a three-year period – a difference of roughly $800 million. And in steel, minimills enjoy $10 to $15 environmental cost per ton advantage over traditional integrated producers.

Complicating the situation for environmental managers is the growing array of choices they have for how and when they will respond to environmental pressures. Managers today have so many choices that they aren't always sure what to do. Old-fashioned command-and-control regulations, which allow managers very little freedom, are giving way to market-based incentives, including tradable permits, pollution charges and deposit refund systems. These new incentives do not tell a company what to do but instead provide a clear set of financial incentives that are designed to influence behaviour positively, much like a capital market.

The result? Senior managers must frequently juggle a number of issues without a means for setting priorities or a method for integrating those issues into business decision-making. In McKinsey's survey, 92 per cent of CEOs and board members stated that the environment should be one of their top three management priorities, and 85 per cent claimed that one of their major goals should be to integrate environmental considerations into business strategy. At the same time, only 37 per cent believed they successfully integrate the environment into everyday operations, and only 35 per cent said they successfully adapt business strategy to anticipated environmental developments.

THE SEARCH FOR SOLUTIONS

Clearly, today's managers lack a framework that will allow them to turn their good intentions into reality. A number of executives are attempting to do just that. Among the most practical of those is Swiss industrialist Stephan Schmidheiny, who led the Business Council at the 1992 Earth Summit in Rio de Janeiro. In *Changing Course*, Schmidheiny and his colleagues at the Business Council, including ABB Chairman Percy Barnevik, retired 3M Chairman and CEO Allen Jacobson, Dow Chemical President and CEO Frank Poppoff and Nippon Steel Chairman Akira Miki, articulate a vision of 'sustainable development', or the ability to meet the needs of the present generation without compromising the welfare of future generations. The authors do not claim that growth and the environment are mutually reinforcing, rather, they argue that economic growth and environmental protection are inextricably linked.

The vision they offer is based on free trade, market prices that reflect the comprehensive societal impact of products and processes, more flexible regulations and investors who pay greater heed to environmental considerations. In the cases Schmidheiny cites, he shows a clear understanding of the environmental issues managers must face. Yet *Changing Course* does not, nor does it aspire to, provide an all-encompassing framework for managers who must daily negotiate the conflicting demands of the market and the environment.

Schmidheiny leaves CEOs with no clear guideposts for which products or processes to work on first and how far to go in cleaning up and at what cost. Without that guidance, even the most environmentally sensitive CEO will be lost. The current crop of environmental texts suggests that competitive advantage can be found in effective environmental management, yet these texts offer only one-dimensional prescriptions. The common rallying cry of many environmental thinkers is that the environment must be integrated into everyday business decisions, yet few specify what that means.

Many corporations view the environment as a discrete functional area generating issues that are treated in isolation from 'core' business issues. Writers on all ends of the spectrum, however, now agree that the outmoded functional approach must yield to a more integrated way of thinking.

In her book *Costing the Earth*, Frances Cairncross, the Environment Editor of *The Economist*, suggests that the total quality movement may be one vehicle through which environmental issues can be integrated into business as a whole. 'In American management terms,' she writes, 'environmental responsibility has become an aspect of the search for total quality.' While Cairncross may be correct, most total quality environmental management programmes have a missionary focus on emissions reductions that doesn't take into account the cost at which that quality is obtained or, alternatively, the value created. Traditional cost-reduction efforts, on the other hand, err too much in the opposite direction by concentrating on quarterly costs without devoting sufficient attention to environmental impact and the longer term costs and liabilities.

THE PATH TO PRAGMATISM

Instead of focusing on win-win solutions, companies would be better off focusing on the 'trade-off zone', where environmental benefit is weighed judiciously against value destruction. Only a focus on value rather than compliance, emissions or quarterly costs can provide managers with the information to set priorities and develop appropriate business responses. This does not mean that managers should obstruct environmental regulatory efforts. Instead, managers must pick their shots carefully. In a world where you cannot do everything, only a value-based approach allows informed trade-offs between costs and benefits.

Much work remains to define all the elements of a value-based approach. Broadly speaking, such an approach must be systematic, integrated and flexible. Managers must set clear priorities based on the potential impact on shareholder value and the amount of discretion they have to deal with the environmental problem at hand; they must make environmental decisions in the context of the company's needs and strategy; and they must be able to exercise different options as an uncertain future unfolds.

Within this framework, environmental issues can be broken down into three broad categories: strategic, operational and technical (see Figure 4.1). Each type requires a distinct managerial approach. Together they represent a way of thinking about the environment that goes beyond incremental, reactive and functional approaches which are now reaching the limits of their cost-effectiveness.

Some environmental issues are *strategic* because their impact on value is high enough either to put core elements of the business at risk or to fundamentally alter a company's cost structure, and because managers have considerable discretion about how to respond. A good example is the issue of chlorine-free paper production facing the pulp and paper industry. Opinion is sharply divided on when, and even whether, government regulation will prohibit the use of chlorine in the paper manufacturing process. The value implications for pulp and

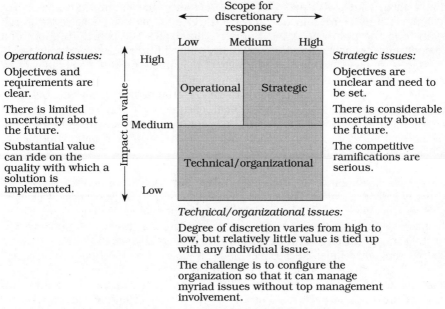

Operational issues:

Objectives and requirements are clear.

There is limited uncertainty about the future.

Substantial value can ride on the quality with which a solution is implemented.

Strategic issues:

Objectives are unclear and need to be set.

There is considerable uncertainty about the future.

The competitive ramifications are serious.

Technical/organizational issues:

Degree of discretion varies from high to low, but relatively little value is tied up with any individual issue.

The challenge is to configure the organization so that it can manage myriad issues without top management involvement.

Figure 4.1 *A Triage of Environmental Issues*

paper companies are enormous, not only because of the absolute cost of chlorine-free production but also because some companies are likely, by virtue of their plant configuration or other reasons, to enjoy a relative competitive advantage in this form of manufacture. Meanwhile, the level of discretion in how to respond is considerable. While Louisiana-Pacific has started to prepare its organization for chlorine-free paper production, many other industry participants are fighting tooth and nail to undermine proposed legislation.

As that situation suggests, one key decision that managers must make about each major environmental problem they face is whether to lead or lag behind their competitors on environmental issues. In some cases, a company will want to pursue an environmental strategy in which it gets well in front of regulations or public opinion, as Louisiana-Pacific did. In other cases, a corporation may be served best by moving in lockstep with industry leaders or by reacting only in response to external pressures. The decision to lead or lag regulations is something of a management catch-22. If a company lags, it may find itself on the receiving end of unfavourable regulations, but if the company leads, its actions could increase near-term production costs and leave the company vulnerable to its competitors.

Managers will find that their options can be broken down into those that help them shape events, like forming partnerships with stakeholders, and those that help them develop an optimal response to events, like reallocating resource dollars and redesigning production processes. To prepare a strategy, managers must decide where they want to be on the spectrum from strict compliance to environmental leadership.

Operational issues are those where the impact on value ranges from medium to high, but where managers' scope for discretionary response is generally low.

Management's task with these issues is to ensure that minimum expenditures achieve maximum environmental impact. The example of broad emissions control, again from the pulp and paper industry, illustrates the point. While annual expenditures for complying with regulations controlling air, water, and solid-waste emissions are measured in the hundreds of millions of dollars, companies often have little choice about whether or how to comply.

The challenge with these issues is to view environmental costs as manageable, not as a set of mandates for which a blank cheque is the only solution. The first step is understanding how much is being spent on emission control and why. The second step is devising an approach that ensures that maximum environmental impact is achieved at minimum cost.

Finally, there are those issues that are largely *technical*, where the degree of managerial discretion varies from high to low, but relatively little value is tied up with any individual issue. The cumulative weight of thousands of these decisions, however, can have an adverse effect on shareholder value. Managers must have the necessary information to make informed trade-offs between cost and environmental control. Business unit managers seldom have adequate information about even current environmental costs, let alone possible future liabilities or pressures. The best way to provide that information is to create systems to track and disseminate emissions data on a cross-functional basis, provide environmental cost accounting and perform thorough, opportunity-oriented – as opposed to compliance-oriented – third-party audits. That approach is in contrast to current 'worst practice', prevalent in the McKinsey survey, which can be summed up with the following attitude: 'There are enough problems that will find us without our having to find new ones.'

For all environmental issues, shareholder value, rather than compliance, emissions or costs, is the critical unifying metric. That approach is environmentally sound, but it is also hard-headed, informed by business experience, and, as a result, is much more likely to be truly sustainable over the long term.

REFERENCES

Cairncross, F (1991) *Costing the Earth*, Penguin, London

Fischer, K and Schot, J (1993) *Environmental Strategies for Industry* Island Press, Washington DC

Gore, A (1992) *Earth in the Balance: Forging a New Common Purpose*, Earthscan, London

McKinsey and Company (1991) *The Corporate Response to Environmental Challenge* (self published) Amsterdam

Schmidheiny, S with the Business Council for Sustainable Development (1992) *Changing Course: A Global Business Perspective on Development and the Environment*, MIT Press, Cambridge, MA

5

The Challenge of Going Green

Various authors

Responding to environmental problems has always been a no-win proposition for managers, report Noah Walley and Bradley Whitehead in 'It's Not Easy Being Green' (see previous article). Help the environment and hurt your business, or irreparably harm your business while protecting the earth. Recently, however, a new common wisdom has emerged that promises the ultimate reconciliation of environmental and economic concerns. In this new world, both business and the environment can win. Being green is no longer a cost of doing business; it is a catalyst for innovation, new market opportunity and wealth creation.

The idea that a renewed interest in environmental management will result in increased profitability for business has widespread appeal. In a new green world, managers might redesign a product so that it uses fewer environmentally harmful or resource-depleting raw materials – an effort that, if successful, could result in cuts in direct manufacturing costs and inventory savings. This new vision sounds great, yet it is highly unrealistic, Walley and Whitehead argue. Environmental costs are sky-rocketing in most companies, with little chance of economic payback in sight. Given this reality, they question whether 'win-win' solutions should be the foundation of a company's environmental strategy.

The following twelve experts assess both viewpoints and offer their comments.

Richard A Clarke
Chairman and Chief Executive Officer
Pacific Gas and Electric Company
San Francisco, California

Much of what is written or spoken about the reconciliation of economic and environmental concerns is oversimplified, and I agree with Noah Walley and Bradley Whitehead that this kind of discourse can create unrealistic expectations. But reconciliation is not a choice. A strong global economy is sustainable only if it integrates economic, social and environmental well-being.

I disagree with the authors' viewpoint that win-win opportunities are insignificant and with their scepticism about the value of a corporate environmental commitment. They point to the 'enormous' and rising costs of environmental compliance, with no positive financial returns, as a reason to argue against any real benefits arising from going beyond compliance. But that argument ignores a key point: complying with environmental or any other law is usually not expected to yield a positive financial return.

Having said that, I do believe that the costs of environmental compliance are unnecessarily high. They are the result of a regulatory system that has become inefficient and ineffective. The solution is creative regulatory reform like that initiated by the Aspen Institute Series on the Environment in the Twenty-First Century and the eco-efficiency work of the President's Council on Sustainable Development. Many of the proposed reforms are aimed at significantly increasing the cost-effectiveness of compliance measures by reducing command-and-control approaches, increasing the flexibility for meeting standards and relying on market-based incentives.

The authors look at win-win opportunities from the rather narrow viewpoint of going beyond compliance in reducing pollution from industrial processes. But a broader approach is necessary, one that focuses on basic changes in products, services and business strategies that offer opportunity, financially as well as ecologically. The shift from building more power plants to increasing energy-efficiency can benefit utility customers and shareholders as well as the environment.

Here at Pacific Gas and Electric, we have installed energy-efficient lighting, heating and cooling systems in the new federal building in Oakland, resulting in annual cost savings of $600,000 and environmental pay-offs that come from saving nearly 6 million kilowatt-hours of energy each year. Among the many win-win pollution-prevention measures we are implementing is the recycling of materials we use – electric conductors, transformers, plastic gas pipes – with cost savings of several million dollars a year.

It is true that economic forces at work in industry are making it more difficult to integrate environmental excellence into a business strategy. Yet the authors choose to treat this challenge, and the lack of a framework for managers to address it, as somehow different from other business challenges that result from changes in the business environment, such as the quickening global economy, a shrinking labour pool or changing technology.

We need a farsighted programme and innovative, creative solutions to address the environmental challenge. We need a comprehensive, forward-looking approach in which current barriers and disincentives are removed; appropriate incentives are provided; and fiscal, economic, environmental and industrial policies are integrated and made mutually supportive.

Robert N Stavins
Associate Professor of Public Policy
John F Kennedy School of Government
Harvard University
Cambridge, Massachusetts

In the 25 years since the beginning of the modern environmental movement, the United States has spent more that $1 trillion to address environmental threats caused by commercial activities. During the latter part of this period, the US economy has shifted from approximate trade balance on a long-term basis to chronic trade deficit. The coincidence of these two trends has led many to suspect that environmental regulation is impairing the 'competitiveness' of US industry.

The conventional wisdom is that environmental regulations impose significant costs on private industry, slow productivity growth and thereby hinder the ability of US companies to compete in international markets. This loss of competitiveness is believed to be reflected in declining exports, increasing imports and a long-term movement of manufacturing capacity from the United States to other countries in the world, particularly in 'pollution-intensive' industries.

A more recent, revisionist view asserts that environmental regulations are not only benign in their impact on international competitiveness but may actually be a net positive force driving private business and the economy as a whole to become more competitive. This argument, articulated most prominently by the Harvard Business School's Michael Porter, has generated a great deal of interest and enthusiasm among some influential policymakers, including Vice President Al Gore.

Now a heated debate has arisen around these two views. Noah Walley and Bradley Whitehead tend to endorse the conventional view of environmental regulations impairing economic competitiveness. In drawing on their extensive experience working with major corporations, they introduce some much-needed reality to the debate, but anecdotal evidence can take us only so far.

Together with my colleagues Adam Jaffe, Steve Peterson and Paul Portney, I recently reviewed the statistical evidence from more than 100 academic and government studies that illuminate this ongoing debate. In our report 'Environmental Regulation and International Competitiveness: What Does the Evidence Tell Us?', we concluded that the truth lies somewhere between the two positions.

We found little to document the view that environmental regulation has had a measurable adverse effect on competitiveness. Although its long-run social costs – including productivity slow-down – may be consequential, studies gauging the effects of environmental regulation on net exports, overall trade flows and plant-location decisions have produced estimates that are small or statistically insignificant.

The picture is bleaker still for the tenet that environmental regulation stimulates innovation and competitiveness. Not a single empirical analysis lends convincing support to this view. Indeed, several studies offer important, if indirect, evidence to the contrary. Natural scepticism regarding this regulatory free lunch should remain unabated.

Rather than advocate either of the two extremes, policymakers should aim to establish environmental priorities and goals that are consistent with the real trade-offs that all regulatory activities inevitably require – that is, policymakers should base environmental goals on the careful balancing of benefits and costs. In so doing, policymakers should seek to reduce the magnitude of those costs by identifying and implementing flexible and cost-effective environmental policy instruments, whether of the conventional type or the newer, market-based breed.

J Ladd Greeno
Senior Vice President
Arthur D Little, Inc
Cambridge, Massachusetts

Walley and Whitehead offer many valuable insights, but their emphasis on the win-win mind-set in corporate environmental management circles does not ring true.

In discussing competitive advantage in the environmental realm, lines must be clearly drawn between activities driven primarily by shareholder value and those driven by regulations, liabilities and public expectations. The authors' lack of a consistent focus on these distinctions leads to misunderstandings about industry's relations with the win-win school of thought.

A sharper picture of the real situation and aspirations of industry can be drawn in four areas:

1. *Compliance and competitiveness.* Most companies focus on compliance, not competitive advantage – for good reason. Environmental managers would welcome a world in which they could 'search exclusively for win-win solutions'. In reality, however, they concentrate on ensuring compliance with current environmental regulations, remediating environmental problems caused by past operations and anticipating the impact of proposed regulations.

   As Walley and Whitehead note, costs in those areas are often enormous, dwarfing potential win-win opportunities. But the authors don't make it clear that when Texaco, for example, invests $7 billion in compliance and emissions reductions, a primary motive is to protect its franchise to operate. Recent fines ($5 million against United Technologies, for example) and criminal enforcement (in 1993, 135 individuals received criminal fines and jail time in environmental cases prosecuted by the Justice Department) show that non-compliance can have significant costs.

   Moreover, the optimistic tone of today's corporate environmental rhetoric reflects management's desire to give its stockholders a unifying vision for a complex array of environmental initiatives. Nevertheless, senior managers are fully aware that many compliance and remediation efforts won't increase, but will protect, shareholder value. They know that any serious discussion about gaining competitive advantage from environmental issues must emphasize future possibilities.

2. *It's never been easy to be green.* The authors claim that in the late 1980s and early 1990s, 'companies were able to make easy, but often very significant, improvements' in areas such as emissions reductions. The result, they say, is a belief that future gains will be as easy. Most companies would be surprised to learn that their environmental achievements have been easy. After all, in the same period, those companies saw compliance costs soar.

3. *Keeping up with the Joneses.* Walley and Whitehead urge companies to enhance shareholder value by improving 'the efficiency and effectiveness of environmental spending'. But their focus on industry-wide statistics for environmental expenditures obscures the key competitive opportunity in those expenditures. Historically, industry has adjusted to the cost of environmental mandates with price adjustments. Companies that can achieve superior efficiency and effectiveness in environmental spending will indeed find themselves in a classic win-win situation, meeting the non-business-driven expectations of the public and the government while besting their competitors' cost structures.

4. *The rest of the world.* The authors focus exclusively on the US environmental context. Increasingly, however, the international dimensions of environ-

mental issues are shaping corporate environmental postures. Companies are taking steps to safeguard against environmental liabilities in countries where regulations are now embryonic. And they are examining how measures, such as the European Union's Eco-Management and Audit Scheme, will raise 'threshold' environmental expectations throughout the world. Just as the United States set an example with its early environmental legislation, other countries are now pioneering approaches in areas such as packaging and environmental reports. As companies globalize their operations, they must account for these developments if they hope to manage environmental costs and opportunities.

Joan L Bavaria
President
Franklin Research & Development Corporation
Co-Chair and CEO
Coalition for Environmentally Responsible Economies (CERES)
Boston, Massachusetts

Walley and Whitehead contribute to the necessary exercise of sorting choices for the future of business, but they veer dangerously towards the shortsighted, operational view of the world that has gotten us into our current pickle. They ignore business people's ability to think creatively and they fail to consider the dimension of time. Similar failures may underlie society's inability to understand the impact of technology and commerce on our quality of life and may impede our success as managers of this planet.

As anyone who has used a spreadsheet to construct a business plan knows, the power of unknown externalities increases beyond one year. Even internal forces over time can seem like fantasy as you create, through mathematical formulas inserted in neat boxes, projections eight, nine, or ten years out. Managers and consultants, trained in the science of computer-aided projections, are understandably more comfortable with knowns than with unknowns and with visible effects than with visions of the future.

But getting us out of the global mess we're in will require a panoply of tactics, technology and innovative partnerships. It will call for the kind of management thinking that doesn't depend on charting known facts against other known facts. We must be willing to think high and wide. Sadly, we are paying for past sins, which doesn't seem fair and is going to be incredibly difficult to allocate, but failing to do so will surely spell disaster in the future, both for companies and shareholders.

The Pollyanna view that going green is a win-win for all corporations at all times deserves to be refuted. For some companies in the short run, changing practices to ensure maximum environmental performance could spell economic disaster. There are some absolutes, however, on what will prove to be a landscape with few clear and obvious short-term solutions to long-term problems. One is that the problem is profound and long term: we are consuming our planet. Even frogs, as the proverb relates, know not to consume the lily pad on which they sit. Ironically, frogs are now one of the indicator species facing possible extinction.

Some industries will bump into scarce resources sooner than others; the fishing industries in New England and the Pacific north-west are aware that they have bitten the hand that feeds them and the hand is no longer extended. Insurance companies are realizing that their short-term costs are directly related to environmental degradation. Managers in other affected industries must grasp quickly the trade-offs available to them and act accordingly.

But most of the choices we as a society must make and businesspeople must make if their companies are to survive are far more complex with far less empirical decision-making support. Companies in some industries must challenge their reason for being or their core competencies. Is an oil company in the oil business long term, or in the fuel business, or in the energy business? Is an automobile manufacturer a transportation company? Read carefully between the lines, Al Gore's book is much more than environmental happy talk; it is a challenge to industry to find solutions by thinking globally and long term.

The use of the traditional business concept of value as the determinant of choices would set the environmental debate back decades. Moreover, calling shareholders the ultimate arbiters of value in this debate is guaranteed to increase the antagonism between environmental activists and businesspeople. That argument ignores concepts of value that include quality of life and resources more properly in the public domain. All participants in the debate must reach new levels of understanding, refuting traditional straw men. Shareholders are no longer just rich folks in Cadillacs; they are also churches, foundations and retired teachers. Similarly, economic trauma is an enemy of the environment in both the short and the long run.

Frances Cairncross
Environment Editor
The Economist
London, England

Win-win is a wonderful concept. It implies that economic oxymoron, a free lunch. No wonder politicians and chief executives long to be told that environmental expenditures are good for business. And no wonder Walley and Whitehead are sceptical. Their article is likely to be less widely quoted than Michael Porter's account of business-boosting regulation, but it is closer to the truth.

Sometimes it is in the commercial interests of the company's shareholders to adopt higher environmental standards. Sometimes, too, companies make money because governments tighten environmental regulations. But those results occur in rather special circumstances. For example, a few companies may make money by making products for that elusive creature, the 'green consumer'. But that strategy has problems. Consumers think 'green' only when buying a limited range of goods. Besides, some 'green' products don't work as well as the non-green sort – think of detergents – but cost consumers more.

It may be in a company's commercial interest to raise its standards mainly for defensive reasons. In most countries, the cost of disposing toxic waste has been rising; the legal liabilities for pollution have become tougher; and companies are increasingly at risk of liability for past contamination. Fear, not greed, has driven most corporate environmental policies.

Politicians would like a more inspiring tale to tell than this. They would like to say that environmental regulation can actually improve corporate competitiveness. So it can, though again, not in the way they hope. For instance, companies selling pollution-control services, whether they be consultants, environmental lawyers or businesses making water filters, find that tougher standards bring in more customers. Companies buying natural resource-based raw materials may want environmental rules to reduce their treatment costs. Water companies gain if farmers must curb polluting run-off from their fields.

Companies that can already meet high standards may lobby to make them mandatory to keep out competitors. The big waste-treatment companies in Britain were aghast last year when the government twice postponed launching a new scheme for licensing the management of landfills. The higher standards of the licensing scheme required extensive capital investment, which small 'cowboy' companies could not afford.

This game can be played internationally too. Germany's 'green dot' scheme, which requires the recycling of waste packaging, has benefited the German paper industry (by providing a large, cheap supply of recycled pulp) at the expense of Scandinavian producers of virgin pulp.

What the free-lunch brigade wants to hear, however, is that environmental rules actually persuade companies to take actions that are in their commercial interest but that they had not previously noticed. Remember the economist and his friend who thinks he sees a $10 bill on the sidewalk? 'It can't be,' says the economist. 'If it were, someone would have picked it up.'

Most of the $10 bills to be had by reducing pollution or saving energy have either been picked up already or can be retrieved only at a cost. That cost may not be cash but management time. If a bright manager must look for ways to reduce waste output, he or she is not available for developing new markets or stream-lining production.

It is not surprising that tougher environmental standards impose costs on companies. The aim of such standards, after all, is to force polluters to internalize costs previously inflicted on society; otherwise future generations inherit them. Environmental policies that are worth pursuing should be introduced for their own sake. To try to improve competitiveness by raising environmental standards is to risk the fate that typically awaits those who try to ride two horses at once.

Daniel C Esty
Associate Professor
Yale School of Forestry and Environmental Studies and Yale Law School
New Haven, Connecticut

Walley and Whitehead greatly oversimplify Michael Porter's argument (with which Al Gore may agree). In addition to rebutting a crude version of Porter's 'innovation hypothesis', they fail to appreciate that his message is as much a prescription for government and a call for new regulatory strategies as a lesson for business. It is true that some environmentalists see seemingly endless environmental investment opportunities for corporations with positive rates of return and will gladly mandate them if companies won't take them on. But Porter understands that regulations have an economic cost. He simply says that properly constructed environmental standards, may, while imposing costs, spur innovation and create business opportunities that offset all or some of the spending on pollution controls.

Porter identifies two kinds of 'innovation offsets'. First, as companies face higher costs for polluting activities due to regulation, they will be pushed to consider new technologies and production approaches that might reduce the cost of compliance. Semi-conductor makers, for instance, forced to abandon the use of ozone-layer-destroying CFCs as a solvent, have discovered several lower cost ways to clean computer chips. More dramatically, Porter suggests that while addressing environmental issues because of regulation, companies may develop entirely new products or processes.

This sort of significant innovation offset is most likely to be found where regulations focus corporate attention on serious environmental problems that others face or will soon face. Quick-responding companies can obtain 'first mover's' advantages by selling their solutions or unexpected innovations to others at home or around the world.

The strength of Porter's hypothesis is that it builds on the dynamic reality of business. In today's global marketplace, the ability to innovate and develop new technologies is a greater determinant of economic success than traditional factors of comparative advantage, such as obtaining low-cost components.

Protecting the environment, moreover, is not a zero-sum game. Many forms of pollution reflect underutilized or wasted resources. Just as Total Quality Management (TQM) helped companies to identify untapped value, break-through thinking in the environmental realm may enable companies to reap real rewards.

The structure of environmental programmes should also be open to scrutiny. Indeed, the government must bear responsibility for establishing regulatory conditions that promote economic creativity and efficient business responses to environmental demands. Regulatory programmes should be flexible and performance oriented or, better yet, based on economic incentives like pollution charges. Integrated regulatory systems that address air, water and waste problems systematically and comprehensively are also more apt to lead to innovation offsets. By regulating with rather than against market forces, the government can help broaden the scope for environmental programmes that spur innovation, reconciling, at least in part, the tension between society's desire for a cleaner environment and business' interest in profits and shareholder value.

Bruce Smart
Senior Fellow
World Resources Institute
Washington, DC

Walley and Whitehead are right: it's not easy being green. But it's also not easy anticipating markets, technologies or social trends. Management is a difficult profession, and the environment is becoming an increasingly important component in decision making.

Nor is a new, unsettling variable such as the environment unprecedented. Imagine the consternation of 19th-century industrialists faced with child labour laws or the dismay of their successors contemplating the new income tax, the Securities and Exchange Commission, and the Wagner Act, all of which dramatically altered their costs and changed their business practices. In such circumstances, farsighted and nimble companies prosper and laggards decline. Such is the way of a dynamic economic system.

Pollution prevention does pay a prompt return on investment – in some cases. And the authors correctly imply that this stream of opportunities hasn't been fished out yet. For example, 3M is still finding projects for its 3P programme, now over 15 years old. Many other companies have barely begun to look. But despite such opportunities, solving the largest environmental problems will require huge investments whose principal economic pay-off will be the right to continue in business. How efficiently these problems are recognized, analysed and addressed will determine the winners.

The costs of change must eventually end up in price: the consumer will pay. Shareholder values may be shifted among players, but they will not be massively destroyed. New capital, properly directed to environmental improvement, will still earn a positive return compared with the alternative of not investing. If it cannot, the proper strategy is to liquidate the business.

To strategize on this undulating playing-field, the prudent manager needs to recognize its underlying forces. Despite some claims to the contrary, major environmental problems are not the creation of some anti-capitalist élite. They are real, founded in science (often not well understood) and globally threatening. They are increasing because of rapid population growth and expanding economic activity. They can be solved only by a common-sense alliance of business, government and environmentalists. Among these, only business has the resources of technology, finances and organizational competence to implement the necessary changes. Herein lies great opportunity as well as great peril.

Policymakers must recognize that environmental resources are often owned 'in common' or not 'owned' at all, and are therefore not priced or underpriced to those who use them. Examples include future fertility and the waste-absorption capability of land; forest, wetlands, coral reefs, oceans and other ecosystems; and the planet's flora and fauna. Where there is inadequate rationing through pricing, use will be profligate, and scarcity will go unrecognized. And because many resources seem 'free', access to them is regarded as an entitlement – 'free as the air we breathe'.

As society sees its quality of life – or life itself – at risk, it will take steps to avert that risk. Companies can choose to 'play', or they can let others shape the game. A company that decides to play can incorporate the environment into strategic planning by taking certain steps:

1. Understand the critical environmental threats.
2. Determine how the company's activities contribute to them.
3. Implement a remedial programme wherever pollution prevention pays.
4. Aim research to develop more environmentally benign processes and products.
5. Design all new investment with environmental effects in mind.
6. Work with government and environmentalists to establish public policies and priorities that address major environmental threats as priorities, seeking a reasonable cost/benefit relationship.
7. Promote implementation mechanisms, especially economic signals – such as subsidies, user fees and taxes – to which business can respond efficiently.

The goal is an environmental protocol that is friendly to both business and society.

Johan Piet
Professor
Institute of Environmental Control Science
University of Amsterdam
The Netherlands

The companies that survive the next 20 years will produce goods and services whose environmental effects are tolerable to all stakeholders. The environmental 'value' of products will have to be weighed against their financial value and consumer preferences. Environmental issues will have to be evaluated according to their relative importance. Executives, therefore, must develop a vision of how a sustainable company operates or at least of how to find the way to do it.

Only win-win companies will survive, but that does not mean that all win-win ideas will be successful. Managers need a methodology for discovering solutions that yield the greatest benefits.

The Pollution Prevention Pays (PPP) programme has been very popular in the Netherlands in recent years. A methodology called PRISMA was developed to trace prevention options. Most savings could be realized by increasing efficiency. Also, in our experience, the most extensive environmental benefits could be attained at only high costs. Objections to PPP include: it measures benefits in terms of cash flow, not environmental impact; it doesn't account for all environmental issues; and improvements may not continue if they are costly.

Another recent development in the Netherlands and elsewhere in Europe is the environmental management system. But an EMS also yields only limited benefits. I prefer a total management system that can fulfil all managerial needs. Win-win solutions are possible for companies that develop a specific corporate environmental strategy, design a system for reliable management information and use a good methodology for evaluating environmental impact. Such a methodology includes:

1. Development of a long-term strategy based on a sustainable environmental philosophy.
2. Selection of specific, dominant environmental issues.
3. Definition of how problems and solutions must be judged.
4. Consideration of the best natural moment when making decisions about environmental improvements (investment, reallocation or replacement, for example).
5. Selection of improvements with the highest chance of success.

Richard P Wells
Vice President
Director, Corporate Environmental Consulting
Abt Associates, Inc
Cambridge, Massachusetts

We have little basis on which to judge whether win-win environmental investment opportunities are rare or plentiful. Most US companies don't have adequate tools to scan their operations for environmental opportunities or to prioritize or evaluate them in terms of contribution to shareholder value. Companies like Polaroid,

DuPont, and J M Huber, however, are demonstrating that rigorous analysis can uncover win-win opportunities. Such analysis looks at the full revenue- and cost-side contributions of environmental initiatives to shareholder value.

Walley and Whitehead largely overlook the product-differentiation contribution of environmental initiatives to the revenue side of shareholder value. Product-differentiation opportunities arise not from domestic regulatory standards but from customer requirements reflected in supplier qualifications, international environmental standards and competition in international markets, where environmental considerations are becoming increasingly important. In a 1991 survey of 85 companies, Abt learned that about 15 per cent of the companies were beginning to find environmental product-differentiation opportunities, 25 per cent were targeting only cost-minimization opportunities and 50 per cent were focusing narrowly on compliance. The product-differentiation category should grow in the 1990s.

The authors also understate the cost-side benefits of environmental initiatives. A December 1993 report from TechKNOWLEDGEy Marketing Services in Orchard Park, New York, indicates that the environmental services industry has lost 56 per cent of the paper value of its stock (or about $50 billion) since its high in the spring of 1991. Why? Because US industry redesigned its products and processes to reduce waste, and the expected market for waste-treatment and disposal services did not materialize. Resources that did not go into waste treatment and disposal have gone into more productive uses in the economy.

I agree that many win-win improvements in environmental performance to date have consisted of harvesting low-hanging fruit, but companies like Polaroid continue to find cost-effective environmental improvements. After the third year of its toxic-use reduction programme, for example, Polaroid had exhausted the low-hanging fruit but went on to adapt best-in-class technologies to its existing processes and research new processes and chemistries. Polaroid has put in place systems to maintain continuous improvement in its environmental performance while funding only the projects that meet corporate ROI (return on investment) objectives.

The key to maintaining continuous environmental improvement is management, not technology. Cost-effective technologies will emerge so long as management systems identify, prioritize and evaluate environmental opportunities.

Environmental performance measures must be tied to financial data to determine whether improvements contribute to shareholder value. On the cost side, TQM, which Walley and Whitehead dismiss much too readily, compares the costs of internal failure (resource waste, and waste treatment and disposal) and external failure (remediation, fines and liability) to the potential savings from prevention. Those costs must be allocated to specific products and processes in capital-budgeting and costing decisions. (In terms of traditional shareholder value, waste-treatment systems also tie up valuable capital compared with less capital-intensive prevention methods.) On the revenue side, TQM helps us understand customer requirements and the contribution of environmental performance to customer satisfaction and shareholder value.

More flexible government regulations create opportunities for environmental initiatives, but corporate management systems must take advantage of them. Traditionally, government regulations have focused on an imbalance between private and social costs as the basis for regulations. Recent initiatives, such as the Toxics

Release Inventory and the EPA's 33/50 Programme, have sought to provide better information for corporate, customer and stakeholder environmental decisions.

With greater flexibility, industry can craft more cost-effective initiatives. In an analysis of over 700 initiatives, DuPont has found that, on average, its internally generated environmental initiatives are three times as cost-effective as those that respond to government regulations.

If we want the world to beat a path to our door because we produce a better environmental mousetrap, we need to improve processes and products, not find better ways to dispose of waste. We do not need to throw money at every environmental opportunity that comes along, but we must develop and implement methods to measure environmental performance and assess the contribution it makes to shareholder value, both by reducing costs and by enhancing revenues.

Rob Gray
Matthew Professor of Accounting and Information Systems
Director, Centre for Social and Environmental Accounting Research
University of Dundee
Dundee, Scotland

Walley and Whitehead's arguments are timely. Enlightened companies have exhausted many of the relatively easy energy, waste and resource-efficiency options. They are now into the harder, longer term investment commitments in which conventional economic and environmental criteria are not necessarily in harmony. Companies – especially chemical industry giants like Dow, ICI, BP and Shell – have been untypically transparent about the costs of staying in business; costs that, as Walley and Whitehead note, are difficult to justify on simple investment-appraisal bases. A steady diet of green-wash propaganda doesn't help companies.

We all want our economic prosperity – which we owe to the enormous success of business – to be compatible with environmental protection. But if we take a broader view and plot any measure of that prosperity against any measure of environmental degradation, we find that the two move, inexorably, in the same direction. After nearly a decade of fairly committed efforts on the part of business and economic communities to reduce their environmental impact, all we find is that the rate of acceleration of environmental degradation throughout the world is slowing down.

Given that we have no way of knowing whether or not the planetary ecology is truly in crisis, and that it is impossible for us to ascertain whether our present ways of doing business can be made compatible with environmental sensitivity, we as a business community have some hard thinking to do. And the sooner we abandon the virtually empty rhetoric of win-win situations the better – for business *and* the environment.

Throughout Europe, as in North America, companies are being driven by a mix of voluntary, semi-voluntary and legislative pressures, all of which attempt to go with the grain of the market. Voluntary environmental reporting is growing steadily. Voluntary supplier-chain audits are placing market pressures on companies to get up to speed on environmental management. The panoply of European Union initiatives – eco-labelling; the Eco-Management and Audit Scheme; initiatives on packaging, waste and contaminated land – are creating a climate of development that more and more companies are finding difficult and expensive to meet.

Enlightened companies are experimenting with the new issues, but many others are unsure of how to react to all the changes. The legislative situation varies among the member states and remains confused over issues like liability for contaminated land. Bank and insurance markets are becoming increasingly complex, too.

Underlying all this are the costs. While there is still confusion over what level of environmental response is being demanded of business, British Gas is spending heavily on its land clean-up, ICI continues to publicize its painful reinvestment programme, British Petroleum continues with its massive emissions reduction, National Power struggles with trying to assess the necessary standards for its new generating plant, and British Airways continues to poke its environmental audit into every nook and cranny. These are expensive and painful experiences for leading, well-run companies. The financial benefits are far from clear for any one of them, but they are the costs of staying in business – the costs of their licence to operate in today's world.

On the other hand, there are still market advantages to be had. Norsk Hydro and BSO/Origin showed real benefits from having been the first companies into substantial voluntary environmental reporting. Ecover and, to a lesser extent, the Body Shop have gained market share from consistently leading in environmental initiatives. But those companies are probably the exception. And this is just the tip of the iceberg. Business has yet to begin to address the issue of sustainability.

As British Telecom and The Body Shop have both noted in recent environmental reports, when you cut through the rhetoric, it is doubtful whether our present ways of doing business can be compatible with sustainable development. The case for business continuing as it is and being sustainable looks very thin. Whether that is a cost or a benefit, a threat or an opportunity, depends on your point of view. Whatever we decide, it won't be easy and it won't be cheap. Walley and Whitehead are absolutely right on that!

Kurt Fischer
US Co-ordinator
Greening of Industry Network
Tufts University
Medford, Massachusetts

Johan Schot
European Co-ordinator
Greening of Industry Network
University of Twente
Enschede, The Netherlands

We agree with Walley and Whitehead, with one caveat. We believe that many companies, especially small and mid-size ones, still have lots of opportunities for win-win solutions. The broader greening of industry will cause a lot of pain and cost a lot of money, but the authors' solution of focusing on environmental efficiency is too reductionist and far too easy.

Business faces many environmental challenges. Regulations will become more stringent and more encompassing, public expectations for environmental performance will rise dramatically and environmental considerations will pervade the marketplace. Companies will be forced to deal with those pressures if they want to thrive.

Take Walley and Whitehead's example, the paper industry. In their article in *Business Strategy and the Environment* (1993), Vincent di Norcia, Barry Cotton and John Dodge showed how environmental demands have changed dramatically the competitive position of the Canadian paper industry. The former advantage of hinterland mill location has turned into a disadvantage because of lack of urban wastepaper supply. Users of paper, such as newspaper companies, are eager to use recycled newsprint, but Canadian producers have not kept pace with that development, viewing it as a threat instead of an opportunity. The paper industry faces a daunting range of environmental issues, including chlorine bleaching elimination, atmospheric pollution and sustainable forest management. Thus, a primary concern for this industry should be how to develop a strategy that integrates these pressures. Of course, efficiency is important, but to emphasize it too much misses the point.

Integrating environmental factors into a business strategy is not only a broad and deep process, but it will also involve big jumps and innovation. We see three crucial elements in this process:

1. Business needs to find ways to continue producing economically valuable goods and services while reducing their ecological impact dramatically. Accomplishing this goes beyond finding smarter and finer trade-offs between business and environmental concerns, as Walley and Whitehead suggest. It calls for developing new products and services.

   Nick Robins offers several alternatives in *Getting Eco-Efficient*, a 1994 report for the Business Council for Sustainable Development (Robins, 1994). They include: miniaturization, drastic weight reduction, design for disassembly, reuse, reparability and ageing with quality. These options challenge most of the conventional wisdom of product development. Also, instead of selling more solvents or cars, for example, businesses need to offer a complete service, such as taking back products or leasing. Such a service approach will change most companies' identities.

2. New standards, which go far beyond shareholder value, must be set for environmental efficiency. Progress (efficiency) needs to be measured on the basis of some kind of value added (money, services, human need) for each unit of ecological cost. Research is well under way to define new measures. As Robins points out, environmental efficiency cannot mean simply getting more from less, since this 'less' may still exceed the ultimate limits of the earth's carrying capacity. Efficiency must encompass absolute as well as relative performance.

3. Companies must develop new relationships with employees, environmental groups, customers, the public at large and governments. Such relationships will widen the scope of accountability and involvement of all parties in a learning process.

Noah Walley and Bradley Whitehead respond:

It's a good sign that so many of the respondents recognize the hard trade-offs between economic growth and environmental improvement. Like Frances Cairncross, we lament that our more sober assessment of these trade-offs is not as 'quotable' as, and perhaps is less inspirational than, the win-win proposition. But, like Rob Gray, we believe that embracing that assessment is more likely to lead to sustainable environmental improvement.

Unfortunately, many of the respondents incorrectly interpreted our views as reactionary and even an attempt to slow environmental progress. Environmental improvement is needed in many areas, and level-headedness and rationality should not be equated with obstruction. Kurt Fischer and Johan Schot miss our point when they warn that a focus on environmental efficiency will lead to incremental and reactionary thinking. And we are not calling for a generally defensive environmental strategy either. A strategy of digging in your heels and drawing lines in the sand is one of the highest risk approaches and it will not maximize value for the companies that adopt it. Moreover, we would never proffer non-compliance as an acceptable option for companies.

The challenge is to figure out how fast and how far to go. Companies must decide what kind of strategy is called for (partnership, pre-emptive move, etc) and what the optimal tactics are. Fischer and Schot argue that business needs to develop new products and services, but they do not tell us at what price we should do that or how dramatically we should act in opposition to, or at least ahead of, consumer interest. Sometimes a bold stroke is the key, such as when the public environmental agenda is clear. At other times, the appropriate path may be in steps, such as in cases of speculative science or unclear linkages between public concern and environmental impact. Unfortunately, few companies are set up to pursue a strategic approach that explores the subtleties of the challenge. Simplistic 'visionary' targets (zero environmental emissions, for example) are overly reductionist and deprive the organization of necessary capabilities.

One of the most vexing challenges for companies is to determine what environmental issues are the most important to society (which may or may not be related to real underlying risks). Involving stakeholders can be an excellent method for finding areas of greatest value and testing the strength of potential responses.

Suggesting, as J Ladd Greeno does, that environmental costs can readily be passed on to consumers and therefore do not bear a value implication for companies, is simply not true. In economic parlance, few goods in today's world are perfectly inelastic, where price is decoupled from quantity sold and where the costs of environmental action (and therefore implied price increase) are identical across companies. Indeed, a major component of our thesis is that environmental costs land unevenly and management has discretion about how it will respond. In most of today's competitive markets, competitors offering substitute products stand ready to seize on such opportunities. Look at the electricity industry where the 'effective price' of using high-sulphur coal has led to massive switching to low-sulphur coal and natural gas.

Richard Clarke observes that complying with regulations is usually not expected to yield a positive return. But that is exactly what the 'false choice apologists' offer. Recall that, in his now-famous quotation, Michael Porter claims that exacting standards can result 'in a process that not only pollutes less but lowers costs or improves quality'.

Indeed, several respondents pick up on this very point. Daniel Esty, for example, claims that environmental standards are an efficient way to spur innovation. He rightly points out that we make our living helping companies find unrealized value across a spectrum of business issues; but it is our real-world experience that makes us sceptical of this seductive argument. While tight environmental standards can spur thinking, the environment is usually one of about 10,000 things that can spur productivity and it seldom provides the best stimuli. And, as Cairncross points out, time spent on the environment is time not spent somewhere else. As we note in Chapter 4, the process engineers at one of our clients spend nearly 80 per cent of their time on environmental issues – time not spent on other, high-return initiatives. That may be important environmentally, but it is not a value-maximizing strategy otherwise.

That argument is akin to telling businesses that in order to spur creativity, they must include a picture of the queen of England and a bell in every product. That might be what one company needs, but it would be a distraction for most, and it would result in a lot of strange products.

Finally, Robert Stavins notes that his research suggests that environmental regulation plays a small role in a country's competitive profile. As national economies compete to provide increasing standards of living, the effects of the environment on international competitiveness are still swamped by factors such as the openness of markets, tax structures and physical infrastructures. For individual companies competing head-to-head, however, the environment can matter a great deal. How companies within an industry respond to environmental regulation can produce real, sustainable competitive advantage. We concur with Smart that environmental costs need to be more transparent and internalized in management processes. When companies have information and incentive systems to ensure that they incorporate environmental costs in their decisions, the result is well-thought-out environmental strategies that can save them millions of dollars each year and help them to capitalize better on market opportunities. These gains, while never approaching the nirvana of win-win, can translate directly into better value to consumers, greater returns for shareholders and a more sustainable platform for ongoing environmental improvement.

REFERENCES

di Norcia, V, Cotton, B and Dodge, J (1993) 'Environmental Performance and Competitive Advantage in Canada's Paper Industry', *Business Strategy and the Environment* vol 2, part 4, pp 1–9

Robins, N (1994) *Getting Eco-Efficient* Business Council for Sustainable Development, Geneva

6

Green and Competitive: Ending the Stalemate

Michael Porter and Claas van der Linde

The need for regulation to protect the environment gets widespread but grudging acceptance: widespread because everyone wants a liveable planet, grudging because of the lingering belief that environmental regulations erode competitiveness. The prevailing view is that there is an inherent and fixed trade-off: ecology versus the economy. On one side of the trade-off are the *social* benefits that arise from strict environmental standards. On the other are industry's *private* costs for prevention and clean-up – costs that lead to higher prices and reduced competitiveness. With the argument framed this way, progress on environmental quality has become a kind of arm-wrestling match. One side pushes for tougher standards; the other tries to roll them back. The balance of power shifts one way or the other, depending on the prevailing political winds.

This static view of environmental regulation, in which everything except regulation is held constant, is incorrect. If technology, products, processes and customer needs were all fixed, the conclusion that regulation must raise costs would be inevitable. But companies operate in the real world of dynamic competition, not in the static world of much economic theory. They are constantly finding innovative solutions to pressures of all sorts, from competitors, customers and regulators.

Properly designed environmental standards can trigger innovations that lower the total cost of a product or improve its value. Such innovations allow companies to use a range of inputs more productively – from raw materials to energy to labour – thus offsetting the costs of improving environmental impact and ending the stalemate. Ultimately, this enhanced *resource productivity* makes companies more competitive, not less.

Consider how the Dutch flower industry has responded to its environmental problems. Intense cultivation of flowers in small areas was contaminating the soil and groundwater with pesticides, herbicides and fertilizers. Facing increasingly strict regulation on the release of chemicals, the Dutch understood that the only effective way to address the problem would be to develop a closed-loop system. In advanced Dutch greenhouses, flowers now grow in water and rock wool, not in soil. This lowers the risk of infestation, reducing the need for fertilizers and pesticides, which are delivered in water that circulates and is reused.

The tightly monitored closed-loop system also reduces variation in growing conditions, thus improving product quality. Handling costs have gone down because the flowers are cultivated on specially designed platforms. In addressing the environmental problem, then, the Dutch have innovated in ways that have raised the productivity with which they use many of the resources involved in growing flowers. The net result is not only dramatically lower environmental impact, but also lower costs, better product quality and enhanced global competitiveness (see the box below).

INNOVATING TO BE COMPETITIVE: THE DUTCH FLOWER INDUSTRY

The Dutch flower industry is responsible for about 65 per cent of world exports of cut flowers – an astonishing figure given that the most important production inputs in the flower business would seem to be land and climate. Anyone who has been to the Netherlands knows its disadvantages on both counts: the Dutch have to reclaim land from the sea and the weather is notoriously problematic. How can the Dutch be the world's leaders in the flower business when they lack comparative advantage in the traditional sense? The answer, among other reasons, is that they have innovated at every step in the value chain, creating technology and highly specialized inputs that enhance resource productivity and offset the country's natural disadvantages.

In selling and distribution, for example, the Netherlands has five auction houses custom designed for the flower business. Carts of flowers are automatically towed on computer-guided paths into the auction room. The buying process occurs in a few seconds. Buyers sit in an amphitheatre and the price on the auction clock moves down until the first buyer signals electronically. That buyer's code is attached to the cart, which is routed to the company's shipping and handling area. Within a few minutes, the flowers are on a truck to regional markets or in a specialized, pre-cooled container on their way to nearby Schiphol airport. Good airports and highway systems may be plentiful elsewhere, too. But the Netherlands' innovative, specialized infrastructure is a competitive advantage. It leads to very high productivity. It is so successful that growers from other countries actually fly flowers there to be processed, sold and re-exported.

Paradoxically, having a shortage of general-purpose or more basic inputs can sometimes be turned into an advantage. If land were readily available and the climate more favourable, the Dutch would have competed the same way other countries did. Instead, they were forced to innovate, developing a high-tech system of year-round greenhouse cultivation. The Dutch continually improve the unique, specialized technology that creates high-resource productivity and underpins their competitiveness.

In contrast, an abundance or a lack of environmental pressure may lead a country's companies to spend its national resources unproductively. Competing based on cheap inputs, which could be used with less productivity, was sufficient in a more insular, less global economy. Today, when emerging nations with even cheaper labour and raw materials are part of the global economy, the old strategy is unsustainable.

The example in the box above illustrates why the debate about the relationship between competitiveness and the environment has been framed incorrectly. Policymakers, business leaders and environmentalists have focused on the static cost impacts of environmental regulation and have ignored the more important offsetting productivity benefits from innovation. As a result, they have acted too often in ways that unnecessarily drive up costs and slow down progress on environmental issues. This static mind-set has thus created a self-fulfilling prophecy, leading to ever more costly environmental regulation. Regulators tend to set regulations in ways that deter innovation. Companies, in turn, oppose and delay regulations instead of innovating to address them. The whole process has spawned an industry of litigators and consultants that drains resources away from real solutions.

Are cases like the Dutch flower industry the exception rather than the rule? Is it naïve to expect that reducing pollution will often enhance competitiveness? We think not and the reason is that pollution often is a form of economic waste. When scrap, harmful substances or energy forms are discharged into the environment as pollution, it is a sign that resources have been used incompletely, inefficiently or ineffectively. Moreover, companies then have to perform additional activities that add cost but create no value for customers – for example, handling, storage, and disposal of discharges.

The concept of resource productivity opens up a new way of looking at both the full systems costs and the value associated with any product. Resource inefficiencies are most obvious within a company in the form of incomplete material utilization and poor process controls, which result in unnecessary waste, defects and stored materials. But there are also many other hidden costs buried in the life cycle of the product. Packaging discarded by distributors or customers, for example, wastes resources and adds costs. Customers bear additional costs when they use products that pollute or waste energy. Resources are lost when products that contain usable materials are discarded and when customers pay – directly or indirectly – for product disposal.

Environmental improvement efforts have traditionally overlooked these systems costs. Instead, they have focused on pollution control through better identification, processing and disposal of discharges or waste – all costly approaches. In recent years, more advanced companies and regulators have embraced the concept of pollution prevention, sometimes called source reduction, which uses such methods as material substitution and closed-loop processes to limit pollution before it occurs.

But although pollution prevention is an important step in the right direction, ultimately companies must learn to frame environmental improvement in terms of resource productivity (Joel Makower, 1993).[1] Today, managers and regulators focus on the actual costs of eliminating or treating pollution. They must shift their attention to include the opportunity costs of pollution-wasted resources, wasted effort and diminished product value to the customer. At the level of resource productivity, environmental improvement and competitiveness come together.

This new view of pollution as resource inefficiency evokes the quality revolution of the 1980s and its most powerful lessons. Today, we have little trouble grasping the idea that innovation can improve quality while actually lowering cost. But as recently as 15 years ago, managers believed there was a fixed trade-off. Improving quality was expensive because it could be achieved only through inspection and rework of the 'inevitable' defects that came off the line. What lay behind the old view was the assumption that both product design and production processes were fixed. As managers have rethought the quality issue, however, they have abandoned that old mind-set. Viewing defects as a sign of inefficient product and process design – not as an inevitable by-product of manufacturing – was a breakthrough. Companies now strive to build quality into the entire process.

---

1 See Makower, (1993) for one of the pioneering efforts to see environmental improvement this way.

The new mind-set unleashed the power of innovation to relax or eliminate what companies had previously accepted as fixed trade-offs.

Like defects, pollution often reveals flaws in the product design or production process. Efforts to eliminate pollution can therefore follow the same basic principles widely used in quality programmes: use inputs more efficiently, eliminate the need for hazardous, hard-to-handle materials and eliminate unneeded activities. In a recent study of major process changes at ten manufacturers of printed circuit boards, for example, pollution-control personnel initiated 13 of 33 major changes. Of the 13 changes, 12 resulted in cost reduction, 8 in quality improvements, and 5 in extension of production capabilities (Andrew King, 1994). It is not surprising that Total Quality Management (TQM) has become a source of ideas for pollution reduction that can create offsetting benefits. The Dow Chemical Company, for example, explicitly identified the link between quality improvement and environmental performance by using statistical-process control to reduce the variance in processes and to lower waste.

INNOVATION AND RESOURCE PRODUCTIVITY

To explore the central role of innovation and the connection between environmental improvement and resource productivity, we have been collaborating since 1991 with the Management Institute for Environment and Business (MEB) on a series of international case studies of industries and sectors significantly affected by environmental regulation: pulp and paper, paint and coatings, electronics manufacturing, refrigerators, dry cell batteries and printing inks (see table 6.1). The data clearly show that the costs of addressing environmental regulations can be minimized, if not eliminated, through innovation that delivers other competitive benefits. We first observed the phenomenon in the course of our research for a study of national competitiveness, *The Competitive Advantage of Nations* (The Free Press, 1990).

Consider the chemical sector, where many believe that the ecology-economy trade-off is particularly steep. A study of activities to prevent waste generation at 29 chemical plants found innovation offsets that enhanced resource productivity. Of 181 of these waste-prevention activities, only one resulted in a net cost increase. Of the 70 activities with documented changes in product yield, 68 reported increases; the average for 20 initiatives documented with specific data was 7 per cent. These innovation offsets were achieved with surprisingly low investments and very short payback times. One-quarter of the 48 initiatives with detailed capital cost information required *no* capital investment at all; of the 38 initiatives with data on the payback period, nearly two-thirds recouped their initial investments in six months or less. The annual savings per dollar spent on source reduction averaged $3.49 for the 27 activities for which this information could be calculated. The study also found that the two main motivating factors for source-reduction activities were waste-disposal costs and environmental regulation.

Innovation in response to environmental regulation can fall into two broad categories. The first is new technologies and approaches that minimize the cost of dealing with pollution once it occurs. The key to these approaches often lies in taking the resources embodied in the pollution and converting them into something of value. Companies get smarter about how to process toxic materials

Table 6.1 *Environmental Regulation has Competitive Implications*

Sector/ Industry	Environmental issues	Innovative solutions	Innovation offsets
Pulp and paper	Dioxin released by bleaching with chlorine	Improved cooking and washing processes Elimination of chlorine by using oxygen, ozone or peroxide for bleaching Closed-loop processes (still problematic)	Lower operating costs through greater use of by-product energy sources 25 per cent initial price premium for chlorine-free paper
Paint and coatings	Volatile organic compounds (VOCs) in solvents	New paint formulations (low solvent-content paints, water-borne paints) Improved application techniques Powder or radiation-cured coatings	Price premium for solvent-free paints Improved coatings quality in some segments Worker safety benefits Higher coatings-transfer efficiency Reduced coating costs through materials savings
Electronics manufact- uring	Volatile organic compounds (VOCs) in cleaning agents	Semi-aqueous, terpene-based cleaning agents Closed-loop systems No-clean soldering where possible	Increase in cleaning quality and thus in product quality 30 to 80 per cent reduction in cleaning costs, often for one-year payback periods Elimination of an unnecessary production step
Refrigerators	Chlorofluoro-carbons (CFCs) used as refrigerants Energy usage Disposal	Alternative refrigerants (propane-isobutane mix) Thicker insulation Better gaskets Improved compressors	10 per cent better energy efficiency at same cost 5 to 10 per cent initial price premium for 'green' refrigerator
Dry cell batteries	Cadmium, mercury, lead, nickel, cobalt, lithium and zinc releases in landfills or to the air (after incineration)	Rechargeable batteries of nickel-hydride (for some applications) Rechargeable lithium batteries (now being developed)	Nearly twice as efficient at same cost Higher energy efficiency Expected to be price competitive in the near future
Printing inks	VOCs in petroleum inks	Water-based inks and soy inks	Higher efficiency, brighter colours and better printability (depending on application)

Source: Benjamin C Bonifant, Ian Ratcliffe and Claas van der Linde

and emissions into usable forms, recycle scrap and improve secondary treatment. For example, at a Rhône-Poulenc plant in Chalampe, France, nylon by-products known as diacids used to be incinerated. Rhône-Poulenc invested 76 million francs and installed new equipment to recover and sell these diacids as additives for dyes and tanning and as coagulation agents. The new recovery process has generated annual revenues of about 20.1 million francs. New de-inking technologies developed by Massachusetts-based Thermo Electron Corporation, among others, are allowing more extensive use of recycled paper. Molten Metal Technology of Waltham, Massachusetts, has developed a cost-saving catalytic extraction method to process many types of hazardous waste.

The second and far more interesting and important type of innovation addresses the root causes of pollution by improving resource productivity in the first place. Innovation offsets can take many forms, including more efficient utilization of particular inputs, better product yields and better products (see the box below). Consider the following examples.

Resource productivity improves when less costly materials are substituted or when existing ones are better utilized. Dow Chemical's California complex scrubs hydrochloric gas with caustic to produce a wide range of chemicals. The company used to store the waste water in evaporation ponds. Regulation called for Dow to close the evaporation ponds by 1988. In 1987, under pressure to comply with the new law, the company redesigned its production process. It reduced the use of caustic soda, decreasing caustic waste by 6,000 tons per year and hydrochloric acid waste by 80 tons per year. Dow also found that it could capture a portion of the waste stream for reuse as a raw material in other parts of the plant. Although it cost only $250,000 to implement, the process gave Dow an annual saving of $2.4 million (Mark H Dorfman, Warren R Muir and Catherine G Miller, 1992).

ENVIRONMENTAL IMPROVEMENT CAN BENEFIT RESOURCE PRODUCTIVITY

Process benefits:
- Materials savings resulting from more complete processing, substitution, reuse or recycling of production inputs.
- Increases in process yields.
- Less downtime through more careful monitoring and maintenance.
- Better utilization of by-products.
- Conversion of waste into valuable forms.
- Lower energy consumption during the production process.
- Reduced material storage and handling costs.
- Savings from safer workplace conditions.
- Elimination or reduction of the cost of activities involved in discharges or waste handling, transportation and disposal.
- Improvements in the product as a by-product of process changes (such as better process control).

Product benefits:
- Higher quality, more consistent products.
- Lower product costs (for instance, from material substitution).
- Lower packaging costs.
- More efficient resource use by products.
- Safer products.
- Lower net costs of product disposal to customers.
- Higher product resale and scrap value.

3M also improved resource productivity. Forced to comply with new regulations to reduce solvent emissions by 90 per cent, 3M found a way to avoid the use of solvents altogether by coating products with safer, water-based solutions. The company gained an early-mover advantage in product development over competitors, many of whom switched significantly later. The company also shortened its time to market because its water-based product did not have to go through the approval process for solvent based coatings (Don L Boroughs and Betsy Carpenter, 1991).

3M found that innovations can improve process consistency, reduce downtime and lower costs substantially. The company used to produce adhesives in batches that were then transferred to storage tanks. One bad batch could spoil the entire contents of a tank. Lost product, downtime and expensive hazardous waste-disposal were the result. 3M developed a new technique to run rapid quality tests on new batches. It reduced hazardous wastes by 110 tons per year at almost no cost, yielding an annual saving of more than $200,000 (John H Sheridan, 1992).

Many chemical-production processes require an initial start-up period after production interruptions in order to stabilize output and bring it within specifi-cations. During that time, only scrap material is produced. When regulations raised the cost of waste disposal, Du Pont was motivated to install higher-quality monitoring equipment, which in turn reduced production interruptions and the associated production start-ups. Du Pont not only lowered its waste generation but also it cut the amount of time it wasn't producing anything (Gerald Parkinson, 1990).

Process changes to reduce emissions and use resources more productively often result in higher yields. As a result of new environmental standards, Ciba-Geigy Corporation re-examined the waste-water streams at its dye plant in Tom's River, New Jersey. Engineers made two changes to the production process. First, they replaced sludge-creating iron with a less harmful chemical conversion agent. Second, they eliminated the release of a potentially toxic product into the waste-water stream. They not only reduced pollution but also increased process yields by 40 per cent, realizing an annual cost saving of $740,000. Although that part of the plant was ultimately closed, the example illustrates the role of regulatory pressure in process innovation.

Process innovations to comply with environmental regulation can even improve product consistency and quality. In 1990, the Montreal Protocol and the US Clean Air Act required electronics companies to eliminate ozone-depleting chlorofluoro-carbons (CFCs). Many companies used them as cleaning agents to remove residues that occur in the manufacture of printed circuit boards. Scientists at Raytheon confronted the regulatory challenge. Initially, they thought that complete elimination of CFCs would be impossible. After research, however, they found an alternative cleaning agent that could be reused in a closed-loop system. The new method improved average product quality – which the old CFC-based cleaning agent had occasionally compromised – while also lowering operating costs. Responding to the same regulation, other researchers identified applications that did not require any cleaning at all and developed so-called no-clean soldering technologies, which lowered operating costs without compromising quality. Without environmental regulation, that innovation would not have happened.

Innovations to address environmental regulations can also lower product costs and boost resource productivity by reducing unnecessary packaging or simplifying designs. A 1991 law in Japan set standards to make products easier to recycle. Hitachi, along with other Japanese appliance producers, responded by redesigning products to reduce disassembly time. In the process, it cut back the number of parts in a washing machine by 16 per cent and the number of parts in a vacuum cleaner by 30 per cent. Fewer components made the products easier not only to disassemble but also to assemble in the first place. Regulation that requires such recyclable products can lower the user's disposal costs and lead to designs that allow a company to recover valuable materials more easily. Either the customer or the manufacturer who takes back used products reaps greater value.

Although such product innovations have been prompted by regulators instead of by customers, world demand is putting a higher value on resource efficient products. Many companies are using innovations to command price premiums for 'green' products and to open up new market segments. Because Germany adopted recycling standards earlier than most other countries, German companies have first-mover advantages in developing less packaging-intensive products, which are both lower in cost and sought after in the marketplace. In the United States, Cummins Engine Company's development of low-emissions diesel engines for such applications as trucks and buses – innovation that US environmental regulations spurred – is allowing it to gain position in international markets where similar needs are growing.

These examples and many others like them do not prove that companies always can innovate to reduce environmental impact at low cost. However, they show that there are considerable opportunities to reduce pollution through innovations that redesign products, processes and methods of operation. Such examples are common in spite of companies' resistance to environmental regulation and in spite of regulatory standards that often are hostile to innovative, resource-productive solutions. The fact that such examples are common carries an important message: today a new frame of reference for thinking about environmental improvement is urgently needed.

DO WE REALLY NEED REGULATION?

If innovation in response to environmental regulation can be profitable – if a company can actually offset the cost of compliance through improving resource productivity – why is regulation necessary at all? If such opportunities exist, wouldn't companies pursue them naturally and wouldn't regulation be unnecessary? That is like saying there will rarely be ten-dollar bills to be found on the ground because someone already will have picked them up.

Certainly, some companies do pursue such innovations without, or in advance of, regulation. In Germany and Scandinavia, where both companies and consumers are very attuned to environmental concerns, innovation is not uncommon. As companies and their customers adopt the resource productivity mind-set and as knowledge about innovative technologies grows, there may well be less need for regulation over time in the United States.

But the belief that companies will pick up on profitable opportunities without a regulatory push makes a false assumption about competitive reality – namely, that all profitable opportunities for innovation have already been discovered, that all managers have perfect information about them and that organizational incentives are aligned with innovating. In fact, in the real world managers often have highly incomplete information and limited time and attention. Barriers to change are numerous. The Environmental Protection Agency's (EPA's) Green Lights programme, which works with companies to promote energy-saving lighting, shows that many ten-dollar bills are still waiting to be picked up. In one audit, nearly 80 per cent of the projects offered paybacks within two years or less, and yet the companies considering them had not taken action (Stephen J deCanio, 1993). Only after companies joined the programme and benefited from the EPA's information and cajoling, were such highly profitable projects implemented.

We are now in a transitional phase of industrial history in which companies are still inexperienced in handling environmental issues creatively. Customers, too, are unaware that resource inefficiency means that they must pay for the cost of pollution. For example, they tend to see discarded packaging as free because there is no separate charge for it and no current lower-cost alternative. Because there is no direct way to recapture the value of the wasted resources that customers already have paid for, they imagine that discarding used products carries no cost penalty for them.

Regulation, although a different type than is currently practised, is needed for six major reasons:

- To create pressure that motivates companies to innovate. Our broader research on competitiveness highlights the important role of outside pressure in overcoming organizational inertia and fostering creative thinking.
- To improve environmental quality in cases in which innovation and the resulting improvements in resource productivity do not completely offset the cost of compliance; or in which it takes time for learning effects to reduce the overall cost of innovative solutions.
- To alert and educate companies about likely resource inefficiencies and potential areas for technological improvement (although government cannot know better than companies how to address them).
- To raise the likelihood that product innovations and process innovations in general will be environmentally friendly.
- To create demand for environmental improvement until companies and customers are able to perceive and measure the resource inefficiencies of pollution better.
- To level the playing-field during the transition period to innovation-based environmental solutions, ensuring that one company cannot gain position by avoiding environmental investments. Regulation provides a buffer for innovative companies until new technologies are proven and the effects of learning can reduce technological costs.

Those who believe that market forces alone will spur innovation may argue that total quality management programmes were initiated without regulatory intervention. However, TQM came to the United States and Europe through a different kind of pressure. Decades earlier, TQM had been widely diffused in Japan – the result of a whole host of government efforts to make product quality a national goal, including the creation of the Deming Prize. Only after Japanese companies had devastated them in the marketplace did Americans and Europeans embrace TQM.

The Cost of the Static Mind-Set

Regulators and companies should focus, then, on relaxing the trade-off between environmental protection and competitiveness by encouraging innovation and resource productivity. Yet the current adversarial climate drives up the costs of meeting environmental standards and circumscribes the innovation benefits, making the trade-off far steeper than it needs to be.

To begin with, the power struggle involved in setting and enforcing environmental regulations consumes enormous amounts of resources. A 1992 study by the Rand Institute for Civil Justice, for example, found that 88 per cent of the money that insurers paid out between 1986 and 1989 on Superfund claims went to pay for legal and administrative costs, whereas only 12 per cent was used for actual site clean-ups (Jan Paul Acton and Lloyd S Dixon, 1992). The Superfund law may well be the most inefficient environmental law in the United States, but it is not the only cause of inefficiency. We believe that a substantial fraction of environmental spending as well as of the revenues of environmental products and services companies relates to the regulatory struggle itself and not to improving the environment.

One problem with the adversarial process is that it locks companies into static thinking and systematically pushes industry estimates of the costs of regulation upwards. A classic example occurred during the debate in the United States on the 1970 Clean Air Act. Lee Iacocca, then Executive Vice President of the Ford Motor Company, predicted that the compliance with the new regulations would require huge price increases, force automobiles for US production to a halt by 1975 and severely damage the US economy. The 1970 Clean Air Act was subsequently enacted and Iacocca's dire predictions turned out to be wrong. Similar stories are common.

Static thinking causes companies to fight environmental standards that actually could enhance their competitiveness. Most distillers of coal-tar in the United States, for example, opposed 1991 regulations requiring substantial reductions in benzene emissions. At the time, the only solution was to cover the tar storage tanks with costly gas blankets. But the regulations spurred Aristech Chemical Corporation of Pittsburgh, Pennsylvania, to develop a way to remove benzene from tar in the first processing step, thereby eliminating the need for gas blankets. Instead of suffering a cost increase, Aristech saved itself $3.3 million.

Moreover, company mind-sets make the costs of addressing environmental regulations appear higher than they actually are. Many companies do not account for a learning curve, although the actual costs of compliance are likely to decline over time. A recent study in the pulp-and-paper sector, for example, found the actual costs of compliance to be $4 to $5.50 per ton, whereas original industry estimates had been as high as $16.40 (Norman Bonson et al, 1988). Similarly, the cost of compliance with a 1990 regulation controlling sulphur dioxide emissions is today only about half of what analysts initially predicted, and it is heading lower. With a focus on innovation and resource productivity, today's compliance costs represent an upper limit.

There is legitimate controversy over the benefits to society of specific environmental standards. Measuring the health and safety effects of cleaner air, for example, is the subject of ongoing scientific debate. Some believe that the risks of pollution have been overstated. But whatever the level of *social* benefits proves to be, the *private* costs to companies are still far higher than necessary.

Good Regulation Versus Bad

In addition to being high-cost, the current system of environmental regulation in the United States often deters innovative solutions or renders them impossible. The problem with regulation is not its strictness. It is the way in which standards are written and the sheer inefficiency with which regulations are administered. Strict standards can and should promote resource productivity. The United States' regulatory process has squandered this potential, however, by concentrating on clean-up instead of prevention, mandating specific technologies, setting compliance deadlines that are unrealistically short and subjecting companies to unnecessarily high levels of uncertainty.

The current system discourages risk taking and experimentation. Liability exposure and the government's inflexibility in enforcement, among other things, contribute to the problem. For example, a company that innovates and achieves 95 per cent of target emissions reduction while also registering substantial offsetting cost reductions is still 5 per cent out of compliance and subject to liability. On the other hand, regulators would reward it for adopting safe but expensive secondary treatment (see the box below).

INNOVATION-FRIENDLY REGULATION

Regulation, properly conceived, need not drive up costs. The following principles of regulatory design will promote innovation, resource productivity and competitiveness:

- *Focus on outcomes, not technologies.* Past regulations have often prescribed particular remediation technologies, such as catalysts or scrubbers for air pollution. The phrases 'best available technology' (BAT) and 'best available control technology' (BACT) are deeply rooted in US practice and imply that one technology is best, discouraging innovation.
- *Enact strict rather than lax regulation.* Companies can handle lax regulation incrementally, often with end-of-pipe or secondary treatment solutions. Regulation, therefore, needs to be stringent enough to promote real innovation.
- *Regulate as close to the end user as practical, while encouraging upstream solutions.* This will normally allow more flexibility for innovation in the end product and in all the production and distribution stages. Avoiding pollution entirely or, second best, mitigating it early in the value chain is almost always less costly than late-stage remediation or clean-up.
- *Employ phase-in periods.* Ample but well-defined phase-in periods tied to industry capital-investment cycles will allow companies to develop innovative resource-saving technologies rather than force them to implement expensive solutions hastily, merely patching over problems. California imposed such short compliance deadlines on its wood-furniture industry that many manufacturers chose to leave the state rather than add costly control equipment.
- *Use market incentives.* Market incentives such as pollution charges and deposit-refund schemes draw attention to resource inefficiencies. In addition, tradable permits provide continuing incentives for innovation and encourage creative use of technologies that exceed current standards.
- *Harmonize or converge regulations in associated fields.* Liability exposure in the United States leads companies to stick to safe, BAT approaches, and inconsistent regulation on alternative technologies deters beneficial innovation. For example,

---

one way to eliminate refrigerator cooling agents suspected of damaging the ozone layer involves replacing them with small amounts of propane and butane. But narrowly conceived safety regulations covering these gases seem to have impeded development of the new technology in the United States, while several leading European companies are already marketing the new products.

- *Develop regulations in sync with other countries or slightly ahead of them.* It is important to minimize possible competitive disadvantages relative to foreign companies that are not yet subject to the same standard. Developing regulations slightly ahead of other countries will also maximize export potential in the pollution-control sector by raising incentives for innovation. When standards in the United States lead world developments, domestic companies get opportunities for valuable early-mover advantages. However, if standards are too far ahead or too different in character from those that are likely to apply to foreign competitors, industry may innovate in the wrong directions.
- *Make the regulatory process more stable and predictable.* The regulatory process is as important as the standards. If standards and phase-in periods are set and accepted early enough and if regulators commit to keeping standards in place for, say, five years, industry can lock in and tackle root-cause solutions instead of hedging against the next twist or turn in government philosophy.
- *Require industry participation in setting standards from the beginning.* US regulation differs sharply from European in its adversarial approach. Industry should help in designing phase-in periods, the content of regulations and the most effective regulatory process. A predetermined set of information requests and interactions with industry representatives should be a mandatory part of the regulatory process. Both industry and regulators must work toward a climate of trust because industry needs to provide genuinely useful information and regulators need to take industry input seriously.
- *Develop strong technical capabilities among regulators.* Regulators must understand an industry's economics and what drives its competitiveness. Better information exchange will help avoid costly gaming in which ill-informed companies use an array of lawyers and consultants to try to stall the poorly designed regulations of ill-informed regulators.
- *Minimize the time and resources consumed in the regulatory process itself.* Time delays in granting permits are usually costly for companies. Self-regulation with periodic inspections would be more efficient than requiring formal approvals. Potential and actual litigation creates uncertainty and consumes resources. Mandatory arbitration procedures or rigid arbitration steps before litigation would lower costs and encourage innovation.

Just as bad regulation can damage competitiveness, good regulation can enhance it. Consider the differences between the US pulp-and-paper sector and the Scandinavian. Strict early US regulations in the 1970s were imposed without adequate phase-in periods, forcing companies to adopt best available technologies quickly. At that time, the requirements invariably meant installing proven but costly end-of-pipe treatment systems. In Scandinavia, on the other hand, regulation permitted more flexible approaches, enabling companies to focus on the production process itself, not just on secondary treatment of wastes. Scandinavian companies developed innovative pulping and bleaching technologies that not only met emission requirements but also lowered operating costs. Even though the United States was the first to regulate, US companies were unable to realize any first-mover advantages because US regulations ignored a critical principle of good environmental regulation: create maximum opportunity for innovation by letting industries discover how to solve their own problems.

Unfortunately for the US pulp-and-paper industry, a second principle of good regulation was also ignored: foster continuous improvement and do not lock in on a particular technology or the status quo. The Swedish regulatory agency took a more effective approach. Whereas the United States mandated strict emissions goals and established very tight compliance deadlines, Sweden started out with looser standards but clearly communicated that tougher ones would follow. The results were predictable. US companies installed secondary treatment systems and stopped there. Swedish producers, anticipating stricter standards, continually incorporated innovative environmental technologies into their normal cycles of capacity replacement and innovation.

The innovation-friendly approach produced the residual effect of raising the competitiveness of the local equipment industry. Spurred by Scandinavian demand for sophisticated process improvement, local pulp-and-paper equipment suppliers, such as Sunds Defiberator and Kamyr, ultimately made major international gains in selling innovative pulping and bleaching equipment.

Eventually, the Scandinavian pulp and paper industry was able to reap innovation offsets that went beyond those directly stemming from regulatory pressures. By the early 1990s, producers realized that growing public awareness of the environmental problems associated with pulp-mill effluents was creating a niche market. For a time, Scandinavian companies with totally chlorine-free paper were able to command significant price premiums and serve a rapidly growing market segment of environmentally informed customers.

Implications for Companies

Certainly, misguided regulatory approaches have imposed a heavy burden on companies, but managers who have responded by digging in their heels to oppose all regulation have been shortsighted as well. It is no secret that Japanese and German automobile makers developed lighter and more fuel efficient cars in response to new fuel consumption standards, while the less competitive US car industry fought such standards and hoped they would go away. The US car industry eventually realized that it would face extinction if it did not learn to compete through innovation. But clinging to the static mind-set too long cost billions of dollars and many thousands of jobs.

To avoid making the same mistakes, managers must start to recognize environmental improvement as an economic and competitive opportunity, not as an annoying cost or an inevitable threat. Instead of clinging to a perspective focused on regulatory compliance, companies need to ask questions such as 'What are we wasting?' and 'How could we enhance customer value?'. The early movers – the companies that can see the opportunity first and embrace innovation-based solutions – will reap major competitive benefits, just as the German and Japanese car makers did (see the box below).

At this stage, for most companies, environmental issues are still the province of outsiders and specialists. That is not surprising. Any new management issue tends to go through a predictable life cycle. When it first arises, companies hire outside experts to help them to navigate. When practice becomes more developed,

THE NEW ENVIRONMENTALISTS

Environmentalists can foster innovation and resource productivity by speaking out for the right kind of regulatory standards and by educating the public to demand innovative environmental solutions. The German section of Greenpeace, for example, noted in 1992 that a mixture of propane and butane was safer for cooling refrigerators than the then prevalent cooling agents, hydrofluorocarbons or hydrochlorofluorocarbons, that were proposed as replacements for chlorofluorocarbons. Greenpeace for the first time in its history began endorsing a commercial product. It actually ran an advertising campaign for a refrigerator designed by Foron, a small refrigerator maker on the verge of bankruptcy. The action was greatly leveraged by extensive media coverage and has been a major reason behind the ensuing demand for Foron-built propane-butane-refrigerator producers in Germany later made to the same technology.

Environmental organizations can support industry by becoming sources of information about best practices that may not be well known outside of a few pioneering companies. When it realized that German magazine publishers and readers alike were unaware of the much improved quality of chlorine-free paper, Greenpeace Germany issued a magazine printed on chlorine-free paper. It closely resembled the leading German political weekly, *Der Spiegel*, and it encouraged readers to demand that publishers switch to chlorine-free paper. Shortly after, *Der Spiegel* and several other large magazines did indeed switch. Other environmental organizations could shift some resources away from litigation to focus instead on funding and disseminating research on innovations that address environmental problems.

Among US environmental groups, the Environmental Defense Fund (EDF) has been an innovator in its willingness to promote market-based regulatory systems and to work directly with industry. It supported the sulphur-dioxide trading system that allows companies either to reduce their own emissions or to buy emissions allowances from other companies that have managed to exceed their reduction quotas at lower cost. The EDF-McDonalds' Waste Reduction Task Force, formed in 1990, led to a substantial redesign of McDonalds' packaging, including the elimination of the polystyrene-foam clamshell. EDF is now working with General Motors on plans to remove heavily polluting cars from the road and with Johnson & Johnson, McDonald's, National Bank, The Prudential Insurance Company of America, Time Warner and Duke University to promote the use of recycled paper.

internal specialists take over. Only after a field becomes mature do companies integrate it into the ongoing role of line management.

Many companies have delegated the analysis of environmental problems and the development of solutions to outside lawyers and environmental consultants. Such experts in the adversarial regulatory process, who are not deeply familiar with the company's overall technology and operations, inevitably focus on compliance rather than innovation. They invariably favour end-of-pipe solutions.

Many consultants, in fact, are associated with vendors who sell such technologies. Some companies are in the second phase, in which environmental issues are assigned to internal specialists. But these specialists – for example, legal, governmental-affairs or environmental departments – lack full profit responsibility and are separate from the line organization. Again, the result is almost always narrow, incremental solutions.

If the sorts of process and product redesigns needed for true innovation are even to be considered, much less implemented, environmental strategies must become an issue for general management. Environmental impact must be embedded in the overall process of improving productivity and competitiveness. The resource-productivity model, rather than the pollution-control model, must govern decision-making.

How can managers accelerate their companies' progress towards a more competitive environmental approach? First, they can measure their direct and indirect environmental impacts. One of the major reasons that companies are not very innovative about environmental problems is ignorance. A large producer of organic chemicals, for example, hired a consultant to explore waste-reduction opportunities in its 40 waste streams. A careful audit uncovered 497 different waste streams – the company had been wrong by a factor of more than ten (Gerald Parkinson, 1990). Our research indicates that the act of measurement alone leads to enormous opportunities to improve productivity.

Companies that adopt the resource-productivity framework and go beyond currently regulated areas will reap the greatest benefits. Companies should inventory all unused, emitted or discarded resources or packaging. Within the company, some poorly utilized resources will be held within plants, some discharged, and some put in dumpsters. Indirect resource inefficiencies will occur at the level of suppliers, channels and customers. At the customer level, resource inefficiencies show up in the use of the product, in discarded packaging and in resources left in the used-up product.

Secondly, managers can learn to recognize the opportunity cost of underutilized resources. Few companies have analysed the true cost of toxicity, waste and what they discard, much less the second-order impacts that waste and discharges have on other activities. Fewer still look beyond the out-of-pocket costs of dealing with pollution to the opportunity cost of the resources they waste or the productivity they forgo. There are scarcely any companies that think about customer value and the opportunity cost of wasted resources at the customer level.

Many companies do not even track environmental spending carefully, and conventional accounting systems are ill-equipped to measure underutilized resources. Companies evaluate environmental projects as discrete, stand-alone investments. Straightforward waste- or discharge-reduction investments are screened using high hurdle rates that presume the investments are risky – leaving ten-dollar bills on the ground. Better information and evaluation methods will help managers reduce environmental impact while improving resource productivity.

Thirdly, companies should create a bias in favour of innovation-based, productivity-enhancing solutions. They should trace their own and their customers' discharges, scrap, emissions and disposal activities back into company activities to gain insight about beneficial product design, packaging, raw material or process changes. We have been struck by the power of certain systems solutions: groups of activities may be reconfigured or substitutions in inputs or packaging may enhance utilization and potential for recovery. Approaches that focus on treatment of discrete discharges should be sent back to the organization for rethinking.

Current reward systems are as anti-innovation as regulatory policies. At the plant level, companies reward output but ignore environmental costs and wasted resources. The punishment for an innovative, economically efficient solution that falls short of expectations is often far greater than the reward for a costly but 'successful' one.

Finally, companies must become more pro-active in defining new types of relationships with both regulators and environmentalists. Businesses need a new mind-set. How can companies argue shrilly that regulations harm competitiveness and then expect regulators and environmentalists to be flexible and trusting as those same companies request time to pursue innovative solutions?

THE WORLD ECONOMY IN TRANSITION

It is time for the reality of modern competition to inform our thinking about the relationship between competitiveness and the environment. Traditionally, nations were competitive if their companies had access to the lowest cost inputs – capital, labour, energy and raw materials. In industries relying on natural resources, for example, the competitive companies and countries were those with abundant local supplies. Because technology changed slowly, a comparative advantage in inputs was enough for success.

Today, globalization is making the notion of comparative advantage obsolete. Companies can source low-cost inputs anywhere and new, rapidly emerging technologies can offset disadvantages in the cost of inputs. Facing high labour costs at home, for example, a company can automate away the need for unskilled labour. Facing a shortage of a raw material, a company can find an alternative raw material or create a synthetic one. To overcome high space costs, Japanese companies pioneered just-in-time production and avoided storing inventory on the factory floor.

It is no longer enough simply to have resources. Using resources productively is what makes for competitiveness today. Companies can improve resource productivity by producing existing products more efficiently or by making products that are more valuable to customers – products customers are willing to pay more for. Increasingly, the nations and companies that are most competitive are not those with access to the lowest-cost inputs but those that employ the most advanced technology and methods in using their inputs. Because technology is constantly changing, the new paradigm of global competitiveness requires the ability to innovate rapidly.

This new paradigm has profound implications for the debate about environmental policy – about how to approach it, how to regulate and how strict regulation should be. The new paradigm has brought environmental improvement and competitiveness together. It is important to use resources productively, whether those resources are natural and physical or human and capital. Environmental progress demands that companies innovate to raise resource productivity – and that is precisely what the new challenges of global competition demand. Resisting innovation that reduces pollution, as the US car industry did in the 1970s, will lead not only to environmental damage but also to the loss of competitiveness in the global economy. Developing countries that stick with resource-wasting methods and forgo environmental standards because they are 'too expensive' will remain uncompetitive, relegating themselves to poverty.

How an industry responds to environmental problems may, in fact, be a leading indicator of its overall competitiveness. Environmental regulation does not lead inevitably to innovation and competitiveness or to higher productivity for all companies. Only those companies that innovate successfully will win. A truly competitive industry is more likely to take up a new standard as a challenge and respond to it with innovation. An uncompetitive industry, on the other hand, may not be oriented towards innovation and thus may be tempted to fight all regulation.

It is not at all surprising that the debate pitting the environment against competitiveness has developed as it has. Indeed, economically destructive struggles over redistribution are the norm in many areas of public policy. But now is the time for a paradigm shift to carry us forward into the next century. International competition has changed dramatically over the last few decades. Senior managers who grew up at a time when environmental regulation was synonymous with litigation will see increasing evidence that environmental improvement is good business. Successful environmentalists, regulatory agencies and companies will reject old trade-offs and build on the underlying economic logic that links the environment, resource productivity, innovation and competitiveness.

REFERENCES

Acton, Jan Paul and Dixon, Lloyd S (1992) 'Superfund and Transaction Costs: The Experiences of Insurers and Very Large Industrial Firms', working paper, Rand Institute for Civil Justice, Santa Monica, California

Bonson, Norman, McCubbin, Neil and Sprague, John B (1988) 'Kraft Mill Effluents in Ontario', report prepared for the Technical Advisory Committee, Pulp and Paper Sector of MISA, Ontario Ministry of the Environment, Toronto, 29 March, p 166

Boroughs, Don L and Carpenter, Betsy (1991) 'Helping the Planet and the Economy' *UP News and World report* 110, no 11, 25 March, p 46

DeCanio, Stephen J (1993) 'Why Do Profitable Energy-Saving Projects Languish?', working paper, Second International Research Conference of the Greening of Industry Network, Cambridge, Massachusetts

Dorfman, Mark H, Muir, Warren R and Miller, Catherine G (1992) *Environmental Dividends: Cutting More Chemical Wastes*, IN FORM, New York

King, Andrew (1994) 'Improved Manufacturing Resulting From Learning from Waste: Causes, Importance and Enabling Conditions', working paper, Stern School of Business, New York University, New York

Makower, Joel (1993) *The E-Factor: The Bottom Line Approach to Environmentally Responsible Business* Times Books, New York

Parkinson, Gerald (1990) 'Reducing Wastes Can Be Cost-Effective', *Chemical Engineering* 97, no 7, July, p 30

Sheridan, John H (1992) 'Attacking Wastes and Saving Money ... Some of the Time' *Industry Week*, 17 February, p 43

7

Strategic Management for a Small Planet

W Edward Stead and Jean Garner Stead

Let's review for a moment. Humankind lives on a small planet, one limited in its ability to supply resources to and absorb the wastes of an exponentially growing population and an exponentially growing economic system. The planet is experiencing what are potentially catastrophic environmental problems. Air and water pollution, climate change, waste-disposal problems, acid rain and species loss are plaguing humankind; people's lives are becoming frantic and fractured; and these problems will likely get worse before they get better. Humankind cannot stick its head in the sand and ignore what is happening; ostrich dynamics will solve none of these environmental problems.

Of course, there are many origins to these problems and solving them will require efforts on many fronts. For example, education, population control, agricultural reform, technological change and political change are all necessary. However, the most basic reforms are required in the economic paradigm. Further, economic reform means management reform because business managers collectively represent the largest group of economic decision-makers. Indeed, our ecological problems are largely management problems.

In the 1990s and on into the 21st century, strategic managers will need new knowledge, new models and new paradigms that allow them to guide their firms to economic success without putting undue stress on the ecosystem. It is necessary that they understand that the economic system in which they function is a subsystem of the living system called earth. As such, the economic system is subject to the laws of thermodynamics, which define the earth's limits for processing energy and wastes. Further, strategic managers need to understand that their values are critical factors in their decisions. Many of their current business values are based on unrealistic economic assumptions; they need to adopt new economic models that allow them to account for the earth in their decision-making.

A new management paradigm is beginning to appear. The new paradigm recognizes the true essence of the free enterprise system: no firm can prosper without serving the needs of its stakeholders; profits come to those firms that can successfully meet the demands of consumers, investors, employees, the political/legal system, and the greater social system in which they exist. Today, these stakeholders are becoming decidedly greener in their attitudes toward business activity. They want less pollution and wastes, they want more recycling, they demand that more renewable energy sources be used and they demand that products be safer for the ecosystem. Based on all of this, what should strategic managers do?

STRATEGIC MANAGEMENT AND SUSTAINABILITY

Strategic management is a continuous process that involves the efforts of strategic managers to successfully fit an organization into its turbulent environment by developing competitive advantages. These competitive advantages should allow the firm to capitalize on its environmental opportunities and minimize its environmental threats. Thus, strategic management involves continuously adapting to, and creating, change. The greening of the business environment is one of the most significant changes in recent times. Thus it follows that successful strategic managers in the decades to come need to adopt and implement strategies based on the core value of sustainability: strategies that address the interrelatedness of the ecosystem and the economic system.

The Vision of Sustainability

Strategic management begins with a vision of what the firm is and of what it will become. Based on the core values of the firm, this strategic vision is essentially an image that guides the firm's decision-making processes at all levels. The strategic management process involves developing the firm's mission, the goals and objectives it decides to pursue, the strategies it implements to accomplish its goals and objectives, the information it considers important and the ways in which it measures its success around its strategic vision. Thus, strategic management involves moulding the firm's core values into actions that assure the firm's survival within its environment.

As we have discussed, sustainability means preserving the ecosystem as well as maintaining the ability to provide humans with the goods and services necessary for a good life, complete with fulfilling work and economic justice. Achieving sustainability requires determining which types of business activity fit into the earth's carrying capacity and defining the optimal levels of those activities. William Ruckelhaus (1991), CEO of Browning-Ferris Industries and former head of the EPA, says that achieving sustainability in industrialized nations 'means transportation without smog, consumer goods without toxic wastes, energy without acid rain' (p 7).

Sustainability should be a core value because it supports a strategic vision of firms surviving over the long term by integrating their need to earn an economic profit with their responsibility to protect the environment. Like a sailing craft in a race, the individual firm would see that the key to being competitive is the efficient and effective use of renewable resources. It would want to be as light and manoeuvrable as it could be, leaving no trace of its operations in its wake.

As can be seen in Figure 7.1, such a vision demonstrates the interconnectedness of economic success and the health of the ecosystem; the organization would see itself as a part of a greater society and natural environment, to whom its survival is tied. Thus this vision would serve as an excellent foundation for a strategic management process based on instrumental values such as quality, smallness, posterity, wholeness and community. A firm with a vision based on sustainability would develop strategies designed to enhance its long-run profitability as well as to protect the ecosystem. We refer to these as 'sustainability strategies'.

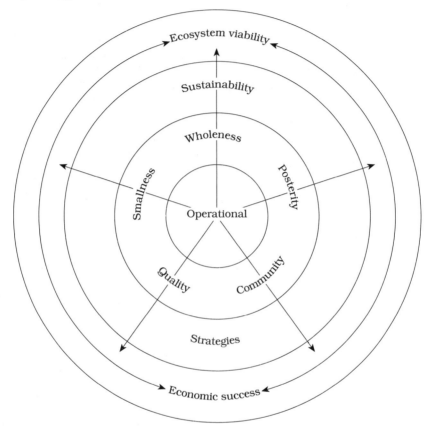

Figure 7.1 *The Vision of Sustainability*

Enterprise Strategy: A Framework for Sustainability

The concept of enterprise strategy has emerged in the past decade as a significant model for describing and analysing the relationship between organizations and their larger environments. Igor Ansoff (1979) first used the term enterprise strategy while discussing the idea that, to be successful in the future, firms must achieve legitimacy within their social and political environments. Edward Freeman (1984) (who has probably contributed most to our understanding of enterprise strategy) says that enterprise strategy is a higher level of strategy that is concerned with what the firm stands for. He identifies three components for understanding a firm's enterprise strategy: (a) values analysis; (b) stakeholder analysis; and (c) issues analysis.

In 1988 Freeman and Gilbert explained that the concept of enterprise strategy ties business strategy to ethics. By determining what it stands for, a firm is able to explicate its purpose, and from that point the firm can develop a strategic management process that supports its purpose. They say:

> *We propose the question 'What do you stand for?' as one that must be answered alongside 'What business are you in?' and one that will link ethics and strategy. 'What do you stand for?' is an explicit appeal for a purpose, and as such, it forms a direct link between ethical reasoning and strategic reasoning. (p 70)*

Menzar, Chrisman and Carroll (1990) point out that determining a firm's enterprise strategy requires an in-depth analysis of the breadth and scope of the firm's relationship with its various stakeholders; this means analysing all of the benefits and costs (economic and social) associated with each stakeholder relationship. They say that a firm can increase its social value by decreasing its social costs and/or increasing its social benefits.

Enterprise strategy provides an excellent philosophical and practical framework for including the planet in the strategic management process. Philosophically, when a firm asks itself what it stands for and then consciously searches for the answer, it has an opportunity to gain a clear, in-depth understanding of the values that form the foundation of its ethical system. Significant clarification and modification of values will be necessary for most firms that wish to develop and implement sustainability strategies, and identifying the values on which the firm's strategies are based is the central focus of enterprise strategy.

Practically, enterprise strategy provides a very good analytical framework for developing sustainability strategies. If the earth is included as a primary stakeholder in the firm, then Freeman's three components for determining enterprise strategy can be used to enhance strategic managers' abilities to develop strategies that recognize the relationship between the firm and the natural environment. First, values analysis assists strategic managers in assessing the degree to which sustainability has emerged as a core value of the firm and which instrumental value changes are required to fully adopt it. Secondly, stakeholder analysis helps strategic managers to better comprehend that the earth is a stakeholder with tremendous breadth. The present human inhabitants on earth would be incorporated as stakeholders in the firm, as would future generations of human beings and other species that exist on the planet; the systems that support life on earth (the air, water, and land) would also be recognized as significant stakeholders in the firm's operations. Also, stakeholder analysis helps the firm to better understand the influences that green consumers, ethical investors and the political/legal system have on the firm. Finally, issues analysis clarifies the relationship between the ecological issues facing the earth and the strategic issues addressed by the organization. Strategic managers would be able to assess the impact of the firm's operations on the earth's resources, species and systems; the results of the assessment could then be incorporated into the firm's strategic decisions.

Thus, analysing the values, stakeholders, and issues related to preserving the earth permits strategic managers to more effectively incorporate these factors into the goals and objectives of the firm. Sustainability values would form the basis of the strategic management process, the costs and benefits of the firm's operations would be measured against the survival needs of the planet's stakeholders, and managers would choose sustainability strategies that allow the firm to operate in profitable, environmentally sound ways.

Sustainability Strategies and Competitive Advantage

It is important to note that sustainability strategies are not compromise strategies; they are not designed merely to earn a profit while doing as little damage as possible to the ecosystem. Rather, they are integrative strategies; they provide competitive advantages to organizations by simultaneously enhancing the quality of the ecosystem and the long-term survivability of the firm. As Art Kleiner (1991) says, 'In the long run, the principles of economic growth and environmental quality reinforce each other' (p 38). Michael Porter (1991) reiterates this point, saying, 'The conflict between environmental protection and economic competitiveness is a false dichotomy' (p 168).

In the front interface with its environment, in which a firm interacts with customers and investors, sustainability strategies can be used to gain an advantage over the competition in several ways. We see in Colin Hutchinson's article (Chapter 8) that consumers and investors are increasingly demanding greenness on the part of organizations. We presented examples (Wal-Mart, Merrill Lynch's Eco-Logical Trust, etc) of how organizations are thriving economically by appealing to these green stakeholders. Further, as Halal (1986) says, smart growth involves turning environmental threats into business opportunities. Many business opportunities exist in industries that are environmentally friendly or are involved in some form of environmental protection and these opportunities will continue to increase over the next decade, providing fertile ground for a variety of entrepreneurial activities.

One example of smart growth is occurring in the recycling industry. As wastes and resource depletion have increased, the recycling industry has prospered; it is projected to grow between 25 per cent and 30 per cent annually between 1990 and 1995. Improved processes for recycling items such as plastics and disposable diapers are rapidly appearing on the scene (Nulty, 1990). Alternative energy sources are also providing smart growth opportunities. Luz International operates a 200 megawatt solar-thermal power generating facility in California that serves 270,000 people. National Energy Associates (NEA) provide power to between 15,000 and 20,000 people by generating energy from 260,000 tons (annually) of low quality cattle manure that cannot be used as fertilizer; the plant saves about 350,000 barrels of oil each year. The president of NEA, Will Parish, points out that this is no do-gooder venture; the firm has paid high returns in order to attract the $100 million in investments it has received.

In addition to recycling and energy, many other industries, such as organic foods and recreation, are providing smart growth opportunities related to our ecological problems ('Growing greener', 1989). In 1991, *Ecopreneuring* by Steve Bennett was published; this book is a guide to green entrepreneurial opportunities in industries such as recycling, water treatment, travel and entertainment. Also, for over a decade a magazine entitled *In Business* has been offering to its readers ideas about environmentally sensitive entrepreneurial opportunities.

At the rear interface with its environment, in which the firm acquires and uses the energy and resources to produce and deliver its goods and/or services, sustainability strategies can also provide several competitive advantages. Reducing the amount of energy and materials consumed in manufacturing and distributing a product or service not only reduces resource depletion, it also reduces costs. The same is true for reducing waste generation and effluent emissions. If production systems can be designed to resemble ecosystems, whereby their wastes and effluents serve as energy sources and raw materials for other processes, then pollution reduction and cost reduction can both be realized (Dougherty, 1990).

Another rear-interface focus that provides both ecological and economic benefits to a firm is the production of high-quality products. High 'conformance quality' (quality based on carefully and precisely conforming to internal specifications) reduces costs because of lower scrap, less rework, less time spent responding to complaints, and so on. It also leads to superior 'perceived quality' by customers and, when customers believe that a product's quality is superior to the competition, a firm can experience higher customer loyalty, more repeat business, opportunities to charge higher prices and market share improvements (Buzzell and Gale, 1987). Add to these economic benefits the ecological benefits that accrue from higher quality (such as the reduction of wastes in manufacturing processes and end-user disposal), and it becomes clear that focusing on quality is a natural strategy for firms concerned about their survival and the survival of our small planet.

In short, sustainability strategies can improve a firm's competitiveness for two reasons: (a) they result in lower costs, and (b) they give the firm the opportunity to differentiate itself and its products from its competitors. According to Michael Porter (1991), cost leadership and differentiation are the two basic competitive advantages firms can develop. Both of these are afforded by sustainability strategies, strategies that not only improve the firm's economic success, but also allow the firm to protect the earth in the process.

REFERENCES

Ansoff, H I (1979) 'The changing shape of the strategic problem' in D Schendel and C Hofer (eds), *Strategic management: A new view of business policy and planning* Little, Brown, Boston, pp 30–44

Bennett, S J (1991) *Ecopreneuring: The complete guide to small business opportunities from the environmental revolution* Wiley, New York

Buzzell, R D and Gale, B T (1987) *The PIMS principles* Free Press, New York

Dougherty, E (April 1990) 'Waste minimization: Reduce wastes and reap the benefits' *R & D Magazine*, pp 62–67

Freeman, R E (1984) *Strategic management: A stakeholder approach* Pitman, Boston

Freeman, R E and Gilbert, D R, Jr (1988) *Corporate strategy and the search for ethics* Prentice-Hall, Englewood Cliffs, New Jersey

'Growing greener' (Autumn 1989) *Exchange*, pp 1, 6–8

Halal, W E (1986) *The new capitalism* John Wiley & Sons, New York

Kleiner, A (July/August 1991) 'What does it mean to be green?' *Harvard Business Review*, pp 38–47

Menzar, M B, Chrisman, J J, and Carroll, A B (August, 1990) *Social responsibility and strategic management: Toward an enterprise strategy classification*, paper presented at the meeting of the National Academy of Management, San Francisco, California

Nulty, P (13 August, 1990) 'Recycling has become big business' *Fortune*, pp 81–86

Porter, M E (April, 1991) 'America's green strategies' *Scientific American*, p 168

Ruckelhaus, William D (1991) 'Quality in the corporation: the key to sustainable development' *Proceedings of the First Conference on Corporate Quality/Environmental Management* Global Environmental Initiative, Washington DC, pp 5–9

8

Corporate Strategy and the Environment

Colin Hutchinson

A SUSTAINABLE FUTURE?

The challenge we face as a world community over the next decade or two is to work towards a sustainable future for the planet. This will require unprecedented co-operation between all nations – hopefully initiated at the 'Earth Summit' in Brazil in June 1992. Co-operation at the level of national governments will not be sufficient. Business organizations and public institutions will have a vital part to play and people in all walks of life will need to review their own life styles and make their adjustments to bring about a future that will be sustainable in world terms.

As Mr Perez de Cuellar, former Secretary General of the United Nations, has said, 'Industrialized countries will need significantly to change their modes of consumption and production as part of the strategy for the environment.'

The role of commercial and industrial enterprises is crucial, as is the role of the many professional institutions with whom they work. The driving force for practical changes must come from business. Industry needs to prove that it is capable of operating in ways that are sustainable. This will not be accomplished by treating environmental issues as a matter for public relations or as an offshoot of Health and Safety. The environmental challenge must be seen as an important strategic decision. Achieving a sustainable future must become part of the agenda for each individual business. In the same way as legality is now accepted as part of business life, so in the future it is likely that 'sustainability' will become an accepted condition of doing business.

Peter Drucker (1995) has suggested that the challenge for every business has three dimensions:

1. to make the present business effective;
2. to identify and realize its potential; and
3. to change it into a different business for a future that will inevitably be different.

All three challenges have to be faced, simultaneously, in the present. These principles can be adapted for the 1990s as shown in the box below.

THE CORPORATE ENVIRONMENTAL CHALLENGE

1. To make your present business effective and its environmental impact acceptable.
2. To identify and realize your potential for a sustainable future, in particular:
   - dealing with wastes and pollution;
   - the procurement and use of resources;
   - developing new business opportunities;
   - providing fulfilling work for employees.
3. To make your business into a different, sustainable business for a future that will inevitably be different.

All three challenges have to be tackled in the present.

Cleaning up the Present Business

In the short term, because of legislation and the need to meet stricter standards in waste management and the control of emissions, the urgent requirement is to look at the business' environmental impacts and to find ways in which these can be made acceptable. An increasing number of companies and local government bodies are adopting environmental policies (Directory of Corporate Environmental Policy). Monitoring the implementation of these policies is often made the responsibility of an environmental department, sometimes linked with Public Affairs or Health and Safety. This work is important both for the performance of the company and for the environment, but it will not be enough.

If a management team decide that their environmental responsibility has been fulfilled by gradually making their enterprise's emissions and waste management acceptable then they are in danger of limiting their business' potential. Most companies seem to be treating the environmental challenge as a threat and failing to realize the opportunities for developing new markets, new products and new processes. There is evidence of this trend in the positioning and job titles of people with environmental responsibilities. The status, location, job title and remit of people with environmental responsibility is a strategic decision. As the box below shows, some job titles indicate that the environment is being seen as a tactical or operational problem.

Exploiting New Business Opportunities

The scale of the opportunity for businesses to tackle environmental problems has been assessed by The Centre for Exploitation of Science and Technology (CEST) in their report *Industry and the Environment: A Strategic Overview*. They described the 12 key problems, the industries which cause them and the technologies which are likely to provide solutions. They also estimated the amount of money likely to be spent on these problems in the next ten years. The figures are given in Table 8.1; Africa, Asia, Latin America and Australasia are not included in these estimates.

TYPICAL ENVIRONMENTAL APPOINTMENTS

Job titles suggesting that the environment is a threat:

* Environmental Safety and Security
* Public Affairs
* Corporate Communications
* Environment Affairs
* Health, Safety and Environment
* Environmental Strategy Manager
* Engineering or Technical aspects
* Quality and Environment

Job titles suggesting that the environment may represent an opportunity:
* Chief Executive
* MD Trading and Marketing
* Business Development

The CEST report provides an indication of the scale of the business opportunities that are likely to arise from the work that needs to be done to reduce environmental damage and to move towards a future that will be more sustainable. This kind of perspective relates to the second dimension of the business challenge. More specifically it gives clear pointers towards reducing pollution, recovering wastes, using resources more efficiently, identifying new business opportunities and, by involving staff more in this kind of work, providing more satisfying work for people at all levels.

Table 8.1 *Business Opportunities in the Environment*

	Estimated expenditure (£bn 1991–2000)		
Issues	*UK*	*EC*	*USA*
Greenhouse effect	48	237	443
Water quality	25	75–100	71
Waste management	19	180–200	120–170
Acid rain	11	51	25
Heavy metals	9	80	52
Ozone depletion	7	70	76
Air quality	7	34	17
Noise	6	32	33
VOCs and smells	3	26	27
Persistent organics	2	23	15
Contaminated land	2	25	150
Major spills	1	7	7
Total	140	860	1060

Source: *Industry and the Environment: A Strategic Overview*, The Centre for Exploitation of Science and Technology

Preparing for a Sustainable Future

The third dimension of the challenge is concerned with changing the business because the future will inevitably be different, and to do this in ways that move closer to a sustainable future.

It is important to appreciate what it means to move an organization towards a sustainable future. In my article in *Long Range Planning* entitled 'Environmental issues: The challenge for the chief executive' (1992), some possibilities for business opportunities were listed. Another way to address this issue is to describe a vision of a sustainable future; a brief outline is given in the box below based on two articles published in *Resurgence* (Lester Brown, 1991). Whilst this is inevitably an oversimplification, it does provide a brief glimpse of what is required. It also suggests possibilities which could help several companies which are seeking new opportunities and would stimulate the creativity of key staff. The overall

---

SUSTAINABLE BUSINESS

Sustainable business achieves the goal of meeting the needs of today without jeopardizing the ability of future generations from meeting their needs. This focuses attention on the way in which non-renewable resources are being consumed and the living world damaged by agricultural and industrial processes.

One of the best indicators of material standards of living is energy consumption. To move towards a sustainable future requires reduction in the use of non-renewable energy (coal, oil and gas especially) and development of renewable sources (solar, wind, geothermal, biomass – according to local endowment).

A major consumer of energy is transport. Reducing the energy used in transportation will be achieved by having fewer cars which travel two or three times as far for each gallon of fuel, relying more on public transport (which would need to be reliable, frequent, clean and efficient to attract customers), by encouraging the use of bicycles for shorter journeys and by replacing some travel with telecommunications.

Other resources should also be used more efficiently and the current acceptance of linear processes which waste resources and produce toxic residues should be replaced by cyclic processes which are resource-conserving and healthy. The goal should be to provide more service for each unit of resource consumed. Changes of this kind will challenge designers and engineers to provide solutions which are compatible with a sustainable future. Guidance will need to come from enlightened top management seeing the environment as an opportunity as well as a threat.

Ultimately it will be necessary to achieve a stable population with life-styles that can be accommodated by the earth's carrying capacity. This will require people all over the world to live peacefully and that will be easier if there is more equitable distribution of wealth. By emphasizing quality of life rather than the quantity of material consumption, the willingness to close the gap between rich and poor will be more acceptable.

In order to accomplish this kind of transformation there will need to be fundamental rethinking of how things are done. Companies should be at the forefront of this challenge. Chief Executives should provide leadership which includes opportunities for managers and staff to re-examine their values, become increasingly involved in refocusing the corporate mission, goals and strategies, to cope with managing change more smoothly and to do it in less time. This will be the area in which companies strengthen their reputation, attract and keep good people and compete effectively in a changing world.

employment pattern will be affected in many developed countries. For example, the proportion of the workforce involved in manufacture, production, agriculture and fisheries could fall to 15 per cent with a rise in skilled manual employment such as reuse, repair, reconditioning and recycling. There is also likely to be a considerable increase in demand for people able to deliver high quality services which contribute to the transformation to a sustainable future.

A COMPANY-WIDE CHALLENGE

In order to respond to the environmental challenge in terms of new business opportunities and to build for the future, management needs to recognize that the issues will pervade all departments. Purchasing departments will need to find raw materials which emanate from sustainable sources of supply and are produced in ways which have a diminishing impact on the environment. They can also find ways to reduce packaging and use more recycled materials.

Research and Development can make their contribution by providing comparative environmental impact data, by identifying processes which use resources more efficiently, by finding new uses for waste products and by contributing to the creation of long-life goods. Those R & D Departments that engage fully with the challenge of sustainable development will be transformed as they tackle the questions relating to 'cradle to grave costing' and a 'total systems approach' to their company's business.

Marketing departments can find out more about the growing consumer preference for environmentally friendly goods, by defining new business opportunities in terms of customer demand and finding marketing, distribution and selling methods which reduce environmental impact. As their company adopts a total systems approach to doing business, they will find much more radical changes to the concepts and methods employed in their departments. These might well include setting up new ventures and using franchising arrangements more creatively.

Production departments need to work with engineers and maintenance people to devise processes which are more efficient and less costly in energy and resource use. In the more radical scenario they will move from using people to fill gaps between machines to seeking ways in which machines can be used to enhance human skills and develop their potential.

Finance and accounting departments need to investigate the benefits of moving towards sustainability in terms of making it easier to raise capital, containing insurance costs, reducing running and maintenance costs and finding new ways to express performance alongside the normal performance criteria. New methodologies and measurements will be required to demonstrate how companies are using resources to optimum effect and minimizing pollution and wastes.

Office and site managers should look into the degree to which energy and lighting is used efficiently and economically, how much paper usage can be reduced by electronic mail, how telephones and fax machines can replace some meetings which involve costly travel. Personnel departments should look at terms of employment and whether company car schemes still make sense or if the policy should be to reduce engine size, stipulate unleaded petrol or even abandon company cars altogether. Training and development departments should appreciate the scale and speed of the requirement for new learning at all levels and how this can be done effectively and economically. Health and Safety Departments are likely to find that the growing consciousness about the environment will add to the importance of their roles and strengthen it in terms of third-party risks.

Legal Departments need to find good ways to keep abreast of legislation and how best to disseminate this information. Public Affairs Departments will become increasingly aware that they need to keep up-to-date with all the above activities if they are to represent accurately what their organization is doing to tackle the environmental challenge.

The overall implication of all this potential activity is that it will not happen if there is no vision, strategic direction and example emanating from the highest levels in the organization. Furthermore, coherence and integration will only be achieved if the strategic plan indicates why it is important, which are the priorities (they will inevitably vary from business to business), the time-scales involved, how the appropriate level of resources will be allocated and how to achieve an appropriate balance between the three dimensions of the business challenge.

Already there are two examples of cross-functional initiatives with which companies are involved. One is Integrated Pollution Control and the second is Life Cycle Assessment. The former adopts a holistic approach to pollution control and considers ways in which wastes can be reused or recycled, thereby reducing environmental impact. The latter is a term that has been used in marketing to describe product life cycles in the marketplace, but is now used widely to mean assessing and reducing environmental impact from the 'cradle to the grave' or from acquisition of materials, through production, use and final disposal after use. Both these approaches raise issues which have strategic significance.

HOW A COMPANY MIGHT MOVE TOWARDS A SUSTAINABLE FUTURE

Every organization has capital tied up in various kinds of fixed assets. For industrial organizations there is a considerable investment in plant and machinery which needs to be renewed periodically. At any given time there will be some that is due for replacement and the expectation will be that the new plant or machines will have a life-span of ten years or more.

Similarly, products have a limited life and new products and services need to be introduced from time to time. Many organizations also change the way they do things because market conditions are different, information technology creates new possibilities and staff have different expectations.

In any given year the business plan will include various items where new plant, machines, products or processes are being introduced. If an organization assumes that the world tomorrow will be much the same as it is now then decisions about replacements and developments will reflect that assumption. Companies with environmental policies which make this assumption, implicitly or explicitly, will find that they continue on an unsustainable path, even though they reduce their environmental impact. For example, a furniture manufacturer might find ways to improve timber usage, reduce effluents and use energy more efficiently, but fail to examine the prospects for sustainable supplies of timber or the market potential for repair and reconditioning of furniture.

As each year passes, the opportunity for incorporating a sustainable development approach is further deferred and in some cases – for example, the continuity of supply of materials or major plant investments – this may be for as long as 30 years. If, however, planned investment is seen as an opportunity to move towards a more sustainable future then appropriate change can be integrated into each year's strategic plan. This will be difficult to accomplish without considerable awareness raising among large numbers of managers before an integrated approach can be adopted effectively. An investment in this awareness raising is itself a strategic decision.

Some companies struggle to achieve the good intentions that are embodied in their business plans. This is often because they have only considered the business dimensions of their plan and ignored the equally important strategic decisions concerning the capability of the organization to achieve its stated objectives. A model which addresses both issues is shown in Figure 8.1. This indicates that as much attention should be paid to the organization's capability and culture as is given to the desired performance and business goals. When the nature of the business, the processes and the marketplace of the future are going to be very different then the investment in developing appropriate capability, organization culture and management behaviour is a very important investment which will only happen if it is part of the strategic plan.

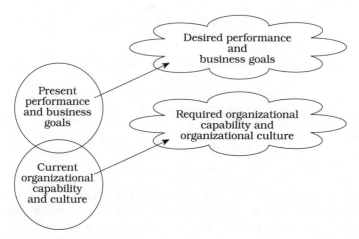

Figure 8.1 *Business Results and Organizational Capability*

If the strategic plan is to include adequate attention to the environmental challenge and give due attention to the development of organizational capability, then the approach to strategic planning needs to be reviewed in order to ensure that these elements are an integral part of the approach being used. Systems thinking is very helpful and any organization already familiar with this concept and using it for planning purposes will find it invaluable.

A STRATEGIC FRAMEWORK

The underlying assumption in this article is that a sustainable future is an appropriate vision for the world community, nation states and for business and other organizations. That vision inevitably influences the perspective from which this article is written. The whole approach to strategic planning described here emanates from this vision. If your vision is similar then the framework and techniques which follow could be relevant to your situation. They are selected primarily for their relevance to business planning. However, two things need to be emphasized. First, the magnitude of the change and the difficulty of the transformation to a sustainable business is daunting. Second, the amount of work that has so far been done to create appropriate and effective concepts and processes is minuscule. This article introduces a few ideas and simple models which do no more than make a start.

In terms of a strategic choice between a sustainable future and an unsustainable future there is no contest. The former is an ethical imperative whereas the latter is collective suicide on a global scale.

It is helpful to have an overall map to appreciate the broad elements which will need to be considered if your company is to make progress towards a sustainable future. Start by building commitment to a vision of this kind. It is essential that the board or top executive team is involved in this process. For those who have never done this before it will be important to do it initially with a skilled facilitator, otherwise a failed attempt will, very likely, result in discrediting a powerful and helpful technique.

This article is written primarily for those who treat the environmental challenge as a fundamental, strategic issue with wide-ranging implications. From this viewpoint it is essential that the top level should be involved. As these top executives realize that radical changes will have to be accomplished if the business is to survive through the 1990s, then commitment to an appropriate degree of involvement of their time and allocation of an appropriate investment in resources will develop. One way to appreciate what it will mean to achieve a sustainable future is to consider the level of per capita consumption that might be sustainable. For example, with a world population of 10 billion, 0.5 tonnes per annum oil equivalent of non-renewable carbon fuels may be the requirement to achieve the traditional level of carbon dioxide in the atmosphere. This compares with figures of (approximately) 8 and 4 million tonnes per annum of oil equivalent for the US and Europe respectively at present. While this appears to be a huge constraint, it does not take account of the degree to which sustainable energy could be developed for many applications for which carbon fuels are used now. Again the scale of the transformation is impressive.

There will be barriers to overcome – many of them will emanate from traditional thinking strongly adhered to by the advocates of a business-as-usual philosophy. As an individual reading this article your first difficulty may well be to find others in your organization who agree that it is a vital issue and should be given attention. Some of you will be pressured to get the urgent matters attended to – they always seem to be given priority – and will struggle to create an opportunity to deal with something that is not urgent but is crucially important. There will be colleagues of yours who may remain sceptical and you will need to find some way to raise the issue so that they are either confronted or links made with matters on their agenda. Overcoming barriers like these will be the inevitable starting point for some, and the best way to begin is often to build a small supportive group who can plan an appropriate approach and gradually widen their sphere of influence.

Having achieved a vision of a sustainable future for your organization it is then appropriate to analyse the environment in which you work as well as your own business. Figure 8.2 shows, in broad outline, how this might be done and some of the important factors to consider. The information collected can then be sorted using a familiar technique such as a SWOT (Strengths, Weaknesses, Opportunities and Threats) analysis. From this it will be helpful to relate back to the box on page 86 and the three dimensions of the environmental challenge. An action plan can then be developed to deal with the key elements listed in the figure.

This framework provides a simplified overview. Each stage will require more detailed tools and techniques which need to be developed. An introduction of one or two possibilities is discussed below.

Exploring values

There has been a tremendous amount of exposure of environmental subjects in the media over recent years and most people are aware of many of the issues. However, few organizations have given their staff the opportunity to share their perceptions, to test the accuracy of their opinions and to relate their concerns to their own business. A few companies (such as ICI) are now beginning to do this and to establish stronger common ground between staff at all levels. They aim to achieve consistency of understanding about the issues, the company's impact on the environment and how company policies and practices are being implemented. Without this kind of an initiative your staff are likely to arrive at their own conclusions which will influence what they say to their work colleagues and to their family and friends. At best any negative views they may have will affect morale adversely; at worst it could, through time, damage corporate image and the ability to recruit and retain good people. A model which introduces the subject of exploring values is given in Figure 8.3. However, this may well prove inadequate for the scale of change that is required, in which case new concepts and language will have to be developed.

It is likely that the environmental scene will continue to develop at a fast pace and information about the issues will emerge over the coming years. Sometimes an issue will prove to be less significant as time passes while other issues will assume much greater importance and occasionally a new factor will arise which had not previously been identified. This turbulent picture is unlikely to settle down in the foreseeable future so it will be important to explore values periodically, hence the circular nature of the diagram in Figure 8.3.

Environmental Trends and Pressures

The environmental challenge affects all departments as has already been indicated. In preparing for the strategic approach it is imperative that all are involved. One way to do this is to undertake an internal review using *Your*

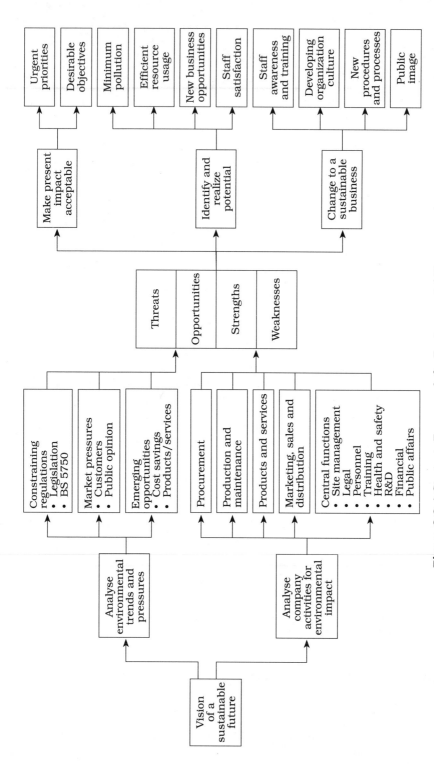

Figure 8.2 *A Strategic Framework for Environmental Management*

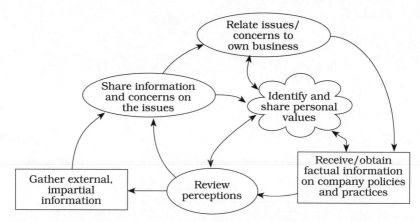

This is a creative way to get people to identify and modify their values as they learn more about the environment and their company's philosophy

Figure 8.3 *Exploring Values Concerned with the Environment*

Business and the Environment – a D-I-Y Review for Companies (Coopers and Lybrand Deloitte, 1991). This excellent publication has been prepared as a work book and contains many useful diagrams and checklists which help to bring important issues into focus. Its value lies in a framework for analysis rather than strategy, but the former is a necessary prelude.

The response to the environmental challenge has already been discussed in terms of job titles. It can also be considered in terms of the orientation overall. There is evidence that the concept of sustainable business has never been considered by some organizations. Others have given environmental issues some thought but dismissed it as irrelevant for their business. Many organizations, mostly the very large ones, are engaging with the challenge but most of these are doing so in a reactive way to trends and pressures. Thus attention is concentrated on compliance with the law, achieving BS 5750, saving money through more efficient use of resources or trying to enhance or preserve reputation and market image. This is illustrated in Figure 8.4.

As the realization grows that the real challenge is to achieve a sustainable future, the struggle will be to balance the viability of the business, in terms of cash flow and profitability, with the health of the environment in terms of ecology and its ability to support life. Figure 8.5 represents this challenge in a simple model.

Those organizations which have had internal projects to strengthen cash flow, improve quality, strengthen customer care, introduce new information systems etc, may well believe that it is just not possible to initiate another major project at this time. For these people it is worth noting that there is some work being done to integrate environmental management with Total Quality Management, thus reducing the feeling of 'not another performance-improving project'. *Corporate Quality/Environmental Management: The First Conference* (1991) published their proceedings and there are several interesting papers from people working with these issues in their companies.

Having gathered the information about the environment and the internal perspectives, it can now be sorted using a SWOT analysis. This will help to focus attention as a stepping-stone towards the areas in which action is needed. The

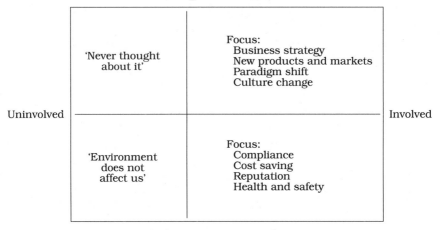

Achieving a sustainable business

	Focus:
'Never thought about it'	Business strategy New products and markets Paradigm shift Culture change
	Focus:
'Environment does not affect us'	Compliance Cost saving Reputation Health and safety

Uninvolved · Involved

Reducing environmental impact

Figure 8.4 *Assessing Environmental Involvement*

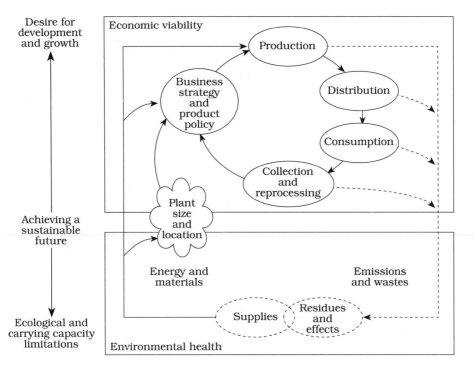

Figure 8.5 *Achieving a Sustainable Future*

final step is to arrange the information in terms of the three dimensions of the business challenge given in the box on page 00. This then provides the basis for action planning.

PRODUCT STRATEGY

A key part of the strategic plan will be the business strategy from which the product strategy is derived. Most organizations will have their established ways of assessing new products and services and these can still be used. However, an additional assessment will be required to consider the sustainability of products and services. More sophisticated concepts and tools will be needed than are available now. However, as a preliminary, a simple framework can be used. The dimensions are potential for sustainability and market potential as shown in Figure 8.6.

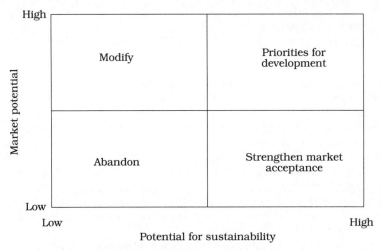

Figure 8.6 *A Product Strategy Matrix*

This model can be used to classify existing products as well as those that are in the latter stages of development. Where the potential for sustainability is low and market potential is also low, the products should be abandoned – this is self-evident and unlikely to create problems. Where the potential for sustainability is high but market potential is low, attention should focus on strengthening market awareness and acceptability. Where the market potential is high but the potential for sustainability is low, product development should be considered to reduce adverse environmental effects. Finally, where the potential for sustainability and the market potential are high, the products should be given priority attention for development. As stated, this is a very simple way of looking at the dilemma but can be helpful as a start.

In reviewing products it is also necessary to consider their environmental impact very broadly. This means looking at the whole product life cycle (or cradle to grave). In other words the assessment should cover all the elements shown in Figure 8.7.

Products	Procuring materials	Production processes	Product distribution	Products in use	Disposal after use
A					
B					
C					
D					
E					

Consider: resource depletion, wastes, pollution of air, water and soil recovery procedures, impact on community and damage to the environment at each stage of the life-cycle.

Quick rating: give scores ranging from 1 (low impact) to 5 (high impact) for each product and each stage of the process. Develop strategies for dealing with all scores of 3 and above for any individual rating and all products which achieve a score of 12 or more.

In-depth analysis: develop descriptive information for each stage of one product. Review the method and the criteria being used. Redefine as necessary to suit your business and then complete the analysis.

Figure 8.7 *A Framework for Product Life-Cycle Assessment*

Descriptive information, quantified where possible, should be recorded for each product in a layout similar to that shown in the figure. In considering this analysis the environmental impact should cover all the important perspectives. These include the rate of exhaustion of energy and materials, the generation and disposal of wastes, pollution of soil, water and air, recovery procedures and community impact in terms of noise, nuisance and convenience. Criteria such as these are being used in the work being done to develop a consistent approach to eco-labelling. The demanding and time-consuming work that is involved in this analysis can be used in three ways – namely for strategic planning purposes, for managing environmental impact and to substantiate claims to use eco-labelling once the standards have been agreed.

In many cases where new products are being devised or where new markets are being developed, the starting point for these initiatives will be the design brief. Once again, many of the existing methods for writing design briefs can be used, but the goals to be achieved will be in accordance with the overall corporate strategy in terms of sustainability through time. This in turn will stimulate a great deal of work on the criteria to be used and how sustainability is defined in particular industries. At some time it may be appropriate for progressive development to occur, at other times new products in new markets may need a newly formed department or company to develop the initiative alongside the established corporate activities.

Suppliers and Contractors

The analyses carried out using Figures 8.6 and 8.7 will have raised the question of suppliers. In this context it is important to recognize that under the Environmental Protection Act 1990 (EPA) the constraints are more strict than they have ever been. For example, processes need authorization, all releases to the environment will be controlled by a single authority, operators will be required to use the Best Available Technique Not Entailing Excessive Cost (BATNEEC) and periodic reviews will take place in order to raise standards as better techniques and technology are developed.

The public will have access to the information and the polluter pays principle will be enforced. Operators can be held liable for the standards maintained by their suppliers and contractors. The maximum fine that can be imposed by a magistrate's court has been raised to £20,000, while in higher courts unlimited fines are available as penalties. Already some larger companies are stipulating the standards that they require from their suppliers and contractors or are asking detailed questions in order to assess whether there is likely to be any infringement of the EPA.

The trading conditions and terms under which contractors and suppliers operate are likely to undergo considerable change. Those companies which already have a quality programme will be familiar with the introduction of new quality constraints into the agreements with third parties. Additional constraints relating to sustainability could be the best way to achieve desired standards.

THE HUMAN DIMENSION

The scale and nature of the environmental challenge facing any organization is such that it becomes apparent sooner or later that the strategic approach can only be adopted successfully if staff at all levels are involved. Some of the large companies which have been addressing their environmental problems for some time have discovered that it can take four or five years to build the understanding and commitment of all employees and that without it the achievement of the desired goals remains an illusion.

To achieve a sustainable business for a future that will inevitably be different means that opportunities should be provided to enable people from top management to the shop floor to come to terms with their changing responsibilities. This should be part of the strategic plan if it is to receive the required amount of attention.

We have already seen in Figure 8.1 that to move an organization from the business that it is doing now to something different in the future will only be achieved if the organization's capability is also developed. This is often neglected or given too little attention. The assumption often is that a clear message given once is sufficient for people to understand what is required and to change what they do and/or how they do their job. It is not. Most people require time with appropriate support and challenge to think through the implications so that they can come to terms with what is involved for them personally and to relate this to how they work with others. Where this sort of opportunity is provided – often as a specially designed course, workshop or seminar lasting from three to five days – then the benefits materialize. These benefits result in stronger commitment, more energy applied to the change, a greater willingness to let go of the old and a new determination to make the changes work. In due course this will be translated into bottom-line results.

It is worth spending some time recognizing how people come to terms with change. In establishing a strategic approach to the environment many people will have their world disturbed. Consider, for example, discontinuing a product to which many people are strongly committed, abandoning machinery or processes which have been painstakingly maintained, a source of supply which has to be discontinued, people who have to be moved to new locations or responsibilities, investment decisions which need to be made using different or additional criteria and greater devolved authority. All these changes have their impact on people who have to find their own ways to come to terms with a new situation which is frequently more demanding. As the rate of change accelerates then the investment of time and resources in helping staff to adjust is a crucial strategic decision which cannot be ignored.

The human responses to change are shown in Figure 8.8 and represent the typical phases through which most people pass, at varying speeds, while coming to terms with changes which affect them. Denial of the validity of these reactions can be counter-productive and result in those who need to change getting stuck at the denial or blame stages.

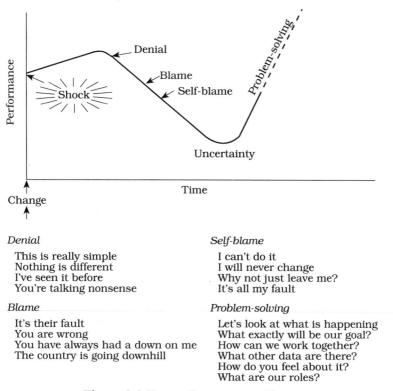

Denial

This is really simple
Nothing is different
I've seen it before
You're talking nonsense

Blame

It's their fault
You are wrong
You have always had a down on me
The country is going downhill

Self-blame

I can't do it
I will never change
Why not just leave me?
It's all my fault

Problem-solving

Let's look at what is happening
What exactly will be our goal?
How can we work together?
What other data are there?
How do you feel about it?
What are our roles?

Figure 8.8 *Human Responses to Change*

The implication arising from the acceptance of this phenomenon is that Personnel Departments and/or Management Development people need to be involved at an early stage of the change process. Their role is to plan and run (possibly with external help) a crucial part of the implementation plan, which they need to understand in some depth in order to create the right kind of experience for staff at different levels.

When an organization decides that it will only achieve its mission if adjustments are made to its organization culture then the magnitude of change is such that it will only be accomplished through sustained effort. Some companies are finding that this is the challenge they face. For example, Dow Chemicals have said that it took four years to bring about the required level of understanding among their staff to implement fully their environmental policies. The scale of culture change that was required proved much greater than expected.

It is likely that many organizations are going to find that the implications of moving towards a sustainable future will only be possible if the issue of culture change is tackled as part of the business strategy. This will involve giving attention to management style emanating from the top, different ways of working, new recruitment and promotion criteria, new performance measurements and revisions to the reward structure.

An Organization Model

Another area of change which is often treated as a subsidiary issue concerns the organization. Many people recognize the need to do something about organization structure in times of change, but few appreciate that this is only one element in organization design. It is helpful to have an organization model which is shared and widely understood by people who work together in the same organization, but this is seldom the case.

There is no single correct model and there is no consistent way in which terms are used. It is therefore necessary for people who work together to agree a model which they understand and to use terms which they have defined in an agreed way so that effective communication can take place. One such model is represented in Figure 8.9. The result of the strategic review as described above will be that significant changes are likely to occur to the way in which organization purpose and the corporate vision are described. This is likely to impact on the broad strategies chosen for implementing the vision and the specific objectives that will be pursued in the business plans. With changes in these areas there will be a consequential impact on the tasks to be performed. As soon as one element of the working organization is altered there is an impact on each of the others. Hence if the work to be done changes then the people required to do the work may be different or, at the very least they need retraining. If the people and tasks change, job categories will be affected and the reward structure – both formal and informal – will need to be adjusted. With changes in these three areas the flow of information will need adjustments and the processes for decision-making will alter. This will have added significance if environmental responsibility is devolved to people nearest to the action – which is what should happen. We return now to the question of organization structure and recognize that the grouping of people into departments and their reporting relationships will need some adjustment as well.

All these changes cannot be left to chance or deferred, they need to be embodied into the strategic plan and the whole question of organization design given attention as part of the implementation plan. This requires some demanding thinking about the way in which the organization will function in practice. A good fit between the working elements is essential if good performance is to be achieved.

Organizations which start early on the challenge to become a sustainable business will gain in stature and enhance their reputation and results in a daunting and challenging world.

Adapted from the work of Jay Galbraith

Figure 8.9 *An Organizational Model for Dealing with Environmental Issues*

REFERENCES

Brown, Lester R (1991) 'A sustainable future' *Resurgence* no 147, July/August, and Capra, Fritjof and Callenbach, Ernest, (1991) 'A sustainable society' *Resurgence*, no 149, November/December

Coopers & Lybrand Deloitte (1991), *Your Business and the Environment – A D-I-Y Review for Companies*, Business and the Environment, 5 Cleveland Place, London SW1Y 6JJ

Corporate Quality/Environmental Management: The First Conference (1991), Global Environmental Management Initiative, Washington DC

Directory of Corporate Environmental Policy, (1991, 1st Edition), Industry and Environment Associates, 77 Temple Sheen Road, East Sheen, London SW14 7RS

Drucker, Peter F, *The Practice of Management*, William Heinemann (1955 & recently reprinted).

Hutchinson, Colin, (1992) 'Environmental issues: The challenge for the chief executive', *Long Range Planning*, Vol 25, no 3, pp 50–59

Industry and the Environment: A Strategic Overview, (1990), The Centre for Exploitation of Science and Technology (CEST), 5 Berners Road, London N1 0PW

Managing Organizational Change (1990) a programme devised by Sheppard Moscow Limited, Beaumont House, Willow Grove, Chislehurst, Kent BR7 5DA.

Part III

Research, Development and Technology

Introduction

Kenneth Green and Ian Miles

Human beings interact with and transform the natural world through the use of technology. Over the course of human history, we have developed increasingly powerful technologies, with greater scope for affecting the state of the natural and human worlds. Technology does not stand outside society; it is the result of social choices concerning what knowledge should be developed. The way in which technologies themselves are applied once they are created is similarly a matter of social choice. Nevertheless, having access to particular technologies makes it possible to do things that could not have been successfully attempted before these means to affect the world were developed. Thus, understanding technological development is essential for environmentalists.

But what is technology? It is misleading to think of it as just 'things' or items of hardware (although in Anglo-Saxon everyday thought, it is usually seen in such 'hard' terms). These 'things' are themselves the result of the development and application of knowledge about how the world works and how it can be affected. Technology thus comprises not only things (or combinations of such artefacts in systems) but also the *knowledge* of how they work (and how to create them), and the learned *skills* of making those things/systems work. These technologies also include the skills of manufacture and design that people have developed, plus the engineering and scientific knowledge of the principles by which devices 'work'.

If technologies are, then, a combination of things, human skills and organized knowledge, they involve an intimate intermingling of the physical world and the social world. To repeat the point: technological evolution is not an autonomous affair of technologies forcing themselves on to society; and technology does not *determine* what society can do. Over the last twenty years, social scientists from disciplines as disparate as history, economics and sociology have shown how economic, political and cultural influences shape the technologies we use. They have shown, in other words, that technologies are *social constructions*. Many of these social factors have clear environmental implications. For example, until recently, our societies happily embraced the notion of 'disposability' in consumer products, appearing contented to provide for its consequences by hugely-expanded waste-management systems. Technological choices reflect and reinforce this situation, with a parallel underdevelopment of alternative technologies which might support, instead, recycling or reuse. We have also embraced beliefs in the economic superiority of large centralized systems, thus justifying, for example, the development of centralized electricity generation and the technologies that support superstore-based retailing. More profoundly, the economic 'benefits' of capital-intensity have been universally assumed, driving the development of technologies of mechanization and automation over the last 150 years.

Some of these socio-cultural beliefs in the benefits of centralization and in the pursuit of capital-intensive production methods are currently under attack. In consequence, there is growing attention to the possibilities for different types of technology. Socio-cultural changes *do* eventually get expressed in different technologies, although we may well be faced with a huge legacy of investments in developing both intellectual knowledge and physical infrastructure in particular ways, with all of the costs that can be entailed in setting out on new trajectories.

Given the urgency of dealing with many of the planet's environmental problems, it is important to speed up the rate of change of technology in directions which are less deleterious to the environment. To do this, we need to know how technologies change and what is possible. Technological knowledge sets limits on what we can do practically to change production and consumption styles. An understanding of how technological knowledge is structured, and how it develops in capitalist industrial societies, is important if we are to come up with credible programmes for change.

The need for changes to our technological systems is slowly being appreciated by industry. Some firms have been responding to consumer and environmentalists pressures, as well as to tighter environmental/health and safety regulation and government incentive programmes, by exploring the notion of clean technology. The principles of clean technology are discussed in Chapter 9 in which Roland Clift and Anita Longley contrast clean technology with the more traditional approach of industrial 'clean-up' and 'remediation' responses, using 'end-of-pipe' technologies. This traditional approach accepts that industry generates environmental problems and tries to find ways of responsibly minimizing the damage that these generate. Clean technology, in contrast, say Clift and Longley, should seek to transform production so as to obviate or reduce the problems in the first place, through such approaches as 'waste minimization' and 'dematerialization'.

Alan Irwin and Paul Hooper (1992) have explored the application of the ideas of 'clean technology' in practice, studying a number of actual examples from UK firms in the late 1980s. They point out that industry has, in fact, interpreted the idea of clean technology in many ways – from changes that are merely 'end-of-pipe' extensions (and thus relatively undisruptive of existing manufacturing practice) to what they call 'innovative' technologies: 'integrated technologies which necessitate the introduction of new production processes or substantial modification of existing processes.' Interestingly, not only can such technologies be environmentally friendlier but also commercially sensible – money may be saved directly (eg by recycling wastes or reducing production inputs such as energy), companies may be able to improve their image and market shares and there may be new market opportunities in 'clean' products and processes.

Technological change, whether made in response to environmental pressures or to other demands and opportunities, can take a number of forms. For example, new technologies can be minor improvements, involving the slow but sure application of new or existing knowledge (so-called 'incremental' changes). They may be major developments often derived from fundamental scientific work ('radical' changes). The development and diffusion of new technologies involves the process known as *innovation.*

Technological innovation is a central feature of modern industrial societies; the larger firms, and many of the not-so-large, are in continuous competition to find successful new products, to find ways of making products more cheaply, and so on. Environmentalists may criticize this dynamic trait – the constant quest for new products and production methods based on ever new technologies is itself seen as a big part of the problem. Certainly new products and processes do often bring with them new and poorly understood risks to the environment; and the 'throw-away' society is reinforced by the way in which innovation renders last year's products obsolescent. However, whatever one's attitude to the pace of technological change, there is still an urgent need to understand how that change occurs. Dismantling, reducing or redirecting modern industry's environmentally disruptive, 'brown' products, processes and systems and replacing them by 'greener' alternatives implies changes in our artefacts, skills and knowledge – in other words, technological innovation.

Influencing the process of innovation means influencing Research and Development (R&D) as early as possible. One issue that is especially important is how the scientists and engineers that work in companies' R&D departments decide which projects they will work on. What they choose (or what the company chooses for them) will have a critical effect on the kinds of technologies and underpinning knowledge that will be at a company's disposal should it wish to move in a new, more sustainable direction. To the extent that R&D begins to consider environmental factors very early on in project selection, it is more likely that the innovations that finally ensue will help move industry in greener directions.

Of course, firms do not choose what R&D to do in a vacuum. When it comes to incremental developments in technology, firms are much affected by what the market is prepared to accept; such innovations are thus typically said to be 'market-driven'. Product improvements are very often the result of feedback from users as to problems experienced or features that are desired. They may represent efforts to modify technologies so that they can be used by new markets. This will be typically by users with less motivation to use the product or with less technical expertise than the pioneers – so the modifications often centre on simplification and cheapening.

However, for many innovations, especially radical ones, 'the market' does not yet exist. But firms still explore technologies that *potentially* can be lucrative for them, should new markets develop. Competition is one source of pressure; other firms may establish the new markets so as to exclude them. And it is difficult for most firms to rest on their laurels; the search is always on for innovations that might bring more financial security. Furthermore, many people in industry are actually challenged by the idea of creating successful new products, especially if these involve interesting technical challenges.

Firms can only exploit technologies where they have an appropriate knowledge base for developing such technologies. Such a knowledge base is typically acquired slowly, through experience, although it is sometimes possible to buy in relevant skills, either by recruitment or by purchase of pioneering companies. But to acquire expertise requires some understanding of what the 'relevant' technologies are. This will be limited by the 'paradigms' or 'regimes' of technological knowledge that scientists and engineers are working within. To change this needs *new technological concepts* and this needs the more vigorous pursuit of environmentally conscious basic research. It also requires some idea of where market demands are heading. These ideas are explored further in Chapter 10.

Even if consumers *claim* to be prepared to purchase environmentally-sustainable products, there may be structural obstacles to their accepting new products that are actually offered to them. Existing products have built around them patterns of use which can be hideously difficult to dismantle without a disruptive and expensive transition. This is especially so in some of the basic infrastructures of our society, such as in energy and transport, even if we can argue that these are *inherently* unsustainable in their present form. However the prospect of such a transition is something that must be faced. In Chapter 11, David Fleming examines whether technical solutions will be enough to deliver sustainability. His Six-Age model suggests that they are likely to be overwhelmed by growth in global output, and that the only alternative to the technical fix is some form of suppression of output. Fleming describes some of the catastrophic consequences that could arise in the event of suppressed or negative growth, but shows that, however reluctantly, the world economy could be forced to make the transition to a 'low output' regime. He then explores the policy options available to business in such changed economic and social conditions. As we have stressed, whatever the appropriate 'balance' between technological and socio-cultural 'solutions' to current environmental problems, it is a balance. Both are necessary: environmentalists need to understand the dynamics of social *and* technological change.

REFERENCES

Irwin, A and Hooper, P (1992), 'Clean Technology, Successful Innovation and the Greening of Industry: a Case Study Analysis', *Business Strategy and the Environment*, vol 1, no 2, pp 1–11

9

Introduction to Clean Technology

Roland Clift and Anita Longley

CLEAN TECHNOLOGY AND CLEAN-UP TECHNOLOGY

There is a useful general distinction between:

1. *Remediation:* repairing damage caused by past human activity (or 'natural disasters').

2. *Clean-up technology:* reducing environmental damage by retrofitting, modifying, or adding 'end-of-pipe' pollution abatement measures to an established plant or process.

3. *Clean technology* (or sometimes 'cleaner technology'): avoiding the environmental damage at source.

The concept of clean technology goes beyond 'clean production' which has been defined by the United Nations Environment Programme (UNEP, see Baas et al) as:

> *a conceptual and procedural approach to production that demands that all phases of the life-cycle of a product or of a process should be addressed with the objective of prevention or minimization of short- and long-term risks to human health and to the environment.*

For reasons explored below, our discussion of clean technology concentrates on the function of providing a human benefit or service, rather than concentrating on products per se as in the UNEP definition of cleaner production. However, the concept of the life-cycle is central to both clean production and clean technology. Environmental life-cycle assessment is introduced below, as a systematic approach to determining all the environmental impacts and resource depletions associated with providing the benefit or service.

To give a simple introduction to the distinction between clean technology and clean-up technology, we assume that the environmental impacts and resource depletions can be aggregated so that they can be represented by a single parameter. This parameter is called here the 'environmental load', but is also sometimes known as 'environmental stress'. Just as for the environmental load, the financial cost of the activity must be based on the total life-cycle cost, including the usual capital and operating costs but also allowing for the cost of decommissioning plant and disposing of waste. For any given activity, the financial cost and environmental load are related by the kind of curve shown in Figure 9.1 (A Warhurst, 1992 and R Clift, 1993) representing the trade-off between financial cost and environmental load. The asymptotic behaviour of the curve at low environmental load arises from the thermodynamic constraint that any human activity involves some environmental impact or resource utilization, so that the environmental load cannot be eliminated completely. Similarly, the asymptotic behaviour at low financial cost simply reflects the non-existence of free lunches: even the most environmentally profligate activity has a financial cost.

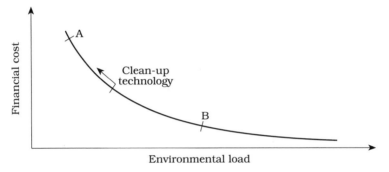

Figure 9.1 *Clean-up Technology and the Efficiency of Environmental Improvements*

Clean-up technology (or end-of-pipe pollution abatement) by definition involves adding something to the process, or treating or reprocessing the product which provides the benefit or service. Thus it involves moving around the curve in the sense shown in the figure, increasing the financial cost to reduce the environmental load. The gradient of the curve is inversely proportional to the efficiency of expenditure on environmental improvements. In general, OECD countries will be represented by points around A, corresponding to high cost but relatively low environmental load. By contrast, the Eastern European countries, for example, are represented schematically by points around B, where the environmental load is higher but the efficiency of expenditure on clean-up technology is also much higher. To take the specific case of electricity generation from fossil fuel, the environmental load parameter will be a measure primarily of emissions of acid gases and, for those who subscribe to the view that carbon dioxide causes global warming, of 'greenhouse gases'. For example, it has been estimated (CEFIC, 1992) that expenditure on improving the environmental performance of power generation and use will achieve many times more reduction in environmental load by investing in Eastern rather than Western Europe. In other words, for this particular environmental load, the gradients at points A and B differ by orders of magnitude. This kind of analysis can be developed further, for example as an aid to formulating international policy (R Lofstedt and R Clift, to be published).

Figure 9.2 illustrates the essential difference between clean-up technology and clean technology (R Clift, 1993 and R Carlsson, 1994). As in Figure 9.1, curve

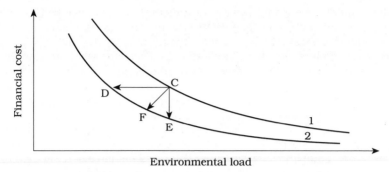

Figure 9.2 *Clean-up Technology (curve 1) and
Clean Technology (curve 2)*

1 represents an established technology to which clean-up can be applied. Curve 2 represents a significantly different technology, which is inherently cleaner in the sense that it is represented by a curve displaced towards the origin. Thus an organization operating at point C with the established technology can in principle, by adopting the clean technology of curve 2, reduce its environmental load without increasing costs (point D), or reduce costs while retaining environmental performance (point E), or reduce both cost and environmental load (point F). Whether this is practicable depends, of course, not only on the availability of the clean technology represented by curve 2, but also on whether there are any barriers to making this change – for example, due to existing investment in technology 1 or investment needed to exploit technology 2. Other organisational barriers to the adoption of clean technologies are discussed later.

Within this context, general features can be identified which distinguish clean technologies from clean-up technologies. Illustrations of these features will be found below. For example, in the process industries, a clean-up technology may capture a potential emission from a process and transform it to another state, such as by 'scrubbing' or filtering a gas stream to collect an atmospheric pollutant as liquid or sludge or solid for disposal by other means. A clean technology will avoid producing the pollutant in the first place or will recycle it within the process.

HOW CLEAN IS THE TECHNOLOGY? ENVIRONMENTAL LIFE-CYCLE ASSESSMENT

The UNEP definition of clean production, quoted above, explicitly refers to the 'life-cycle of a product or of a process'. Environmental life-cycle assessment is a formal approach to defining and evaluating the total environmental load associated with providing a service, by following the associated material and energy flows from their 'cradle' (ie primary resources) to their 'grave' (ie ultimate resting place, as solid waste or dispersed emissions). Life cycle assessment (LCA) is increasingly being used as a decision support tool in improving environmental performance, primarily by reducing the environmental load associated with specific products (B Pedersen, 1993, and G A Keoleian and D Menerey, 1993), with an accepted methodology (SETAC, 1992 and 1993) and recognized internationally as the essential basis for awarding 'ecolabels' as a public recognition of products or services with improved environmental performance (R Clift, 1994). LCA aspires to be an objective quantitative approach (J B Guinee et al (1), 1993 and J B Guinee et al (2), 1993). The idea behind LCA is that, by considering all activities 'from cradle to grave', it is possible to determine whether a product or service genuinely causes reduced environmental load, or whether the environmental load is merely transferred from the immediate supplier to the 'upstream' suppliers or to 'downstream' disposal. LCA must be used to establish the environmental load used as a parameter in Figures 9.1 and 9.2.

Environmental life-cycle assessment is a form of environmental system analysis. The basic concept of LCA (and of other forms of analysis, including site-specific environmental impact assessment (EIA)) is summarized in Figure 9.3. The productive system which provides the function (ie the benefit, service or product) is identified. In order to provide the function, the system will require inputs of materials and energy. It will also generate undesirable outputs in the form of emissions to air and water and solid wastes. For site-specific EIA, the system boundary is drawn around the manufacturing plant, so that the productive system takes the simple form shown in Figure 9.4. However, this level of analysis cannot represent the total environmental load: providing the inputs of energy and materials must involve some environmental loads, while if the output is a tangible product it will eventually become a waste. Environmental life-cycle assessment attempts to account for these 'upstream' and 'downstream' environmental effects, as well as those directly associated with manufacture. For life-cycle assessment, the system boundary must therefore be drawn around the whole life-cycle of the materials and energy flows used to provide the function. The system now takes the general form shown in Figure 9.5, and must also include the environmental effects of the transport steps involved.

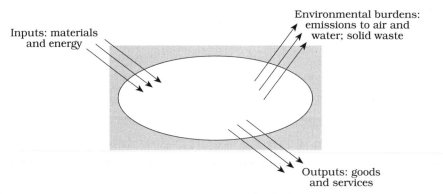

Figure 9.3 *Environmental System Analysis*
(after Azapagic and Clift, 1994)

The formal procedure of carrying out and applying an LCA involves the following steps:[1]

1. *Goal definition.* In terms of Figures 9.3 to 9.5, the first step is to define the boundaries of the system to be studied. At this stage the functional unit

---

1. The steps in carrying out an LCA summarized here are simpler than the formal steps identified in the SETAC Code of Practice (SETAC, 1993) but are those suggested by Guinee et al((1) and (2), 1993)

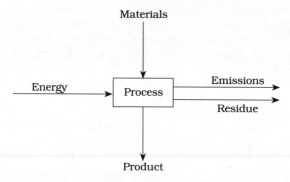

Figure 9.4 *Site-Specific Environmental Impact Analysis*

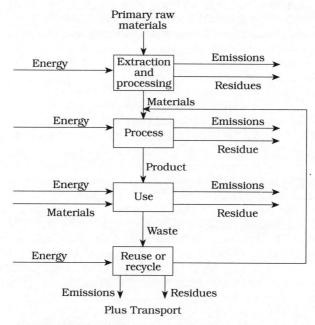

Figure 9.5 *Environmental Life-Cycle Analysis*

must also be defined: the unit of service on which the analysis is to be based. This is not necessarily a quantity of material or a number of manufactured items. For the example of packaging, the functional unit must be defined as a quantity of material packaged, not as a number of packets or a fixed weight of packaging material. When LCA is used to compare completely different ways of providing the same service, then definition of the function unit can be difficult or contentious (R Clift, 1994 and H A Udo de Haes et al, 1994). In any case, the goal definition step is critical, because it can determine or even prejudge the outcome of the study.

2. *Inventory.* Next, the inputs of primary resources and the outputs of emissions and solid residues must be defined and quantified. In effect, this

amounts to carrying out a material and energy balance over the system defined at the goal definition step, allowing for flows of trace components which may have significant environmental impact. The result of this step is an inventory table which quantifies the inputs and outputs per functional unit provided.

3. *Classification.* Once the inventory table has been compiled, the contributions of the inputs to and environmental outputs from the system (see Figure 9.3) to recognized environmental and health problems are quantified. For example, all atmospheric emissions which could contribute to global warming are weighted according to their 'greenhouse warming potential'. By this process, the detailed data in the inventory table are aggregated into a much smaller number of so-called effect scores which defined the environmental profile of the system.

4. *Valuation.* Ideally, the effect scores are now weighted to give a simple estimate of the environmental effect of delivering the function; in other words, to determine the environmental load parameter shown in Figures 9.1 and 9.2. This step inevitably requires relative values to be placed on completely disparate environmental effects and resource usages.

5. *Improvement analysis.* Ideally, when LCA is used within a company, the result is used to identify changes in the product or productive system which will reduce the total environmental load.

Of the five steps above, goal definition and inventory analysis are established processes (although some problems of detail remain to be resolved in inventory analysis; see, for example, Udo de Haes et al, 1994). Classification is less well developed, but standard methodologies are emerging (see, for example, Guinee et al, 1993). However, serious difficulties arise in valuation. The original aspiration in developing LCA as a decision-support tool in environmental management was that the same relative weightings could be assigned to different environmental effects wherever they occur, ie that valuation could be carried out on a 'global' basis. The environmental economics approach can be regarded as one way to address valuation. However, it is increasingly becoming clear that valuation must be carried out locally rather than globally (Udo de Haes et al, 1994). Thus the 'environmental load' parameter in Figures 9.1 and 9.2 actually conceals a substantive problem in environmental management.

Overall, environmental life-cycle assessment is a complex procedure and is not fully developed. Nevertheless, the discipline of setting out the life-cycle, from cradle to grave, is an important part of identifying where effort should be applied to make a technology cleaner and which stages in the life-cycle should be changed or eliminated. A specific example is summarized in Table 9.1: an LCA study carried out to establish ecolabel criteria for washing machines (UKEB, 1992). Four stages in the life of a machine were considered, with the environmental loads 'classified' by aggregating into five broad categories. In this case, it is clear that the great majority of all the environmental loads arise at the use stage, so that valuation to combine the five categories of environmental load is not needed in this case. Furthermore, most of the air pollution and much of the solid waste arise from generating the electric power which the machine uses. Therefore the analysis leads to the four key criteria, A to D. Criteria A to C indicate the environmental efficiency in use, while criterion D recognizes the solid waste associated with manufacturing and disposing of the machine is not negligible. Because the environmental load is dominated by the use stage, it follows that a clean technology approach to cleaning clothes will concentrate on the actual cleaning process rather than on the equipment in which the cleaning is carried out. We return to this example below.

Table 9.1 *Distribution of Environmental Loads through the Life-cycle of a Typical Machine for Washing Clothes*

Categories of environmental load:

1. Energy consumption.
2. Air pollution.
3. Water pollution.
4. Solid waste.
5. Water consumption.

Typical contribution of stages in life-cycle (as percentages):

	1	2	3	4	5
Production	4.1	1.5	3.7	7.2	2.1
Distribution	0.3	0.1	0.7	0.6	0.1
Use	95.5	98.4	95.6	87.2	97.8
Disposal	0.1	0.0	0.1	5.0	0.0

Hence 'key criteria' indicating environmental performance:
A. Energy consumption during use.
B. Water consumption during use.
C. Efficiency of use of detergent.
D. Recyclability of materials.

SERVICES AND COMMODITIES

The essential distinction between providing a service or human benefit rather than supplying a product or artefact has already been introduced as the basis for defining the 'functional unit' in environmental life-cycle assessment.

This distinction is central in developing the idea of clean technology and arises with remarkable ubiquity. The differences will now be illustrated by some simple examples.

Herbicides

For the first example, we are indebted to Dr Geoff Randall of Zeneca, for pointing out a simple calculation by Corbett et al (1984). Herbicides used to control wild oats, a common weed in cereal crops, typically are recommended for application at rates of the order of kilograms per hectare. However, the quantity of herbicide actually needed – in the sense of entering the system of the wild oat seedlings to kill them – is estimated as a few micrograms per hectare.[2] In other words, we apply more than 109 times as much of the herbicide as reaches its target. If the functional unit is taken as unit mass of herbicide, then the emphasis will be based on manufacturing and distributing the herbicide, ie on cleaner production. However, the functional unit should be taken as a number of wild oat seedlings killed or an area of cultivated land treated or, perhaps most appropriately, a quantity of cereal crop produced without damage by wild oats. The calculation is now based on the whole weed-control system and it becomes clear that the limiting step is controlling the weed rather than producing the herbicide. Thus a cleaner technology might focus on selective delivery or on overcoming the wild oats' defences against systemic toxin, or on pesticides whose action is triggered by contact with the pest, but not on product per se. Put starkly, there is little benefit in containing emissions during production if the herbicide is subsequently, quite literally, sprayed all over the countryside. One of the most significant environmental developments in agrochemicals over the years has been the reduction in application rates rather than cleaner production.

Organic Solvents

The idea of providing a service rather than a product can also be illustrated by developments in the use of industrial solvents – for example, for degreasing metals. Traditional organic solvents, which are commonly chlorinated, can represent a substantial environmental load. One trend in recent years has therefore been towards use of water-based solvents. However, the environmental load arises not from the use of organic solvents but from their release or escape. An alternative approach to environmental improvement is therefore to concentrate on 'closing the system' to contain the solvent completely and to reprocess it for reuse. This is properly a clean technology because it reduces environmental load and is economically attractive, even though the degree of technical innovation involved may be relatively small. The innovation lies primarily in the business practice. Rather than being sold to the consumer, the solvent – in this case kerosene (see below) – is leased to the user and then taken back for reprocessing, sometimes with the user paying a premium for any material lost. Equipment for using and containing the solvent is also leased to the user. Thus the life-cycle has been closed in the commercial as well as the material sense. The supplier retains responsibility for the material from cradle to grave. Sometimes, the solvent residue left after reprocessing may be used as fuel (see below). Thus the shift to what Glarini and Stahel (1989) have called 'the new service economy' (see below) is virtually complete: the service or use is traded, not the commodity. This particular case is explored in more detail below, as an example of industrial ecology.

2. The basis for this estimate is as follows (Corbett et al, 1984):
   1. A three-week-old wild oat plant contains 3 x 106 cells.
   2. Assume one molecule per cell gives a toxic response
   Therefore 3 million molecules need to enter each plant.
   3. Assume 10 per cent of the chemical falling on a plant actually gains entry.
   4. Only 10 per cent of the chemical gaining entry survives inactivation by metabolism or storage at an inert site.
   5. Half of the plant's leaf area is available to chemical sprayed from above.
   6. Take representative molecular mass of herbicide as 250 Daltons.
   The lower limit for herbicidal action is then 2.5 x 10.6 grams per hectare.

Cleaning Clothes

To take a further, partly hypothetical, illustration, we will consider the service used above as an example of LCA: removing soil from human clothing. The basic process is a simple separation, shown schematically in Figure 9.6. The soil is mainly animal fats excreted by the body, plus whatever external dirt the clothes have acquired. If the solid could be kept together, it could be used – for example, as food for chickens or to make candles. However, the familiar process for washing clothes does not do this; it disperses the soil into the water system, with the aid of hot water and detergents (see Figure 9.7). It was noted above that the environmental loads associated with washing-machines arise primarily in use, and Figure 9.7 shows why: effect chemicals (the components of the detergent) and energy are used once, and then emitted as waste. This represents an example almost as stark as that of pesticides: while it is important to contain releases to the environment from detergent manufacture, there is an inconsistency because the product is subsequently flushed down the drain with hot water. A clean technology approach to cleaning clothes will therefore concentrate on the function of separating soil from fabric, rather than on clean production of detergents.

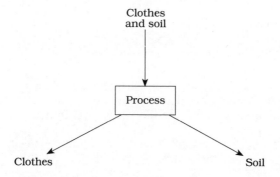

Figure 9.6 *Basic Operation of Cleaning Clothes*

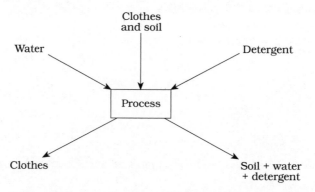

Figure 9.7 *Traditional Approach to Washing Clothes (Schematic)*

An alternative approach is suggested by a different technique: dry cleaning. In this case, a solvent is used to detach the soil (see Figure 9.8). Although dry cleaning is not usually seen as environmentally benign, the environmental load arises not because organic (and often chlorinated) solvents are used but because they are emitted. Hence, just as for metal degreasing, dry cleaning can be made a clean technology by containing the solvent, separating it from the soil (for example, by evaporation), and reusing it.

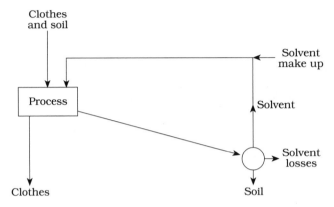

Figure 9.8 *Dry Cleaning of Clothes (Schematic)*

With this example in mind, a cleaner approach to wet washing might be as shown in Figure 9.9. If the soil is separated at source from the water waste, perhaps using a membrane process, then the hot water plus unused detergent can be reused, while the wet effluent keeps the soil concentrated, perhaps with sufficient surfactant to keep it in micellar form. This difference in technology now opens up a number of further possibilities, which go beyond purely technological changes:

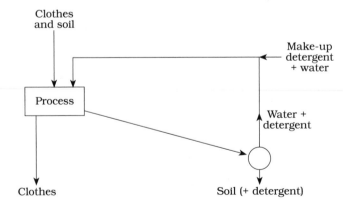

Figure 9.9 *Cleaner Technology for Washing Clothes (Schematic)*

1. The detergent chemicals could now be replenished rather than added in fixed proportions for each wash. The machine would then incorporate

dispensers for the main groups of agents making up a detergent, so that their quantities and proportions could be selected for the load according to the nature of the fabric and soil.

2. If the soil stream is concentrated, then dedicated water treatment at source can be considered. This suggests in turn that fabric cleaning might return to being centralized within a local community rather than distributed throughout individual households. Signs of this trend can be found in the revival in some countries of 'diaper services' instead of disposable or home-washed diapers.

3. If 'fabric care' becomes centralized, then it becomes possible to consider further approaches to achieving the basic separation of soil from fabric (Figure 9.6). Super-critical fluid solvents would reduce the energy requirement to separate solvent from soil (Figure 9.7), opening up the possibility of completely different approaches to providing this particular service.

This example has deliberately been pursued beyond current practice to demonstrate that clean technology depends at least as much on rethinking commercial and social habits as on introducing technological developments. For example, as developed here, a clean technology from cleaning clothes would introduce completely different relationships between the manufacturers of detergents and washing machines: they would combine to provide the service, rather than each selling their own product.

MATERIALS REUSE: THE NEW INDUSTRIAL ECOLOGY

One of the goals in clean technology is to provide a service with minimum consumption of energy and primary materials, a goal which has been called dematerialization of the economy (O Glarini and W H Stahel, 1989, and T Jackson (ed), 1993).

Some reductions in consumption can be achieved by life-cycle containment (with minimal and controlled purge from the cycle of recovery and reuse, as in the examples of degreasing solvents and Figure 9.8). Prolonging the service life of machines represents an analogous approach for services which are provided by manufactured items. However, given that service life will remain finite, clean technology requires a systematic approach to reuse of materials and components. Like the example of cleaning clothes explored above, this approach implies changes not only in technology but also in commercial relationships. The term 'industrial ecology' has been coined to denote a relationship in which systems providing different services and products 'metabolize' successive uses of materials and energy.

Beyond Recycling: Cascades of Use

The 'once-through' use of resources which characterizes the profligate behaviour of much human activity is represented by the 'open loop' system of Figure 9.10. An ideal 'dematerialized' system would be represented by the 'closed loop' system

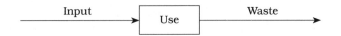

Figure 9.10 *'Once Through' Use of Resources: Open-Loop System*

of Figure 9.11. However, this popular view of recycling is obviously a simplistic misconception. Very rarely does reuse or recycling entail no resource consumption or environmental load. Even reusable drinks containers, such as the traditional milk bottle, must be transported, washed and sterilized before refilling. Furthermore, a completely closed loop is impossible; even in the everyday (at least in the UK) example of the milk bottle, bottles can be broken or chipped. Therefore a real closed-loop recycling system must take the general form shown in Figure 9.12. It is now necessary to enquire whether the resource depletion and environmental load entailed in recycling may offset the benefit of material recycling. In some cases, particularly involving products from renewable resources, recycling may arguably be environmentally damaging; ie recycling is not necessarily a clean technology, or even a best environmental option. To take a specific example, it has been argued that paper derived from sustainably farmed forests should be burned as a renewable biofuel, not recycled as a waste material (R Clift, 1993, Y Virtanen and S Nilsson, 1993, and E Daae and R Clift, 1994).

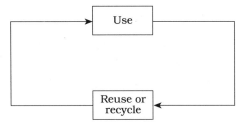

Figure 9.11 *Idealized View of Recycling: Closed-Loop System*

Recognizing the practicalities of reuse and recycling leads to the general concept of industrial ecology shown in Figure 9.13. On its passage through the human economy, a material will ideally pass through a series of uses, usually with progressively lower performance specification (see, for example, Stahel and Jackson, 1993). This general concept is familiar in process engineering, exemplified by a counter-current washing or extraction cascade. Industrial ecology extends the concept to encompass more than one process. There may be some recycling around any step in the cascade, and it could be desirable to reprocess the material to raise its specification so that it can be returned to a higher level in the cascade. Ultimately, however, the material will leave the economic system as waste or, if combustible, as fuel. For example, paper products and hydrocarbon-based polymers should be regarded as materials which pass through one or more uses on their way to being used as fuels (R Clift, 1993).

Recognizing that a material should pass through such a cascade of use introduces another component of clean technology: avoiding contaminating

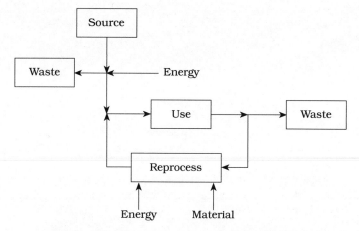

Figure 9.12 *Real Closed-Loop Recycling System*

materials with unnecessary additives which will increase the environmental loads associated with subsequent uses. An obvious example is eliminating toxic heavy metals from printing inks, recognizing that paper ultimately should be burned. Life-cycle design goes beyond environmental life-cycle assessment, designing the whole use cascade rather than optimizing a single use of the material.

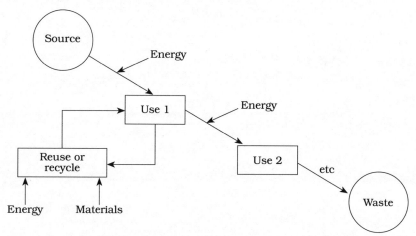

Figure 9.13 *General Industrial Ecology for Material Use*

Example 1: Organic Solvents

The example used above, of reprocessing degreasing solvents, can be examined in more detail as an example of the development of an industrial ecology and the associated commercial relationships. The following account is a simplified version of the development described by Roberts and Lewis (1994).

The business of leasing and reprocessing kerosene used as degreasing solvent

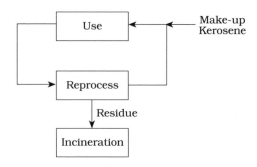

Figure 9.14 *'Metabolized' use of organic solvents*
(a) Reprocessing of degreasing solvents

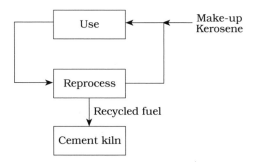

Figure 9.14 *'Metabolized' use of organic solvents*
(b) Fuel use of solvent residue

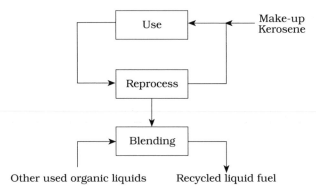

Figure 9.14 *'Metabolized' use of organic solvents*
(c) Incorporation of other used organic liquids

is shown schematically in Figure 9.14a. The leasing relationship closes the loop in the life-cycle, so that the used solvent is returned for reprocessing and subsequent reuse. At this early stage of the commercial relationships, the residue from reprocessing must be incinerated. However, the residue contains a large proportion of kerosene, in addition to aqueous and solid components removed in degreasing, and therefore has a substantial fuel value. As a first development, it can therefore be used as a specification fuel, for example in cement kilns, in this case with the same supplier providing the fuel system to the cement manufacturer – see Figure 9.14b. Thus the solvent supplier has retained 'duty of care' for the organic material throughout its life-cycle.

This concept can be expanded further, as shown in Figure 9.14c. Other organic liquid wastes, such as used in lubricating oil or paint thinners, may be bought in and blended with degreasing solvent residue to increase the quantity of recycled liquid fuel available. The industrial ecology has now drawn in other materials which would otherwise be incinerated or stored, to provide a useful conclusion to their life-cycles. Provided that the import of other materials is carefully controlled, the output from this cascade of use is still a recycled liquid fuel produced to specifications. Whether this fuel is treated as a waste then becomes a question of legal definition only, although the legal status of the material determines the applicable regulations or directives, and therefore affects its commercial utility. Legal constraints on the practice of clean technology represent a broader area than can be addressed here.

Example 2: Office Equipment

Different technical and organizational changes are necessary for manufactured products. We consider next the specific case of photocopiers. We are indebted to Geene and Kummer (1994) for this example, which we have attempted to generalize here as an approach which could be followed for other manufactured products. The user of the equipment self-evidently obtains it for its functions: the purpose is to make photocopies, not to have a photocopier. Thus the end-user buys or leases the equipment to obtain a service. When the machine reaches the end of its service life (ie it no longer provides the function), it becomes scrap hardware without the service value. Unless it is returned to the supplier, or equivalent agent at this stage, the machine becomes undifferentiated scrap and joins the general waste stream. These broad aspects are common to the example of organic solvents.

If the machine is returned to the supply system as shown in Figure 9.15, then the assembly and components may be reusable. Machines which have only been subject to light use may be partially dismantled, to remove worn or damaged parts, and reconditioned or returned to the assembly line. However, it requires an uncommon flexibility in the manufacturing process to accept incomplete machines into the assembly line. Machines which have received more use are disassembled completely. Components can then be fed back into the assembly line, preferably with no distinction from new components. Components which cannot be used, for example because they contain compounds which are no longer used or permitted, leave the system as solid waste. Otherwise, the material is reused or 'cascaded' to another use. In the latter case, the material is preferably returned to the supplier, who can blend it in to fresh material or reprocess it for other applications. The component manufacturer would then be required to accept material which, wholly or partially, has been used before.

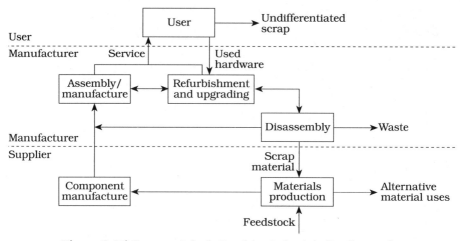

Figure 9.15 *Commercial relationships in 'metabolized' use of a manufactured product*

Thus Figure 9.15 also shows the business relationships necessary to bring about an industrial ecology. It is essential that the used machine is returned to the supply system. For photocopiers, this step is part of the normal commercial process, because some 80 per cent of photocopiers are leased rather than sold (Geene and Kummer, 1994). This is another example of leasing the service rather than selling the product, and it can represent a barrier to adopting clean technology for an industry (such as automobiles) where the accepted commercial relationship involves selling ownership rather than leasing use. It is also important that the manufacturer is able to accept partially dismantled machines and used or reconditioned components into the manufacturing process. This in turn demands quality control procedures in disassembly which equal those in original supply. Furthermore, the material and component suppliers must be involved in the reuse of the material content of components which cannot be reused directly. This requirement demands that individual components contain as few different materials as possible, preferably a single material.

The requirements of designing for easy disassembly and minimizing the number of different materials used in any component diverge from conventional design procedures, but emerge as key elements of clean technology on the manufacturing sector.

WASTE REDUCTION AT SOURCE

The preceding discussion has concentrated on changing to new technologies and new commercial relationships. For an organization to improve its environmental performance on a time-scale which is shorter than its capital cycle, it is necessary to concentrate on improvements to existing processes and products. Rather than clean technology in the broad sense, this section concentrates on clean production and specifically on reducing waste at source (T Jackson (ed), 1993).

The European Union recognizes a hierarchy of waste management options. In order of decreasing importance these are:

1. Prevention.
2. Minimization.
3. Recycling.
4. Disposal.

Following the discussion earlier in this chapter, recycling must be approached in the context of industrial ecology, while disposal is considered elsewhere in this book. We concentrate here on prevention and minimization. A more closely defined hierarchy, due to Crittenden and Kolaczkowski (1992) is given in Table 9.2. A classification due to Freeman (1993) is shown in Figure 9.16, again making the basic distinction between source reduction and recycling.

In terms of Table 9.2 and Figure 9.16, the clean technology approach concentrates on source reduction (with some attention also to prompt recycling, ie recycling within the process itself). Figure 9.16 recognizes four components of source reduction.

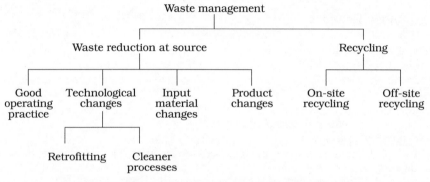

Figure 9.16 *Practical Techniques for Waste Minimization*

Table 9.2 *Hierarchy of Waste Management Practices*

	Top priority
Elimination	Complete elimination of waste.
Source reduction	Avoidance, reduction or elimination of waste, generally within the confines of the production unit, through changes in industrial processes or procedures.
Recycling	Use, reuse and recycling of wastes for the original or some other purpose, such as input material, materials recovery or energy production.
Treatment	The destruction, detoxification, neutralization, etc of wastes into less harmful substances.
Disposal	The discharge of wastes to air, water or land in properly controlled or safe ways such that compliance is achieved; secure land disposal may involve volume reduction, encapsulation, leachate containment and monitoring techniques.
	Lower priority

Input Material Changes

These can be considered where it is possible to substitute a material which provides the required function but results in reduced environmental load. Examples are the replacement of chlorinated organic solvents by non-chlorinated or aqueous media[3] in cleaning operations or paints; the replacement of chemical biocides or oxidants by ozone or hydrogen peroxide which decompose to leave no residues or emissions; and the elimination of toxic heavy metals, for example, in electrolytic processes and devices. In each case, the whole life-cycle of the material must be considered to ensure that one environmental problem is not simply being exchanged for another elsewhere. Although a substituted material may be more expensive, the increased material cost may be offset by savings in waste treatment and disposal costs. In this case, material substitution constitutes a change to a cleaner technology.

Technology Changes

These include the kinds of major changes in practice discussed in earlier sections of this chapter. Less radical changes which may be 'retrofitted' to an existing process include:

1. Improving chemical synthesis – for example, by using a more selective catalyst, to reduce by-product formation.
2. Improving process control.
3. Redesigning or reconfiguring the process to improve heat recovery or to avoid dilution of process streams.
4. Improving the selectivity of separation processes.

In addition to avoiding producing waste, technology changes include containing wastes and retaining them in a concentrated form, rather than diluting them for dispersion into the environment or mixing wastes for subsequent treatment. Throughout the manufacturing and process industries, there is a general trend towards treatment of waste at source, recognizing that a process to treat a specified waste is likely to be more effective and less expensive than treatment of a mixed waste stream. The move away from the 'dilute and disperse' approach to the strategy of 'concentrate and contain' usually also requires changes in operating practice.

Good Operating Practice

This includes preventing unnecessary releases, and therefore merges into on-site recycling. Returning to the example of replacing organic by water-based solvents, this kind of material substitution may not represent an environmental

---

3. While it is generally considered a good practice to replace organic by aqueous solvents, especially if the organic solvents are chlorinated, it was pointed out earlier in the chapter that, consistent with the life-cycle approach, it is the escape rather than the existence of the organic material which causes the environmental load. The discussion here therefore refers to cases where it is impractical or uneconomic to contain the solvent.

improvement if the solvent is simply discharged after use. The discussion of approaches to cleaning clothes earlier in this chapter was a 'domestic' example. If the organic or aqueous medium is used as a cleaning agent, it should be contained and reused; depending on the nature of the cleaning operation, mechanical or membrane filtration may suffice to collect the soil so that the liquid can be reused. A particular environmental problem arises with 'clean-in-place' treatment, for example, of food-processing or brewing equipment. Emissions of the cleaning fluids can constitute the main environmental load from the equipment. The most urgent issue for improving environmental performance is then management of the cleaning process. Waste stream segregation may represent a minor technology change which yields a disproportionately large improvement in environmental performance.

Product Changes

These include changes in final or intermediate products to reduce waste generation and other environmental loads arising elsewhere in the life-cycle. The approach here is usually product-specific and therefore commercially sensitive. Ecolabelling is an attempt to identify consumer products which genuinely have improved environmental performance, without revealing commercially sensitive information (see R Clift, 1993).

CONCLUDING REMARKS

This introduction to clean technology has invoked examples from several different industrial sectors. However, a number of features characterizing clean technology emerge, whichever sector is considered:

1. Clean technology is really an approach to providing services and benefits, not a recognizable set of technologies.
2. To ensure that a technology is really clean, it is necessary to consider the whole life-cycle of the materials or objects which provide the service or benefit.
3. An organization intending to apply clean technology must concentrate on the service which it provides rather than on the products or artefacts which it sells. It should also retain responsibility for the products or artefacts which provide the service and either reuse them or pass them on to another organization for a different use within the industrial ecology.
4. Wherever possible, waste should be avoided at source rather than cleaned up at the end of the pipe. If a waste is unavoidable, it should be concentrated and dispersed into the environment.

REFERENCES

Baas, L, Hoffman, H, Huisingh, D, Huisingh, J, Koppert, P and Newman, F (1990) 'Protection of the North Sea: Time for Clean Production', Erasmus Centre for

Environmental Studies, Erasmus University, Rotterdam, Netherlands

CEFIC (1992) 'Carbon/Energy Taxation: The Position of the European Chemical Industry', European Chemical Industry Council, Brussels

Clift, R (1993) 'Pollution and waste management', *Science in Parliament*, no 50

Clift, R (1994) 'Life-cycle assessment and ecolabelling', J Cleaner Production, no 1, pp 155–159

Corbett, J R, Wright, K and Baillie, A C (1984) *The Biochemical Mode of Action of Pesticides*, Academic Press, London and Orlando, p 343

Crittenden, B D and Kolaczkowski, S T (1992) *Waste Minimization Guide*, Institution of Chemical Engineers, Rugby

Daae, E and Clift, R (1994) 'A life-cycle assessment of the implications of paper use and recycling', I Chem E, Environmental Protection Bulletin no 28, pp 23–25

Freeman, H M (1990) *Hazardous Waste Minimization*, McGraw-Hill, New York

Geene, F and Kummen, K (1994) personal communication on behalf of Rank Xerox Ltd

Glarini, O and Stahel, W R (1989) *The Limits to Certainty*, Kluwer Academic Publishers, Dordrecht

Guinee, J B, Heihungs, R, Udo de Haes, H A and Huppes, G (1993) 'Quantitative life-cycle assessment of products – 2; classification, valuation and improvement analysis', J Cleaner Production, no 1, pp 81–92

Guinee, J B, Udo de Haes, H A and Huppes, G (1993) 'Quantitative life-cycle assessment of products – 1: Goal definition and inventory', J Cleaner Production, no 1, pp 3–13

Jackson, T (ed) (1993) *Clean Production Strategies*, Lewis Publishers, Boca Raton, Florida

Karlsson, R (1994) 'LCA as a Guide for the Improvement of Recycling' in *Proceedings of the European Workshop on Allocation in LCA* (eds G Huppes and F Schneider), SETAC, Brussels, pp 18–28

Keoleian, G A and Menerey, D (1993) *Life Cycle Design Guidance Manual*, US Environmental Protection Agency, Cincinnati, Ohio

Lofstedt, R and Clift, R, An Analysis of the Efficiency of International Environmental Aid, to be published

Pedersen, B (ed) (1993) *Environmental Assessment of Products*, UETP-EEE, Helsinki

Roberts, K and Lewis, R (1994) personal communication on behalf of Safety Kleen UK Ltd

SETAC (1992) *A Conceptual Framework for Life-Cycle Impact Assessment*, Society of Environmental Toxicology and Chemistry, Pensacola, Florida

SETAC (1993) *Guidelines for Life-Cycle Assessment: A 'Code of Practice'*, Society of Environmental Toxicology and Chemistry, Brussels and Pensacola

Stahel, W R and Jackson, T (1993) *Optimal utilization and durability – towards a new definition of the service economy*, Chapter 14 in Jackson, T (1993)

Udo de Haes, H A, Bensahel, J F, Clift, R, Fussler, C R, Griesshammer, R and Jensen, A A (1994) *Guidelines for the Application of Life Cycle Assessment in the EV Ecolabelling Programme*, DGXI of the Commission of the European Communities, Brussels

UKEB (1992) *Ecolabelling Criteria for Washing Machines*, UK Ecolabelling Board, London

Virtanen, Y and Nilsson, S (1993) *Environmental Impact of Waste Paper Recycling*, Earthscan Publications Ltd, London

Warhurst A (1992) *Environmental management in mining and mineral processing in developing countries*, Natural Resource Forum, Feb, pp 39-48

10

A Clean Break? From Corporate Research and Development to Sustainable Technological Regimes

Kenneth Green and Ian Miles

INTRODUCTION

A vital element of the shift towards sustainable development is technological change. The creation of new technologies has to be better informed by the environmental consequences of the application of these technologies in production processes and in the use and disposal of products. These consequences must be taken account of in the process of Research and Development (R&D).

R&D has various sources. Publicly-funded R&D is mostly a matter of 'pure' research, although over recent years the emphasis on applicable science has grown remarkably. One result is that such research is often carried out within firms which use public funds as a way of boosting the money they put into corporate R&D. Public funds for applied research have mushroomed with large programmes in Information Technology like the UK's Alvey and the EC's Esprit programmes, and their successors. In recent years, public R&D funds have increasingly been devoted to environmental problems and 'clean technology' on the assumption that knowledge generated here can inform technological choices.

However, it is still overwhelmingly *firms* who commercialize and mass-produce technologies. For firms to reorient their technological development, it will be necessary for them to redirect their corporate R&D. To do this is not a straightforward matter; to understand how it can take place, you need some understanding of how technological change takes place.

HOW TECHNOLOGIES EVOLVE

The growth in the study of technological innovation over recent years has revealed many inadequacies in the conventional economist's view of technology. Conventional economics assumed that information about technological options was freely available and could be assimilated with practically no costs. It saw the choice of technology as a fairly simple matter, with firms somehow able to

1 Acknowledgements for supporting the research on which this paper draws are due to: the Commission of the European Communities (SEER programme), the UK's Economic and Social Research Council (Joint Panel and SPSG programmes) and the Technology Strategy Forum. Thanks to Alan Irwin and Andrew McMeekin for their comments.

establish exactly the optimum mix of resources and inputs to use, and selecting exactly the right technology to use these proportions of resources. But historical analyses, case studies and large-scale surveys showed that the picture was far more complex. One result has been the emergence of a body of thought which called 'evolutionary economics'. This provides a number of useful approaches for understanding the relationship between environmental pressures, technological innovation and corporate R&D (G Dosi et al, 1988).

Evolutionary approaches draw an analogy between the processes of natural selection in Darwinian thought and the selection processes that take place in markets. The analogy can be put in terms of firms who compete for survival like organisms do, or it can be developed to consider competing technologies. For example, the VHS and Betamax video formats could be said to have been competing for market share, with the former eventually winning out. It is quite common for two or more fairly similar products to be released at roughly the same time by competing firms which have been developing more or less substantial variants of the same technology in parallel. The battle is on for the new market, and while it is common for one design to end up predominating – the so-called 'dominant design' – there are cases where different types of design flourish in different 'niches' (eg different personal computer systems in homes, businesses and schools). Another sort of competition is revealed when one product supplants another – a famous case is the substitution of the motor car for the horse and cart and, more recently, the CD player could be seen as a newcomer that has driven vinyl records out of their 'habitats'. In such cases, we are often seeing a quite new type of technological 'solution' to a market 'requirement' – a recently-developed type of knowledge is being applied to help do something that consumers or firms want or need to do.

Of course, the technologies themselves are not consciously struggling for survival; it is firms and alliances of firms (and sometimes governments) that are promoting particular technologies. But what happens in the market is important, in that purchasers are utilizing their discretion to acquire the best deal they can for their cash. Playing fields are not always level, and there is no guarantee that what seems to be technically the superior product will win out. Regulations may influence choices, too, by outlawing certain products as not meeting safety or environmental standards, for example. Within firms, product development relies upon managers choosing to invest money, having drawn the best conclusions they can about the likely acceptability of their products to markets and regulators. Thus, as well as selection processes taking place in markets, within firms there are also (earlier) selection processes, as options for technological development are generated and then screened in an effort to second-guess markets. This is sometimes referred to as a '*search process*' within firms. More precisely, firms seeking to create technologies that will achieve success, rather than trying to 'discover' successful technologies.

Another idea spelled out in the evolutionary approach is that technologies, and the innovative efforts of firms and industries, tend to follow trajectories of development. Such trajectories can usually be traced out once a particular sort of product has been established in a market, and the manufacturing or service processes used to create it have been established in an industry. As a result of firms in that industry pursuing 'incremental innovation', making continual but usually small changes in the product and/or the process, the typical trend is for the products to become cheaper (through processes that economize on machinery, labour and material inputs) and/or to have improved quality or performance. Computer technology is a striking illustration of this – the pace of change in performance has been so steady and rapid that 'Moore's Law' has been coined to describe the trend.[2]

But what produces trajectories? The specific trajectory followed by a specific firm will be governed partly by the skills and knowledge that have been accumulated in the company, and partly by what is happening in the world outside the firm – in the external 'selection environment'. This comprises those factors outside a firm that influence which products and/or processes it chooses to innovate, and includes:

- Changes in the prices of raw material inputs.
- Changes in the prices of capital equipment.
- Changes in demand for the firm's products.
- Competitive pressures from rival firms.
- Changes in all the laws, regulations and public-political pressures which bear on a firm's products, processes and organizational routines.

A related idea in the evolutionary approach is the technological regime: managers, engineers and scientists come to develop a set of more-or-less common assumptions as to what technological principles can be applied to solving particular 'problems', where performance gains and costs savings might be forthcoming, and what improvements will be valued by markets or compatible with trends in resource costs. Such a 'regime' involves both a particular set of products and processes, and the assumptions and experience that are associated with developing and using them. It leads to decisions as to where, from the vast range of possible technological developments to concentrate technological efforts. Innovation is said to move forward through narrow 'corridors' which tend to maintain the regime.

These ideas can contribute to thinking about the prospects for clean technology, and how these can be maximized. The performance characteristics that structure the direction of technological development that firms choose are shaped by the technological regime concerned. For example, the electronics industry, from the 1970s, has been heavily focused on miniaturization and speed of processing and massive cost reduction by process automation. For chemicals, since the 1940s, the focus has been on cost reduction for basic raw materials through refinery automation (see C Freeman, 1982, and R U Ayres 'Industrial Metabolism' in J H Ausubel and H E Sladovich (eds), 1989). For many industries, disposability (in the sense of 'throw-away-ability') has been a performance characteristic which has guided product development. Can 'cleaner' performance characteristics similarly be the focus of effort?

Evolutionary economics suggests that what is now needed are shifts in technological regimes. A few one-off improvements in polluting and resource-consuming technologies will not suffice for sustainable development. Technologies

---

2 'Moore's Law' purports to describe the steady exponential increase in the power of microchip technology from the 1960s. D MacKenzie, in 'Economic and Sociological Explanations of Technical Change' in R Coombs et al, 1992, argues that for some writers it is indeed treated almost as a 'law' of technical development.

would still be evolving along trajectories that are affected only indirectly by environmental considerations. Furthermore, if single products only were being improved, then the whole complex of technologies (including complementary products which are required for the effective functioning of these products) would still continue on established tracks. What is required is a shift in a whole series of interrelated technologies – and in the ongoing directions of technological changes. Such a shift in technological regime is clearly a more daunting challenge than simply inventing a less polluting internal combustion engine (or whatever). But it is the sort of change that sustainable development is going to require.

What are the prospects for such change? The evolutionary approach also provides some insights here, especially in its less economistic versions. While some evolutionary economists have seen technological choice as following from rational calculations or even following *natural* trajectories, others (especially sociologists and historians) have stressed the cultural and political elements of choice. In their view, an industry's technological regime is an institution,

> sustained, not through any internal [ie, natural] logic, or intrinsic superiority
> to other institutions, but because of the interests that develop in its
> continuance and the belief that it will continue. Its continuance becomes
> embedded in (technologists' and managers') frameworks of calculation and
> routine behaviour, and it continues because it is thus embedded.[3]

This way of looking at technological development provides approaches to examining how technological regimes change. Thus, if a given regime is indeed an institution, then it can be seen as an inextricably social *and* technical resource for technologists active in industrial innovation. The regime will therefore constitute a set of 'socially' agreed, if broad, objectives as to what the parameters of an industry's products will be, how they would be typically made and (crucially for R&D) on which features of the product and process technological development should focus. In other words, this specifies which 'performance characteristics' will serve as a heuristic for R&D attention.

The technological regime is thus a knowledge resource and an organizational resource to use in deciding which particular directions should be pursued in technological development – and thus what technological trajectories emerge (once the results of the choices of competing firms have been subject to the selection processes of the market).

CHANGING TECHNOLOGICAL REGIMES

Technological regimes are not eternal, though they are usually quite long-lasting. Under certain circumstances, the technologists that work within firms may be obliged to 'reconsider' the technological regime within which their research, development and design teams work. Major rethinks of which performance characteristics to focus on, or how to achieve them, will be necessary. External 'shocks' are one circumstance which may have such an effect; an example was the large increase in crude oil costs in the early 1970s, which had the effect of focusing innovative attention on economising the use of petroleum products

---

3 D MacKenzie, op cit, emphasis added.

(whether as raw material or as energy source) with which many firms had previously been rather profligate.

A rather different sort of 'shock' is the development elsewhere in the economy of a new technology which can be applied effectively to products, processes and purposes which were previously handled in very different ways. Microelectronics is a case in point, which has had wide reverberations. While this technology can be viewed as a further step in the development of a trajectory that began with transistors, its implications extended well beyond the traditional electronics industry. To take a notable example, the long-established wrist-watch industry, based on a centuries-old technology of clockwork, was decimated by the arrival of new electronic timepieces – fashionable (at least for a while), cheap and rapidly becoming cheaper, accurate, without problems of winding, and often incorporating new functions like alarms, calculators, etc. Microelectronics similarly led to shifts in the technological regime in typewriters, cash registers, electromechanical controls, and many other industries. It has been central to the most profound technological revolution (the term for simultaneous change in numerous regimes, associated with the development of new underpinning technological knowledge) since the development of electric power.

In some cases, it will be possible to accommodate such 'shocks' by innovation which stretches the existing technological regime to the limit. Solutions can be found (for example, recycling waste heat) by drawing on the resource of knowledge that the regime 'prescribes'. However, in other cases, the regime may become increasingly vulnerable as a substantial revision of the technological basis becomes necessary. Then, the search for new product and/or process designs is on and rival technologies are offered as solutions. (The current 'struggle' between chemical and biotechnological techniques in the food and chemical industries can be seen as the struggle of two rival regimes.) Some firms are liable to promote more radical innovations; if these succeed, other firms may follow, leading eventually to new dominant designs and a new technological regime.

How is one technological regime overthrown and replaced by another? Anderson and Tushman (1990) argue that it is not a matter of one regime being 'naturally' or obviously technically superior to another. Rather, one regime comes to dominate due to 'social, political and organizational dynamics....of compromise and accommodation between actors of unequal influence'. Which one wins, they propose, depends on a contingent mixture of such factors as:

- Market demand (which in no sense can be reduced to 'wants' or 'needs', but which is itself subject to construction by many social actors – markets are 'created').[4]
- Corporate producer power (ie large firms can crowd out rival regimes merely because they can spend more on R & D and capital investment).
- User or purchaser power (ie large users – like governments, especially in their military departments – can, by their purchases, favour one technological design over another).[5]
- Industry-wide agreement over standards (the winning 'dominant design' will often be confirmed by industry standards; the struggle to establish a new dominant design will thus be visible as a struggle over standards, over

4 See K Green, 'Creating demand for biotechnology: shaping technologies and markets' in R Coombs, et al, 1992, op cit
5 An example of this is the development of NC-machine tools described in D Noble, 1984

supplier/ customer networks and over criteria for efficient production).

- Industry alliances (in cartels of producers or producers and major purchasers).
- Regulatory frameworks (stricter regulations can favour one regime over another).
- These are all external, 'selection environment' factors. We can add a further factor which is 'internal' to the firm: institutional assumptions about potential markets and technological directions and the desirability of different courses of action (ie internal firm debates/disputes about strategies).

The relationship between changes in the selection environment and the pursuit of a particular trajectory inside individual firms is not a mechanical one. The signals from the selection environment are not necessarily clear or unambiguous; the firm, as an organization (rather than an organism, as might be concluded from the use of the evolutionary metaphor) has, of course, to be structured so as to absorb and act on the signals in the first place. Systems have to be in place to identify selection environment changes (by means of intelligence-gathering on markets, regulations, political factors and scientific/technological developments). There must be the capability to interpret the information gathered (by means of a variety of techniques in marketing, regulatory affairs and R&D departments). Making sense of all the interpreted data requires strategic action (often via committees that formulate and disseminate corporate and business strategies). In short, firms require appropriate organizational structures, practices and cultures to look for and create discontinuities and co-ordinate them with technological possibilities.

The question that concerns us here, then, is: 'What changes in the organization of R&D are needed to meet the challenges which green/environmental pressures pose to existing technological regimes?'

WHY CHANGE R&D?

We will argue that substantial reorganization of R&D structures and practices is called for in order to meet these challenges. But it could be suggested that the needed shift in the directions of R&D could be effected by three features of the 'selection environment', without any particular reorganization of R&D structures being necessary. The factors are market demand, technological trajectories and changing prices of inputs.

The Magic of the Market

First, it can be argued that market demand alone will automatically guide technological development on to new paths. For example, if consumers make it clear through their spending choices that they prefer greener products or environmentally responsible firms, changes will sooner or later sweep through industry. The power of consumer choice – and of organized action like boycotts – should not be ignored. But there are problems here: there may be limitations in consumer information about products and processes; indeed firms often exploit such limitations to actively create 'greener-than-thou' images. These limitations are hopefully being addressed in new labelling and auditing schemes. Even so, consumers are having to integrate environmental concerns (themselves many-sided) into decisions in which factors like prices and convenience play a role, alongside other features such as brand image and other political considerations (eg do these products come from a military dictatorship?).

Furthermore, as illustrated in the discussion of technological regimes above, R&D efforts tend to follow particular established patterns of activity. Research staff will have been recruited with particular technological competencies, which are liable to focus their efforts in particular directions. Furthermore, formal and informal reward structures will exist which reinforce particular strategies of technological search. Changing the regime thus requires considerable effort. New criteria need to be incorporated into R&D for environmental issues to be taken into account in the search process and thus to be reflected in a reshaping of technological regimes.

Such a shift in direction in R&D is required if clean technology is to be an underlying principle of a new technological regime. Otherwise, we may repeatedly face the choice between more and less damaging technologies each time a purchase is being considered. There is no guarantee that technological progress will be continually pushed in more sustainable directions as a consequence of this. The environmental signal that comes from the consumer purchase decision is liable to be too weak and too readily confounded with signals about other properties of the technology for its salience to be recognized and thus to shape the search process within R&D.

Technological Revolutions

A second argument suggests that current directions of technology search are already becoming markedly 'greener' than was heretofore the case, so that no further adjustment of R&D structures would be necessary. The argument here is that major trajectories of technological change have become well-established in advanced industrial economies in the past few years, as a consequence of the development of significant new technological knowledge which is inherently 'greener' than the knowledge it supersedes.

It is commonplace to hear of the three 'technological revolutions' of Information Technology (IT), Biotechnology, and Advanced Materials. There are intriguing similarities and differences between the three underlying technologies. All of them involve the application of knowledge to engineer their key factors – data, biological organisms and products, and materials – in far more intricate ways than previously possible. Each of these key factors underpins numerous economic and social activities. Of the three technologies, IT appears both to offer most scope for application (because information is intrinsic to all economic activities) and to be undergoing the most rapid pace of innovation.[6]

What is the significance of this for clean technology and sustainable development? Compared to the 'supply-push' signals coming from these technolo-

---

6 See I Miles, 'Characteristics and Dynamics of Contemporary Technological Revolutions' in M R Bahagavan (ed) (1995)

gies, the 'demand-pull' of environmental concerns may appear to be rather weak. But proponents of these technologies argue that they are particularly well suited to addressing environmental concerns. A few examples will suffice to make the point. IT allows for the improved monitoring of emissions and energy use, and for control systems that can adjust production processes to minimize these. Biotechnology can substitute for highly intrusive use of pesticides and other chemicals in agriculture, and genetically modified organisms can be applied to remediating contaminated land. New materials provide dramatic increases in the lifetime of blades, in the ratio of strength to weight, and in the temperatures at which equipment can operate, and thus allow for reduction of replacements and increase in energy-efficiency.

Such potentials are extremely important, and may well contribute significantly to a cleaner technological regime. But in many cases they result from the almost promiscuous search for 'problems' to which the three technological revolutions can be 'solutions'. The new technologies, furthermore, hardly have unblemished environmental records, and the supply-push dynamics associated with them may well mean that they will be sources of new environmental problems. While the IT industry has done much to clean up its act, it is well-known that considerable contamination of groundwater occurred in Silicon Valley as a result of the operation of electronics industries. These industries were also major CFC users, though they have phased this out rapidly. The general 'push' of computers (with relatively short product lives) into all sorts of applications means a proliferation of energy-using technologies in activities which previously required mainly mental effort. Even if PCs and other IT equipment are being rendered more energy efficient – 'green' computers are currently in vogue – the share of IT in office energy costs is continuing to expand significantly.

In the case of the other two revolutionary technologies – Biotechnology and Advanced Materials – experience is less systematic, but there are numerous fears about the environmental consequences of the diffusion of some of the innovations they promise (K Green and E Yoxen, 1992). For instance, the release of genetically modified organisms may disrupt existing ecosystems – it has even been suggested that bacteria (engineered to reduce frost damage to leaves) might percolate into the upper atmosphere, changing its crystallization dynamics, ultimately affecting the weather! New long-lasting materials may well cause disposal problems – what do you do with a ceramic car shell? – and more complex materials may be less well suited for reuse and recycling than simpler, familiar products. A broader concern is that the three 'revolutionary' technologies may contribute to global environmental degradation by undermining agriculture and industry in many Third World countries, unless these countries receive assistance enabling them to apply the new technologies productively themselves.

Powerful forces drive on the development and application of these revolutionary R&D decisions are being taken on the basis of expectations about their trajectories. There is no doubt that the new technologies can be applied to 'clean' ends. But without incentives to this end it is likely that the problems to which these 'solutions' are applied will be determined by the existing R&D culture rather than according to environmental objectives. The challenge of building such objectives into the R&D process remains.

Energy efficiency

The third argument also suggests that current technological trajectories are inherently cleaner than their predecessors. In this case, however, the issue is changing prices of key resource inputs to the production process. The best example is that of energy because this is the most pervasive issue.

Powerful economic incentives are pressing firms toward finding ways of achieving more energy efficiency in their processes. These coincide in large part with the aim of reducing energy consumption – though not specifically with the phasing out of fossil fuels. Energy use has some features in common across a wide range of industries. Perhaps the most universal applications are those for lighting/heating and for transport. Many branches of manufacturing industry share energy requirements for machining and/or heating materials in order to transform them. Because the energy issue has strong generic features, there can be common changes in trajectories across many industrial sectors.

Some widely applicable innovations here may also serve energy conservation, such as IT-enhanced controls for greater efficiency and IT-supported systems for design so as to minimize waste (transport logistics are rather similar to this). Other innovations may be more localized, such as process redesign to reduce the number of transformative steps that are involved (for example, through the use of new materials). Some energy uses are highly specific to particular process industries – for example the cryogenic cooling of air in order to manufacture industrial gases where there are considerable efforts in hand to save energy costs by means of membrane technology.

There are common problems, but whether common, generic, radical technologies will emerge to support industrial energy conservation remains uncertain. Such developments might trigger a strong supply-push consolidating technological trajectories toward reduced energy use. However, the goal of increased energy efficiency has already been incorporated into many industries, who strive for it in their processes and products. The application of IT control systems and lightweight materials are frequently elements of the solution – and could well continue to be major instruments for energy conservation.

In *processes*, energy-saving represents cost-saving. In products, benefits may be offered to users. For example, manufacturers of components for automobile systems, such as brake drums and parts of engines, are strongly motivated to decrease the weight of their products, so that greater mileage per gallon can be promised to final consumers. This may involve the use of new ceramic materials, or even familiar substances such as aluminium. Household appliances, too, are increasingly being marketed with energy efficiency (and other environmental characteristics) to the fore, as are items of office equipment such as PCs and copiers.

The argument then is that even if firms have little interest in environmental impacts, let alone green marketing; they are still likely to be motivated to pursue energy efficiency in their products and processes. This technological trajectory may be built into R&D practice, then, without any more general environmental pressure on management.

Such an impetus is clearly present, but it will vary with energy costs rather than with the environmental costs (externalities) associated with energy use. Cheapening of energy – even as a result of breakthroughs in 'clean' technology, such as solar cells or fuel cells – would reduce the impetus.

In any case, the impact of energy efficiency measures on fossil fuel use may be less than would result from more environmentally-informed decision-making. Nor does the drive for energy efficiency necessarily mean that other environmental concerns are being satisfied – lightweight materials may have disposal problems, new production processes may mean new pollutants. Energy concerns which are motivated mainly by financial considerations do not substitute for broader 'green' concerns. Research efforts directed toward energy efficiency may often provide useful contributions. But the question of how environmental issues are incorporated into business R&D remains fundamental to the development of cleaner technologies, in energy production and use and in other environmentally sensitive areas. How can such an incorporation take place?

THE PROBLEM OF RESEARCH AND DEVELOPMENT

The crucial role of R&D is poorly reflected in the environmental management literature.[7] Recent years have seen a flood of books, articles and reports on how companies can respond to the environmental challenge. But even the books which purport to deal with all aspects of a company's operations usually neglect R&D. Total systems principles are discussed, sometimes within the context of quality control or environmental management standards schemes, but their detailed applicability at the level of the various management subsystems tends to be limited to 'marketing' or 'personnel/training'.

There is hardly any published literature on the links between strategic environmental issues and R&D – the first conclusion reached in Winn and Roome's (1992) comprehensive review of the field. They suggest that this reflects environmental issues tending to be *board level* issues which 'reflect senior management's vague concerns about societal issues'. This is perhaps not surprising, given the time it would take to 'translate' top-level commitments into practical action over the technological content of a company's products and processes. R&D management interests have focused on finding 'techniques' to deal with the environmental issues. Less concern has been given to the question of the adequacy of organizational design, training, managerial competence and organizational values.

Several authors suggest that firms are (or should be) evolving toward more environmentally aware practices, and that this evolution can be described in terms of a set of stages through which companies supposedly pass on their way toward 'greenness'. It is simplistic to assume that all companies move through the same sequence, let alone at similar rates. But these accounts do highlight some key styles that differentiate one firm from another, and suggest steps that can be taken in the course of the greening of industry. However, R&D is notably absent from most such approaches.

One exception is Roome (1992), who identifies five strategies that businesses can adopt in response to environmental pressures, which can readily be seen as such a sequence of steps from non-compliance, through compliance, compliance

---

7 More generally, although internationally competitive firms spend between 2 and 15 per cent of their turnover on R&D, surprisingly little attention is given to the management of such a large resource in management literature of any kind; the environmental management case is an extreme version of a common blind spot.

plus, and commercial and environmental excellence to leading edge.

Roome suggests that the last three strategies all have clear implications for the kind of technology development strategy which a firm might follow. A 'compliance-plus' strategy will require some change of direction for the firm's R&D, though Roome suggests that no organizational changes are likely. 'Commercial and environmental excellence' and 'leading-edge' strategies, however, have implications both for the direction and for the form of organization of R&D. A 'leading edge' strategy requires all this, but also calls for a fundamental change of 'organizational values'. Which strategy is adopted is partly dependent, argues Roome, on internal company factors, (such as degrees of personnel commitment to environmentalism) and on the nature of the environmental driving force (which involves both public perceptions of the environmental impact of a business' processes and products and the scientific significance of the environmental impact of some product, process or technology).[8]

Another relevant account is given by Chatterji (1993), who presents a 'five step' model of the evolution of the R&D laboratory as a firm moves from compliance to strategic leadership. (His stages are: reactive, participative, active, innovative and leadership.)

Roome and Chatterji present classifications that are evolutionary, implying that firms move through the various stages – from 'compliance' to 'leading edge' or 'strategic leadership'. However, a straightforward evolution through the stages is difficult to imagine. Strategies – whether corporate or technology – that a firm adopts in response to environmental issues have to take account of a number of factors. Such factors must include:

- The continually shifting environmental agenda and priority list; some issues become less important due to more research, government regulations and, crucially, changing public perceptions as reflected in public opinion or in consumer markets; an R&D strategy and technology management system has to be flexible enough to deal with these changes.
- The controversial nature of many environmental issues – in terms of the scientific 'facts', and in terms of their system/temporal boundaries. (How far into the future do you seek to predict environmental impact? How do you incorporate notions of sustainability and inter-generational equity into an R&D strategy?) Such things are inherently difficult to know how to respond to; they account for the confusion that many businesses admit to at the moment and their demand for government to be clear and consistent about the direction of its regulatory policies.
- The differences between different businesses in a firm; not all businesses will require the same strategy.

There has been disappointingly little empirical research into such issues.[9]

---

8 'Scientific significance' is not as clear-cut as it might appear; the significance of some environmental problem can change over time, going 'in and out of fashion' as new scientific evidence accumulates or is reviewed. Scientific interpretations themselves can be controversial, with some scientists considering some issues trivial and others of great import.

9 A few surveys are suggestive as to how firms currently stand in terms of such classifications; see B M Rushton, 1993

INNOVATING UNDER PRESSURE

Case studies of individual firms' R&D responses to environmental pressures make interesting reading. Perhaps the most dramatic is that of ICI.[10] The specific pressure was the requirement to phase out CFCs. ICI was a major producer of these ozone-depleting substances, and its efforts resulted in the commercialization of a CFC substitute – Klea – in half the time previously accepted as the industry's norm for a new product (ie in five years instead of ten).

This required the creation of a highly integrated team of over 80 members by 1990; in 1985, when the decisions to press ahead with the project was taken, the relevant team had been half this number. Team integration was facilitated by team-building exercises, counselling support, and ground-rules, including a 'no-blame' regime. The team covered several disciplines, based at one location under one technical manager. Researchers and engineers had to reverse their normal operating practices, bypassing the conventional procedure whereby engineers would only begin to design a plant after the process for producing a chemical was determined. Plant design was begun by the engineers on the understanding that the chemists would be able to provide details of catalysts by a specified date.

The project was overseen by a Business Team that included members from Marketing, Sales, Production and Technical functions. Tight project planning (using project engineering planning techniques) was used, to meet specific deadlines. In 1987, a date of 1995 was set for the first commercial plant to open – but shortly after the signing of the Montreal protocol (on CFC phase-out) this was accelerated to 1993, and later to 1991. This target has been exceeded – the first commercial plant opened in 1990, giving ICI a lead in the competitive race with rival chemical producers. ICI simultaneously developed the chemistry and the engineering technology for plants in the UK, the USA and Japan.[11]

Perhaps ironically, given the strong commitment of ICI researchers to helping solve global pollution problems, their CFC substitute has come under criticism from environmentalists, on account of its being a powerful greenhouse gas. Greenpeace, in particular, has been promoting the use of radical alternatives to CFCs in refrigeration, such as propane/butane systems, which German firms have now adopted. ICI's considerable efforts and achievements were still, it seems, constrained by the technological regime dominating the company, rather than constituting an alternative regime.

ICI's achievement certainly should not be minimized, and its team required 'a very different commitment and culture' – in other words, organizational innovation. How unique is this response? ICI was under tremendous pressure to respond to demands of the phasing out of CFCs, and thus introduced innovations in the organization of R&D. It may be that such dramatic innovations, forming a hot-house system of organizational change, are most applicable to crises such as this, where the 'replacement' of one product/technology by one that is more environmentally friendly has become urgently necessary. Environmentalism required a radical rethink of R&D organization, meaning finding ways to:

---

10 We draw on our own research, together with the helpful inside account by A Foster, 1991.
11 Important developments also took place in the relations between chemical firms, as well as in their internal integration. Unprecedented collaboration was developed between chemical companies who were otherwise hotly competing to capture markets resulting from the regulatory control of CFCs. While the chemical producers competed on specific substitutes and production processes, they collaborated in pooling resources for toxicity and environmental assessment.

- Break down barriers between disciplinary divisions within firms;
- collaborate with rival firms;
- incorporate new knowledge from universities and elsewhere.

Such a system of organization might be most applicable to those crises where rapid 'replacement' of one product/ technology by a more environmentally-friendly one is necessary, where a number of (probably large) firms are moving in slightly different ways along the same technological frontier, and where there is high redundancy in acquiring costly information and/or presenting such information to the regulating authorities.

Most other cases that have been described seem to be far more 'incremental' in organizational terms. This is true, for example, for the programme launched by GEC–Marconi for finding CFC substitutes for the cleaning of electronic assemblies even though this also involved intensive and collaborative work (B P Richards et al, 1993). But, the ICI case may indicate a sort of response that will become more common in the future, if environmental crises become more frequent and intense. Such hot-house systems may be tried out in other cases where rapid innovation is sought, and not only in extreme 'crisis' situations.

Environmental concerns necessitate changes in technology. The most common and dramatic example which firms have confronted in recent years is the need to phase out CFC use. At one extreme such a change may have few knock-on effects: for example, a search is made for the most effective CFC substitute that will allow for processes to continue as before. For sophisticated users, however, there may be more analysis of the processes in which CFCs are used. It may be discovered that quite different solutions are possible. Firms may go further still, and recognize business opportunities in marketing CFC substitutes or technologies supporting alternative processes to those requiring CFC (or CFC-substitute) use. ICI's development of Klea is an example of the former; Greenpeace's solution is one of the latter.

Another distinction that is commonly drawn in the discussion of clean technology is that between 'end-of-pipe' and 'integrated' solutions, with the former involving minimal process change other than the addition of 'clean-up' elements once the waste has been produced, while the latter aims at waste minimization by various means. We have seen that firms typically prefer the former solution, which is easier to accommodate within familiar production processes. As Irwin and Hooper (1992) note, end-of-pipe solutions, in the short term, tend to be cheaper, to serve better as external demonstrations of environmental commitment, to be less disruptive to current processes/practices, and to be available from a well-developed market. Furthermore, current regulatory systems tend to favour them. As recognition of these problems grows, pressures for cleaner technologies is also likely to grow. More substantial changes in R&D may then be required for more radical changes.

The response to environmental pressure may be relatively one-off and discrete. Often it is at present. Or, at the other extreme, it may be part of a more sustained process, where clean technology involves a change in the technological regime prevailing in a firm. A long-term improvement in the environment-friendliness of products and processes requires that many more firms approach the latter end of the continuum. This is, arguably, itself a precondition for continuing economic growth. Growing output without such continuous improvement is liable to impose high costs on the environment.

CONCLUSIONS

The incorporation of environmental concerns into R&D, effectively reshaping the research base and technological trajectories of the firm, will be crucial to the achievement of environmental sustainability. But even when environmental issues seem to be most deeply rooted in management decision-making processes, these priorities are embodied in R&D strategy at present only to a limited extent. One indicator of this is the practical absence of R&D in the topics covered in company environmental policy statements.

There may well be no single best model for incorporating the new agenda into management priorities. Companies have to evolve from their own specific starting-points, and deal with their own specific circumstances. While there has been little empirical research into these issues, several studies make recommendations how environmental issues should be incorporated into R&D management. Thus, the EIRMA study recommended:

- Companies should have an environmental and safety R&D strategy covering five years.
- Environmental and safety R&D programmes should be integrated into overall R & D strategy.
- Companies should have a central environmental and safety R&D unit to establish and monitor appropriate R&D programmes, though the work itself could be done by central and local facilities; the programmes should be generated by business units and R&D centres jointly but with major funding from business units.
- R&D should input into management and public discussions of environmental issues.

To achieve sustained impacts of environmental concerns on R&D means that environmental signals need to be either explicitly or implicitly built into the R&D process. They may be built in implicitly by virtue of an environmental objective being largely consonant with some other business objective – most frequently energy efficiency pursued on cost-saving grounds. They may also be built in implicitly by means of a learning process, such that the researchers and engineers come to internalize criteria that are employed to evaluate their project proposals. This may be the first stage in the achievement of impacts from the environmental methodologies being introduced by several leading firms.

Our studies indicate that large and R&D-intensive firms are groping for appropriate methodologies to use to incorporate environmental concerns routinely into their R&D planning. These include, for example, simple metrics of waste compared to materials input, through to complex life-cycle analyses; attempts at detailed audits of particular sites, through to company-wide environmental reports.

There is limited literature on most of these methods (auditing has attracted most attention), especially as they are more intimately related to R&D. One indicative account reports on approaches being adopted by Philips Corporate Design Senior Director (The ENDS Report, 1993). His design principles are:

1. cleaner production cycles;

2. enhanced disassembly techniques;
3. longer-life or more recyclable products;
4. reduction of material and energy (eg by miniaturization, and by use of service carriers eg telecommunications rather than transport).

A design handbook lists criteria for designers to consider. This includes general rules, like 'develop long-life products', as well as specifics such as 'redesign battery packs' or 'avoid cadmium plating'; the manual includes a scoring chart which can be used to rate proposed projects. Similar methods of appraisal are being tried out in numerous companies, and may well be a viable strategy for embedding environmental concerns into R&D.

Such methodologies, rather than generic new technologies themselves, may be fundamental to the establishment of a new, cleaner, technological regime. In other words, rather than expecting widely applicable breakthroughs in core technologies, we anticipate a reshaping of existing technological trajectories in consequence of the routine application of new criteria and appraisal methods in R&D and its management. It would be rather simplistic to see this as a 'demand-pull' trajectory, rather than a 'supply-push' one, but it undoubtedly requires a marked change in the way that radical innovations are being developed. A major challenge for the coming decades will be to refine and apply such management methodologies in such a way that they can 'tame' the technological regimes emerging from generic technologies such as IT, biotechnology, and new materials.

Finally, what is the place for public R&D in all of this? Recent years have seen the development of important programmes of support for clean technologies in many countries. Some of these are targeted at specific issues – for example, waste minimization is a current theme being pursued by the Engineering and Physical Sciences Research Council in Britain, through its Clean Technology Unit. Some are targeted at particular industries – for example, again in Britain, the Department of the Environment has undertaken initiatives supporting research in, and for, the construction industry on environmentally sensitive building design, construction and use. Other relevant programmes are supported by other government departments and research councils, and the European Commission is also a major player in these fields.

Such public R&D can be important in many circumstances. Some sectors, like construction, perform relatively little R&D of their own, and government funds can be important in facilitating innovation and diffusion. Such research may also be tied to the development of regulations and standards, sometimes leading to the development of more stringent criteria for materials, processes or products. In other cases, public funds help pay for more basic research that opens up pioneering areas of development, and generates knowledge that can subsequently be exploited by firms. Demonstration programmes can be used to iron out problems which may deter firms from adopting a new technology, as well as being used to raise awareness more generally; and they may also provide attractive new markets which firms can use to explore the possibilities and practicalities of alternative technologies. Such contributions can be extremely significant, especially if the knowledge that is generated can be made accessible and relevant to companies. It can then be fused with the R&D efforts of more innovative firms to help reorient technology more generally.

Public R&D may lead to breakthroughs, or even to less earth-shattering demonstrations of the viability of technologies, which force themselves upon corporate R&D managers. Sustained public R&D into clean technologies may help to create continual infusions of such knowledge, as well as increasing the general visibility of, and availability of skills in, this area. But without a reorientation of corporate R&D practices towards more environmentally sensitive criteria, public funds will not be sufficient to shift the trajectories of corporate technology development. Thus a better understanding of how corporate R&D and innovation operate, and how they may be influenced in 'cleaner' directions, remains a priority.

REFERENCES

Anderson, P and Tushman, M L (1990) 'Technological Discontinuities and Dominant Designs: a cyclical model of technological change', *Administrative Science Quarterly*, vol 35, p 617

Ausubel, J H and Sladovich, H E (eds) (1989) *Technology and Environment*, National Academy Press, Washington DC

Bahagavan, M R (ed) (1995) *New Generic Technologies in Developing Countries*, Macmillan, London

Chatterji, D (1993) 'R&D Management and the Environmental Imperative', BOC, mimeo

Coombs, R et al (1992) *Technological Change and Company Strategy*, Academic Press, London

Dosi, G et al (1988) *Technical Change and Economic Theory*, Frances Pinter, London

EIRMA Working Group 44 (1992) *Environmental and Safety Considerations in Industrial R&D*, EIRMA, Paris

ENDS Report, The (1993) 'Philips: integrating eco-design into product development' ENDS Report, September, no 224, pp 22–24

Foster, A (1991) 'Managing R&D and Technology development' paper presented at The Economist conference, December, London

Freeman, C (1982) *The Economics of Industrial Innovation*, Chapters 2 and 3, Frances Pinter, London

Green, K and Yoxen, E (1992) 'The Greening of European Industry: What role for biotechnology?' *Futures*, vol 22, no 5, pp 475–495

Irwin, A and Hooper, P (1992) 'Clean Technology, Successful Innovation and the Greening of Industry' *Business Strategy and the Environment*, vol 1, no 2, pp 1–11

Noble, D (1984) *Forces of Production: a social History of Industrial Automation*, Knopf, New York

Richards, B P et al (1993) 'Technical options for replacing CFCs for cleaning electronic assemblies' *GEC Review*, vol 9, no 1, pp 3–20

Roome, N (1992) 'Modelling business environmental strategy' *Business Strategy and the Environment*, vol 1, no 1, pp 11–24

Rushton, B M (1993) 'How protecting the environment impacts R&D in the US' Research–Technology–Management, May–June, pp 13–21

Winn, S and Roome, N (1992) 'R&D Management responses to the environment: current theory and implications to practice and research' *R&D Management*, vol 23, no 2, pp 147–160

11

Beyond the Technical Fix[1]

David Fleming

INTRODUCTION

With good reason, this could be described as the Golden Age of environment policy. In every developed country, companies are improving their eco-efficiency (output per unit of environmental impact); in some cases, progress in eco-efficiency is so great that they are able to reduce their total environmental impact while still enjoying the benefits of growth.

However, even in the best-performing industries, the rate of eco-efficiency improvement is hard to sustain and, on a global scale, it is being overwhelmed by output growth. If this mismatch between eco-efficiency and growth continues, it could lead to a failure to sustain growth or even to a destabilizing decline in output; these consequences could be a direct outcome of environmental damage, or they could be due to measures to suppress growth in order to prevent further damage.

We are in a world of uncertainty here, so this paper is built on the precautionary principle: if market economies *should* find themselves in conditions of long-term zero or negative growth, they would be better placed to deal with the problem if it had been thought through in advance. The implications for business are far from attractive and, for that reason, they have not so far merited serious consideration. But silence on strategic options which could play a decisive role in environmental protection, and which may be imposed in any event, can no longer be justified. In breaking the silence, this paper will outline some of the fundamental problems of a 'low-output' regime, in which growth in gross domestic product (GDP) has been suppressed or even reversed.

The paper begins with the Six Age Model, suggesting that eco-efficiency improvements are likely to be overwhelmed by growth; the consequences – or, more exactly, the problems – of low output are then briefly indicated and survival strategies for companies are discussed in Part 3. Dematerialization and solutions for the economy as a whole are then considered. The conclusion aims to place the sequence of argument into perspective. A long-term trend of growth is an indispensable condition of stability in the competitive market economy, so a discussion of policy responses for companies in a regime of suppressed growth addresses what may be an impossible agenda. It is hoped that this will be accepted as an excuse for discussing some unlikely-sounding solutions.

---

1 Comments by Andrew Gouldson, Nick Robins, Edward Roth, Richard Starkey and Lawrence Woodward are acknowledged with thanks.

THE SIX AGES OF ENVIRONMENT POLICY

For a general account of the shape of technical change in an industry and, in particular, its relationship with environmental impact, there can be no better example than the airline industry, blessed by outstanding technology, cursed by rising environmental impact; the industry's experience and expectations of continued growth are used as the basis for the Six Age Model, which is set out in terms of three interdependent variables:

(a) The volume of output, measured in revenue passenger kilometres (RPKs).
(b) Eco-efficiency, which is primarily the result of learning and investment in improved technology and systems, but which is also in part an outcome of growth itself since this provides the funds for research and development. It is measured in the model as the impact ratio – environmental impact per unit of output.[2]
(c) The environmental impact of the industry (such as the airline industry's high altitude emissions of carbon dioxide, nitrous oxides and water vapour); this is the product of (a) and (b).

1. Early Growth

The technology employed by a new industry is inefficient, and offers rich opportunities for improvement. This is vividly illustrated by the case of the airlines industry between 1936 and 1971. The mean cruise speed of the DC3, which entered service in 1936, was 282 km/h, and the aircraft's productivity was 527 tonne-kilometres per hour (tkm/h); the DC10, introduced in 1971, had a mean cruise speed of 915 km/h and a productivity 45 times that of its forebear, at 24,730 tkm/h. During that period, the total output of the world airline industry grew about 60-fold to 340 billion revenue passenger kilometres (RPKs).

Productivity, which is the product of an aircraft's speed and load it carries, is a quite different thing from the impact ratio of the industry, although the two are likely to be correlated, since they are both dependent on technological advance. Impact ratio is hard to measure directly, not least because the complex environmental impacts cannot be represented by a single number; the record of fuel efficiency (RPK per tonne of fuel) is therefore used as an approximate guideline for

---

2 Sources for the output statistics are based on the following series: 1950–1970: International Civil Aviation Organization; 1970–2013: International Air Transport Association; the estimate back to 1936 is by the author, with reference to Rigas Dogarnis (1991); this is also the source of the productivity statistics. Fuel efficiency estimates are based on conversations in the industry, especially with Swissair. This model is an intentional but radical simplification of the issues of growth in the airline industry. For example, it does not take into account loading factors and ancillary impacts such as road traffic; it makes the unjustified assumption that varied environmental impacts can be aggregated into a single number for eco-efficiency, and the use of estimates of fuel-efficiency as a proxy for eco-efficiency is at best an approximation. For a rigorous study of the environmental impact of the airline industry, and comparisons with other industries, see Leonie J Archer, 1993 and Mark Barrett, 1991.

The estimates used in the model are set out in Table 11.1. Impact ratio (environmental impact per unit of output) is the inverse of eco-efficiency, and is used in the Six Age Model because output is the independent variable; that is, the airlines first maximize their output, and then try to minimize its environmental impact. In the low-output economy, by contrast, environmental impact is fixed, and the dependent variable is output; for this, eco-efficiency (output per unit of environmental impact) is the better measure.

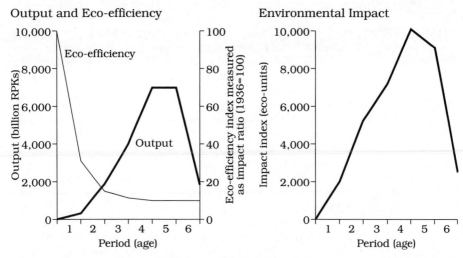

Figure 11.1 *The Six Age Model*

Age	...ending in year	Output (bn RPKs) (a)	Eco-efficiency (as impact ratio) (b)	(c) = (a) x (b)	Impact index (eco-units)
	1936	6	100.0	600	100
1	1970	360	33.3	12,000	2,000
2	1990	1,894	16.7	31,567	5,261
3	2005	3,972	11.1	44,133	7,356
4	2020	7,572	7.9	60,095	10,016
5	2035	7,572	7.2	54,632	9,105
6	2055	1,893	7.2	13,658	2,276

Table 11.1 *The Six Age Model*

eco-efficiency, providing the basis for a calculation of eco-units, measured as an index, where 1936=100.

Fuel efficiency tripled during the period, forcing the impact ratio down to 33 from its base of 100. Environmental impact is therefore estimated to grow from its base of 100 to 2,000.

2. Development

In the Development Age, (when productivity in tkm/h doubled), the output of the airline industry grew to about 1,900 billion RPKs. Fuel efficiency improved by about 100 per cent, halving the impact ratio, but this improvement fell far short of the rise in output, so environmental impact rose from 2,000 eco-units to 5,216.

3. The Golden Age

The Golden Age of environmental policy began in earnest in 1990. Although the eco-efficiency of companies has improved steadily alongside their technological advance, it is only in the 1990s that the aim of improving environmental performance has become widely established as a central objective of company policy. As many industries have discovered, corporate environmental policy offers new targets for performance and progress; it makes available new criteria for competition and for differentiation between companies, which would otherwise risk being jaded by homogeneity – a convergence in techniques and products. There is a feeling of optimism in the Golden Age, a hope that eco-efficiency will be the key to the problem of growth, fulfilling the hope of sustainable development. The case for sustained growth, along with investment in environmental performance, appears now to be spherically sensible, borne out from every point of view: environmental investment tames the impact of growth, which finances the cost of environmental investment, which provides opportunities for further growth.

Certainly the airline industry is no exception to this corporate culture, with emphasis being placed on environmental performance, not only in response to legislation and genuine public concern about climatic effects, but also as an instrument of competitive marketing. The model suggests a further 33 per cent improvement in impact ratio: this is less than the halving in the index achieved in the Development Age, and it reflects the problems of diminishing returns on investment in eco-efficiency improvements, but research and development in the leading companies is dedicated to achieving this improvement, even though the easier gains have already been made. As the technical director of one airline admitted, 'We don't yet know how we are going to do it.'[3]

However, the example of the industry suggests that the confidence and hopes of the period may have been overstated. The hard-won impact ratio improvement will be overwhelmed by rising output, which is forecast to grow from 1,900 to 4,000 billion RPKs in 2005, producing a rise in eco-units to 7,356.

4. Late Growth

In the fourth period, sustained advances in environmental performance become much harder to achieve. Eco-efficiency progress continues (a generous 30 per cent improvement is suggested by the model), but it is overtaken by sustained growth in the output of an already large industry, with contributions to growth being made by the younger and rapidly growing industries of the developing countries. The International Air Transport Association's projections of growth run out in 2013, when output is expected to be growing at 4.7 per cent per annum, but a projection of the series to 2020 at an annual growth of 4 per cent produces an output forecast of 7,500 billion RPKs. Adjusted downwards by the improvement in impact ratio, this gives a total environmental impact of 10,000 eco-units.

Given the scale of this environmental impact, Late Growth could be a period of heightened tension between the needs to contain environmental impact and to maintain the momentum of growth. The industry's contributions to the greenhouse effect and to ozone destruction have already reached the point at which the prospect of regulation to suppress growth in the industry is causing concern

---

3 Willi Schurter, Technical Director, Swissair (personal communication).

(Douglas Cameron, 1992). By the end of the period, the tension between the imperatives of growth and environmental protection could reach breaking point.

The end of the Late Growth period does not occur at the moment when it becomes clear that the only way of halting the rise in environmental impact is to set a ceiling on output; that is an insight which will have been growing since the 1990s. It ends when, given the choice between intensified environmental impact and loss of growth, the latter seems to be, in terms of immediate pain, the lesser of two evils.[4]

5. Standstill

Standstill – an imposed growth ceiling beginning in 2020 – would produce a financial crisis in the airline industry, and would sharply reduce the resources available for improvements in eco-efficiency, not least because there would be a collapse in the demand for new aircraft, with their higher standards of environmental performance. Nonetheless, the model assumes a further 10 per cent improvement in impact ratio so, for the first time, the environmental impact falls, but it remains well above the level reached in 2005, and it is well short of the fall required to reduce the total level of *cumulative* environmental burden, which would continue to rise strongly in the standstill phase.

6. Correction

The scale of cumulative environmental impact has now (say, 2035) reached the point at which there is no choice but to correct it by a reduction in volume. The correction could develop from public policy – with governments very reluctantly insisting on reduced output in order to protect the environment from further damage; or it could arise from direct environmental damage to production, or from a combination of the two. One possible scenario might be a threshold event,[5] such as the marine flooding of a coastal city or a prolonged drought, leading to food shortages and a crisis in water supply, which is regarded as a sign of worse to come, finally opening the way to public tolerance for suppressed growth, and giving governments the mandate to impose it. Alternatively, the economic consequences of the lack of growth in the standstill phase may be so destabilizing that output could begin to fall, with little delay between Late Growth and Correction. Another possibility would be for the standstill phase to be extended for a long period, with economies becoming increasingly unstable as (for reasons explained in the following section), unemployment continued to rise.

In the unstable conditions of the correction phase, it is likely that standards of environmental performance would fall; there would be massive cost-cutting programmes and the conditions of the time would encourage a culture of making-do – surviving the moment, without too much concern for the future; this would replace the current culture of making-better, with its environmental reports and audits, and its targets solemnly committing companies to small incremental improvements in enviromental performance. However, there is no basis other than guesswork on which to forecast the actual fall in eco-efficiency, so the model gives

4 Mark Barrett (1991) concludes his study of the environmental impact of the airline industry with a time horizon of 2020: 'The officially projected growth of demand in terms of distance travelled by passengers and aircraft will offset any technical improvements, increasing pollution ... Demand management [viz some suppression of growth] is essential to prevent aircraft pollution emissions from greatly increasing.'
5 Defined as a shock which rises above the threshold of confidence in business-as-usual.

the industry the benefit of the doubt, by assuming that it will be unchanged. This still means that the whole of the improvement in environmental impact has to come from the fall in output: advances in eco-efficiency are no longer making their contribution.

LOW OUTPUT AND ITS CONSEQUENCES

The model suggests that the good results being achieved in the Golden Age of environmental policy could be giving a profoundly misleading message – a case of overvaluing the present. Improvements in eco-efficiency appear to hold out the hope of a dream ticket of growth *and* environmental protection – mutually dependent and mutually consistent – the ideal goal of current policy. And yet experience in the airline industry, combined with official forecasts of future output, suggest that the effect of eco-efficiency improvement is to sustain the rise in environmental impact on a roughly linear path, compared with the more rapid geometrical growth in output – approximately 10 per cent per annum in 1950-1995 and approximately 5 per cent per annum in 1996-2020.

A slowing-down of growth in environmental impact is a substantial achievement for environmental technology, but it falls short of being a solution to the environmental burden imposed by industrial economies.[6] As growth continues, the double bind faced by industry gets tighter, since:

- growth in the scale of output, together with the accumulated environmental impact of previous output, will require greater improvements in eco-efficiency, just at the moment when...
- previous advances in eco-efficiency will make further improvements harder to achieve.[7]

Any suppression of growth would be radically destabilizing:

- Unemployment would rise relentlessly (see the box below).
- There would be falling incomes and loss of taxation revenue on a scale which would threaten critical government commitments such as the system of transfer payments for the unemployed.
- Firms would be progressively forced into liquidation.
- Both the funds and the regulatory regime required for environmental protection would be at risk.

Clearly, society depends on growth every bit as much as it depends on environmental protection.

---

6 The inference that the airline industry can be used as a model for the global economy, if properly argued through here, would extend well beyond the scope and purpose of this paper. But other industries do appear to be on a similar trajectory (see Archer, 1993); moreover, air transport is a core industry, underpinning tourism, by some calculations by far the largest industry in the world, employing 1 in 9 of the world's working population (John Naisbitt, 1995). A faltering of growth in the airline industry would profoundly affect almost all other industries.
7 For a discussion and references on the diminishing returns to problem-solving see, for example, Joseph A Tainter, 1995.

LOW OUTPUT AND REDUNDANCY

Market economies have to grow in order to prevent a relentless rise in unemployment.[8] The reason for this lies in productivity improvements, illustrated in Figure 11.2.

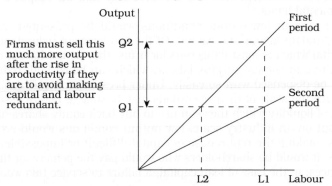

Firms must sell this much more output after the rise in productivity if they are to avoid making capital and labour redundant.

Figure 11.2 *Rising Productivity and the Need for Growth*

Productivity is indicated in the diagram with production functions, giving the conversion ratio between labour and output. When a firm installs new technology or systems, or just becomes more skilled as a result of practice,[9] it is able to get more output from the labour it is using. That is to say, productivity improves (ie the production function become steeper), so the labour used (L1) produces a higher quantity of output, which rises (in the schematic terms of the diagram) from Q1 to Q2.

The firm now has to sell this *higher* output (in other words, the firm has to grow) if it is to keep its *original* quantity of labour employed; the problem is that it may not be able to achieve that higher level of sales. It might be able to sell, say, only Q1 – the amount that it was selling before the productivity improvement, so that it has redundant labour (shown by the gap between L1 and L2). In the past, this released labour has been redeployed into other, faster-growing industries, but if those industries themselves are prevented from growing (by, for example, an environmental constraint), then the released resources will not be used, and will become unemployed and a charge on the state.

In the case of the individual firm or industry, the idea of low output is somewhat ambiguous, since an industry in this situation will inevitably adjust downwards to the lower level of output, with many or most of its companies going out of business, adapting its capacity to the new level of output. An industry that has gone through this process (for example, the British coal industry) cannot be said to be working under low output conditions. The only unambiguous case of low-output, therefore, is that of an entire economy, since economies, unlike firms, cannot adapt by off-loading their unemployment problem, or by simply going out of business.

A similar story may be told for capital as the unemployed resource. This is more complex, since productivity advance is in part due to new capital investment but, at the same time, each unit of capital becomes more productive, along with each unit of labour, so that higher output is required if capital is to avoid the prospect of redundancy.[10]

---

8 The Delors White Paper (Commission of the European Communities, 1993) suggests that growth of 3 per cent is required to stabilize unemployment.

9 A discussion of productivity improvement as the driver of growth is in Moses Abramovitz, 1989.

10 Moses Abramovitz, (1989).estimates that total factor productivity can account for 90% of productivity advances.

Low-output conditions could take a variety of forms, ranging in intensity between the extremes of an insufficient long-term rate of growth, through zero growth and negative growth, to a steep fall in GDP. The programme required to stabilize economies would vary in each case, in intensity but not in principle and, for the purposes of the present discussion, it is assumed only that the output ceiling is set by environmental limits.[11]

Firms operating in low-output conditions would be presented with the problems of redundant labour and capital. Of the two forms of redundancy, it is redundant capital which is most dangerous for firms: they do not have a responsibility to continue to employ surplus labour, which can be laid off; redundant capital cannot be dispensed with so easily. Under present economic conditions, firms that reduce the scale of their operations may be able to realize assets and acquire a fund of liquidity which they can use to buy back equity shares or repay loan capital, but on an industry scale, low-output conditions would erode the value of assets, making the repurchase of capital difficult or impossible. In the case of equities, it would be shareholders who would pay the penalty for this with falling asset prices; in the case of loan capital, a failure to service this would lead to liquidation.

Moreover, the whole structure of investment, pensions and asset management – that is, systems for storing value – depends on the corporate sector, which would be fundamentally destabilized by low output. The problem of unemployed financial assets has not yet received the attention paid to unemployed labour, but it could be as significant, especially in view of the projected rise in the proportion of the population at or beyond retirement age. The indispensable role of a healthy and stable system for storing value is a definitive argument (as if one were needed) for sustaining growth. However, since growth may not be sustained indefinitely, uncomfortable and unfamiliar possibilities demand inspection.

One of the advantages enjoyed by a prosperous firm is that the diverse interests of stakeholders can be fulfilled without unmasking the potential collisions of interest between them. In low-output conditions, this consensus would begin to unravel, with stakeholders urging different and conflicting priorities such as continuity of employment, vs prompt realization of assets, vs protection of core skills and resources. For present purposes, it will be assumed that the objectives of firms (represented by management and backed by shareholders) would be (a) to survive in some form and (b) to maximize expected profits.

Since economies cannot wash their hands of redundant labour as companies can, rising unemployment on an economy-wide scale would take government finance into the double-bind of reduced receipts and higher demands for payment; this is a problem which would reach a critical threshold at some level of unemployment – say, 2–4 million greater that the present – testing taxpayers'

---

11 The ceiling could also be set by demand inertia – that is, by demand lagging behind the advance in productivity. Classical economics recognizes market imperfections but rules out demand inertia as a primary cause of unemployment, on the grounds that consumer demand is insatiable – non-satiation is one of the axioms of neo-classical economics. Yet demand inertia could develop, for example, as a result of households directing a smaller proportion of their incomes into the consumption of produced goods and services in order to compete for non-produced positional goods, such as housing. This principle is explored in David Fleming, 1988. The assumption in this paper that the ceiling is set by environmental limits is to avoid further twists in an already complicated argument.

consent up to or beyond the limit and raising questions about government solvency. Priorities for the economy would therefore be to minimize the fall in employment, to sustain government revenues on a scale which would enable it to finance its commitments, to develop acceptable means of distributing the static (or declining) national income, given a declining employed population, and to develop ways of using the static (or declining) flow of available resources in the economy as effectively as possible.

STRATEGIES FOR COMPANIES IN LOW-OUTPUT CONDITIONS

The prospect of low output is unattractive in the extreme – at least, from the point of view of economic and corporate stability. But if it should occur, what options would be open to companies? Six types of survival strategy are discussed in this section; special emphasis is given to the first two, because they are constructive strategies, with possible wider application to the low-output economy.

Employment Intensity

In its White Paper, *Growth, Competitiveness and Employment* (1993) the European Commission develops the idea of employment intensity – the ratio between jobs and output. An increase in employment intensity (more jobs per unit of GDP) would protect or create jobs and, as the White Paper argues, there is nothing necessarily inconsistent between a rise in employment intensity in some sectors, and a fall in other sectors where productivity improvements are generating growth in output without a matching growth in jobs. Although the role of employment-intensive work acknowledged by the White Paper is only marginal, the sector may offer an important strategic option for companies, and it would be particularly relevant under low-output conditions. Three main features of employment-intensity are discussed here – but the issue raises a problem of vocabulary, and suggested solutions to this are contained in the box below.

The employment intensity sector can be competitive...

The labour-intensive sector, which is large and growing, includes most of the professions, the arts, trades such as gardening, repairs, some construction and many administrative jobs. It also includes most aspects of household production, used in the broad economic sense, which includes activities such as housekeeping, child rearing, gardening, leisure and entertainment – in fact almost everything which households do for themselves.[12]

Although employment intensity is particularly associated with very small businesses and the self-employed, it thrives also in technology-intensive industries, where employment-intensive services are supplied as a complement to the company's core product. An illustration of this is offered by the case of the airlines, where there is intense pressure to increase yield – that is, to raise the revenue generated by each seat sold – and an important way of doing this is to offer a premium service. A recent study found that a 5 per cent improvement in

---

12 As discussed, for example, in Gary Becker, 1965.

HANDS-ON AND HANDS-OFF(I): NAMING NAMES

The distinction between employment-intensive and productivity-intensive jobs turns on the proportion of the value added which is attributable to the worker, rather than to the equipment: teachers and airline pilots can be assumed to stand at opposite ends of the spectrum.[13] Labels that can be used for the two limited cases include:

- *Employment-intensive vs technology-intensive.* The problem here is that 'employment-intensive' jobs do not necessarily involve employment; they may be forms of self-employment, or belong in the informal economy. 'Technology-intensive' seems to deny that (in most cases) even employment-intensive jobs use some form of developed technology.
- *Labour-intensive vs information-intensive.* Problems here, too: 'labour-intensive' invites a romantic vision of teams of people working with a wilful neglect of efficiency under the paternal gaze of Count Tolstoy; 'information-intensive', where information refers to the degree of technological sophistication used in an industry, is possibly the best label, but could be misconstrued as referring only to the information industries.
- *Hand-on vs hands-off.* This has the advantage of brevity: 'hands-on' (indicating employment intensity) contains the appropriate image of hands doing the actual work of production, rather than processing information which will lead eventually to production. 'Hands-off' is problematic, since virtually every job involves some 'hands-on' engagement.

All these pairs have their disadvantages and there is no ideal label, so each will be used, depending on the context.

---

yield can contribute as much to an airline's profits as a 10 per cent cut in overheads, or a 25 per cent increase in sales (Philip Shearman, 1992). British Airways' programme of increasing yield has included a 'well-being in the air' service, featuring such labour-intensive services as an exercise programme and aromatherapy (Ron Katz, 1994). Swissair's emphasis on premium service enabled it to increase its revenue from passengers by 8 per cent in 1991, despite a decline of 5 per cent in the passenger-kilometres sold.

The main factor driving the growth of hands-on employment is the advance in productivity of the hands-off sector; productivity improvements in hands-off output lead to (real) cost reductions, which are passed on to consumers as lower (real) prices, leading in turn to higher (real) incomes, which in turn enable households to switch some expenditure into hands-on goods and services. The longer the rise in real incomes continues, the more can households spend on hands-on goods and services which could emerge as the characteristic employer of the stable mature post-industrial economy.

---

13 On a strict interpretation of the White Paper's understanding of employment intensity, an operatic superstar, a highly paid lawyer or a successful artist would be low on the employment-intensity scale, because in these cases the level of employment per unit of GDP is low. However, such jobs, which are clearly labour-intensive rather than technology-intensive, are included in the present discussion. In this sense, at least, the labels 'labour-intensive' and 'hands-on' are closer to the intended meaning than 'employment-intensive'.

...and it is a provider of high quality and environment protection

A second characteristic of the employment-intensive sector is that it may, in certain circumstances, produce goods and services to an exceptionally high standard of quality. There are some goods and services where any notion of raising productivity would be inappropriate, and where only hands-on labour will do. Hand-tailoring, furniture restoration, cuisine, crafts and traditional trades, the live arts, can all claim to be able to produce a high, even luxurious standard, where productivity improvements have their place, but are not to be expected. As one economist wrote in a classic paper, 'A horn quintet calls for 2.5 man-hours in its performance, and any attempt to increase productivity here is likely to be viewed with concern by critics and audience alike' (W J Baumol, 1967).

Quality in this sense extends, critically, to environmental protection. In low-output conditions, the output ceiling is set by environmental impact, and the problem is to maximize output, subject to the binding constraint on environmental impact – the opposite problem to (at the kindest interpretation) current policy, which is to minimize environmental impact, subject to the prior commitment to maximized growth. In an economy which is already operating at the given limit of environmental impact, improvements in the eco-efficiency of output can have the effect – if only marginal – of easing the output ceiling.

Employment-intensive trades and professions, as a general rule, have minimal direct environmental impact per person employed. They do not use large quantities of materials or energy per unit of output; if they did, that would suggest a level of dependency on equipment which would place them in the productivity-intensive sector. Indeed, employment-intensive output may actually have a benign environmental impact. There is some flexibility of method: labour-intensive farming, for instance, is in a position to be more tolerant of landscape features which are a problem for machinery, and it can use methods of horticulture involving diversity and attention to the small scale of plants and predators, in preference to the large-scale technology of pesticides. The relative abundance of labour means that the business is tolerant to a high level of detail – selective cultivation and felling of trees, individual attention to each carrot and vole – which would be out of the question for more price-sensitive alternatives. The high value added to a smaller resource means that a correspondingly high level of income is derived from it: the wood used for making a chair, for example, could keep a factory worker employed for an hour or a craftsman employed for days.

There is a similar environmental effect in the example of commercial fishing, where advanced technology is focused on saving labour, rather than saving the natural resource. Fisheries which, without benefit of developed technology, are labour-intensive, have a direct interest in the sustainability of their fish stocks, since they cannot move their fleet or capital elsewhere so that a small area of sea can sustain jobs indefinitely (Simon Fairlie et al, 1995).

Hands-on output can therefore accommodate itself to the environmental agenda in ways which are outside the scope of hands-off output. This does not mean that labour-intensive output is inherently more environmentally benign; as discussed in the section on dematerialization (below), many forms of advanced technology, not least the environment-protection technologies, have overwhelming environmental advantages and employment-intensive service, such as parts of the tourism industry, can be environmentally destructive in the extreme. For the present, it is enough to note that the employment-intensive sector, with its flexibility and its relative inefficiency, can include environmental protection in its claim to be able to deliver goods and services to a characteristically high quality.

But its growth is limited by cost and income distribution

The third characteristic of the employment-intensive sector is that its goods and services tend to be expensive; hand-made clothes, cars and furniture, for example, may cost an order of magnitude more than the standard versions. Worse still, every productivity improvement in the hands-off sector makes hands-on output even more expensive. This is because the Retail Price Index falls in response to productivity improvements in the hands-off sector;[14] as a result, the RPI-adjusted price of employment-intensive output, which does not benefit from productivity improvements, rises steadily.

The high and rising relative cost of output of the hands-on sector has substantial implications for the distribution of income. The ideal conditions for the expansion of the sector are probably those in which there is a sharply unequal distribution of income, with purchasers earning multiples of the incomes of the labour force in the sector. Indeed, under low-output conditions, the need to locate and develop demand for labour in the sector could encourage much greater tolerance of income inequality; there is clearly a potent mixture for political conflict here, with the claims of equity being balanced against those of jobs.[15]

The high cost of output in the hands-on sector does not mean that development of the sector would necessarily require trade protection, since it may be a complement to the hands-off sector, or a hybrid with it. Hybrid forms include not only labour-intensive add-ons to mainstream products and services – such as the luxury services provided by airlines – but also the use of information technology to provide personal service, such as the individual specification of cars and other goods and services backed by design systems based on virtual reality (William H Davidow and Michael S Malone, 1992). This use of intelligent systems as a foundation for personal service to form a hybrid can bring the cost of the employment-intensive sector within range of conventional technology-intensive industry.

In cases where it is a substitute, however, and particularly where the high quality concerns the process more obviously than the product (as in the case of food grown to high standards of environmental protection), hands-on output is fatally

---

14 As so often in economics, this statement must be qualified by the *ceteris paribus* condition; in fact, the RPI almost never falls, because the improvements in productivity are overwhelmed by other factors, chiefly inflation; a rise in the cost of raw materials, aggressive wage bargaining by producers, or a profound change in the composition of goods and services purchased by households could also help to mask the effect of productivity improvement on prices. However, in the absence of these complications, rising productivity would produce a fall in prices; in theory this lowered price platform should be the base from which inflation is measured – but it is not, and it follows that a rise in RPI actually understates inflation. For a taster of the complexities see Vanessa Fry and Panos Pashardes, 1986.

For these reasons, the cost of labour-intensive public services such as the health service and teaching rises progressively in response to productivity improvement elsewhere in the economy, unless they can make corresponding improvements in their own productivity. This is one reason for the intensive pressure on governments to reduce costs in these sectors.

15 The evidence that jobs are created by lower wages is dubious (see Alan Manning, 1994). However, from the point of view of people in labour-intensive industries such as the crafts, the existence of customers with incomes many times as great as their own is desirable.

vulnerable to low-cost competition. Government intervention, providing protection in some form, as part of a wider programme of economic stewardship, would be indispensable to serious growth of turnover in the sector. Nonetheless, the high cost is a reflection of the sector's usefully high labour content and its important potential role in maintaining turnover in conditions of declining business.

The significance of the hands-on sector, then, can be summarized as follows. It has potential as an employment-creator; it is associated with high quality of output and high standards of environment protection. However, its intensive use of labour means that it has high unit costs; it can develop strongly as a complement to more technology-dependent forms of output, but it could not compete as a substitute or alternative to hands-off output without some form of protection.

Competitive Efficiency

The second type of strategy open to companies in a declining market appears at first to be contradictory to the employment-intensity strategy, but it is in fact complementary with it: it is to develop high levels of efficiency (in both senses of efficiency: (a) capital and labour per unit of output, and (b) output per unit of environmental impact, in order to remain in business through direct competitive advantage in difficult market conditions. The strength of this strategy derives not only from the use of advanced technology to reduce waste, but also from the development of complex and efficient organizational systems. In low-output conditions, requiring companies to develop radically new relationships with stakeholders, new organizational systems would prove their value, and it is worth pausing for a moment to sketch some outlines of this organizational change. Their relevance is greater than it may seem.

Productivity improvements are being achieved through organizational change

One of the effects of the new information technology has been to transform the ability and potential of groupings within a firm. Many complex operations which have previously had to be carried out by specialist functions in different departments or firms can now be integrated into self-managing teams, and even those functions which cannot be integrated physically can be linked by computer-supported co-operative systems. The information technology keeps the team informed, not only about the process, but also about its context – its links with suppliers, the market and other teams, so it becomes substantially independent of the control and co-ordination formerly imposed by management. This transformation in the competence of teams has been described as the productivity breakthrough of the 1990s (B Dumaine, 1990).

It is important to recognize that self-managed teams are not the only organizational solution to the search for greater efficiency. Some of the most successful international companies stick closely to a system of rules, giving minimal scope for initiative, not least because the companies concerned have moved far beyond the creative exploratory phase of their development, and are engaged in applying a tested formula.[16] In some companies, the computer networks which enable people to work directly with each other, rather than referring decisions up and

---

16 For example, McDonald's: Paul Vallely, 1995.

down a management hierarchy, are also used as instruments of authoritarian control, enabling a senior central management to prescribe and monitor the activities of their work-force, the time spent on each job, their location at each hour of the day, their decisions, and their consequences.[17] These are the 'new monarchies' – with senior management who use the information networks as their power base in an apparently decentralized organization (Anthony Sampson, 1995).

But, even if the self-managed team is not adaptive for all businesses, it has already had a profound impact on some organizations, particularly those companies in which flexibility and the development of new technologies and markets are at a premium, and where the complexity of the issues facing the company is beyond the competence of any central management organization, however gifted. As Peter Senge, introducing the principle of organizational learning, writes, 'It's just not possible any longer to figure it out' from the top, and have everyone else following the orders of the 'grand strategist'; instead, organizations must 'discover how to tap people's commitment and capacity to learn at *all* levels in an organization' (Peter Senge, 1990).[18]

The successful self-managing team, whose work is directly co-ordinated electronically, can be expected to develop a sense of 'efficacy' – with members of the team recognizing not only that their own role is significant but that the team itself is competent, and that it is responding to complex situations in its own characteristic way. Boundaries between the team and others (such as suppliers and customers) become ill-defined, and flexible thinking takes over from the hard concepts of order that have to be laid down in organizations where functions are widely separated. In these 'soft' systems, decision-making moves towards 'a continuous process that integrates actions with shared knowledge'.[19]

The culture of organizational learning accommodates itself to circumstance instead of waiting for instructions; the emphasis is on adaptation, even muddling through (Steven A Cavaleri, 1994). Established distinctions (as between management and workers, producers and customers) are eroded and, as Frank Blackler writes, organizations, 'independent of geographical location, devoid of conventional hierarchy, and with no obvious boundaries between themselves and other organizations, [become] increasingly difficult to understand' (Frank Blackler, 1994). Blackler's summary of the distinctiveness of the new management approach is set out in Table 11.2.

Self-managing teams could be building blocks for radical new corporate structures

The emergence of self-managing teams may have implications extending well beyond the matter of industrial efficiency. The teams have a dual personality in that they have (a) autonomy as functioning systems, acting in their own best-interest as a stable and cohesive group, and at the same time (b) belonging, or dependency, as part of a wider organization which requires their co-operation. This could be said, too, of the old functional departments, but the balance has shifted towards autonomy, and the structure of the teams is complex, involving a range of different functions. They therefore qualify as Arthur Koestler's 'holons'

---

17 See, for instance, Emma Cook, 1995.
18 See also Alex Trisoglio (1995), *Managing Complexity*, draft paper presented at the LSE Strategy Seminar, 25 January.
19 de Waele 1994, p 154.

Table 11.2 *Two Faces of Organization Theory*[20]

Modernist Organization Theory	Post-modernist Organization Theory
Organizations as machines	Organizations as flux and change
Monologue	Dialogue
Planning	Improvization
Homogeneity as strength	Heterogeneity as strength
Certainty	Ambiguity
Integration	Collective learning

(1967) – sub-assemblies which are both complete in themselves, with their own stability, and are also part of a larger structure, representing a higher level of complexity.[21]

Holons, balanced between autonomy and belonging, may be the key to a complex evolution of companies under conditions of low output. Self-managing teams, with this balance, and with their lack of dependence on direct financial incentives,[22] could be the basis for profoundly different organizational structures; they could, for instance, extend beyond the workplace to other stakeholders, and in particular to customers.

This has already reached early stages in some relationships between companies and their industrial customers; co-operation and long-term commitment now often override immediate cost criteria, and companies, notably in the chemical industry, are changing their role from that of suppliers of goods, to providers of services – helping customers to achieve their aims with the minimum use of chemicals, and recycling or disposing of the chemicals at the end of their life cycles. There is also a precursor in the form of demand-side management (DSM), in which utilities suppliers, working within a common regulatory system, help households to maximize the service they derive from reduced purchases of fuel.[23]

A logical but radical extension of this would see direct co-operative relationships between suppliers and households: the survival and well-being of the community in co-operation with suppliers would be the aim of a new and advanced form of self-managed team which straddles the boundary between producer and household and blurs the distinction between them. This extension of the self-managed team in low output conditions is sketched in the final section, A Wider Application?.

---

20 From Frank Blackler (1994).
21 Arthur Koestler, 1967. This has much in common with the grid-group structure in Michael Thompson, Richard Ellis and Aaron Wildavsky's *Cultural Theory*, (1990). And yet, at the intersection between the two dimensions of authority and belonging, they see the hermit. The holon, the autonomous-dependent group, seems to be a more promising find at this central point of balance.
22 They work within a competitive market economy, but their superior performance relative to incentive schemes is emphasized by A Kohn, 1993.
23 See Dow Europe (1994) Environment Progress Report for closer co-operative links with industrial customers and London Economics (1994) 'Demand-Side Management: A Survey of the US Experience', report prepared for Ofgas

Other Strategies

The four other strategies open to a company faced with low-output conditions can be briefly listed.

Reduce Scale

The natural responses to low-output conditions would be to reduce the scale of operations. This can be very expensive, requiring the company to redeem its equity and loan capital or to service it out of the proceeds of a smaller business. The first companies to reduce scale are the most likely to have the necessary funds to finance the transformation; in the case of companies in a weak market, already faced by low output conditions, liquidation may be a better option, or the only one.

Merger

Merger, and the compromise of alliances, are well established as methods of cost reduction, notably in the airline business.[24]

Monopoly

Companies in low-output conditions can attempt to protect their turnover and independence through making maximum use of market power: the large company, with distribution, high volume, and resources for investment can do much to distance itself from the fraying edge of an industry in low-output conditions; the advantages accruing to suppliers that are already dominant in the market are manifest in many industries, notably retailing (Rosemary D Bromley and Colin J Thomas, 1993) and dairy farming (David Fleming, 1994).

Selling on the Margin

A company whose fixed costs are a high proportion of total costs, and where there is excess capacity in the industry, may be tempted to compete by cutting prices to below average cost, inviting retaliatory action from competitors, and setting off cascading cost reductions which will lead to bankruptcy of some of the companies involved, and probably to poor performance and service by all of them. This can have the advantage of postponing the demise of the most ruthless firm, but the cost is borne by the industry as a whole, its shareholders and customers. It is a strategy which is particularly associated with capital-intensive industries such as airlines and container shipping.[25]

Of the six strategies for survival, two – labour intensification (hands-on) and business efficiency – are interesting in that they are constructive, rather than purely defensive. Note that they are not mirror images of each other; the relationship between the two is discussed in the box below. But they share the major disadvantages that they are winner-takes-all strategies, making business survival in low-output conditions a positional good, where one company's survival depends

---

24 'Alliance fever is hotting up again: airlines that don't have strategic partners are rushing to find them' *Airline Business* (1995), January, editorial.
25 For a description of the 'empty core' phenomenon in airlines, see Timothy K Smith, 1995.

HANDS-OFF AND HANDS-ON (II): TECHNOLOGY AND SYSTEMS

Two technology-selection objectives have been discussed: (1) to develop labour-intensive output, and (2) to maximize business efficiency. It is important to recognize that these two strategies are not simply limit cases in a spectrum of labour intensity, because business efficiency makes use of organizational change as well as technological change. Soft management structures are particularly associated with highly developed information technologies, but they could also develop in a firm which uses labour-intensive methods or hybrid forms of hands-on and hands-off.

In other words, the technology and the organization are on different dimensions, and there is room for debate as to how they relate to each other. One possible model is set out in Figure 11.3. Here the two axes lie in the spaces, respectively, of:

- *management system,* ranging between hard systems (conventional management hierarchy, based on functions) and soft systems (horizontal organization, based on teams);
- *technology,* ranging between labour-intensive and information-intensive (using advanced electronic systems as the primary tool in most functions).

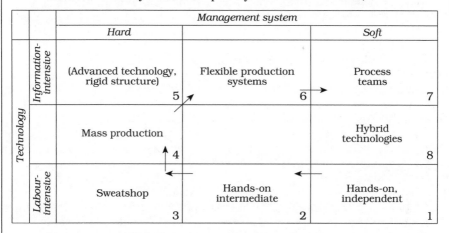

Figure 11.3 *Technologies and Systems*

The model can be described in terms of industrial change. Pre-industrial output is unambiguously employment-intensive, but may be organized in forms ranging from the co-operative, self-managing craft enterprise (1) to the rigidly managed sweatshop of the early factory (3). Technological advance then leads to (4) – deterministic and hierarchic systems, culminating in mass production, where the nature and pace of work is essentially defined by the limitations of the equipment; more advanced technology enables either (5), a rigid, controlled hierarchy monitored by information technology, or a gradual softening of the organizational structure, producing the long transformation between (4) and (7), moving through flexible production systems as a transition phase.

The new horizontal, information-intensive organization is at (7); but within this management system, it is possible to employ a range of technologies, from the information-intensive, down through hybrids (8) back to the skilled craft (1). However, it should be noted that the possibility of paradigms (1–3) remains open, and that in the post-industrial, low-output economy, there could be renewed pressure to re-establish low-wage work within a rigid hierarchy.

For the purposes of the present discussion, hands-off and hands-on technology should be understood to refer, respectively, to paradigms (7) and (1), although the darker, authoritarian possibilities (5) and (3) remain.

on another's failure in a zero-sum game. They would have no wider application in low-output conditions unless they could be in a form which offered solutions not just for winners of the positional contest,[26] but also for the broad range of companies at risk and for the people who depend on them.

Is broader application possible? Some pointers will be set out in the final section, but first it would be useful to take a closer look at 'dematerialization' and the relationship between the two extremes – hands-on and hands-off technology.

DEMATERIALIZATION

Two main forms of technology have been discussed: (a) labour-intensive (hands-on) and (b) technology-intensive (hands-off), as part of the strategy of the efficient firm. These technologies have an important feature in common, namely, that they are both capable of delivering eco-efficiency: hands-on production (for reasons discussed in the previous section) and hands-off technology (because it is a discipline of 'dematerialization' – progressive minimization of all inputs as a ratio of output). Although both technologies also have potential for devastating levels of environmental impact, the contribution they can both make to eco-efficiency seems to be very significant.

The eco-efficiency of both technological extremes relative to the intermediate forms is borne out by a classic historical study of the environmental impact of industrial economies since the start of their industrialization. Wilfred Malenbaum showed that their changing resource intensity (resource consumption per unit of GDP) can be tracked by a curve rising sharply during the early years and then falling away from a peak as dematerialization develops in the mature economy Malenbaum, 1978).[27] This view of the matter has an immediate cogency, suggesting progress from the small-scale crafts-based technologies at the start of industrialization, followed by the crisis of the inefficient smoke-stack industries, and reaching out towards cleaner production systems.

Pre-industrial economies proved to be eco-efficient and durable. They operated on a small enough scale for renewable resources to be able to recover from the environmental impact they impose; their use of natural materials simplified their waste problem, and their poor transport links required them to maintain a high degree of natural diversity. This is not a claim that the pre-industrial model is necessarily eco-efficient; on the contrary, its dependence on a narrow renewable resource base could make them highly destructive when they grew faster than the rate at which the resource could be renewed.[28] For instance, the energy base of the UK was critically – almost terminally – threatened by the emerging wood-fuel famine of the early eighteenth century. However, the containment of environmental impact was a significant feature of pre-industrial economies and their technologies, which had a good record of underpinning sustainable economies for many centuries.

---

26 The idea of positional goods was introduced by Fred Hirsch, 1976. In positional contest, one person's success depends on another's failure. In fact, this is not necessarily a zero-sum game, since total outcomes could add to greater or less than zero, although the sum of the benefits of both choices is less than it would be if the relationship between the costs and benefits were linear. A review of the meaning of positional contest is set out in David Fleming, 1988.

27 The model is discussed fully in Oliviero Bernardini and Riccardo Galli, 1993.

28 See Clive Ponting, 1991, for a narrative of environmental destruction by pre-industrial economies.

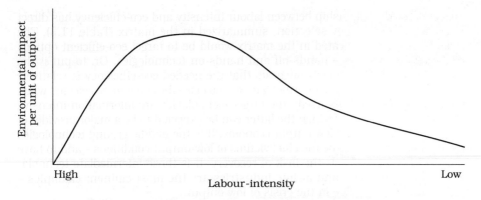

Figure 11.4 *Labour-intensity and Environmental Impact*
A Suggested Relationship (after Malenbaum)

As economies start to industrialize, they use technologies that are wasteful in energy and materials; they stay with them for a time as they build their industrial base, and then move ahead through a long process of dematerialization, with decreasing 'intensity of use' as they mature. Malenbaum's original study of this has been borne out by many other studies since then, and Bernardini and Galli's review of them (1993) concludes that the future will see not only a declining trend in the rate of *growth* in material and energy consumption at the world level, but also the possibility of 'a decline in absolute terms in the rate of material consumption over the next half century or so'.

They overstate their case, since (a) even falling environmental impact would contribute to the gross cumulative impact; (b) historical studies are likely to over-emphasize the record of the mature OECD countries, which could prove to be insignificant when placed beside the massive, and perhaps decisive, new impact of the industrializing countries, notably China; and (c) eco-efficiency improvements are likely to be overwhelmed by sustained growth, as the Golden Age model suggests. But a vital implication of the Malenbaum model which has not been brought out is that the two extreme cases of low environmental impact apply not just in terms of historical change, but also in terms of the industrial economy in cross-section (Figure 11.4); it lends weight to a central argument of this paper – that the best eco-efficiency standards are achieved at the high and low extremes of the spectrum of technology.

Table 11.3 *Technology Selection Matrix*

Labour intensity	Eco-efficiency		
	High	*Intermediate*	*Low*
High	1. Target	2. Select	3. Reject
Intermediate	4. Select	5. Review	6. Reject
Low	7. Target	8. Review	9. Reject

This suggested relationship between labour intensity and eco-efficiency has direct relevance to technology selection, summarized in the matrix (Table 11.3). The focus of policy as indicated in the matrix would be to target eco-efficient options in the two limit cases – hands-off and hands-on technologies. Or, to put it the other way round, the matrix suggests that the needed eco-efficiency is relatively unlikely to be found in the intermediate technologies (but should be selected when the opportunity presents itself): the target technologies are information-intensive and labour-intensive, of which the latter can be expected to be a major provider of the jobs required in the low output economy. It is the middle-ground technologies that can be expected to be the chief victims of low-output conditions – and to have the least to offer towards the task of recovery. It is those intermediate technologies – the automobile and airline industries are the most eminent examples – which face obsolescence in the crisis of low output.

A WIDER APPLICATION?

Is there any possibility that, in the commercially poisonous environment of low output, with economies committed to stagnation or even negative growth, strategies could be found to enable companies to survive and employment to be stabilised? The answer to that is 'don't know'. Given the absolute imperative of growth embedded in the market economy, that answer could reasonably be described as wildly optimistic. And yet there are (and there need to be) possibilities to explore, and stabilization solutions may usefully be sought in two directions implicit in the discussion so far: (1) labour intensity, and (2) service intensity.

Labour Intensity

Labour intensification has a larger role to play than the one conceded to it by the EC White Paper, because it could extend to the sectors where it would be used as a substitute for – and not simply as a complement to – the less eco-efficient intermediate technologies. However, this would require government or community support in a programme of economic stewardship, which would include protection of the industries concerned against predatory competition. Labour intensification – and the related policy of reallocating working time, using a shorter standard working week (or working lifetime) to soak up redundant labour – would directly raise the cost of output (the *indirect* impact on costs, after taking into account taxation and the cost of unemployment, is more complex); it is therefore intensely vulnerable to competition from suppliers working in other economies, who are able to produce output at lower costs by the simple means of reneging on any standards of labour intensity and environmental protection being developed by other economies.[29]

All forms of policy requiring co-ordination between governments contain an element of instability, in that they are vulnerable to free riders. Hands-off technology (segment 7 of Table 11.3) can look after itself in international trade;

---

29 The Social Chapter to the Treaty of Maastricht offers the opportunity for this form of free riding, giving a competitive advantage to member states that do not comply.

indeed, the stimulus of international competition in cost and performance is helpful to it, but the hands-on sector, with its high unit costs, would be dependent on some form of protection if it is to stand a chance of climbing out of the niche, and becoming a realistic substitute for eco-inefficient intermediate technology. Economic stewardship, a policy of economic protection which distinguishes between sectors that need protection and those that do not, and which ensures that stabilization policy is actually implemented in practice despite the ever-present threat of dissidents, would become central to the mandate for government in low-output conditions.

Service Intensity

'Efficiency' has been used in this paper in two senses in common currency: (1) the capital and labour employed per unit of output and (2) eco-efficiency – output per unit of environmental impact. But there is a third sense: household efficiency – the well-being obtained by households per unit of consumption; in other words, the use to which households put the resources available to them. Industrial development is dependent on a progressive decline in household efficiency, since it needs the household to consume increased quantities of goods and services, even though there is no expectation that their well-being will rise at a corresponding rate. (Indeed, rising consumption may even be associated with a decline in well-being (Richard Douthwaite, 1992). Under low-output conditions, the direction of change in household efficiency would be reversed: the overriding objective for households would be to sustain their well-being, despite the binding limit on consumption. Firms' strategy (in fulfilment of their survival and profit objectives), would be to maximize the yield obtainable from their low level of material sales, to assist consumers in their aim of maximizing household efficiency, and to help them to maintain some liquid spending power, rather than dropping out of the market.

The motivations of firms and households would therefore be complementary, and they can be brought together in a constructive relationship through developed forms of demand side management (DSM), reinterpreting output in terms of the service it provides, rather than in terms of the product. This changes the relationship between firms and households from that of market exchange to the closer range co-operative links that are already being developed in industrial marketing, and in the marketing of energy to households.

In the conventional, high-output economy, the problem is that this DSM policy is too efficient: fully implemented, it would drastically depress sales. However, in the low-output economy, output is already reduced, so barriers to the extension of DSM have already fallen: the ceiling to output has been set, and the task is to assist households to make the best use of the diminished flow of material resources available to them. The logic of extending DSM would include a major breach in the boundary between supplier and consumer, recruiting households themselves into the self-managing, multi-functional teams discussed on p157-9 – bringing industrial production and household production within a policy of service intensity, organized in part on a localized basis.

How companies could make the quantum jump from non-market relationships in a self-managing team working within the company, to a wider self-managing team in which the non-market relationship extends to customers, lies far outside the scope of this paper. But it has been a characteristic of industrialization that radical new technologies have developed just at the moment when the need for them has reached crisis point. The new technology – a cultural and economic technology this time, rather than an applied scientific one – may give a new meaning to eco-efficiency, securing acceptable levels of well-being within a drastically reduced level of output. This would unquestionably meet one requirement of organizational change – that companies should acknowledge and achieve 'outrageous goals'.[30]

CONCLUSION

In a market economy, companies are under continual pressure to achieve improvements in their productivity. In order to absorb the labour (and, in many cases, capital) freed by these advances, companies and the economies to which they belong have to grow. The successes of environmental policy which are taking place at present provide encouragement for the paradigm of sustainable development, offering the double and interdependent benefits of growth and environmental protection. This paper has suggested that, as eco-efficiency improvements are overwhelmed by growth in the volume of output, growth may cease to be a feasible option. In the absence of growth, economic chaos could be expected to follow, and the paper has considered a problem that is at best difficult, and may be impossible: are there survival strategies available to companies in the chaotic conditions of growth failure?

Hardly surprisingly, the paper has not answered that question. However, it has suggested some directions that might be explored, and which might have relevance for companies faced with the prospect or reality of low output. Labour-intensive output was considered, as was the strategy of survival through competitive efficiency, for which technology-intensive (labour-saving) technology is likely to be central. The two technological extremes of high and low labour-intensity, it was suggested, have the feature in common that they may both be eco-efficient relative to intermediate technologies. But there are also other interesting features in the corporate strategies that were discussed: for instance, the organizational learning and soft systems employed in the strategy of competitive efficiency may provide the foundation for a radically new type of relationship between firms and customers, in which the household itself is brought into direct co-ordination with the supplier.

The fundamental conclusion of this confessedly speculative paper may be that the new generation of technology, which will address the critical nexus of economics, societal stability and environmental sustainability, will not be in the form of technical fix, but of cultural change.

---

30 Discussed in the context of total quality management by David Jackson, 1994.

REFERENCES

Abramovitz, Moses (1989) *Thinking about Growth*, Cambridge University Press

Archer, Leonie J (1993) *Aircraft Emissions and the Environment*, Oxford Institute for Energy Studies

Barrett, Mark (1991) *Aircraft Pollution: Environmental Impacts and Future Solutions*, WWF Research Paper

Baumol, W J (1967) 'The macroeconomics of unbalanced growth: the anatomy of urban crisis', *American Economic Review*, June, vol 57, pp 515–426

Becker, Gary (1965) 'A Theory of the Allocation of Time', *Economic Journal*, no 75, pp 493–517

Bernardini, Oliviero and Galli, Riccardo (1993) 'Dematerialization: Long-Term Trends in the Intensity of Use of Materials and Energy', *Futures*, vol 25, no 4, pp 431–448

Blackler, Frank (1994) 'Post-Modern Organisations: Understanding How CSCW [Computer Supported Co-operative Work] affects organisations', *Journal of Information Technology*, no 9, pp 129–136, p 133

Bromley, Rosemary D and Thomas, Colin J (eds) (1993) *Retail Change*, UCL Press, London: see Neil Wrigley 'Retail concentration and the internationalization of British grocery retailing'. See also Raven, Hugh and Lang, Tim with Dumontil, Caroline (1994) *Off Our Trolleys: Food Retailing and the Hypermarket Economy*, SAFE Alliance/Institute of Public Policy Research, London

Cameron, Douglas (1992) 'No Smoke Without Fire', *Airline Business*, September, pp 86–88

Cavaleri, Steven A (1994) 'Soft Systems Thinking: A Pre-Condition for Organizational Learning', *Human Systems Management*, no 13, pp 257–269; p 262

Commission of the European Communities (1993) White Paper *Growth, Competitiveness and Employment*

Cook, Emma (1995) 'Bosses Spy on Time Thieves', *Independent on Sunday*, 11 June, p 23

Davidow, William H and Malone, Michael S (1992) *The Virtual Corporation*, Harper Business, London

de Waele, Martin (1994) 'Self-Management: Road to Productive, Healthy and Self-Sustaining Organizational Milieu?' *Human Systems Management*, 13, pp 133–144

Dogarnis, Rigas (1991) *Flying Off Course*, 2nd edition, HarperCollins, London

Douthwaite, Richard (1992) *The Growth Illusion*, Green Books, Hartland, Devon

Dow Europe (1994) *Environment Progress Report*. See also London Economics (1994) 'Demand-Side Management: A Survey of the US Experience'

Dumaine, B (1990) 'Who Needs a Boss?' *Fortune*, pp 52–60. Quoted in de Waele (1994).

Fairlie, Simon, Hagler, Mike and O'Riordan, Brian (1995) 'The Politics of Overfishing', *The Ecologist*, no 25, 2–3, pp 46–73; p 49

Fleming, David (1988) *After Affluence: A Study of the Market for Positional Goods*, unpublished PhD dissertation, University of London

Fleming, David (1994) 'Pint of Your Best, Farmer, Please' *Country Life* 8 September 1994, revised in 'The Dairy Industry: a Question of Scale' *Strategy Workshop Discussion Paper*, available from the author

Fry, Vanessa and Pashardes, Panos (1986) *The RPI and the Cost of Living*, Institute for Fiscal Studies, London

Hirsch, Fred (1976) *Social Limits to Growth*, Routledge, London

Jackson, David (1994) 'BPR: Hype or Reality?' *The TQM Magazine*, vol 6, no 6, pp 19–22

Katz, Ron (1994) 'The Fine Art of Profit', *Airline Business*, pp 24–29

Koestler, Arthur (1967) *The Ghost in the Machine*, Hutchinson, London

Kohn, A (1993) 'Why Incentive Plans Cannot Work', *Harvard Business Review*, September–October, pp 54–63

Lancaster, Kelvin (1966) 'A New Approach to Consumer Theory', *Journal of Political Economy*, no 74, pp 132–157

Malenbaum, Wilfred (1978) *World Demand for Raw Materials in 1985 and 2000*, McGraw-Hill, New York

Manning, Alan (1994) *Estimating the effect of minimum wages on employment from distribution of wages: a critical review*, Centre for Economic Performance, Discussion Paper 203, London School of Economics

Naisbitt, John (1995) *Global Paradox*, Nicholas Brealey, London

Ponting, Clive (1991) *Green History of the World*, Sinclair-Stevenson, London

Sampson, Anthony (1995) *Company Man*, HarperCollins, London, pp 331–334

Sen, Amartya (1985) *The Standard of Living*, Cambridge University Press, Cambridge

Senge, Peter (1990) *The Fifth Discipline* (1992 edition) published in the UK by Random House, London

Shearman, Philip (1992) 'Costs and Yields', *Airline Business: The Skies in 1992*, pp 17–21

Smith, Timothy K (1995) 'Why Air Travel Doesn't Work', *Fortune*, 3 April, pp 26–36

Tainter, Joseph A (1995) 'Sustainability of Complex Societies', *Futures*, vol 27, no 4, pp 395–407

Thompson, Michael, Ellis, Richard and Wildavsky, Aaron (1990) *Cultural Theory*, Westview Press, Boulder, Colorado

Trisoglio, Alex (1995) *Managing Complexity*, draft paper presented at the LSE Strategy Seminar, 25 January

Vallely, Paul (1995) 'The Big Mac', *Independent*, 10 June, p 13

Part IV

Techniques for Environmental Improvement

Introduction

Richard Welford

Previous chapters of this book have already demonstrated that there is a need for a change in the way in which the internal organization of the firm is defined and operated. It has been suggested that new forms of organization need to be explored and techniques developed which are capable of moving the firm towards a more sustainable pattern of business activity. Whatever the ultimate management structure and ethos of the organization, there will be a key role for management in binding the various parts of the organization together and ensuring that the ultimate objectives of the organization are realized. The next three chapters therefore outline some of the steps which can be taken to build a more sustainable organization.

A common thread which runs through all the articles in this part of the book is that there is a real difference between environmental management and management consistent with sustainable development. The latter is less well developed and all the authors point to the need for further research and development in this area.

According to Rob Gray in *Corporate Reporting for Sustainable Development*, from which the following chapter is taken, reporting is an important technique for environmental management. Such techniques, it is argued are both essential and practicable. Moreover, in the spirit of openness, accountability and creditability we should simply expect companies to disclose information about their environmental performance. Gray makes a clear distinction between environmental reporting and reporting for sustainability but notes that to date efforts to encourage organizations to voluntarily undertake either have not been successful. Gray argues that every enterprise needs to report on its policy, plans and structure, finances, activities, and management. Ultimately, however, reporting for sustainability must consist of statements about the extent to which corporations are reducing (or increasing) the options available to future generations.

Rolf Marstrander in 'Industrial Ecology: A Practical Framework for Environmental Management' (from which Chapter 13 is taken) notes that increasingly our focus has shifted from the local regulation of industrial pollution to concern with sustainable development. He argues that the industrial organization needs to create a culture based on pro-active, ecology-oriented participation. Like Hawken therefore, Marstrander sees industry as a leader, co-operating with all stakeholders, establishing new social insights, new tools for decision making, training systems and techniques for organizational development and a greater understanding of environmental issues. All these challenges represent possible threats to the individual company but also provide huge new opportunities. A shift in thinking away from the local and towards the global and a re-examination of the way in which our societies develop and consume is needed.

My own view, outlined in 'Breaking the Link Between Quality and the Environment: Auditing for Sustainability and Life-Cycle Assessment' (see Chapter 14) goes even further, arguing that although contemporary environmental management systems techniques may be useful they do not go far enough if our ultimate aim is to achieve sustainable development. Central to that achievement is an increased emphasis on life-cycle assessment and the development of techniques associated with auditing for sustainability. Moreover, there is a need for a new ideology in the business world which puts a greater emphasis on environmental protection, equity and futurity.

The authors all agree that ultimately, corporate environmental management requires a new, more fundamental approach and a commitment within every firm to go through radical change in its corporate culture. This requires a paradigm shift which sees the world as integrated rather than a dislocated collection of parts which compete rather than co-operate. Environmental management can sometimes be a shallow form of environmentalism which accepts a mechanistic paradigm and tends to endorse the ideology of economic growth. The implicit message of this part of the book is that we need to see industry expanding its horizons and developing a clearer, holistic world view. Some of the techniques for achieving that are outlined but others are still to be discovered.

12

Corporate Reporting for Sustainable Development: Accounting for Sustainability in AD2000[1]

Rob Gray

INTRODUCTION

The concept of 'sustainability' rose to prominence following the Brundtland report in 1987.[2] It has rapidly become the core concept in discussion of mankind's interaction with the physical environment. Further, on the face of it, it is a concept that is universally accepted as a desirable, even essential, yardstick by which to assess mankind's actions. However, there is considerable disagreement over the actual operationalization of the concept and over its implications for the way in which mankind orders its life. Any serious discussion about sustainability must first expose this disagreement and then attempt to resolve it.

The general definition of sustainability is *not* in dispute, namely that humanity must:

> '... ensure that [development] meets the needs of the present without compro-
> mising the ability of future generations to meet their own needs.' (World
> Commission on Environment and Development, 1987, p 8)

How this might be achieved at national and international levels is widely discussed. There is, however, an increasing recognition that the pursuit of sustainability must be continued at community, household and organizational levels as well. Corporations are crucial in any progress towards sustainability. They account for a large proportion of the world's economic activity and (in the case of the major multi-national corporations) hold much of the international power; they control much of the world's resources, technology and innovation and they have considerable influence over many of mankind's choices.

If corporations are to contribute fully to humanity's attempts to seek a sustainable existence then a strong case can be made for the development of accounting and reporting systems which will support this process. In broad terms

---

1 In what follows, I acknowledge the considerable influence of Tony Clayton, The Centre for Human Ecology and The Institute for Policy and Development and their work on the operationalization of the concept of sustainability. I also acknowledge the considerable support of the Chartered Association of Certified Accountants for the research into environmental accounting upon which much of the enclosed is based. An earlier version of this paper was commissioned by and presented to the International Institute for Sustainable Development.
2 United Nations World Commission on Environment and Development 1987.

this will require the monitoring and recording of data that relates to the extent to which an organization is acting (un)sustainably. This data will form the basis of information for both management and the external participants of the organization who should then be in a position to monitor and assess the organization's progress towards sustainability (or away from unsustainability) and make judgements and take steps, in the light of the information, as they see fit.

This broad outline, while perhaps having an overall plausibility, is far too general to be of any practicable value. In this paper I shall attempt to examine each of these stages and to turn each of them into more practical options so that any organization could adopt and apply a reporting system for sustainability. This should enable, in so far as current knowledge permits, each organization and organizational participant to obtain a clearer idea of the nature of the relationship between the organization, its environment and the pursuit of sustainability.

Throughout this paper I will be approaching the problems as an accountant who sees accounting and reporting as two sides of the information systems coin. The two sides are mutually dependent – it is impossible to report until one has something to report, to give an account until something is accounted for. Both depend upon and are themselves information systems. I will not, however, be restricting 'accounting' to 'financial accounting' – the demands of sustainability are too critical to be restricted to plausible financial measurement techniques (or to await the derivation of such).

The paper is structured as follows. The following section reviews the 'light green' environmental accounting and reporting initiatives and relates these to the corporate social reporting experiments of the last two decades. There is then a review of the current environmental accounting and reporting options available to any organization. However, sustainability is not about being light green – it is a far more profound concept. A review of what is meant by sustainability and some of the ways in which the concept can be operationalized is attempted. Then follows a critical review of our current reporting institutions and frameworks. The purpose of this is to highlight the necessary tension between (i) conventional conceptions of current reporting, (ii) the actuality of current reporting and (iii) the sort of frameworks – notably, stewardship, accountability and transparency – we will need if we are to report for sustainability. Finally, the paper proposes some practicable ways of approaching accounting and reporting for sustainability.

THE STATE OF THE ART IN SOCIAL AND ENVIRONMENTAL REPORTING

At its simplest, the current accounting and reporting activity depends upon four factors.[3]

1. Organizations: the organizations that are accounted for (the 'accounting entities') are defined in space and time. Events which do not fall within the defined organization are ignored.
2. Economic events: the only events which accounting recognizes are the 'economic events' which are tautologically defined as those events which have *financial* effects on the organization.

---

3 The following is adapted from Laughlin and Gray 1988.

3. Financial description: the events that accounting recognizes are further limited to those economic events which can be described in financial terms, or, more particularly, those which have generated in the past, do generate now or will generate in the future cash receipts or cash payments.
4. The users of information: the way in which the events are recognized and then processed is (largely) determined by sets of assumptions about the eventual users to whom this information will be communicated and by whom it will be used. The users are predominantly assumed to be management, investors and lenders and their interest is assumed to be of a predominantly financial nature.

Thus, at a simple level, we can envisage the accounting activity as recognizing and recording the financial attributes of a particular set of economic events as they flow across the imagined boundaries of the organization for which we are accounting. This recorded data is then processed, rearranged, summarized and manipulated and adjusted to put it into a form that management can use (eg cost data, budgetary data, activity centre performance data, etc) or that external financial stakeholders can use (eg profit and loss, costs and revenues, assets and liabilities etc).

The relatively short history of social and environmental accounting and reporting has been, at its simplest, about questioning each of these characteristics. That is:

*   How do we define organizations? To what extent can we include externalities?
*   Why account for only economic events? How might we account and report on social and environmental events as well?
*   What are the consequences of restricting our accounting and reporting to only financial description? How might we account in other ways?
*   Why do we restrict our reporting to a selected set of participants? How might we set about accounting and reporting to society, other countries, employees, communities or future generations?

In the early 1970s there was considerable debate, speculation and actual experimentation with the elements of this framework – principally in North America.[4] Corporations tried many forms of reporting: within the annual report or within a separate booklet; in financial numbers, in non-financial quantities, in words and pictures; the reports were for employees or management or society-at-large; some were audited, some not; they covered one or more of: plans, policies, interactions with communities, charitable giving, levels of pollution and emissions, energy usage, employment data, health and safety at work, etc. There was virtually no regulatory back-up to these experiments and by the mid- to late-1970s the experiments had all but disappeared and interest in the field had waned to a vestigial level all over the world.[5]

In the current growth of excitement and interest in environmental reporting it might be well to recall that we could learn a great deal from this earlier experience.

4 For more detail see Gray, Owen and Maunders 1987, Estes 1976, Johnson 1979, Belkaoui 1984.
5 The evidence suggests that the overall average level of social and environmental accounting and reporting did not actually alter much – one simply saw an upsurge in 'outliers', one-offs who undertook major initiatives or particularly interesting experiments. For more detail see Gray 1990b.

1. The examples of significant environmental reporting[6] which we are now beginning to see (especially in Europe) echo those earlier (predominantly North American) experiments.[7]

2. The short-lived but energetic enthusiasm for 'social accounting' made little in the way of long-term impact. Perhaps corporate reporting now emphasizes social issues a little more, but if so, it is marginal. With virtually no exceptions, it is only the regulated changes in reporting that actually bring about widespread change in behaviour or reporting practice. There is much talk currently of leaving developments in environmental reporting 'to the market'. As far as I can see the market will largely ignore the development of environmental reporting (for more detail see below) and I would have thought the 'market case' rather than the 'regulation case' was the one that had to be made.

3. A considerable body of research evidence has been accumulated over the last twenty years on (a) whether social and environmental reporting could be associated with profitable or unprofitable organizations, and (b) whether bankers, investors and stock markets in general (ie the financial participants) reacted to social and environmental disclosure. The results are largely inconclusive.[8] It is possible to conclude, as does Mintzberg, 'that it pays to be good, but not too good'. Or, more brutally, one can conclude that financial participants in organizations do not currently express anything other than the very mildest concern for the social and environmental effects of the organization that they own or to which they lend unless it is likely to directly or indirectly (through public image, regulation or whatever) influence financial returns. (Even the current experience with ethical funds does not run counter to this conclusion).[9]

4. The social reporting agenda of the 1970s was predominantly controlled by the companies. This is not meant to impugn the corporate integrity but to emphasize that throughout the debate the interests of 'business', of the companies, came first. Thus the examples of organizational social and environmental reporting that we have to draw from are largely self-congratulatory.[10] One need not be surprised by this but a very clear message is that one must be clear as to why one is pursuing a development in reporting. If the development is to achieve social change of some sort then there is no evidence to support the idea of leaving it to the companies. If the purpose is

---

6 For more information on environmental reporting initiatives in the UK see Owen 1992 and Harte and Owen 1991.

7 European companies like Norsk Hydro, BSO/Origin, The Body Shop, Rhône Poulenc etc all have their counterparts in earlier experiments by North American companies like Philips Screw, Clark C. Abt, First National Bank of Minneapolis, Eastern Gas and Fuel Associates and so on. For more detail see Gray, Owen & Maunders 1987; Owen 1992, Gray et al. 1993.

8 For more detail see, Gray et al. 1987; Owen et al. 1987; Mathews 1987; Mintzberg 1983.

9 For more detail on ethical funds, and the green funds in particular, see Harte et al. 1991, Owen 1990, Burman 1990, Rockness and Williams 1988.

10 There are exceptions to this, but explanations can usually be found. For example, the Atlantic Richfield social/environmental report, one of the best in the mid-1970s, contained data which did not necessarily show the organization in a good light. The Atlantic Richfield company had recently experienced a major environmental disaster. This echoes the Norsk Hydro case – a company who have produced a most wide-ranging report that contains data detrimental to the company. The company had experienced a recent environmental disaster in Norway. Such negative explanations cannot always be found of course but it is noticeable that those more 'honest' social and environmental reports were rarely repeated for more than a year or two.

to smooth over a simple but troublesome issue without causing business any great worries then a voluntary approach will work perfectly well.

This is a critical dilemma and I shall return to it later. In the meantime we can now turn to look at the way things in the corporate sector are currently moving with regard to environmental accounting and reporting.

ENVIRONMENTAL ACCOUNTING AND REPORTING

Accounting and reporting cannot act in isolation. Organizational change is necessary to enable and/or encourage the internal information and reporting systems to be both developed and used while institutional, regulatory and market changes are necessary to encourage organizations to report and for financial participants to respond positively. The regulatory changes will be considered later. For the moment, in order to give some indication of the sort of organizational change that is needed, John Elkington's 'Ten Steps to Environmental Excellence' are shown in the box below.

THE TEN STEPS TO ENVIRONMENTAL EXCELLENCE

1. Develop and publish an environmental policy.
2. Prepare an action programme.
3. Arrange organization and staffing, including board representation.
4. Allocate adequate resources.
5. Invest in environmental science and technology.
6. Educate and train.
7. Monitor, audit and report.
8. Monitor the evolution of the green agenda.
9. Contribute to environmental programmes.
10. Help build bridges between the various interests.

Source: Elkington (1989)

In such an organizational climate, then, the following suggestions of ways in which accounting might take greater cognizance of environmental issues become realistic possibilities (see the box below).

While these suggestions *are* largely experimental, most of them are in current use somewhere in the world. So, for example:

- many organizations are finding considerable direct, financial, short-term benefits arising from energy accounting;
- Rhône-Poulenc, one of the world's major chemical companies, is famous for its pioneering work in introducing accounting systems for its wastes and effluent;
- environmental impact assessment is becoming increasingly a regular fact of organizational life;
- the costs incurred by the chemical industry in investing in new, cleaner technology received considerable press coverage throughout the early 1990s;

SOME POSSIBILITIES FOR ENVIRONMENTAL ACCOUNTING AND INFORMATION SYSTEMS

1. *Compliance and ethical audits.* Reviews of the organization's performance against legal and consent requirements and its own code of conduct.
2. *Waste and energy audits and accounting systems.* Reviews of organizational energy use and waste outputs. development of information systems which record waste and energy, communicate it to line managers and, as appropriate, charge to activity centres.
3. *Environmental costs.* Separate identification of costs and potential liabilities that are environmentally related.
4. *Emissions information recording and communication systems.* Establishment of monitoring systems recording emissions to water, air and land (including noise). Regular reporting of this information to line managers.
5. *Environmental budget and performance appraisal systems.* Establishment of environmental criteria as part of management performance appraisal. Identification of environmental targets, environmental allowances and environmental spend as part of the organizational budgetary control system.
6. *Environmental impact assessment, environmental hurdle rates.* Best Practicable Environmental Option (BPEO), Best Available Technique Not Entailing Excessive Cost (BATNEEC), Environmental Risk Assessment etc. Bring environmental criteria into investment and project choice and post-audit in order to establish whether the organization's investment policy is environmentally sensitive.
7. *Financial environmental and social reporting.* Introduction of separate items in financial reports that identify, for example, environmental expenditures (separating compliance and other costs), environmental investments (actual, proposed and committed, and again identifying compliance-related costs) and potential environmental liabilities (such as reparation, fines for consent overrun or contingent, 'Superfund', clean-up liabilities).
8. *Non-financial environmental and social reporting.* Establishment of wider reporting of environmental interactions including, for example, compliance with legal and consent standards, environmental policy and plans, environmental activities undertaken etc.
9. *Accounting for accountability and transparency.*
10. *Accounting for sustainability.*

---

and, most visibly,

• environmental reporting has taken on a new lease of life.[11]

The suggestions and initiatives in the box above relate principally to internal environmental management by corporations and, while information systems such as these are prerequisites for developments in environmental reporting, they do not *in themselves* progress the reporting issues. Items 7 and 8 in the box are concerned with reporting issues.

---

11 For example, the USA experience with Superfund is being echoed in the European experience. Increasing numbers of organizations recognise that the EC moves towards freedom of information, environmental audit and corporate liability to clean up environmental damage will have a significant impact on the legislative framework of external reporting. Further, major reporting initiatives from companies such as Norsk Hydro, British Petroleum, Dow Chemicals and BSO/Origin have updated the standards in voluntary external reporting. More detail on these matters can be found in Gray 1990b, Gray et al. 1993 and Owen 1992.

Recent developments[12] in both voluntary environmental disclosure by companies and the intentions of regulatory bodies can be considered as falling into three categories of reporting:

- *General narrative reports.* Perhaps including statements of policy[13] and selected elements of 'hard' quantitative data, these are the most popular forms of environmental reporting.[14]
- *Non-financial quantitative and qualitative data.* Might include such things as emission statements and/or reports on environmental audits, for example. This is the form taken by the British company Norsk Hydro and a version of this approach is discussed below.[15]
- *Financial disclosure of environmental information.* This is not yet widespread outside the influence of the USA's 'Superfund' Act. While a number of companies may give selected items of financial data[16] and, at the other end of the spectrum, the Dutch company BSO/Origin have made attempts to report 'complete environmental accounts', it is only a matter of time before other parts of the globe follow suit.[17]

A degree of synthesis of these three approaches to reporting is provided by the United Nations Centre for Transnational Corporations' recent initiative in environmental accounting and reporting. Their proposals are summarized in the box below.

THE UNITED NATIONS PROPOSALS ON ENVIRONMENTAL ACCOUNTING

Financial information
- Disclosure of amount spent on environmental matters (possibly enabling capitalization due to spend impact on EPS – earnings per share), will possibly be split between regulated and voluntary costs.
- Disclosure of environmental contingent liabilities, most especially those arising from remediation costs under 'Superfund' type legislation.
- Disclosure of anticipated pattern of future environmental expenditure (possible split between regulated and voluntary costs).

Non-financial information
- Disclosure of environmental policy for the organization.
- Disclosure of organizational activity in the environmental field, including such matters as emissions statements.

---

12 See Roberts 1991 for a European view and, for a more global perspective, see UNCTC 1992.
13 The most popular 'off the shelf' policy statements are the Valdez Principles and the ICC Business Charter for Sustainable Business.
14 See, for example, recent Annual Reports or supplementary reports from Sainsbury's, Allied Lyons, Ciba-Geigy, Sandoz, British Steel, Hoechst, ICI, Rhône Poulenc, British Gas.
15 This approach is less popular but British Nuclear Fuels Ltd and a number of the UK Water Companies have adopted an approach something along these lines. ICI is moving in this direction and the Chemical Industries Association is encouraging this form of reporting.
16 Examples include ICI, RTZ and Glaxo in the UK.
17 For example, the EC's investigation of and proposals for a 'European Superfund Act' force European companies to follow the USA lead in disclosure of environmental contingent liabilities.

Thus, if the UN is successful in getting nations to adopt their proposals, all companies can be expected to increase their financial disclosure within the current financial statements while *also* being required to provide statements of environmental policy and statements of environmental performance. This last would almost certainly follow the general sort of direction suggested for the statement of compliance-with-standard.

The compliance-with-standard approach to social and environmental reporting is derived from the concept of the accountability of the corporation to society (see below). At its simplest, the organization would include a report (probably with the annual report) of the extent to which it had met the performance standards required of it. The standards would relate to (*inter alia*) emissions, spills, accidents, dumping, species habitat etc, and they would be derived from federal, national or supra-national law, regulatory body consents and standards set by trade associations.[18]

This approach to reporting is not only theoretically sound but there have been a number of experiments in this direction. The most notable of these in the 1970s was the Philips Screw Report in the USA although, in the UK, Social Audit Ltd used the concept to great effect in their social audit reports. Environmental reporting initiatives in the early 1990s are certainly headed in this direction.[19] In practical terms it seems that a compliance-with-standard (CWS) report must consist of a summary report plus more detailed data available to serious enquirers.[20] An idea of how a CWS report might look is given in Table 12.1.

Table 12.1 *An example of an Environmental Compliance-with-Standard Report Summary*

Area of standard	1990 level	1990 std	1991 level	1991 std	Source of standard	Description
Ground water:					NRA consent levels	(eg) X dies when BOD exceeds Y
Discharge 1						
Character a	w	a	y	c		
Character b	x	b	z	d		
Discharge 2						
Discharges to mains, etc						
Discharges to air, etc						
Disposal of wastes, etc						
Discharges to sea, etc						

18 For an introduction to these ideas see Gray et al. 1986, 1987. The relationship with concepts of accountability is developed more fully in Gray et al. 1988 and 1991.
19 See, for example, Gray et al. 1993.
20 This seems necessary because of the sheer complexity of many organizations and the dangers that any accessible summary may over-simplify complex matters. Thus the British Nuclear Fuels Ltd report is really very complex for the lay-person whereas the summary data they report give a much quicker impression.

The United Nations proposals taken together with the CWS report represent current best estimates of the way in which environmental reporting could develop in ways commensurate with both the practical constraints on corporations and the demands of environmental accountability.[21] However, it is essential to note that this is only environmental reporting, it is not reporting for sustainability. While such reporting (and the other suggestions in the box on page 178) could most usefully guide corporations and external participants towards more environmentally sensitive – and, thus, less unsustainable – activity, there is no element of such reporting which will link the concepts and demands of sustainability with corporate activity. For that, it is necessary to take further, more intrusive – or even radical – steps.

This is what suggestions 9 and 10 in the box are directed towards. That is, reporting for sustainability requires two major elements. First, it must be explicitly directed towards sustainability – the connection between activity and sustainability cannot be assumed. Second, the *actual* sustainability of actions cannot be known.[22] Sustainability involves trade-offs and personal valuations. Corporations cannot be expected to either know the ultimate sustainability of their actions or, necessarily, to act sustainably on behalf of future generations. Therefore, any reporting for sustainability must involve transparency and accountability – that is, it must be society in the widest sense that makes the choices – not just management and financial participants.

In order to develop these notions it is necessary to first examine the concept of sustainability before moving on to consider the reporting framework for corporate reporting and the implications of accountability and transparency. Only then can we consider what reporting for sustainability might actually look like.

THE NATURE OF SUSTAINABILITY

... a large selection of quotations from recent writing on sustainability shows that there is no general agreement on exactly what sustainability means. This fuzziness is useful in forging a consensus to promote sustainable development but it also obscures the political, philosophical and technical issues that still remain unresolved from the 'environment versus growth' debate of the early 1970s. (Pezzey, 1989, p 1)

Pezzey goes on to show where the agreements and disagreements lie. The essence of the problem is the extent to which one believes (or is willing to believe):

• that what (Western, business) man conventionally considers to be success – growth, profits, economic activity, conventional material well-being etc – derives ultimately, not just from man's activities, but from the physical environment; and,

---

21 This is perhaps graphically illustrated by the high degree of agreement between recommendations for environmental reporting from groups as diverse as the UK 100 Group of Finance Directors, the UK's Advisory Committee on Business and the Environment, The Institute of Chartered Accountants in England and Wales, The Chartered Association of Certified Accountants Environmental Reporting Awards and the Society of Management Accountants of Canada.
22 It is this which has led Ekins and Hueting to recommend attempting to calculate un-sustainability and to measure movements towards and away from un-sustainable activities. See Gray et al., 1993, Ch.14.

• the extent to which that physical environment can continue to support the activities which have generated these things.[23]

At one extreme we have conventional economic theory which assumes that all wealth derives from man and the use of (generally) unlimited resources. This theory is embedded in our ways of thinking about business and economies and leads to the assumption that continued economic growth is an inalienable right and duty which must not be challenged on any grounds. This extreme position is further bolstered by a touching faith in the ability of markets and technology to solve problems. Thus the current panoply of environmental concerns are seen as neither systemic nor critical. Under this view, humanity can carry on doing exactly what it is doing although there is some necessity for sticking-plaster solutions to mitigate the worst of the immediate environmental concerns. This is the 'business-centred' or 'economics-centred' view and it is widely disseminated through political, economic and business writing. It needs no further illustration here.

At the other extreme, and working from exactly the same data, is the view that humanity is likely to be extinct within current lifetimes and that the planet the race leaves behind will be a badly-wounded cess-pit. That is, the environmental concerns are systemic and critical. The issues listed in the box below, for example, *are* connected, worsening and critical. Furthermore, despite an apparently growing concern with environmental management they are continuing to get worse and will do so for the foreseeable future. This extreme view sees the current activities of mankind as profoundly *unsustainable*.

SOME EXAMPLES OF CURRENT ENVIRONMENTAL PRESSURES

Most environmental pressures are increasing exponentially. Thus, mankind is faced with an accelerating:

• rate of ozone depletion;
• rate of species extinction;
• rate of habitat depletion;
• rate of increase in technological catastrophe and scientific ignorance;
• desertification;
• deforestation;
• incidence of acid rain;
• depletion of fishing stocks;
• decline in the planet's waste-sink-absorption capacity; erosion of soil;
• pressure on water resources;
• rates of poverty and starvation;
• rate of usage of non-renewable resources; etc.

---

23 Two points should be emphasised here. First this analysis will, in common with much of the concern with environmental issues, be anthropocentric. That is, we look at the problem from the point of view of the environment's ability to continue to support human life and 'value' the environment in human terms. That is we do not give other life forms and the planet itself any rights or value independent of man's existence. This is a narrow view; for more detail see, for example, Maunders and Burritt, 1991; Lovelock, 1982; 1988. Second, this analysis is also very western-centred – also in common with most commentators on the subject. When the gross inequalities between peoples are considered and the role that environment plays in that, the subject becomes more complex still, see, for example, Angell et al., 1990. I would suggest any allowance of these two factors must make the pursuit of sustainability more radical and threatening to western humans' ways of living.

The problem is that neither extreme view is provable – except *in extremis*. Therefore, if we are concerned with practicable action as a way forward we must try to find some realistic middle ground that can be articulated in ways that enable real-world policy to be derived from it. There is a group of environmental economists – including Daly, Pearce and Turner – who have sought to do just this and whose work is widely recognized as occupying a 'reasonable middle ground'.[24] It is their views of sustainability which will be used here to enable us to move forward.[25]

Pearce et al have produced what is probably the most widely quoted and accepted principle of sustainable development:

> ... the necessary conditions as 'constancy of natural capital stock'. More strictly, the requirement as for non-negative changes in the stock of natural resources such as soil and soil quality, ground surface waters and their quality, land biomass, water biomass, and the waste assimilation capacity of receiving environment. (Pearce et al., 1988; quoted in Pearce et al., 1989)

Pearce et al and then Turner further developed this by employing the concepts of 'capital' and we can relate this to Daly's work using the concept of 'income'.

The 'capital' available to humanity can be thought of as falling into three categories:[26]

- *Critical natural capital.* Those elements of the biosphere that are essential for life and which, for sustainability, must remain inviolate (examples include the ozone layer, a critical mass of trees, etc).
- *Other (sustainable, substitutable or renewable) natural capital.* Those elements of the biosphere which are renewable (eg non-extinct species, woodlands) or for which reasonable (however defined) substitutes can be found (perhaps, for example, energy from fossil fuels versus energy from renewable sources given the right capital investment).
- *Man-made capital.* Those elements created from the biosphere which are no longer part of the harmony of the natural ecology which includes such things as machines, buildings, roads, products, wastes, human know-how and so on.

The general point is that man-made capital (which is largely covered by priced transactions and thus is dealt with and measured in conventional economics and accounting) is created and expanded at the expense of the natural capitals. It is man-made capitals that are measured by GNP and by profit, and which Western

---

24 Examples of their work are included in the bibliography at the end of this paper. The political and intellectual dangers of seeking a `middle ground' are well argued in Tinker et al 1991.
25 I should be honest here and mention that I personally subscribe to the second of the 'extreme views'. Furthermore, although the work of Daly, Pearce and Turner is excellent and very important in many ways, I have profound doubts about some of its basis, see – for example, Gray 1990f, 1992.
26 Sustainability is, of course, a concept rather wider than just the physical environment. It refers to ways of life, societies and communities and the general quality of the life of humanity. Included in what follows there should also be, therefore, reference to 'social' capital – qualities of lives, education, culture, built environment etc. The analysis without these things is difficult enough and I, in following Turner and Daly, have also left them out. Most 'deep greens' see sustainability as embracing these wider social and, it must be said, spiritual concepts through a realigning of Western values and the pursuit of smaller community levels of activity.

capitalism has been excessively successful at creating and expanding. But, as man-made capital expands so it becomes almost inevitable that the natural capital *must* decline – unless some way of managing sustainably can be found. It then follows that for sustainability to be achieved, the critical capital must not be touched and all diminutions in other natural capital must be replaced, renewed or substituted for.[27] Under current economics and accounting that cannot happen. Further, Daly's point (which can be added to this analysis) is the commonly accepted notion in economics, business and accounting that prudent behaviour suggests we only take as income that which is left over after maintaining our capital intact – capital maintenance. What we currently measure as 'income' does *not* leave our *natural* capital intact – it leaves it depleted. It must follow, therefore, that our measure of income is wrong and the level of consumption that we have enjoyed has been paid out of capital. Sustainability requires that we maintain our capital and only spend the income that allows us to do so.[28]

The operationalization of a concept as complex as sustainability is bound to over-simplify the concept and, perhaps, lose some of the essential ingredients in the process. As societies show no inclination to revert to a level of peasant existence where sustainability is much easier to achieve, it is necessary to devise some method that can be seen to approximate the concept of sustainability in a practical way within our current institutional and structural arrangements. This is what Pearce, Turner and Daly achieve. The concepts can then be translated to a corporate level. This is where *accounting and reporting for sustainability* can perhaps help and to which the last section of this paper is directed.

But before suggesting some ways in which organizations might account for and report their (non-) sustainability, it seems essential to consider the actual institutional arrangements for reporting. Without a serious appraisal of these arrangements there is the very real danger that there may be no actual change in reporting practice or else that matters will simply become so trivialized as to be irrelevant. A major reason for this is that systematic environmental reporting for sustainability cannot sit easily and comfortably within current reporting arrangements and practices.

THE CURRENT FRAMEWORK OF CORPORATE REPORTING

Current reporting by corporations is, in the main, a highly regulated activity governed by law and professional pronouncements. In the majority of large corporations, the regulated, and principally, financial data are augmented by

---

27 One point of departure from the economists' approach would be the notion that one can substitute for natural capital. While, for example, the energy use in coal (non-renewable natural capital) could be substituted by the energy use of solar panels (man-made capital) there is no way in which the total 'use-value' that future generations may derive from coal can be known. Until that is known, future generations cannot be compensated for our use of their coal. Other aspects of natural capital, species for example, cannot be substituted for. Attempts to put a financial value on all of the natural capital lead to arguments about how that valuation should be done, whether it is ethical and whether we really want to be in a position to trade 'n' Mutant Ninja Turtle toys for 'm' golden eagles. Finally, there is a critical problem of deciding what is really critical capital. For the 'deep green' observer, a considerable major proportion, if not all, of the biosphere is critical capital.

28 For more detail, see the references to Daly, Daly and Cobb, Pearce et al., Turner, Turner and Pearce in the references. See also Gray, 1990e, 1990f, 1991 and 1992.

voluntary reporting. This voluntary reporting consists, again in the main, of information that it would appear the corporate management wish the readers of the report to know about. This is dominated by general operational information, explanations of downturns, fanfares for successes and general image-related data on products and processes. (Of course, there is also social and environmental data but, beyond legally required disclosure this tends to vary between corporations, vary over time and to be, on average, less than half a page of the annual report.)[29] The dominant audiences for the annual report are presumed to be the financial constituents – mainly the investors but also, it would appear, investment analysts, prospective investors, bankers and other financial (and to an extent, trade) creditors.

As I have already stated above, there is no evidence to suggest that corporations as a whole will systematically report data which are difficult and which have a potentiality to reflect negatively on the reporting entity. Furthermore, as also mentioned above, there is no evidence to suggest that the financial community has any interest in environmental data except in so far as those data reflect a potential financial gain or loss that the corporation might suffer in the future. Therefore, I can see very little evidence that would suggest that corporations would voluntarily undertake (or that the 'market' would encourage them to undertake) significant, systematic reporting that might reflect badly on the organization and/or have negative financial consequences. This may seem pessimistic with respect to the potential for voluntary reporting for sustainability but the current reporting framework is generally assumed to be related exclusively to financial gains and losses. This has become more and more the case as the older concepts of 'stewardship' have been pushed out by talk of 'efficient capital markets' and 'the information needs of investors'.

There would therefore appear to be a series of conundrums. First of all, *if* we assume that 'markets' are efficient and that they will respond to new information and thus allocate funds to those companies with the best prospects then reporting by corporations about their environmental activities and the extent to which they are acting sustainably *might* influence the way in which capital is allocated in markets. *But*, we are in no position to assess, absolutely, how sustainable organizations are *and* there is no evidence to suggest that corporations will supply the information voluntarily. How then could the markets react? And, critically, why should they act? There is obviously a need for the ball to be set rolling and all the evidence suggests that this has to be done through regulations.

Secondly, and equally critically (if perhaps more theoretically) the evidence suggests that (a) assumptions of market efficiency are overstated and are, in fact, acts of faith; and (b) that the purportedly efficient allocation of scarce resources through capital markets cannot be shown to be either allocatively efficient in particular or in society's interest in general – whether self-interest, short-term interest, long-term interest or anything.[30] Therefore, if we cannot show that financial information helps financial markets to allocate financial funds in a suitable way for the purpose of financial self-interest we have little or no justifica-

---

29 These data are taken from Gray 1990b which is based upon a UK survey of annual reports over a ten-year period. These results appear to be broadly consistent with practices in other countries. See also Owen, 1992 and Gray, 1993.

30 This matter is expanded a little in Gray & Kouhy, 1993 and Gray, 1992.

tion for the current rationale for accounting reporting by corporations.[31] There is certainly no evidence to suggest that markets per se will allocate environmental resources successfully.

Therefore, it seems to me that the current framework of corporate reporting cannot and will not accommodate the essential changes in reporting that are needed – whether we continue to talk of environmental reporting or talk of reporting for sustainability. For this reason, I believe that any reporting framework must take on board the concepts of stewardship and accountability – but not just to the financial community. This stewardship and accountability is owed to the financial community *and* to society, to communities and to future generations. Only a framework which acknowledges rights to information of a wider constituency can be assumed to encourage the new forms of reporting which are necessary. Furthermore, the very critical nature of the environmental problems that one is seeking to address plus the sheer complexity of the issues and the increasing level of ignorance of humanity's interaction with the biosphere do not lend themselves to the assumption of 'rational', allocative decision-making by selected groups of the privileged, (as is assumed by the traditional financial reporting model). Information and decision-making must be *democratic* in the widest sense of the term because it is society as a whole which must make the choices and trade-offs that are essential in the path to sustainability. The concept of accountability can acknowledge easily that all of society has rights to information about actions taken on its behalf. This is then developed as organizations become more *transparent*. That is, information is used to reduce the distance between the organization and external participants so that society can 'see into' the organization, assess what it is doing with the resources that determine future options and react (or not react) accordingly.

Because there *will*, as Pezzey[32] concludes, be trade-offs that have to be made if sustainability is to be pursued. Thus, it is surely absolute nonsense to argue that the West can carry on expecting the same continuing rise in our standard of material well-being while profoundly reversing the direction of our impact on the biosphere. If it *can* be done, nobody has yet explained how. Not only do we need more knowledge about these things but society will have to be informed, through reporting, about the extent of the issues at stake.

It is not likely that corporations will find such a prospect attractive. However, if this accountability and transparency can be accepted then the corporation will find itself (depending upon how you look at it) more closely in tune with its wider constituents or under considerable pressure from employees, consumers, communities and society through democratic processes. This, rather than the financial interests of investors will produce the forces that are necessary to help corporations move towards sustainability.

---

31 Gray & Kouhy, 1993, develop this by referring to the many attempts by the accounting profession to develop a Conceptual Framework for accounting. They have all had two things in common: they start from the assumption that the wants of investors are paramount in efficient capital markets and that they have been expensive but abject failures. Investors' wants, governed by their own short-term financial self-interest, are not compatible with accountability, with stewardship, with any ethical argument or with any assumptions about the maximization of social welfare. The current framework for accounting practice is therefore very hollow and no basis for the development of other forms of reporting. For more detail, see Gray, Owen and Maunders, 1986, 1987, 1988, 1991, Gray 1991 and 1992.

32 Pezzey, 1989, is probably the authoritative study of definitions of sustainability.

Much more could be said about these matters[33] but for now it seems that enough has been said to illustrate that there is some hard thinking and bargaining to be done and, perhaps most importantly from the position of this paper, there is at least some significant doubt as to whether the conventional accounting and reporting frameworks currently in operation have anything to offer.

If we can assume that there is at least a will to regulate in order to bring corporations more in line with concepts of accountability, then we can now turn to look at some ways in which we might account for and report upon an organization's sustainability.

REPORTING FOR SUSTAINABILITY

Ultimately, reporting for sustainability must consist of statements about the extent to which corporations are reducing (or increasing) the options available to future generations. This is a profoundly complex, if not impossible, task. However, there do appear to be three major ways in which any organization could try to approximate this in a fairly practicable and systematic way which would potentially lend itself to reporting. These are the Inventory Approach and the Sustainable Cost Approach – which are both based around the categorization of man-made and natural capital discussed earlier – and the Resource Flow-through/Input-Output Approach, which is more general. (In a broad sense, one might bear in mind that the first two are attempts to report *about* sustainability while the last is an attempt to move towards reporting *for* sustainability.) These will be briefly examined in turn *but* it must be stressed that each is still very experimental.[34] Until corporations are willing to work alongside researchers with these exploratory models, it is inevitable that they will remain experimental. It should also be recalled that no reporting can take place until it has a related accounting/information system to back it up and supply the data. Finally, it should be recalled that the thinking behind the reporting I have discussed in this paper is related to providing information to which society has a right and which will enable society – in the broadest sense – to make judgements about the activities of its organizations. It is, thus, an utterly *democratic* approach which sees accountability in general and sustainability reporting in particular as part of the dialogue between a society and its organizations.[35]

The Inventory Approach is concerned with identifying, recording, monitoring and then reporting, probably in non-financial quantities, the different categories of natural capital and their depletion and/or enhancement.[36] The different elements of: critical; non-renewable/non-substitutable; non-renewable/substitutable; and renewable natural capital which could be thought of as being under the control of the organization would first be identified by the corporation. These,

---

33 For more detail, see Gray, Owen & Maunders, 1987, 1988, 1991 and Gray, 1990d, 1990e, 1990g and 1991.

34 Other experiments are taking place in, for example, Canada and New Zealand, which have yet to produce anything that looks like a corporate reporting approach. These are early days, though.

35 This should not be confused with a development of the mid-1990s in which companies began to label sections of their annual reports 'sustainable development'. These varied between genuine attempts to acknowledge the frightening challenge of sustainability for most corporations through to trite misinterpretations of the term in order to capture and control the term.

36 The only experiment in this area so far of which I am aware is that undertaken in New Zealand with regard to local authority reporting.

INVENTORY OF X CORPORATION'S SUSTAINABILITY INTERACTIONS

Critical Natural Capital

Ozone depletion. The level of CFC use emission for 1991 was XXX (1990, YYY). The corporation is committed to total elimination of CFCs by 1995 and HCFCs by 1997.

Tropical hardwood. The corporation has eliminated all use of tropical hardwood in its own processes (1990, YYY used). Supplier audits have established that all hardwood use by suppliers is from sustainably managed sources as accredited by ABC & Co.

Greenhouse gases. (See also compliance-with-standards report on emissions)

Critical habitats species,...., etc.

Non-renewable/Non-substitutable Natural Capital

Oil and petroleum products.

   Product 1: use, comparative figures, plans for reduction or substitution, funds or efforts expended to provide substitute.

   Product 2: ditto, etc.

Other minerals and mineral products,...., etc.

Non-renewable/Substitutable Natural Capital

Energy usage. Use details, changes in usage, plans to change, efforts towards renewable sources.

Disposal of wastes. Levels of wastes produced and types, changes and plans. Efforts towards discovery and access to new sources of resources (typically minerals), and extending longevity of use, repairability and recycling might appear here. Etc.

Renewable Natural Capital

Timber products. Use, harvesting, recycling, etc.

Species exploitation: ditto.

Habitat destruction/remediation:

Leisure and visual environment, built environment, water, air, noise... etc.

---

plus changes therein, likely impacts upon and steps to mitigate effects or replace/renew/substitute the elements involved, could then be reported. The box above provides a tentative illustration of the way this might look.

As with the compliance-with-standards (CWS) report discussed above, there may well be a need for some means of providing summaries but with detailed back-up data available to serious enquirers. Also, as with the CWS report, there is a critical need for corporations to engage with researchers in experimenting about the feasibility of the approach and working out methodologies.

The second of the approaches to *accounting for sustainability* mentioned above is the Sustainable Cost Approach. This is easier to explain but may very well prove to be exceptionally difficult in practice. Its attractions though are that it can fit within current reporting practice, it is a simple concept and the accuracy of the actual sustainable cost is probably not important.

The notion of sustainable cost derives directly from accounting concepts of capital maintenance and the need, within all the definitions of sustainability, to maintain the natural capital for future generations. Translating the most basic concept of sustainability to the level of the organization we could say that *a sustainable organization is one which leaves the biosphere at the end of the accounting period no worse off than it was at the beginning of the accounting period.* It must be the case then that the vast majority of, if not all, organizations do not comply with this. The extent of this 'failure' can be quantified. That is, it is theoretically possible to calculate the amount of money an organization *would* have to spend at the end of an accounting period in order to place the biosphere back into the position it was at the start of the accounting period. We are, thus, dealing with a *notional* amount but one which is based on *costs* not *values*. The resultant number could be shown on the income statement as a notional reduction of profit or notional addition to operating expenditure. It is probable that the number would be very large and would wipe out any profit the organization has earned in this (or any previous) year – dividends are, and have been, paid out of 'capital'. But broadly speaking, that is the 'right' answer. It is widely accepted that current organizational activity is *not* sustainable and the calculation of sustainable cost provides some broad 'ball-park' quantification of the degree to which this is the case.

This will not be a simple matter. First, any use of 'critical natural capital' will, by definition, have to be included at infinite cost because it is irreplaceable. Although that might be an uncomfortable conclusion it strikes me as being morally correct (and, perhaps, practically correct in terms of the survival of humanity). Second, there may be a very large number of ways of replacing a part of the biosphere, there may equally be no simple way. (What, for example, is the cost of replacing a net full of cod?) Third, there is no simple agreement on the level at which resources can be sustainably harvested. Fourth, the system, rather like life-cycle assessment, involves an infinite regress as each element in the calculation is dependent upon a set of earlier, prior environmental interactions. These are major practical problems and there is a real need to explore them in corporations but until organizations are willing to work alongside researchers on matters of this sort, basically simple ideas like sustainable cost will remain academic pipe-dreams.

The third and final suggestion for approaching the problem of *reporting for sustainability* is the Resource Flow/Input-Output Approach. This is derived from both a method well-established in economics and an approach used in many environmental audits. It is based upon a systems conception of the organization and attempting to report the resource flows of the organization. *It does not directly report sustainability* but provides a transparency to the organization which focuses upon resource use. This is done in a way that will enable participants to assess resource use – and, ultimately, therefore the sustainability of the organization's activities.

What one is seeking here is a catalogue of the resources flowing into an organization, those flowing out of the organization and the 'losses' or leakages (wastes and emissions, for example) from the process. Such an 'account' would again be quantified – probably in both financial and non-financial numbers (including the profit and other distributions generated). The non-financial numbers would in many ways be the most useful, being the most easily accessible and understandable, but the use of financial numbers may help in providing summary data. Table

Table 12.2 *Resource Flow Statement for XYZ Lodge Ltd (Extract)*

Inputs Brought f/d	Loss/theft Breakages	Leakages Emissions	Wastes	Outputs Carried f/d
Building				Building
Fixtures	Deterioration			Fixtures
Furniture				Furniture
Fittings				Fittings
Furnishings	Deterioration			Furnishings
Sheets				Sheets
Crockery etc	Breakages			Crockery, etc
Additions to non-consumables				
Repairs				
New sheets			Packaging	
New crockery, etc			Packaging	
Consumables				
Meat			Scraps	2700 bed-nights
Groceries			Packaging	
Canned food			Cans	
Canned drink			Alu cans	
Milk			Bottles	
Bottled drink			Bottles	
Cleaning materials		Sewage	Plastics	
Electricity		Heat		
Oil		Gases, heat		
Gas		Gases, heat		
Car miles		gases		
Laundry, etc		Water		
				Profit/loss Taxation paid

As far as possible all inputs, leakages and outputs would be described and/or quantified.

12.2 is a tentative outline illustration of how a summary of this might look for a small hotel.[37]

Such a summary would probably need to be backed up by detail which analysed each of the categories and each category would need quantification – in simple numbers, in weights and measures or in financial numbers. While perhaps the major problems with this suggestion are (a) it is cumbersome, and (b) it would

---

37 The approach taken here has a very similar intellectual heritage to the German and Austrian attempts at Okobilanz. The hotel referred to in the text is an actual organization and the example is used because it allowed access and a degree of experimentation with its resources and flows.

probably be wholly unacceptable to organizations on the grounds of confidentiality, it is a method which organizations could use for internal reporting and *it does fulfil the requirements of transparency and of allowing society to make choices about resource use.*

The Resource Flow/Input-Output Approach has been independently pursued by Paul Ekins and New Consumer Ltd. Their approach is much more sophisticated and is far more refined and developed than the approach described above. Under the New Consumer proposal, the resources used by an organization/product and their flow is further separated into their source of origin, their function in the organization and their ultimate destination. The idea is to produce product/organization data sheets which can provide references for consumers and others wishing to assess the potential sustainability of an organization or product they intend dealing with (similar in intent to life-cycle assessment). Yet again, the idea is experimental and the data shown in Table 12.3 (taken from a 1990 New Consumer Ltd research proposal) have been collated from the public domain.[38]

In its concern with transparency, with informing the public and allowing society to decide, the New Consumer approach is clearly not a reporting *of* sustainability but a move towards reporting *for* sustainability.

At the time of writing, these three broad suggestions represent the full extent of the methods for reporting for sustainability of which I am aware.[39] We are therefore in a period when experimentation and research are critical. Until organizations take that need more seriously than they appear to be doing at present we must, of necessity, continue to work for, buy from and own organizations which are blatantly unsustainable. There is only one conclusion to such practice.

SOME WAYS FORWARD?

The foregoing has attempted to demonstrate that (*inter alia*):

* While *environmental reporting and reporting for sustainability* are clearly related concepts there is quantum difference in their scope, focus and impact.
* Environmental reporting has been experimented with for many years (under the guise of 'social reporting') and, thus, there is a wide although patchy experience from which to learn.
* The current conventional reporting framework offers no likelihood of organizations voluntarily producing – on a widespread and systematic basis – environmental reporting of any seriousness.
* The proposals for reporting for sustainability are embryonic and research and experimentation are critically needed.
* No organization, to my knowledge, has approached, or is likely to approach, reporting for sustainability in the foreseeable future.
* If reporting for sustainability is to be any more than a rather comforting form of arm-waving, a substantial regulatory initiative will be necessary.

---

38 I understand that funding and access are preventing the experiment from being developed further at this stage.
39 There has also been a UN CTC funded experiment in Canada involved with a forestry company undertaken by Dan Rubenstein. To a large degree that experiment attempted to combine all three elements above. Its practical implications are still being worked out.

Table 12.3 Example of Ekins/New Consumer Sustainability Report Proposal

Emulsion Paint Dulux, ICI		Raw materials/extraction	Processing/manufacture	Packaging	Use	Disposal
Resources	Renewable	Water Brine Sulphur dioxide Hydrogen sulphate	Chlorine gas Sulphuric acid			
	Non-renewable	Titanium dioxide (ilmenite, rutile) Oil (acrylates) Mercury	Oil (acrylates) Gas Coal (coke)	Metal (tin) Oil (plastic)		Chalk to neutralize metal salts)
Wastes	Emissions		Acrylic acid, Sulphuric acid Chlorine gas, Sulphur dioxide			
	Pollution		Acrylic acid, Sulphuric acid Chlorine gas, Sulphur dioxide			Sulphuric acid Heavy metal salts
Impacts	Global services					
	Species/ecosystems	Mining (open cast and dredge)				Marine life Marshland
	Amenity	Mining (open cast and dredge)		Landfill sites		Landfill sites
Policy	I		Tioxide to spend £220m over 5–10 years on environmental improvements. ICI spends 10 per cent of the capital cost on safety and environmental protection			
	II		ICI's initiatives include developing alternatives to CFCs, Aquabase car paint and Biopol, a biodegradable plastic			

STEPS IN ENVIRONMENTAL ACCOUNTING AND REPORTING

Policy
- Statement of environmental policy (or steps being taken). The Valdez Principles are the current state of the art.
- Steps taken to monitor compliance with policy statement.
- Statement of compliance with policy statement.

Plans and Structure
- Structural and responsibility changes undertaken in the organization to develop environmental sensitivity – for example, Vice President of environment; committees; performance appraisal of line managers.
- Plans for environmental activities: introduction of environmental impact assessment; environmental audit; projects; investment appraisal criteria, etc.
- Talks with local green groups; plans to work with community, etc.

Financial (The best initiatives here are covered by UN papers 1991–1995)
- Amount spent on environmental protection: capital/revenue; reaction to anticipation of legislation; voluntary/mandated; damage limitation/pro-active (enhancement) initiatives.
- Anticipated pattern of future environmental spend: to meet legislation, as voluntary; capital/revenue.
- Assessment of actual and contingent liabilities – for example, 'Superfund' type problems, impact on financial audit; impact on financial results.

Activity
- Compliance with standards audits, procedures for, results of and issuance of compliance with standards report.
- Environmental audit and issuance of summary/results.
- Physical units analysis on, for example, materials, waste and energy.
- Analysis of dealings with regulatory bodies/fines/complaints.
- Awards/commendations received.
- Analysis of investment/operating activity influenced by environmental considerations.
- Analysis/decription of voluntary projects undertaken – for example, tree-planting; schools liaison.

Sustainable management
- Identification of critical, natural sustainable/substitutable, and man-made capital under the influence of (not necessarily 'owned' by) the organization.
- Statement of transfers between categories.
- Estimates of sustainable activities.
- Estimates of 'sustainable costs' which would have to be incurred to 'return the organization (and thus future generations) to same position as they were in before the activity.
- Assessment and statement of input/output resource-flows and changes therein.

An alternative or complementary reporting form might recognize the different dimensions of environmental impact, such as resources used; emissions; waste energy; products; transport; packaging; health and safety; toxic hazards; biosphere; built environment; visual environment; community interaction.

So the question arises – assuming that the pursuit of sustainability is a genuine one – how might we move forward from here? Currently, to all intents and purposes, environmental reporting is little more than the slightest of murmurs worldwide and reporting for sustainability is non-existent. Therefore, any developments in environmental or sustainability reporting would be progress – if such developments did not prevent further development through a misplaced sense of achievement and complacency.

A number of references have been made to current or past experiments which are in the public domain and, further, a number of specific suggestions have been outlined here. These are more than enough to provide ideas and guidance for any organization looking to start the process towards sustainability reporting. It seems to me that organizations might well find it easier if they took discrete steps towards the goal, passing through simple forms of light green reporting, through financial reporting and on to CWS reports, eventually coming to the challenge of reporting for sustainability. The box below provides a minimal checklist that might aid an organization embarking on this process.

It would be nice to believe that organizations and the 'market' will voluntarily move organizations towards much greater reporting and disclosure about their environmental impacts and about the degree of their sustainability. There is really no evidence to suggest that this will actually happen. In so far as voluntary efforts are making progress (as, for example, with the ICC Business Charter for Sustainable Development) the progress is not leading to substantive reporting – at least not yet – and the initiatives themselves are remarkably cautious and timid in the face of the enormity of the issues. It would be very nice to be proved entirely wrong but it seems to me that the most crucial step forward, the prerequisite for other steps, must be a major initiative by an influential (perhaps regulatory) body establishing the need, beyond question, for substantial, systematic reporting that approaches the question of whether or not an organization is acting sustainably. Without this, the world's organizations will continue to be patently un-sustainable. There is no future in that.

REFERENCES

Angell, D J R, Comer, J D and Wilkinson, M L N (eds) (1990) *Sustaining Earth: Response to the Environmental Threats*, Macmillan, London

Belkaoui, A (1984) *Socio-Economic Accounting*, Quorum Books, Connecticut

Burman, V (1990) 'Budding friends of the earth', *Money Marketing*, 24 May, pp 9–10

Daly, H E (ed) (1980) *Economy, Ecology, Ethics: Essays Toward a Steady State Economy*, W H Freeman, San Francisco

Daly, H E 'Ultimate confusion: The economics of Julian Simon', *Futures* 10/85: pp 446–450

Daly, H E and J B Cobb, Jr (1990) *For the Common Good: Redirecting the economy towards the community, the environment and a sustainable future*, Greenprint, London

Elkington, J (with Tom Burke) (1987) *The Green Capitalists: industry's search for environmental excellence*, Victor Gollancz, London

Estes, R W (1976) *Corporate Social Accounting*, Wiley, New York

Gray, R H (1989) 'Accounting and democracy', *Accounting, Auditing and Accountability Journal* vol 23, pp 52–56

Gray, R H (1990a) 'Greenprint for Accountants', *Certified Accountant*, March 1990, p 18

Gray, R H (1990b) 'Corporate Social Reporting by UK Companies: a cross-sectional and longitudinal study – An Interim Report', paper presented to British Accounting Association, University of Dundee, April 1990

Gray, R H (1990c) 'The accountant's task as a friend to the Earth', *Accountancy*, June 1990, p 65–69

Gray, R H (1990d) 'Business ethics and organizational change: Building a Trojan horse or rearranging deckchairs on the Titanic?', *Managerial Auditing Journal* vol 5, no 2, Spring, pp 12–21

Gray, R H (1990e) *The Greening of Accountancy: The profession after Pearce* (Certified Research Report 17), ACCA, London

Gray, R H (1990f) 'Accounting and Economics: The Psychopathic Siblings – A Review Essay', *British Accounting Review* vol 22, no 4, pp 373–388

Gray, R H (1990g) 'Corporate social reporting in the UK: The British Petroleum Company plc', in Taylor & Turley (eds) *Cases in financial reporting* Phillip Allan, Oxford, 1990, pp 98–122

Gray, R H (1991) 'Sustainability: Do you REALLY want to know what it means?', *CBI Environment Newsletter* no 3, January, pp 10–11

Gray, R H (1992) 'Accounting and environmentalism: an exploration of the challenge of gently accounting for accountability, transparency and sustainability', *Accounting Organizations and Society*, vol 17, no 5, 339–425

Gray, R H and Kouhy, R (1993) 'Accounting for the environment and sustainability in lesser developed countries', *Research in Third World Accounting 2*, pp 387–399

Gray, R H, Owen, D L and Maunders, K T (1986) 'Corporate social reporting: the way forward?', *Accountancy* December 1986, pp 6–8

Gray, R H, Owen, D L and Maunders, K T (1987) *Corporate Social Reporting: Accounting and accountability*, Prentice Hall, Hemel Hempstead

Gray, R H, Owen, D L and Maunders, K T (1988) 'Corporate social reporting: emerging trends in accountability and the social contract', *Accounting, Auditing and Accountability Journal*, vol 1, no 1, pp 6–20

Gray, R H, Owen, D L and Maunders, K T (1991) 'Accountability, Corporate Social Reporting and the External Social Audits', *Advances in Public Interest Accounting 4*

Harte, G, Lewis, L and Owen, D L (1991) 'Ethical investment and the corporate reporting function', *Critical Perspectives on Accounting*, vol 2, no 3, pp 227–254

Harte, G and Owen, D L (1991) 'Environmental disclosure in the UK: A research note', *Accounting, Auditing and Accountability Journal*, vol 4, no 3, pp 51–61

Johnson, H L (1979) *Disclosure of corporate social performance: survey, evaluation and prospects*, Praeger, New York

Laughlin, R C and Gray, R H (1988) *Financial Accounting: method and meaning*, Van Nostrand Reinhold, London

Lovelock, J (1982) *Gaia: A New look at life on Earth*, OUP, Oxford

Lovelock, J (1988) *The ages of Gaia*, OUP, Oxford

Mathews, M R (1987) 'Social responsibility accounting disclosure and information content for shareholders', *British Accounting Review*, vo 19, no 2, pp 161–168

Maunders, K T and Burritt, R (1991) 'Accounting and Ecological Crisis', *Accounting, Auditing and Accountability Journal*, vol 4, no 3

Mintzberg, H (1983) 'The case for corporate social responsibility', *The Journal of Business Strategy*, vol 4, no 3, pp 3–15

O'Riordan, T and Turner, R K (1983) *An Annotated Reader in Environmental Planning and Management*, Pergamon Press, Oxford

Owen, D L (1990) 'Towards a theory of social investment: a review essay', *Accounting, Organizations and Society*, vol 15, no 3, pp 249–266

Owen, D L (1991) *Green Reporting: The challenge of the nineties*, Chapman & Hall, London

Owen, D, Gray, R and Maunders, K (1987) 'Researching the information content of socially responsibility disclosure: A comment', *British Accounting Review*, vol 19, no 2, pp 169–176

Pearce, D (1977) 'Accounting for the future', *Futures* vol 9, pp 365–374, reprinted in O'Riordan & Turner (op cit)

Pearce, D (1985) 'Resource scarcity and economic growth in poor developing countries', *Futures* vol 10, pp 440–445

Pearce, D (ed) (1991) *Blueprint 2: Greening the World Economy*, Earthscan, London

Pearce, D, Markandya, A and Barbier, E B (1989) *Blueprint for a Green Economy*, Earthscan, London

Pezzey, J (1989) *Definitions of Sustainability*, no 9, UK CEED

Roberts, C B (1991) 'Environmental disclosures: a note on reporting practices in Europe', *Accounting, Auditing and Accountability Journal*, vol 4, no 3, pp 62–71

Rockness, J and Williams, P F (1988) 'A descriptive study of social responsibility mutual funds', *Accounting, Organizations and Society*, vol 13, no 4, pp 397–411

Tinker, A M, Lehman, C and Neimark, M (1991) 'Corporate social reporting: Falling down the hole in the middle of the road', *Accounting, Auditing and Accountability Journal*, vol 4, no 1, pp 28–54

Turner, R K (1987) 'Sustainable global futures: common interest, interdependence, complexity and global possibilities', *Futures*, vol 10, pp 574–582

Turner, R K (ed) (1988) *Sustainable Environmental Management: Principles and Practice*, Belhaven Press, London

Turner, R K (1989) 'Interdisciplinarity and holism in the environmental training of economists and planners', Symposium on education for economists and planners, International Environment Institute, University of Malta, December

Turner, R K (1990) 'Review of Blueprint for a green economy', *Environment*, vol 32, no 5, pp 25–26

Turner, R K and Pearce, D W (1990) 'Ethical foundations of sustainable economic development', International Institute for Environment and Development/London Environmental Economics Centre, Paper 90-01, March

United Nations World Commission on Environment and Development (1987) *Our Common Future* (The Brundtland Report), OUP, Oxford

United Nations Centre for TransNational Corporations (1992) *International Accounting*, UNCTC, New York

13

Industrial Ecology: a Practical Framework for Environmental Management

Rolf Marstrander

During the last years an important shift in environmental thinking has taken place. We see this in the declarations from the UN conference in Rio, where energy conservation, global warming, biodiversity, economic development and technology transfer, world population growth and food supply, became the key themes. We have received the concept of sustainable development from the UN Commission on Environment and Development. The title of their report, *Our Common Future*, is in itself a reflection of the same trend. We see the same idea in more detail in the industrially developed economies, where life-cycle assessments of products, energy conservation, the limitation of waste from households, agricultural pollution and global pollution related to ozone depletion and greenhouse effects, get more attention than direct emissions and discharges from industrial activity.

THE SHIFT IN THINKING

As shown in Figure 13.1, we have moved from an environmental approach where interest was directed at industry and local pollution, to an environmental view which focuses on global problems related to the way our societies consume and develop. This new perspective confronts industry and society at large with new challenges because the environment has become a third dimension integrated with the two traditional divisions of technology and economics as the critical factors for industrial development.

In the 'local pollution-by-industry' era, environmental improvement in industry was initiated to a large extent by government authorities. In the 'society's-global-concerns' era, which we are entering, this is no longer a viable approach. The solutions have to be found through co-operation between the public, authorities, industry and the users of industrial products, and society represented by the final consumers. Industry is needed as a pro-active partner to help solve the environmental and ecological challenges and threats which we face globally. Implicit in this conclusion is the belief that technology, and the ways we apply it, will be part of the solution.

The change in focus from local to global and from industry to society represents a dramatic shift. But more than that, it represents an increased

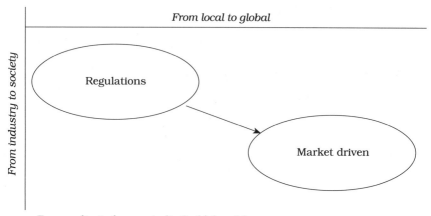

From local to global

From industry to society

Regulations

Market driven

- From unlimited space to limited/closed loop
- From linear thinking to systems thinking
- From economics to sustainability

Figure 13.1 *The Shift in Environmental Thinking*

realization of the fact that we are living on a planet which sets its own limits – limits that make it necessary to restrain the amount of waste we produce. Our planet has always faced this sort of challenge and it has been solved through ecology. Now that our industry-based culture is faced with a global challenge, the concept of industrial ecology has come to the surface.

The focus on global issues raises a series of new challenges:

- If industry is to take the role of a pro-active ecology-oriented partner co-operating with markets and authorities, management will require new social insights, new tools for decision-making, new technologies, and a higher general understanding of environmental issues.
- In industry we are used to thinking in terms of single companies competing in the market. That viewpoint will persist, but we need to add new dimensions to our thinking. The car user wants the car to function, but society wants the car to be produced, used and recycled with a minimum use of resources and generated waste. This will require new co-operative alliances which will exist alongside traditional competition.
- In industrial companies we have developed cultures which deal with challenges in the field of economics, technology and an improved environment. We must develop this culture further to achieve a pro-active ecology-oriented participation from our organizations. Training systems and techniques for organizational development must be created for this purpose.

All these challenges represent possible threats to the individual company if we fail, but much more important is the fact that any threat is an opportunity. These questions point to an embryonic situation; we are really at a turning point.

In this chapter we will look more closely at these challenges to industry and possible solutions to them, taking the idea of 'industrial ecology' as our starting point.

We will do this by:

- Looking more closely at the evolving concept of industrial ecology. What does it mean in terms of concepts, development of new methods, new technologies and analytical tools?
- Discussing how this relates to some of industry's experiences in the traditional field of safety, health and environment (SHE).
- Finally, we will discuss management practices that combine the SHE experiences with ecology-related approaches.

THE CONCEPT OF INDUSTRIAL ECOLOGY

During the last years, we have seen regulators call for life-cycle analyses and life-cycle assessments of products. We have seen ideas formed around clean technology, environmentally clean manufacturing and design for the environment. All these broadly based ideas point towards a shift in thinking from a clearly process-oriented focus to a more systems-oriented view. Lately, these trends have been brought together into the broader idea of industrial ecology.

Harbin B C Tibbs (1992) describes an 'industrial ecosystem at Kalundborg' that has very limited losses of energy and waste, because of its integration with a series of industrial activities. These activities include an electric power plant, an oil refinery, a bio-technology plant, a plasterboard factory, a sulphuric acid producer, cement producers, local agriculture and horticulture, and district heating.

A collection of cases from companies around the world shows how business has embarked on a path to sustainable development. The book by Willums and Golüke (1992) discusses the role of 'The business charter for sustainable development' drafted by the International Chamber of Commerce, and the actions needed to fulfil Agenda 21 from the UN Rio Conference. It presents a series of cases from different companies, the actions that were taken and the results achieved. The majority of cases demonstrate the capacity of organizational dedication and technical ability to improve processes, utilize waste and to co-operate with customers, suppliers and the surrounding community. An important message is the need to formulate clear goals related to identified areas for improvement. Examples of this are Dow's 'Waste reduction always pays' programme (WRAP) and Du Pont's targets in the same area. Both companies have publicly committed themselves to targeted reductions of waste, and both companies reflect these targets in their inter-company programmes for improvement.

The proceedings of the National Academy of Sciences of February 1992 has references to a colloquium entitled 'Industrial Ecology'. In the introduction to the colloquium, industrial ecology is described as

> '*a new approach to the industrial design of products and processes and the implementation of sustainable manufacturing strategies. It is a concept in which an industrial system is viewed, not in isolation from its surrounding systems, but in concert with them. Industrial ecology seeks to optimise the total material cycle from virgin material to finished material, to component, to product, to waste product, and to ultimate disposal*' (Jelewski et al, 1992).

The concept of industrial ecology stems from the definition of ecology and the similarities we face between ecology and an industrially developed society in the obvious limitations which exist if we want our industrial system to become really sustainable. A biological ecosystem is a natural system in balance, but dependent on energy input from the sun. Some organisms in this system use water and minerals to grow, others consume these organisms along with minerals and gases. The waste of these organisms again are food for others, etc. The whole system is a network of inter-related processes in which everything produced is used in another process. This balance is dynamic. We can see dramatic changes in the system, but the system as a whole adapts.

In the 19th century, we allowed ourselves to run industry as if we had unlimited resources and we could produce unlimited waste without doing any harm. The smoke from the plants was a good sign; it meant healthy business. Today we are learning by experience that landfills are limited, and long-range pollution like acid rain sets obvious restrictions to what we can emit from our smokestacks, etc. We are entering a period in which we want to base our industrialized society on a model which has limited energy and limited resources as inputs, and limited waste as its final output. This is described as an 'industrial ecosystem' as represented in Figure 13.2. The main areas of activity in an industrialized society are identified as the raw-material producers, the processing and manufacturing industry, the consumers and the waste-handling industry. In each of these four areas we will find activities where we can improve environmental performance. We may also find activities between the areas, as shown in the Kalundborg example, or as in all sorts of activities related to the recycling of used products.

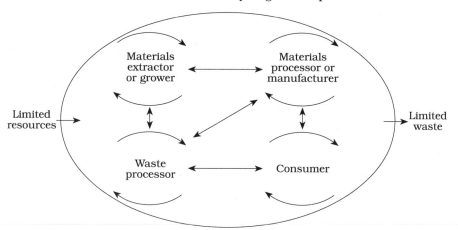

Figure 13.2 *A Model of an Industrial Ecosystem*

In order for it to function properly, the industrial ecosystem will require a major improvement in communication between the different areas of activity, and between the often competing actors in each of the four areas. If we add to this the fact that society at large, often represented by the public authorities, also has its role to play, it is clear that the biggest challenge will be one of communication and education – showing individuals and groups how different activities can each contribute to the end-result by limiting the consumption of non-renewable resources and reducing the generation of waste. The rewards will be seen in the increased economic activity which will be developed to support the new interchanges in this industrial ecosystem.

A NEW INDUSTRIAL ECOSYSTEM

The challenges we will face in establishing this new industrial ecosystem have been listed by Jelewski et al (1992). They concentrate on the following topics:

- The development of an industrial infrastructure for recycling and remanufacturing. We see this developing today for some categories of products and for valuable metals.
- Evolving models and methods that will enable us to measure the value of natural resources in economic units. Without this development, we cannot use our normal economic and financial techniques to take decisions in an industrial ecology system.
- The development of methods and rules for the use of life-cycle analyses, life-cycle assessments, or systems studies of the application of alternative materials to specific products. These systems studies will be based on the engineering and scientific data which is needed to assess environmental effects.
- Logistics and transport studies, including risk assessments, related to an industrial process.
- The analysis of production systems and their use of energy. This will include energy-efficiency measures in a single process, as well as the efficiency improvements which can be achieved by redesigning the complete industrial system.

All these topics will have to be studied by the different actors in the industrial ecosystem, from a practical point of view. Universities and research institutes will also have an important role to play in the development of an industrial ecosystem. John R Ehrenfeld (1992) describes some of the R&D topics he sees for Massachusetts Institute of Technology (MIT) which are needed for the education that is necessary for supporting the development of industrial ecology:

- *Data acquisition.* Develop data networks that can assess and combine relevant information from different sources.
- *Analysis and transformation of data.* Develop approaches to indicate and quantify the material flows across industrial sectors. Research on life-cycle assessment (LCA) to provide a systematic framework for analysing the product and for processing the implications of LCA will be part of this development.
- *National accounts.* Development of 'sustainable' performance measures, including standard account systems for national economics and the integration of these into management information systems for the public service.
- *Policy analysis.* New and improved processes for negotiating and purchasing upon ecological values and criteria. Processes that help introduce scientific analysis into policy discussions and processes to deal with uncertainty will be included.
- *Implementation studies.* Studies of organizational behaviour in choosing among technologies. Many alternative 'clean' technologies exist but are not used, in spite of the potential cost savings and product quality gains.

Research into reasons behind these decisions, including studies of
innovation and design practices, is needed.

This brief summary of the concept of industrial ecology indicates some of its
characteristics. Industrial ecology is a *systems approach* to guide the development
towards a more sustainable industrial system. The concept, and the solutions it
points towards, are very much in an embryonic state, but it is a pro-active
concept. It can act as the framework for strategy which will embrace technology
development, the positioning and development of relationships between
industries, and communication with public authorities and potential markets for
individual companies as well as industries.

The concept of industrial ecology is complicated because we must deal with a
very complex system that we cannot yet fully describe. Also industrial ecology is a
system in dynamic adaptation. The management of a company that wants to be
'environmentally pro-active' in line with the concept of industrial ecology will be
faced with challenges in two dimensions:

- *Expertise.* One dimension is related to the exploration of concepts and the
  development of the in-house expertise which is needed to be able to handle
  the systems and solutions required. This is the same task we face in any
  R&D effort.
- *Communication and education.* The other dimension is the task of building
  an organizational understanding of industrial ecology, including all the
  employees and communicating this to our customers and to society. This is
  a matter of communication and education.

The challenge related to the development of expertise needs to be seen in a longer
time horizon. The development of expertise does not solve any immediate problem.
It is related to the strategic choices about future market positions, future
products, technologies and services.

The challenge of building understanding in our organizations is also long
term, but it can give more immediate feedback. An important factor in any ecology-
oriented development will be our present efforts on safety, health and
environment. We will discuss in some depth how we can relate these efforts to the
larger concept of industrial ecology.

SOME CHARACTERISTICS OF SAFETY, HEALTH AND ENVIRONMENTAL WORK

So far, we have been occupied with the general concept of industrial ecology
without being company-specific. Seen from the individual company's point of view,
industrial ecology is a system like the one indicated in Figure 13.3. The 'value' of
the end-product is defined by the sum of the processes needed to make it, its
properties in use and the possibilities of the end-product being reused or recycled.
By 'value' we mean its economic, technical and environmental characteristics.
When discussing the role of safety, health and environmental work (SHE) in this
system, we see that SHE work is part of all the processes and so must also be
represented in the end-value of the product.

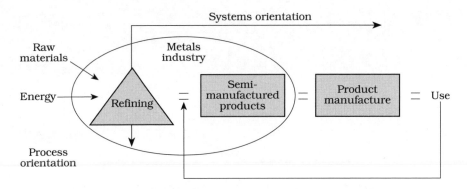

Figure 13.3 *SHE is an Integral Part of Ecology-Orientation*
Safety, health and environmental work is process-oriented; ecology is
system-oriented

It is important to remember that the authorities' approval of SHE work has been related to the regulation of discharges, the use of dangerous substances, etc, for each particular process or plant. Similarly, each company has been concerned with SHE work related to its own processes and based on its own organization. This also reflects the fact that the product's performance is not directly linked to the emissions and safety hazards related to making it. But the SHE value may be an important factor in marketing, or may be demanded by the authorities, as we see in demands for LCAs or eco-labels. The experiences and philosophies behind SHE work are discussed elsewhere. Here, however, we will focus on one characteristic of SHE responsibilities as seen in safety work.

Most major companies in the Western world have achieved impressive improvements in safety performance during the last ten years. Most of these gains have come as a result of a very simple but effective management approach. It has been a focus on a single common denominator, accidents per million hours worked, and the responsibility has been defined as part of the line manager's job in all departments of the company.

The use of a common denominator has made it possible to establish a simple control loop as shown in Figure 13.4. This control loop is traditional and well understood. It gives us the basis for a systematic approach to continued improvement. The definition of line responsibility ultimately leads to every employee from the CEO down through the company. But it is obvious that the safety performance of a sales representative spending most of his time in a car is different from that of a mechanic using his spanner tightening nuts, or an operator watching his control panel. For the design engineer, safety in the processes he designs is different again. The important lesson from this analysis is that the safety denominator, combined with line responsibility, has helped us to identify and explain to every employee the complex field of safety improvement. Also, the experience gained in safety is helping companies to implement and develop an understanding of the wider concept of total Environmental quality assurance.

An example of this can be taken from the refining of aluminium oxide into primary aluminium. In this process fluorides are needed and they are costly. Emissions of fluorides as particulates, and as gas, can cause harmful effects in the environment. The refining process has therefore been linked to cyclone

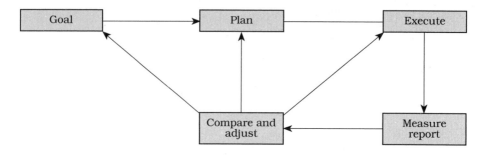

Figure 13.4 *The Control Loop*
Developing policies and systems for environmental management

batteries and a dry-scrubber system, using aluminium oxide to catch as much as 97 per cent of the fluorides in the off-gases coming from the reduction cells. The aluminium oxide from the dry scrubber is used as raw material in the reduction process. This is an example, as indicated in Figure 13.5, of a closed-loop process reducing the loss of a costly raw material that can also be harmful to the local environment. The process is dependent upon a minimum loss of off-gases containing fluorides before they have been recaptured. With the overall goal of reducing the amount of fluorides lost, we get a common goal for the total quality in the closed-loop system consisting of

oxide silo ➡ reduction cell ➡ gas transport system ➡ dry-scrubber system ➡ oxide silo

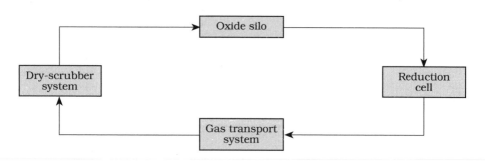

Figure 13.5 *The Refining of Aluminium*
A closed-loop system to eliminate fluoride emissions

BUILDING ORGANIZATIONAL UNDERSTANDING TO ECOLOGY-RELATED INDICATORS

Implementing the concept of industrial ecology depends very much on the relationships the individual company has with its customers and with the end-users of the product. If we want to make an analysis of an end-product in a supply-chain like the one shown in Figure 13.3, we can use the kind of a matrix illustrated in Table 13.1.

Table 13.1 *Life-Cycle Assessment Data*

LCA data for each material and product	Energy efficiency	Recyclability	Environmental factors waste/emissions	Safety	Food preservation
Process related	☐			☐	
Recycling related		☐	☐		
Transport related					
Product use characteristic	☐		☐	☐	

That sort of matrix presented in combination with the systems-based concept of industrial ecology can be complicated and difficult to communicate to the different organizations in the supply chain. The complete concept of industrial ecology will be useful mainly in strategic analyses, and in the development of concepts for new products and new processes.

In an operational setting on the shop floor, or in our communication with a specific customer, our local community or to the public at large, we need a simpler vehicle to get our message across.

If we take the lessons learned from the safety and environment-related activities about goal-setting, we should look for simple indicators which relate to the whole system and use them to reduce the complexity of the industrial ecosystem. Experience in metal fabrication and other material-producing industries suggests indicators like:

- energy use and energy efficiency;
- waste reduction;
- recyclability;
- transportation of materials and products.

All of these relate to all the processes in the system and to the use and handling of end-products.

We have seen in *Business and Sustainable Development* (Willums and Golüke, 1992), in Dow's WRAP-programme and Du Pont's goals for waste reduction, examples of big corporations using similar indicators in their environmental policies. The policies also involve goal-setting and line responsibility as we found with regard to safety. In preliminary studies of energy use and logistics in hydro aluminium, we found that these parameters could be used in the same way.

It is reasonable to assume that for any company we could define a set of relevant ecology-related factors that should measure: the raw materials, the manufacturing processes, the end-products, the recycling possibilities and the links between them. If they were applied as we described in our safety example, we would produce:

- similar approaches to those used in safety, health and environment work;
- access to indicators that can help to reduce the complexity of the system;

- a basis for communication with customers and suppliers on ecology-related matters.

The management challenge will be to give the process some priority in resource allocation, and to provide the necessary expertise and status for the ecology programmes. The industrial ecology programmes will require systems studies, communication and educational activities, both outside and inside the company.

PRACTICAL IMPLICATIONS

Our focus here is on environmental management. The challenges we face in this are derived from the challenges we also face in the environment. In recent years we have seen a change of emphasis away from local issues to global challenges, and a focus away from industry-specific concerns towards a view of industry as an integral part of society. This change-over is a consequence of taking an ecological perspective, and seeing industry as a total system. This had led to discussions around the concept of 'industrial ecology'.

Our discussions clearly demonstrate that we are at a very early stage in the development towards an industrial ecosystem, but we can also see that the concept which is rooted in industrial ecology is likely to raise some new challenges related to:

- a new industrial infrastructure for recycling and the reuse of all sorts of waste;
- increased co-operation between industries and between companies;
- a more clearly defined role for the consumer in the industrial ecosystem eg, in recycling waste and conserving energy.

These challenges require us to develop approaches which will enable us to include performance measures for environmental factors in our established process of techno-economic planning, and strategic analysis.

All these challenges are identified and discussed in the literature, but the concept of industrial ecology can provide the basis for a more comprehensive and systematic approach.

Ecology is a concept that implies dynamic change. Dynamic change has two different dimensions:

- The strategic long-term dimension; and
- The immediate dimension of education and increased awareness.

The strategic long-term dimension contains the traditional R&D elements. The management challenge is very much one of giving vision and support to the development of technology, and providing techniques for planning and analysis. The concept of industrial ecology will provide a conceptual framework for co-ordinating these strategic efforts.

The dimension of education and ecological awareness is different. From our experience with traditional safety, health and environment work, we can see that the principles of environmental management, as expressed in setting goals on identifiable parameters and giving responsibility to line management, can also be applied to the concept of industrial ecology. This concept suggests that we might choose to set goals in terms of elements that bind the industrial ecosystem together, such as:

- Energy use and energy efficiency;
- Recycling and waste; and
- Transport.

Experience indicates that each of these parameters can be used as a measure to reduce the complexity of the message for involving employees, customers and suppliers, defining clear goals, policies that can be understood, and results that will encourage further improvement.

Developed and used as indicated in this chapter, the concept of industrial ecology is one that can help management to build on the foundation of policies and practices already established for environmental management.

REFERENCES

Ehrenfeld, John R (1992) 'Implementing Industrial Ecology/Design for Environment: Roles for the University', *MIT Program on Technology, Business and Environment*, MIT, Cambridge, Massachusetts, prepared for the National Academy of Engineering Workshop on 'Industrial Ecology and Design for Environment', July 13–17

Jelewski, L W, Graedel, T E, Landise, R A, McCall, D W and Patel, C K W (1992) 'Industrial Ecology: Concepts and Approaches', *Procedures of the National Academy of Sciences*, USA, vol 89, February, pp 793–797.

Tibbs, Hardin B C (1992) 'Industrial Ecology – An Agenda for Environmental Management', *Pollution Prevention Review*, Spring

Willums, Jan-Olaf and Golüke, Ulrich (1992), *From Ideas to Action: Business and Sustainable Development*, ICC report on the Greening of Enterprise, ICC Publishing and Ad Notam Gyldendal, Oslo

World Commission on Environment and Development (1987) *Our Common Future*, Oxford University Press, Oxford

14

Breaking the Link Between Quality and the Environment: Auditing for Sustainability and Life Cycle Assessment

Richard Welford

INTRODUCTION

In what has become an increasing trend in businesses, environmental management (defined in this paper as the management of environmental issues as they impact on business) seeks to improve the environmental performance of companies in order that the planet on which we live remains habitable for future generations. Indeed environmental strategies have received increasing attention as the degradation of the planet has accelerated. At the core of this strategic approach has been the central role of environmental management systems whereby companies put into place systems and procedures which ensure that environmental performance is improved over time. Management systems aim to pull a potentially disparate system into an integrated and organized one. To that end, the system covers not only management's responsibilities but the responsibility and tasks of every individual in an organization.

While accepting the need for management systems to control and monitor environmental performance, this article argues that the emphasis put upon them is greater than their role deserves. The argument developed below is that concentration on a management systems approach and an environmental auditing methodology based around those systems may be sub-optimal if our ultimate objective in society is to get businesses to behave in line with the concept of sustainable development.

The arguments in favour of a systems-based approach are nevertheless clear: an integrated system which covers the totality of operations helps management and workers to clearly see their place in the organization and recognise the interdependence of all aspects of an organization. Through establishing clear communications and reporting channels it should pull a potentially tangled web of structures and tasks into a clearly defined matrix of relationships with clear horizontal and vertical links. This means that functions are less likely to be lost in a maze of mini organizations and that a key aspect of an organization's tasks are not forever lost in a black box labelled 'nobody's responsibility', either leading to inefficiency which has negative environmental impacts or its revelation by a mistake, accident or disaster.

An effective management system is therefore central to the avoidance of disasters, accidents and environmental degradation, in so much as it pulls together all the other tools and strategies for the avoidance of risks. Quite simply, a management system should be developed and implemented for the purpose of accomplishing the objectives set out in a company's or organization's policies and these must include the avoidance of environmental damages. Each element of the system will vary in importance from one type of activity to another and from one product or service to another.

THE LINK BETWEEN QUALITY AND THE ENVIRONMENT

Many commentators, including some earlier work of this author, have stressed what they see as natural linkages between quality management and the improvement of environmental performance (Welford, 1992). It has been argued that this link exists through the need for environmental management systems and their associated auditing procedures, and that the general approach taken in philosophies such as total quality management mirror the desired approach for environmental improvement. The aim of both approaches is to achieve a continuous cycle of improvement achieved through the commitment of everybody involved in an organization.

The theory behind a Total Quality Management (TQM) system is that as quality improves costs actually fall through lower failure and appraisal costs and less waste. The concept that defects in the production process cost more to remedy if a product has left the factory gates seems obvious. But TQM is much more than assuring product or service quality; it is a system of dealing with quality at every stage of the production process, both internally and externally. TQM is a system requiring the commitment of senior managers, effective leadership and teamwork and this is also true of any system which aims for environmental improvements. This sort of generic approach integrating environmental issues, where pollution, for example, is viewed as a quality defect, has engendered a strong link between quality and the environment and has become the dominant ideology amongst industrialists.

This same link has led to the development of BS7750 and the EU eco-management and audit scheme. Such standards have been heralded as the major step forward which will provide incentives for businesses to improve their environmental performance. Fundamental to both schemes is a need to develop an environmental management system (EMS) and to undertake periodic audits of undefined measures of environmental performance and the management system itself. Both standards specify environmental improvement as their aim rather than the achievement of a set threshold below which firms may not fall. In parallel with this, while the environmental auditing methodology which has been based on the management system approach does provide for continuous improvement, it also means that major polluters who are producing extremely unsustainable products are able to gain the award and the prestige which such a badge brings them. Moreover, we know from the experience of BS5750 (the British quality systems standard), that certificates of compliance are often pinned to the wall and subsequently forgotten about until the auditors are due again. There is no reason to suppose that the same will not happen with BS7750 and the EU scheme, rather than provide for environmental improvement that may lead to environmental negligence by the very firms which have been accredited by the 'highest' standards.

Rather than stress the quality approach which is based on management systems aimed at continuous improvement, an alternative might be to go back to the key concept of sustainability and audit for sustainability. Auditing for sustainability is a holistic approach predicated on a clear world view and an understanding of the need for a 'paradigm shift' in business culture (Commoner, 1990, Wheeler, 1994, Welford and Gouldson, 1993). Organizations auditing for sustainability should be committed to integrating environmental performance to wider issues of global ecology and make specific reference to the concepts associated with sustainable development. Thus, as a starting point, energy-efficiency should be focused on the need to minimize NO_x, SO_x and CO_2 emissions and avoid nuclear waste. Waste minimization, reuse and recycling should be driven by the need to conserve non-renewable resources. Product design should prioritize the use of renewable resources. Sourcing of raw materials should have no negative impacts on global biodiversity, endangered habitats or the rights of indigenous peoples. Overall corporate policies should examine the business's impact on both the developed and underdeveloped world, both now and into the future.

The key question relates to the extent to which EMSs can actually deliver sustainability. Where they are based on a continuous cycle of improvement, sustainability may take a very long time to achieve. Moreover, the auditing process encompassed in the quality driven EMS, is dominated by the audit of the system, procedures, documents and management rather than environmental damage. The fact that many firms are embracing management systems such as BS7750 is explained by the fact that they are easily achievable, particularly in organizations where a quality management system is already in place, and they highlight the idea that an organization is doing something rather than nothing.

The EMS approach stresses the continuous cycle of improvement. Progress continues to take place, therefore, unless that cycle is interrupted. However, that cycle can sometimes break down and one of the biggest challenges of the TQM approach is to keep up momentum. Common reasons for the breakdown in the continuous cycle range from simple complacency through to alternative competing agendas which push the original objectives down the list of corporate priorities.

There is a contradiction which arises when, as so many firms have done, organizations commit themselves to sustainable development, often signing the ICC's (International Chamber of Commerce) Business Charter for Sustainable Development, and then opt for an approach which does not necessarily achieve these fundamental aims. One of the key problems that has arisen is that, by adopting a quality-driven environmental management system approach, firms believe that they are adopting principles of sustainable development. They seem to be of the view that environmental improvement equates to sustainable development. This is clearly not the case, as a closer look at the sustainable development concept reveals.

RE-EXAMINING THE CONCEPT OF SUSTAINABLE DEVELOPMENT

The belief which lies behind the concept of sustainable development is that there is a trade-off between continuous economic growth as experienced to date and the sustainability of the environment. Over time, growth has traditionally caused increases in pollution and atmospheric damage. The concept of sustainable development stresses the interdependence between economic growth and environmental quality. It is possible to make development and environmental protection compatible by following sustainable strategies and by not developing the particular areas of economic activity that are most damaging to the environment.

The Brundtland Report (World Commission on Environment and Development, 1987), commissioned by the United Nations to examine long-term environmental strategies, argued that economic development and environmental protection could be made compatible, but that this would require quite radical changes in economic practices throughout the world. They defined sustainable development as development that meets the needs of the present without compromising the ability of future generations to meet their own needs. In other words, mass consumption is not possible indefinitely and if society acts as if all non-renewable resources are plentiful, eventually there will be nothing left for the future. But more importantly than that, mass consumption may cause such irreparable damage that humans may not even be able to live on the planet in the future.

The challenge that faces the economic system and industry is how to continue to fulfil its vital role within modern society while working towards sustainability. Complying with the principles of sustainability cannot be achieved overnight. However, both for entire economies and for individual businesses, there is hope that it can be achieved within the time-scales which appear to be necessary if environmental catastrophe is to be avoided. Nevertheless, the approach needed is a radical one and not a piecemeal one (the approach we have seen to date) and such a radical approach can only be changed via culture shift and a re-examination of the dominant ideology surrounding environmental management strategies. Tinkering with commonly accepted approaches such as quality management may be insufficient.

Sustainable development is made up of three closely connected issues:

- *Environment.* The environment must be valued as an integral part of the economic process and not treated as a free good. The environmental stock has to be protected and this implies minimal use of non-renewable resources and minimal emission of pollutants. The ecosystem has to be protected, so the loss of plant and animal species has to be avoided.
- *Equity.* One of the biggest threats facing the world is that the developing countries want to grow rapidly to achieve the same standards of living as those in the West. That in itself would cause a major environmental disaster if it were modelled on the same sort of growth experienced in post-war Europe. There therefore needs to be a greater degree of equity and the key issue of poverty has to be addressed. But it seems hypocritical for the West to tell the Third World that it cannot attain the same standards of living and consumption. What therefore is the solution?
- *Futurity.* Sustainable development requires that society, businesses and individuals operate on a different time-scale than currently operates in the economy. While companies commonly operate under competitive pressures to achieve short-run gains, long-term environmental protection is often compromised. To ensure that longer-term, inter-generational considerations are observed, longer planning horizons need to be adopted and business policy needs to be pro-active rather than reactive in response to a

recognition that the environment is a dynamic and not a static entity.

The Brundtland Report concludes that these three conditions are not being met. The industrialized world has already used much of the planet's ecological capital and many of the development paths of the industrialized nations are clearly unsustainable. Non-renewable resources are being depleted, while renewable resources such as soil, water and the atmosphere are being degraded. This has been caused by economic development but in time will undermine the very foundations of that development.

The Brundtland Report calls for growth which is environmentally and socially sustainable rather than the current situation of unplanned, undifferentiated growth. This means reconsidering the current measures of growth, such as gross national product (GNP), which fail to take account of environmental debits like pollution or the depletion of the natural capital stock. While concern about the depletion of materials and energy resources has diminished since the 1970s there is, nevertheless, now concern surrounding the environment's capacity to act as a sink for waste.

One major obstacle preventing sustainability from being achieved is the overall level of consumption. However, Western consumers are apparently reluctant to significantly reduce their own levels of consumption. While governments are increasingly adopting economic instruments such as taxes, subsidies and product-labelling schemes to reduce and channel consumption towards more environmentally friendly alternatives, industry itself must be encouraged to further increase environmental efficiency.

Sustainability challenges industry to produce higher levels of output while using lower levels of inputs and generating less waste. The problem that remains is that while relative environmental impact per unit of output has fallen, increases in the absolute level of output, and hence environmental impact, have more than offset any gains in relative environmental efficiency (Welford and Gouldson, 1993). However, if we examine the ways in which environmental efficiency has been improved, then we can begin to understand some of the key practical elements with which sustainability may be better promoted.

While much may be achieved on the environment front through an approach based on a continuous cycle of improvement it is difficult to see how this deals with the other two central aspects of the concept of sustainable development, namely, futurity and equity. Moreover, the environment, futurity and equity are inseparable concepts and all of them must be tackled if we are to prevent further degradation of the planet. But to date, industry has largely ignored two out of three of these important concepts.

THE CORPORATE RESPONSE TO SUSTAINABLE DEVELOPMENT

Companies are faced with a challenge of integrating considerations based on the three elements of sustainable development into their production and marketing plans. There is always an incentive, however, for profit-maximizing firms seeking short-term rewards, to opt out and become a free rider (assuming that everyone else will be so environmentally conscious that their own pollution will become negligible). European Union environmental legislation is increasingly plugging the gaps which allow this to happen and firms attempting to ignore their pollution are now subject to severe penalties. What is really required though is a shift in paradigms towards an acceptance by industry of its ethical and social responsibilities. If that is an insufficient reason for change in a profit driven world then businesses should recognize that it is not only ethical to be environmentally friendly, but with the growth of consumer awareness in the environmental area, it will also be good for sales (see, for example, Welford and Gouldson, 1993 and Peattie, 1992). Such an approach continues to leave aside the key concepts of futurity and equity however.

Firms clearly have a role to play in the development of substitutes for non-renewable resources and innovations which reduce waste and use energy more efficiently. They also have a role in processing those materials in a way which brings about environmental improvements. For many products eg cars and washing machines, the major area of environmental damage occurs in their usage (coupled, of course, with the public authorities' failure to tackle the root causes, such as the absence of public transport). Firms often have the opportunity of reducing this damage at the design stage, and when new products are being developed there is a whole new opportunity for considering both the use and disposal of the product. But this all ought to be done in the context of ensuring that operations do not exploit the developing world and its peoples. Moreover, environmental costs ought to be properly accounted, that is, they ought to be measured on a time-scale which has not to date been considered. The real cost of using non-renewable resources when measured over time therefore approaches infinity since once used they are lost forever. This is rarely considered.

According to Wheeler (1994) this sort of approach inevitably leads on to the question as to whether ecological performance can be measured quantitatively at all. Some environmental inputs and outputs to and from the organization may be amenable to full cost accounting. Some of the costs of environmental impacts (usually externalized by industry) might then be included in the annual reports and financial statements of the company. However, the full cost-accounting option remains speculative and highly controversial and there are many ecologists and environmental managers who doubt both the wisdom and practicality of attempting to reconcile all ecological impacts with conventional financial indicators for a number of reasons. Firstly, it is not possible to make realistic financial estimates of the intrinsic value of numerous important ecological assets eg unique habitats, endangered species, the ozone layer or the homelands of indigenous peoples. Secondly it is not possible to predict what value would be placed on these assets by future generations.

Thus, the view of many commentators (eg Wheeler, 1994) is that it is impossible to envisage all key indices of sustainability emerging from cost accountancy. For this reason, the approach to environmental auditing and reporting is never likely to be more than passing attention to financial indicators. However, we ought to be committed to devoting increasing efforts to the definition of ecological impacts with respect to true indices of sustainability. Moreover, where there is a benefit of doubt over the true costs of an economic action on the environment, the precautionary principle is central. Any benefit of doubt should be given to the planet and people and not to short-term benefits arising out of production opportunities. That is the radicalism which is demanded. It is a radicalism which may mean that some products and industries are lost for ever. If that is the case then so be it. It is better to have lost an industry than to lose the planet.

AUDITING FOR SUSTAINABILITY AND LIFE-CYCLE ASSESSMENT

The majority of firms who are doing anything at all to try to improve their environmental performance have now adopted auditing procedures based on a systems approach. Such an approach may take a business around in circle after circle of incremental improvement but where the starting point for this environmental merry-go-round is fundamentally unsustainable, it is unlikely to result in the significant step up in environmental performance which the world needs. The alternative approach is to undertake environmental audits based not on the principles of management systems but on the fundamental principle of sustainable development. That is not to suggest that management systems are not important – they are – but they should be seen as the vehicle which drives environmental improvement and not the measure of success themselves.

Auditing for sustainability requires firms to look at their overall impact on the environment, on equity and on futurity. It challenges firms to prioritize their actions in ecological terms rather than management systems terms. Moreover, it must be recognized that while bad systems may worsen environmental degradation, it is not the systems themselves which cause the damage but the products and services for which the system is designed. Rather than auditing management systems we ought to place more emphasis on auditing products and processes and therefore there is a central emphasis on the need for life-cycle assessment (LCA).

The LCA process is necessarily quite complex and requires commitment to detailed measurement. It requires the active co-operation of suppliers, and collaboration and co-operation are prerequisites for progress. However, since life-cycle assessment has been taken seriously by businesses, there is increasing concern that LCA may become a non-ecological activity. For example, it is clearly in the interest of suppliers of bulk commodities to draw the boundaries of LCA quite tightly in order to focus attention on those factors which are most easily controlled: wastes, polluting emissions and energy consumption. However, a full ecological consideration of product life-cycles also has to take into account the impact of raw material procurement on biodiversity, endangered habitats, human and animal rights and non-renewable resources. Ignoring these issues may be convenient (especially to the agrochemical, petrochemical, chemical and mining industries), but it is not tolerable from an ecological perspective (Wheeler, 1994).

Life-cycle assessment brings with it a number of advantages often overlooked by traditional environmental auditing methodologies. The concentration on the product, rather than the production system, facilitates direct measurement of environmental impact. Being directly linked to products also means that environmental strategy can be linked into the marketing system and therefore marketing and environmental strategy become intertwined. LCA also widens the environmental analysis beyond management systems and site-specific production attributes which can so easily hide environmental damage up or down the supply chain. The product specific approach also aids environmental communication because of the clear link between LCA and eco-labelling.

A concentration on products also allows us to track the inputs into the production process, allows us to track the sources of those inputs and therefore allows us to say something about possible impacts on underdeveloped countries and the concepts of equity and futurity. Tracking the life cycle of the product forward enables us to say much more about environmental damage than we can in a traditional assessment of processes. Again, it fundamentally places the concept of futurity within our overall measurement of performance.

The process of life-cycle assessment puts more emphasis on the role of design and re-design. It is often accepted that 80–90 per cent of the total life-cycle costs associated with a product are committed by the final design of the product before production or construction actually begins (Fabrycky and Blanchard, 1991, Gatenby and Foo, 1990). Similarly, waste resulting from the product creation, use and disposal are largely determined by original design. To date this has not been the central focus of the design phase; however, nor have designers commonly thought about futurity and equity implications of the products which they are developing. However, the LCA and auditing for sustainability approaches raise these issues and push them to the forefront of the design task. Traditional auditing methodologies perform no such function.

Life-cycle assessment is, however, to date, a very underdeveloped area in terms of research and the development of methodologies. For this reason it has not been taken up by that many organizations. It is useful at this stage to highlight one of the key problems with the LCA approach which has dogged its inception. The problem concerns how impractical LCA can be if it is unbounded. In a far-reaching life-cycle assessment absolutely everything connected with a particular product would have to be measured and all measurements and impacts would have to be assessed according to an unlimited time horizon. While this is perhaps desirable in measures associated with sustainability, it is none the less impossible. Unless bounds are placed on the assessment, the inventory of impacts grows exponentially. There is therefore a fundamental need to put boundaries in place and this will involve fundamental decisions to be made. Such decisions are not easy when our ultimate aim is measurement with respect to the environment, to equity and to futurity. This is therefore an area where we need some fundamental research and debate which would begin to define workable measures, data-bases of environmental impacts and a recognition of acceptable boundaries to measurement.

However, the barrier to such research and development is the very economy-environment nexus which we seem to have created for ourselves over the past few years. That framework is achievable, manageable and has the backing of an all-powerful industry. It is a nexus which fits well into present systems both at the company level as well as at the level of the economy. The fact that that comfortable nexus goes only a small way to achieving the fundamental need to audit for sustainability is the flaw in the approach. Such a piecemeal approach may satisfy the demands of the customers of some companies; it may well give companies a good feeling about some of the ethics involved in their activities. It does not go very far in achieving real sustainable development however.

THE NEED FOR A NEW IDEOLOGY

Significant evidence exists that management trends which become popular exert a strong influence on the on-going techniques of corporate management. New concepts which are successfully implemented in certain organizations become accepted, become dominant and, even when they are inappropriate, become the norm (Mintzberg, 1979). DiMaggio and Powell (1983) offer three explanations for this phenomenon. Firstly, organizations will submit to both formal and informal pressures from other organizations upon which they depend. Secondly, when faced with uncertainty organizations may model themselves on organizations that have seemed to be successful and adopt the sorts of techniques which they see being introduced. Thirdly, normative pressures which stem from a degree of professionalism among management can cause the adoption of 'fashionable' management techniques. Universities, training institutions, standard setters and professional associations are all vehicles for the development of these normative rules.

These are precisely the trends which we are seeing in the adoption of the quality driven approaches to environmental management. It has been argued that this approach is not entirely appropriate to the concept of sustainable development in that it does not go far enough. But this approach is becoming the accepted ideology because it is being adopted by leading firms, espoused by academics and legitimized through standard setters such as the BSI and the EU.

Moreover, this trend is further reinforced by so-called benchmarking analysis which is becoming increasingly common in industry. As a principle, benchmarking can be valuable, but it can also reinforce inappropriate general techniques. It has been argued that current standards are not high and that this in turn gives the impression to imitators in industry that the environmental challenge facing industry is actually quite weak. Actually the reverse is quite true and what is needed therefore is a change in the dominant ideology.

Such a change in ideology is, of course, difficult to achieve because environmental management standards have been set largely by industry itself. They have been designed to be voluntary and not to conflict with the ideology associated with profit maximization in the short to medium term. Arguments such as the ones outlined above, suggesting that industry has not gone far enough, will therefore be treated with derision by industry and sidelined. The power which industry has in the current economic system is therefore a barrier to further development of the concepts of sustainable development. Thus the only way to bring about a change in this suboptimal dominant ideology is to challenge the very basis of that power. Without a fundamental revolution in the way we organize our society, such a challenge can only come about through a legislative process.

THE LEGISLATIVE FRAMEWORK

The premise taken here is that there is a need for tougher legislation which would include requirements on businesses to measure their environmental impacts widely defined. Moreover there is a need for national legislation which not only protects domestic economies but also those of developing countries. Such an approach represents a radical shift in the foundations of industrial policy and firms will, of course, complain that the real requirements for sustainable development will impose severe costs and competitive disadvantage on them. On the other hand a number of commentators tell us that improved environmental performance is also a source of competitive advantage (eg Welford and Gouldson, 1993, Stikker, 1992, Davis, 1991). Whatever the view about competitive advantage or disadvantage, businesses will not, however, disagree on the need to create the ubiquitous 'level playing-field'. The clear implication of this is that industry itself should have a vested interest and should be campaigning for a tougher legislative stance on the part of governments across the whole world. Such a campaign should be based on making sure that the whole of industry faces a common set of minimum standards. The problem associated with alternative voluntary approaches is that some firms can create a cost advantage for themselves simply by not adopting those voluntary codes, which further weakens adherence in the whole industry.

There is a need to develop a new set of environmental standards which take us beyond the piecemeal approach identified here. Part of those new standards should insist on the public disclosure of environmental information about the performance of businesses, verified by third parties. Compulsory environmental auditing and public reporting of audit results should be introduced in those industries identified as having particular negative environmental impacts. This will add to the information about the products and processes which are more environmentally responsible which is identified by Roberts (1992) as central to achieving sustainable development. Moreover, these new standards must be common across countries and mandatory and must be based on the three fundamental principles of sustainable development, not the environment in isolation.

There will be arguments which will suggest that such common standards may be achievable at the level of the individual member state, or even across the whole of the EC. There will be those who will argue that companies or even whole countries operating in the less developed world will simply escape these minimum standards. We must recognize though that such standards are fundamental to the continuance of life on the planet and as such are fundamentally superior to the interests of international trade. For companies and countries not willing to comply with environmental standards, protectionist measures are therefore justified.

CONCLUSIONS

This article is not suggesting that current environmental management practice is bad or that innovations such as the EU eco-management and auditing scheme and BS7750 are a waste of time. They do provide principles which all firms should work towards. The issue is whether they go far enough. The EU scheme is clearly superior to BS7750 because of its requirement for verification and reporting but it is still overtly management-system driven. The key concept of sustainable development requires a new approach to business and we have seen little evidence of a radical paradigm shift either in the eco-management and auditing or the BS7750 standards. Indeed it has been argued that current approaches are suboptimal and inappropriate but that they are still likely to be adopted widely because they will become part of a dominant ideology. A responsible and pro-active approach to the environment requires new and radical approaches to doing business. This will include the need for increasing not decreasing legislation which industry itself should be campaigning for in order to protect notions of competition and ensure a level playing-field.

Rethinking business strategy along the lines of sustainable development does require a change in corporate cultures and it therefore opens up new opportunities to reassess other aspects of business. Issues that need also to be addressed in line with environmental demands include worker participation, democracy in the workplace, the treatment of women and minority groups, animal testing, public accountability, and the impact on the Third World and indigenous populations. Indeed, these issues should not be seen as separate entities but as part of a new overall strategy to doing business ethically and holistically. Moreover, the very power which endorses a piecemeal approach to environmental improvement is the same power which continues to deny rights to workers and to the less developed countries. Many of these issues will necessarily challenge the very foundations of the system which we too often see as immovable and will therefore be opposed by vested interests. Nevertheless, such ideas are achievable and indeed fundamental to the very existence of the planet on which we live.

REFERENCES

Commoner, B (1990) 'Can capitalists be environmentalists?' *Business and Society Review*, no 75, pp 31–35

Davis, J (1991) *Greening Business*, Blackwell, Oxford

DiMaggio, P J and Powell, W (1983) 'The Iron Cage Revisited: Institutional Isomorphism and Collective Rationale in Organizational Fields', *American Sociological Review*, no 48, pp 147–160

Fabrycky, W J and Blanchard, B S (1991) *Life cycle cost and economic analysis*, Prentice Hall, New York

Gatenby, D A and Foo, G (1990) 'Design for X: The key to competitive, profitable markets', *AT&T*, Technical Journal, vol 69, no 2, pp 2–11

Mintzberg, H (1979) *The Structuring of Organizations*, Prentice Hall, New York

Peattie, K (1992) *Green Marketing*, M&E Handbooks, London

Roberts, P (1992) 'Business and the Environment: An Initial Review of the Literature', *Business Strategy and the Environment*, vol 1, no 2, pp 41–51

Stikker, A , (1992) 'Sustainability and Business Management' *Business Strategy and the Environment*, vol 1, no 3, pp 1–8

Welford, R J (1992) 'Linking Quality and the Environment' *Business Strategy and the Environment*, vol 1, no 1, pp 25–35

Welford, R J and Gouldson, A P (1993) *Environmental Management and Business Strategy* Pitman Publishing, London

Wheeler, D (1994) 'Auditing for Sustainability: Philosophy and Practice of The Body Shop International' in *Environmental, Health and Safety Auditing Handbook*, McGraw-Hill, Mass

World Commission on Environment and Development (1987) *Our Common Future*, Oxford University Press, Oxford

Part V

Business and the Economy

Introduction

Richard Starkey

The final part of this Reader looks at the interactions of business with other actors in the wider economy. The relationship between business and government is of fundamental importance to the issue of environmental protection and the three articles chosen here look specifically at business interactions with three levels of government: local, national and the European Union.

Jim Skea and Tony Ikwue, in their paper entitled 'Business and the Genesis of the European Community Carbon Tax Proposal' (Chapter 15) look at the role of business in the policy process surrounding the EU's formulation of its proposal for a carbon/energy tax. They point out that the EU is keen to extend the range of policy instruments away from pure command-and-control mechanisms and advocates a shared responsibility between governments and industry in reducing environmental impacts and greater industry involvement in the regulatory process. However, the story of the carbon/energy tax, they suggest, appears to confound all these trends. (When the formal tax proposal appeared in May 1992 the business reaction was, in the authors' words, 'a concerted attempt to kill the tax idea'.) The article discusses whether business actions around the tax illustrate 'a fundamental objection to new models of policy-making and implementation, or whether they point the way towards a richer and more complex view of regulatory instruments and processes'.

Although business adopted a 'highly negative approach' to the proposed measures the new business desire to demonstrate a pro-active approach to environmental policy making was evident. There was very little attempt to exploit ambiguities in scientific evidence surrounding global warming and deny that there was a problem. Business broadly accepted EU policy goals and proposed alternative measures which might be adopted including the setting of voluntary sectoral agreements. Business is increasingly advocating the use of voluntary agreements as its preferred method of achieving environmental improvements and there is likely to be an extensive debate between business, the EU, national governments and NGOs over the next few years about the most suitable policy instrument(s) for environmental protection.

In his article 'Green Jobs? The Employment Implications of Environmental Policy' (Chapter 16), Michael Jacobs looks at the employment implications for business of government policy (both national and EU). He analyses the employment effects of three principal types of government environmental policy:

regulatory measures (legal standards, financial incentives etc), environmental public spending and 'eco-tax' reform (a shift in taxation away from labour, VAT and/or income towards energy, resources, waste and pollution) and concludes that economic development and environmental protection are not the mutually antagonistic goals that in the past they were considered to be. His article shows that environmental policies do not, in general, destroy jobs.

> *On the contrary, many environmental measures are likely to be job-creating. Even more importantly, it shows that environmental improvement is likely to become an essential part of economic development over the next twenty years, to the extent that failure to enact environmental protection measures may lead to worse economic performance, and therefore ultimately fewer jobs.*

In Chapter 17, Roger Levett examines the relationship between business and local government in his article 'Business, the Environment and Local Government' (Chapter 17). In the first part of the article he describes what local authorities are doing to make the local economy more sustainable and shows that there is a great deal of innovative and creative work being done at the local level that brings real benefits for both business and the environment. However, in the second part he argues that considerable limits are placed on the ability of both local government and business to take on the sustainable development agenda by central government policy. Looking at business, Levett argues that 'the pro-environmental actions of companies are directed towards exactly the same end as their anti-environmental ones: commercial security and success'. The trouble is that commercial viability does not dovetail with environmental protection on nearly enough occasions. As he points out:

> *All the frustrations and limitations discussed point to one simple message. There is no substitute for active management of the economy by government to make sustainable behaviour commercially viable. Many of the local actions described should be seen as pathfinders for central government action rather than alibis for central government inaction.*

Business must not be expected to take sole responsibility for sustainable development. Governments have a vital role to play in devising a legal and economic framework that allows business to co-operate in implementing the sustainable development agenda, an agenda necessary to successfully carry us forward to the 21st century.

15

Business and the Genesis of the European Community Carbon Tax Proposal

Dr Anthony Ikwue and Jim Skea

INTRODUCTION

The Commission of the European Community's proposal for a combined carbon/energy tax ranks as one of the most controversial in the history of Community environmental policy. The tax concept is simple in essence. Taxing fuels according to their carbon content will, in principle, lead to the selection of a cost-effective set of abatement measures through the operations of the market. A non-coercive measure such as a tax leaves decisions about which pollution-abatement measures to undertake in the hands of business and individuals. The tax will favour the selection of less carbon-intensive fuels and technologies. Where no alternative fuels or production technologies exist, costs will rise and demand for such products will decline in relative terms.

The Community's carbon tax proposal was made against a complex background. The respective roles of Community institutions on the one hand and the Member States on the other were being vigorously contested as part of a wider debate on 'subsidiarity'. A round of negotiations on 'fiscal harmonization' which formed part of the Single European Market process was just concluding. The Community was also in the middle of a recession and there were widespread concerns that high costs in traditional industries were making them uncompetitive. The proposal proved notoriously unpopular, especially with the business sector. In an attempt to accommodate concerns, it became ever more complex.

The process which began in 1990 is ironical in several respects:

- A non-command and control instrument which was intended to leave maximum discretion with business will be implemented only if the views of business are over-ridden.
- Rather than 'shared responsibility' between public authorities and private enterprise as espoused in the Community's recent programme of action and policy towards the environment (CEC, 1993a), the tax proposal has resulted in a confrontational process of a very traditional kind.

The central purpose of this paper is to examine the role of business in the regulatory process associated with the carbon tax proposal. First however it is necessary to describe the wider context. After identifying the key features of Community environmental policy, the first part of the paper examines climate change policy which was the prime motivation for the tax proposal, the evolution of the draft proposal from 1990 onwards and the key features of the formal proposal presented to the Council of Ministers in June 1992.

The second part of the paper addresses the specific role which business played in influencing the development of the carbon tax proposal. The paper identifies the potential impacts of the tax on business, the implications for corporate strategies and the specific channels of business influence. The final part of the paper assesses what the carbon/energy tax case study tells us about: the business position in relation to large scale environmental problems such as climate change; business responses to economic instruments such as the carbon/energy tax; and the wider relationship between public authorities and business in regulatory processes. The question of whether this relationship has entered a new phase or whether there is still 'business as usual' is addressed. The paper concludes with a brief assessment of the prospects for the carbon/energy tax proposal, or a variant of it, ever being put in place by the European Community.

EUROPEAN COMMUNITY CLIMATE CHANGE POLICY

Environmental Policy

Community environmental policy now has a long history (Haigh, 1993). The original Treaty of Rome which established the European Community made no mention of the environment. Nevertheless, an explicit environmental policy has been pursued since 1973 using general powers relating to 'the establishment and functioning of the common market'. The 1987 Single European Act provided a firm legal basis for environmental policy (Haigh and Baldock, 1989), while the Maastricht Treaty changed decision-making procedures, reducing the political hurdles to the introduction of new environmental measures. Environmental measures must be proposed by the European Commission. Most can now be agreed on the basis of a qualified majority vote in the Council of Ministers. The European Parliament, which has generally adopted a positive position on environmental matters, has been granted powers of 'co-decision'.

The debate about the Maastricht Treaty has highlighted the question of 'subsidiarity' and the appropriate level of decision-making in environmental and other matters. In several areas, Member States guard their sovereignty jealously. Reflecting this, there are three types of environmental measure which, under the Maastricht Treaty, must be agreed unanimously by the Council of Ministers and for which Parliament does not enjoy powers of co-decision:

- Provisions primarily of a fiscal nature;
- Measures concerning town and country planning, land use and management of water resources; and
- Measures significantly affecting a Member State's choice between different energy sources and the general structure of its energy supply.

The tax measure would therefore have to be agreed unanimously by the Member States. It impinges on two policy domains – taxation and energy – which have been of the greatest sensitivity during the debate on the respective role of the Community and its Member States.

The European Community has agreed a new approach to environmental policy-making as part of its Fifth Environmental Action Programme (CEC, 1993a). The new programme places greater emphasis on involvement and 'creat(ing) a new interplay between the main groups of actors (government, enterprise, public) and the principal economic sectors'. Past environmental action has largely been based on traditional 'command-and-control' instruments exercised by government over manufacturing industry. There is an aspiration to use a wider range of instruments, notably market-related incentives. The proposed carbon/energy tax fits in with the Commission's aspiration to move away from traditional instruments, but the process by which the tax has been developed demonstrates little 'involvement' or creative interplay between the key economic actors.

Climate Policy Objectives

Community interest in climate change began in 1988–89, coinciding with hot summers and a strong performance by Green Parties in the European elections. In 1988, the Commission took stock of the scientific state-of-the-art regarding climate change and reviewed wider global diplomatic activity (CEC, 1988). A formal programme of policy studies began in 1989. At this stage, the Community was well behind some of its Member States which had already published detailed policy papers on the climate issue (Enquete Kommission, 1988; Netherlands Second Chamber of the States General, 1989).

By 1990, the intention of signing a Framework Convention on Climate Change (FCCC) at the UN Conference on Environment and Development (UNCED) in June 1992 had emerged. Prompted by its more environmentally ambitious Member States, the Community determined to take a pro-active role in treaty negotiations. Recognizing the close linkages between climate change and energy policy, an unprecedented joint Council of Environment and Energy Ministers took place in October 1990.

This meeting agreed a Community-wide target of stabilizing carbon dioxide (CO_2) emissions at their 1990 levels by the year 2000. However, there was no agreement regarding either the means for achieving this target, or the distribution of the target round individual Member States. There was an acknowledgement that emissions from some Member States at a lower level of economic development (Greece, Spain, Ireland, Portugal) would inevitably increase. However, it was hoped that this would be compensated by more ambitious emission reduction targets set in countries such as Belgium, Germany, Denmark, and the Netherlands.

Developing a Strategy

In the absence of any guidance from the Council of Ministers, the Commission was given the task of devising a strategy for achieving the stabilization objective. The production of a formal strategy proposal took until May 1992, a matter of days before UNCED. The document had to be agreed collectively by the European Commission. However, the interests of the individual Directorates-General (DGs) for which individual Commissioners are responsible diverged. Internal Commission discussions were led by DGXI (Environment) which had an obvious interest in promoting a vigorous Community policy and securing a viable Community negotiating position in wider international discussions. DGXI initiated the carbon tax concept. However, the issue was also of great concern to DGXVII (Energy), DGII (Economic and Financial Affairs) and DGXXI (Customs Union and Indirect Taxation).

The internal Commission process between October 1990 and October 1991 was dominated by energy sector concerns, though the debate about competitiveness was beginning to open up. The climate change issue presented both threats and opportunities to the Energy Directorate. Since the decline in oil prices in 1986, strategic energy objectives had slipped down the Community's political agenda and DGXVII had tried, and failed, to get a specific energy chapter included in the Maastricht Treaty. Climate change offered a chance to revitalize progress towards the Community's energy efficiency objectives (CEC, 1986). On the other hand, the continuing rise in environmental concerns was pushing security of energy supply, DGXVII's distinctive policy theme, off the political agenda.

During 1991, the objective embodied in the title of the strategy document changed from 'to limit Community carbon dioxide emissions and to improve the security of energy supply' to 'to limit carbon dioxide emissions and to improve energy efficiency'. This reflects the waning of the energy security issue and, more specifically, the determination that the Community's climate policy would not become a vehicle for boosting the economic prospects of nuclear power. Nuclear policy was essentially a no-go area for the Commission given the deep and strong differences between Member States.

The initial work resulted in a Communication from the Commission to the Council in October 1991 (CEC, 1991). Apart from energy sector concerns, there was little business input to this document. Specific elements of the proposed climate strategy were put forward very tentatively. The discussion of 'a new fiscal initiative' in particular was couched almost entirely in terms of general principles. At meetings of the Economics and Finance Council and the Environment Council in December 1991, the Commission was encouraged to develop its strategy further.

At this stage, two other Directorates were drawn more deeply into the process. The Economic and Financial Affairs Directorate (DGII) was concerned with the macro-economic effects of the tax and its impact on the competitiveness of the Community. DGII's macro-economic analysis of the tax was published just as the formal policy proposals appeared in May 1992 (CEC, 1992c).

At the same time, lead responsibility passed to DGXXI (Customs Union and Indirect Taxation). Previously, this DG's attention had been focused on harmonizing value added tax (VAT) and excise duties, notably those on various types of fuel, under the Single Market initiative. For DGXXI, the proposed carbon/energy tax was an unwelcome addition to an already full and complex agenda. Integrating a carbon/energy tax into its broader remit was difficult in both technical and political terms, as the initial proposal for the Community to raise tax revenue itself broke with all precedent. Although the European Commission collectively backs the tax proposal, taxation Commissioner Christine Scrivener has been scrupulously lukewarm in discussing the proposal, emphasizing the importance of first 'exhausting' other non-fiscal measures (Forum Europe, 1992). It is ironic that DGXXI has had to take the lead in promoting the carbon tax proposal.

The Policy Framework

The basic elements of the Commission's strategy presented to the Council of Ministers in May 1992 were:

- A monitoring mechanism for CO_2 and other greenhouse gas emissions (CEC, 1993b).
- A set of 'conventional' measures relating to the promotion of energy efficiency (the SAVE programme, CEC, 1993d) and renewable energy sources (the ALTENER programme, CEC, 1993c).
- A fiscal measure, the carbon/energy tax (CEC, 1992b); and
- The use of 'cohesion' funds which could be used to stimulate development in economically less-favoured regions of the Community which could be adversely affected by the tax proposal.

Of the four draft measures proposed in 1992, only the carbon/energy tax proposal remains to be agreed. However, the SAVE and ALTENER programmes are considerably weaker than those proposed by the Commission and rely much more on the discretion of individual Member States.

The Carbon Tax Proposal

The idea of a carbon/energy tax is simple in principle, but it was a remarkably complex proposal which emerged in June 1992. The tax marks the point of convergence of several different strands of thought:

- The idea espoused by green groups and academics that energy prices ought to reflect external environmental costs.
- The observation in some countries that energy consumption and environmental emissions represented a new and possibly more reliable base for raising tax revenue.
- A study conducted by the Energy Directorate of the Commission in early 1990 (CEC, 1990) which showed that conventional measures would not, by themselves, be sufficient to secure a stabilization of Community CO_2 emissions. A substantial increase in energy prices would also be required.

These factors helped to determine that the Community's strategy included a fiscal instrument. Environmental issues enjoyed a high political profile at the time and a measure as innovative as a carbon tax appeared attractive. The choice of a tax level of $10 per barrel of oil equivalent appears arbitrary, and the best justification which has been obtained is that '$5 was too soft, $20 was too hard' (the 'Goldilocks' principle).

The other arbitrary factor is the division of the tax into its carbon and energy components. The Environment Directorate initially proposed a pure carbon tax. However, there was concern about the impacts of such a tax on vulnerable markets for coal and lignite. From the point of view of the Energy Directorate, these sources contribute to the security of energy supply in the Community. Equally, an energy tax could help to revitalize the Community's flagging efforts on energy efficiency. The Commission finally approved a proposal for an energy component which 'should not exceed 50 per cent' in October 1991. The formal proposal in May 1992 was for a 50/50 carbon/energy tax.

The ultimate choice is explained by differences between Member States as well by debates within the Commission. A pure carbon tax can be supported on economic efficiency grounds and is favoured by Member States such as France, which has a high nuclear component in its energy mix. Some other Member States, such as Spain, which makes high use of solid fuels, favour a pure energy tax.

The ultimate shape of the proposal was dictated by three sets of forces:

- The need to reconcile the basic concept with existing taxation practice.
- The need to take account of the very substantial industrial opposition to the tax by devising 'neutralizing clauses' which would serve to weaken criticisms.
- The need to take account of opposition from individual Member States for which the tax was uncomfortable domestically or which felt that their sovereignty in tax issues was threatened (the subsidiarity principle).

As a result, the following underlying principles were established:

- The tax would be levied analogously, but in addition to, existing excise duties on energy products.
- The tax would to be collected by the Member States.
- Introduction of the tax would be conditional on main competitors within the OECD introducing a similar tax or measures having a similar financial effect.
- The tax would be phased in gradually to avoid economic dislocation.
- The overall package should be revenue neutral; other direct or indirect taxes should be reduced or tax incentives for CO_2 reducing measures should be introduced.
- Energy used as feedstocks and renewable energy sources would be exempt.

The tax would be introduced at a rate equivalent to $3 per barrel (October 1991 money) and would be raised by an amount equivalent to $1 per barrel in each of the seven following years. 50 per cent of the total initial tax of 17.70 ECUs per tonne of oil equivalent would be based on CO_2 emissions, while the other half would be based on calorific value.

The energy component of the tax would not be levied on the heat inputs to electricity generation. Electricity output would be taxed instead. This proposed arrangement arises from the 'destination principle' which underlies Community tax policy. Tax revenue should accrue in the country in which the consumption, rather than the production, of electricity takes place. However, the fact that this arrangement would reduce incentives to improve the efficiency of electricity generation has caused some concern.

The possible impact of the tax on international competitiveness was, and still is, the focus of considerable lobbying efforts by energy-intensive industrial sectors. As well as the basic conditionality principle, other safety-nets for energy-intensive industry are built into the draft directive:

- If specific firms were to be disadvantaged by an increase in imports from non-OECD countries, they could be granted graduated exemptions from the tax as shown in Table 15.1. These exemptions would be banded in relation to the firm's energy cost/value added ratio.
- Firms which are very dependent on external trade could receive a full exemption as long as they could demonstrate substantial efforts to save energy or reduce carbon dioxide emissions.
- Member States would also be required to allow companies to set a proportion of investment in energy saving/CO_2 reductions against the carbon/energy tax.

Table 15.1 *Graduated Tax Exemptions for Disadvantaged Firms*

Energy cost/value added ratio band	Per cent tax reduction
8–12%	25%
12–17%	50%
17–30%	75%
>30%	90%

Source: Commission of the European Communities

Positions of the member states

National positions with respect to the tax are highly correlated with the ambitiousness of national emission targets. Table 15.2 shows that the six countries which favour the introduction of the tax – Germany, Denmark, Belgium, the Netherlands, Italy and Luxembourg – have the most ambitious CO_2 emissions reduction targets. France aims to stabilize per capita CO_2 emissions at two tonnes of carbon equivalent per head by the year 2000. It would prefer to see a pure carbon tax, without the energy element, reflecting its major investment in nuclear power. The UK is prepared to *return* its CO_2 emissions to 1990 levels by 2000, but will not promise a stabilization beyond that date (UK Department of the Environment, 1994). The UK expects uncontrolled CO_2 emissions to rise rapidly beyond the year 2000 (UK Department of Trade and Industry, 1992). VAT was extended to household heating fuels in the UK's March 1993 Budget and the Government's current position is that further tax increases on energy products are not necessary. The application of VAT to household gas and electricity, and the consequent impact on lower income households, has met with considerable opposition, and the UK Government would now find it politically difficult to apply the carbon/energy tax as currently proposed.

The rapidly growing economies – Greece, Portugal, Ireland and Spain – anticipate significant rises in CO_2 emissions during the 1990s. Spain, the largest

Table 15.2 *Projected Community CO_2 Achievements*

CO_2 (mt/year)	Target	Dates	1990	2000	Position on tax
Germany (W)	–25%	1987–2005	709	674	Pro–tax
Denmark	–20%	1988–2005	51	48	Pro–tax
Belgium	–5%	1990–2000	112	106	Pro–tax
Netherlands	–3–5%	1990–2000	182	177	Pro–tax
Italy	Stabilize	1990–2000	400	400	Pro–tax
Luxembourg	Stabilize	1990–2000	13	13	Pro–tax
UK	Return	1990–2000	587	587	Opposed to tax
France	2tC/head	2000	366	425	Pro carbon tax
Greece	+25%	1990–2000	74	92	Seeking exemptions
Portugal	+29–39%	1990–2000	40	55	Seeking exemptions
Ireland	+20%	1990–2000	31	37	Seeking exemptions
Spain	+25%	1990–2000	211	263	Prefers energy tax
EC	Stabilize	1990–2000	2775	2878	

Source: Commission of the European Communities

of these countries, is opposed to the concept of a carbon/energy tax. Coal and lignite play a significant role in the country's energy balance and the consumption of solid fuels is expected to increase. It would therefore prefer a pure energy tax. These countries have recently been offered exemptions in an attempt to bring them behind the tax proposal (Environmental Data Services, 1993).

THE ROLE OF BUSINESS IN INFLUENCING THE DEVELOPMENT OF THE CARBON TAX PROPOSAL

Potential Impacts on Business

All economic analyses of the $10/barrel carbon/energy tax have shown that the aggregate effects would be small, as long as the tax is phased in gradually and the principle of revenue-neutrality is observed. On average, direct energy costs make up only 2 per cent of industrial production costs. However, there are individual sectors which would be significantly affected. These are:

- The energy industries.
- 'High-impact' industries, such as iron and steel, cement, glass and clay products, for which energy makes up 10–20 per cent of costs.
- 'Moderate-impact' industries such as chemicals, paper and ceramics, where energy accounts for 5–10 per cent of costs.

These broad groupings disguise considerable variations, both within sectors and across Member States. Some specific sub-sectors of the chemicals industry have very high costs. Broadly speaking, energy costs are relatively more important in the southern Member States (Spain, Portugal) than they are in the north (Britain,

Germany). Some industries would be affected by the tax indirectly, through rises in the cost of transport and the price of intermediate goods.

Table 15.3 shows the full first-round impact of the proposed tax on the prices of fuels used by industry and the power sector in the UK. For manufacturing industry, the tax would raise the price of premium fuels (distillate oil, gas sold on 'firm' contracts) by around 30 per cent and electricity by around 20 per cent. However, the price of bulk fuels (coal, residual fuel oil, interruptible gas) would rise by 50-80 per cent. Apart from the effects on manufacturing costs, these price changes would significantly affect the relative competitiveness of individual fuels. Coal markets, already threatened by competition from gas and the likely withdrawal of subsidies, would be particularly threatened. The introduction of a tax could also force oil refiners to re-consider their strategies for marketing residual fuel oil, particularly if tighter sulphur controls were developed in parallel.

Table 15.3 *Price Impacts of Full $10 per Barrel Carbon Tax*
(All prices pence/gigajoule)

Fuel	UK base price	Final price	Increase
Power industry			
Domestic coal	174	295	69%
Imported coal	119	240	101%
Gas	194	283	46%
Manufacturing			
Firm gas	258	347	34%
Gas oil	320	425	33%
Interruptible gas	163	252	55%
Fuel oil	155	264	70%
Coal	158	279	77%
Electricity (pence/kWh)	4.11	4.97	21%

Source: SPRU

However, the rise in energy costs is only one of the factors which would influence the overall economic impact of the proposed tax on specific sectors. The composition of final demand would be affected by the way in which tax revenue is recycled, ie whether payroll taxes, income taxes or value added taxes are reduced. Changes in international competitiveness would obviously be affected by the nature of measures adopted to combat climate change outside the European Community.

Table 15.4 shows the projected impact of the tax on wholesale prices and production volumes in various sectors 12 years after the phased introduction of a tax. While there is a high correlation between those sectors with high energy costs and those most adversely affected by the tax, the exposure to international competition is also important. The projected impact on European manufacturers of office and electronic data equipment, for example, is quite high. On the other hand, the non-metallic minerals sector is somewhat protected due to limited international trade. There are some potential winners from the introduction of the tax, though the positive effects are small and diffuse. The service sector may benefit because the prices of services will fall relative to those of goods and because it is sheltered from international competition.

Table 15.4 *Sectoral Effects in the Community of a Policy Package to Reduce CO_2 Emissions*

Per cent change from baseline	Producer wholesale price	Production volume
Agriculture	3.4	−1.1
Energy	8.1	−7.0
Ores and metals	5.7	−4.5
Non–metallic minerals	4.2	−1.1
Chemicals	8.6	−3.2
Metal products	3.2	−0.8
Mechanical engineering	3.3	−0.6
Office and electronic data processing	2.3	−3.0
Electrical engineering	2.8	−0.6
Transport equipment	3.3	−1.5
Food, drinks and tobacco	3.8	−0.8
Textiles and clothing	2.9	−0.5
Pulp, paper and printing	3.3	−1.2
Miscellaneous products	2.3	−1.1
Rubber and plastics	5.0	−1.5
Construction	3.3	0.1
Transport services	3.5	−0.1
Retail, tourism and finance	3.2	−0.5
Communication services	2.4	−0.7
Government services	2.8	0.0

Source: Commission of the European Communities

The business response to the proposal

The business sector response to the tax has been hostile. The intensity of the anti-tax campaign has surprised some national governments and parts of the Commission. Predictably, activity has been particularly strong in those sectors where energy costs form a high proportion of production costs and competitive considerations are important. There are various possible classes of response to the current policy initiatives on climate change:

1. To argue that conclusive evidence for climate change does not exist and that any action is unwarranted.
2. To adopt a neutral position on the scientific evidence for climate change and to propose the use of a 'no-regrets' strategy.
3. To support the Community's target of CO_2 stabilization but to oppose the mix of measures chosen, in particular the proposed carbon tax.
4. To emphasize the risks of climate change and to support fiscal measures such as the carbon/energy tax.

The coal industry in Europe has generally taken the first position, while the nuclear industry has supported the idea of fiscal measures. These positions are predictable. More interestingly, against a background of increased corporate sensitivity to environmental issues, manufacturing industry has tended to fall somewhere between the second and third positions. These positions have been reflected in the positions taken by individual companies, national trade associations and Community trade associations.

The Position of Business

Business reactions to the tax are essentially a 'gut response'. Not much credence is given either to the economic analyses which were used to justify the tax or to those carried out by independent analysts. In addition to the uncertainties inherent in economic models, there remains considerable debate and uncertainty over detailed aspects of the tax, such as the point of application (upstream or downstream in the energy sector), the treatment of electricity and the operation of industry- or country-specific exemptions.

The Need for a Tax

Many in industry are sceptical of claims that the world is on the brink of a catastrophic increase in global temperatures. However, given the possible consequences of global warming, it is accepted that governments would be prudent to adopt a precautionary approach. The preference is for measures taken on a no-regrets basis, ie measures should make economic sense even if the fear of global warming should prove unfounded.

Industry has pointed out that energy intensity and energy inefficiency are not synonymous. The motivation should be to increase efficiency rather than to force cuts in domestic output, as might be the case for processes already close to the theoretical limits for energy efficiency. In any case, it is argued that, in industries where energy accounts for a large proportion of costs, there is already a sufficient incentive to look for savings. A tax would reduce profitability and hence the ability of companies to invest in energy efficiency measures.

Conventional Energy-Efficiency Measures

Following on from the point above, business is not convinced that enough is being done to promote the adoption of beneficial energy-efficiency measures by companies. They point out that there is still a large untapped potential for energy conservation projects with short to medium paybacks at current energy prices. Governments are accused of not doing enough to reduce non-market barriers to energy efficiency. The watering down of the Community's conventional energy efficiency (SAVE) and renewable energy (ALTENER) programmes is used to reinforce this point.

Some industrial sectors are offering to introduce voluntary measures to reduce CO_2. They consider a combination of appropriate government action (educational campaigns, tax incentives for energy-efficiency investments etc) coupled with private sector initiatives to be the way forward. Several companies also note that, as the greenhouse effect is a global problem, it may be more efficient and cost-effective to concentrate energy-efficiency efforts in developing countries. Dollar for dollar, measures taken in these regions are likely to be far more effective than is the case in Europe.

Several long-term agreements on energy efficiency have been reached by industry and the Ministry of Economic Affairs in the Netherlands (Netherlands Ministry of Economic Affairs, 1992). While Dutch industrial practices might be difficult to replicate elsewhere, there is considerable interest in other parts of the Community. However, it is notable that the Dutch Government supports the use of carbon/energy tax in addition to these agreements.

Economic Efficiency

Many companies argue that a pure carbon tax would be preferable on economic efficiency grounds. However, it is pointed out by others that the economic efficiency argument is weakened by existing anomalies caused by taxes and subsidies in energy markets. Without reform, these distortions will reduce the efficacy of price signals. As an example, uniform application of the proposed carbon/energy tax will increase the price of fuels such as gasoline and diesel by only 5–10 per cent compared to 40–60 per cent for coal. This is seen as perverse given the large contribution of transport to Community CO_2 emissions.

Fiscal Neutrality

The Community has no competence to raise taxes, although it can address the compatibility of fiscal policies in the Member States. Industry believes that Member States would decide if and how reductions in the overall tax burden would be made. It judges that governments are unlikely to forgo the opportunity to utilize this additional revenue for budgetary purposes. They therefore consider it unlikely that the tax will be revenue neutral in all countries, leading to distortions in competitiveness. The degree of distortion to intra-Community trade could be made even more severe if there were temporary exemptions for the less developed Member States, as is currently proposed.

Conditionality

Although the proposed directive is conditional on similar moves in other OECD countries, it is not clear whether some or all OECD members need to take action. There are ambiguities relating to the precise meaning of 'equivalent measures'. In any case, companies point out, much competition comes from areas outside the OECD, eg the Middle East, Eastern Europe and East Asia. A tax would lead to a competitive advantage for companies operating in these regions. This could lead to increased production in these regions and, for some products, an *increase* in global CO_2 emissions, defeating the object of the tax.

The Business Strategy

There was remarkably little business input to the debate about the carbon/energy tax until the proposal was quite well developed. During the early stages, those sectors which were primarily concerned (mainly energy) focused on the wider issues surrounding the CO_2 debate. The view at this stage appeared to be that, since the Community produced only a small proportion of global CO_2, drastic action was unlikely, especially at a time of economic recession. There was a general belief that the tax idea was the brainchild of the Commission's 'environmentalists'. It was too innovative and the barriers to its adoption by the Commission as a whole were too great. The anticipated barriers included: the divergence in interest between different parts of the Commission; differences in the energy structure of the Member States; and the north/south divide within the Community. To the extent that the tax idea became a formal proposal, business intelligence about the Community's policy-making system appears to have failed.

When the proposed Community strategy was tabled in October 1991, there was genuine surprise. When the formal tax proposal appeared in May 1992, there was further surprise at how 'serious' it looked. The reaction was a concerted attempt to kill the tax idea. The channels of influence which the business sector used were varied. They included discussions with the administrations of national governments which were potentially hostile to the tax, discussions with sympathetic Directorates within the Commission – DGXVII (Energy) and DGIII (Industry) for sectors such as chemicals – and less official representations from high-level company officers to politicians.

Industry's position on the tax proposal has been greatly influenced by larger companies operating in the energy-intensive sectors. This is no surprise given their resources and their facility at managing public affairs. The lead was taken by European-level industrial associations – for example, EurElectric, EuroPIA (petroleum refiners), CEFIC (chemicals), EuroMetaux, IFIEC (industrial energy consumers) – and Brussels-based company officers who could exploit their contacts within the Commission. This stage of lobbying was emotionally highly charged.

International and national federations of industry – UNICE (European employers' federation), BDI (Federation of German Industry), CBI (Confederation of British Industry), ICC (International Chamber of Commerce) – joined the criticisms of the tax, though the positions of these more broadly based organizations were more measured. Many of these associations had to reconcile differences of opinion between a wide range of interest groups within their membership. This reduced their effectiveness as they struggled to develop a common position.

The position of business has been strengthened however by the fact that there is no strong pro-tax lobby. Environmental groups have backed away from the carbon tax debate, conscious of the unpopularity of tax measures and the uneven impact of the tax on different social groups. Industrial sectors and trade associations which, on the surface, would appear to be winners from the tax have not lent any support. Manufacturers of insulation products, for example, believe that more targeted regulatory measures or financial assistance schemes would better promote their activities (Grubb, 1992). Such companies are often members of larger industrial groupings which, in aggregate, would be adversely affected by the tax.

Following the formal proposal of the tax measure in May 1992, tactics switched away from broadly based criticisms towards detailed aspects of the proposal. Pro-active suggestions for alternatives to the tax – conventional command-and-control regulation and voluntary initiatives – were also made. At the same time, lobbying activity began to focus on national representatives and those at the highest level in the Commission.

Business Responses in the UK

Business response in the UK to the tax proposal provides a useful illustration of the national dimension to the tax debate. As in most Member States, the business response to the tax did not really take off until draft legislation was tabled in 1991. First off the mark were the energy-intensive industries. Internal analysis of the proposal and consultations with their trade associations had led them to the conclusion that it would be detrimental to their activities. They quickly made their feelings clear to sponsoring departments within government. Some success at this stage is evident as their submissions were used in Whitehall's initial analysis of the issue. This early industry/government dialogue was soon followed by a wider, more formal consultation on the CO_2 reduction issue by the Department of the Environment (DoE) and the Department of Trade and Industry (DTI).

The anti-tax lobby readily used an extensive set of networks which spans government and Community institutions and national and international trade associations. In the main, individual companies have kept a low profile, leaving the major public role to trade associations and broader-based industry groupings, such as the CBI and the Advisory Council on Business and the Environment (ACBE). Company influence within these bodies ensures that their views are adequately represented. Professional lobbyists were not employed to any great extent. Instead, companies have utilized their personal contacts with politicians and other influential individuals in the policy-making network. Great value has been placed on this type of contact, but it has been used sparingly, especially at the ministerial level. Representations are also made to other Member State governments via subsidiary companies and relevant national trade associations.

To the extent that the UK Government has come out firmly against the tax, business strategy in the UK has been successful. However, it is difficult to know the extent to which this was due to sympathy for industry's position or the tax's incompatibility with government policy in other areas (sovereignty over tax affairs).

ENVIRONMENTAL TAXATION AND GOVERNMENT-INDUSTRY RELATIONSHIPS

The current ambition within the European Community is for shared responsibility between governments and industry in reducing environmental impacts, greater industry involvement in the regulatory process and an extension of the range of policy instruments away from pure command-and-control mechanisms. The story of the carbon/energy tax appears to confound all of these trends. This section considers whether developments illustrate a fundamental objection to new models of policy-making and implementation, or whether they point the way towards a richer and more complex view of regulatory instruments and processes.

Industry and market instruments

Organizations such as the Business Council for Sustainable Development (BCSD) have endorsed, in *general* terms, the idea of making a greater use of market instruments (Schmidheiny, 1992). However, the case of the carbon tax shows that specific proposals for an economic instrument can encounter substantial opposition. This raises the question whether business has truly 'changed course' or whether it has simply developed a more sophisticated understanding of the way in which external pressures, particularly those of an environmental nature, influence its pursuit of traditional goals. The case of the carbon tax strongly suggests the latter hypothesis. In its discussion of energy and the market-place, BCSD notably avoids any endorsement of specific economic instruments such as the carbon tax, while urging 'a better mix of energy prices, stricter standards and better information' (Schmidheiny, 1992, p 53).

There are several market-based measures with which business is content. These may include tradable permits, pollution charges (as opposed to taxes) or externality adders used in heavily regulated industries such as power generation. These examples all serve the objective of reducing compliance costs which, from the business perspective, is the main virtue of market instruments (Stavins and Whitehead, 1992). Tradable permits, as long as transaction costs are not too high, move money round *within* industry. Externality adders change incentives for specific types of investment but do not reduce profitability. The revenue from earmarked pollution charges is generally recycled back into the industry in the form of financial support for environmental investments.

However, a measure such as the carbon/energy tax *increases* compliance costs for most sectors of industry because companies pay for residual emissions (which were previously free) as well as the costs of cleaning up. This revenue loss is the principal reason why industry will not support such a measure and why companies within the European Community have been asking for traditional command-and-control regulation as well as, predictably, financial support for clean investments. It is the very feature which makes environmental taxes theoretically attractive – the fact that demand for products which are more environmentally damaging will be reduced – which makes them unattractive to business.

Industry-Government Relationships

Although there are incentives on both sides for a more co-operative relationship between business and public authorities, the carbon/energy tax case-study shows that there are still conditions under which older, more antagonistic modes of operation are likely to apply:

- When policies are made under conditions of urgency and political pressures lead to a lack of consultation with interest groups. This is particularly likely to happen with large-scale, headline-grabbing issues like climate change or acid rain.
- When the economic consequences of policy are large and manifestly obvious to the stakeholders.
- When politicians have opted out of making decisions in a contentious field.

The carbon/energy tax proposal was left to officials of the European Commission who did not have the political legitimacy to carry through such an innovative and potentially divisive proposal by themselves.

- When public authorities are not clear themselves about their objectives. In the case of the carbon tax, this was perhaps inevitable because the tax lay at the boundaries of environmental, energy, industrial and fiscal policy. Early consultations were internal to the public administration, and failed to take into account the views of business and the public.
- When, in a federal mode of government such as that which effectively exists in the European Community, there are fundamental differences between the different levels, in this case the Community vis-à-vis its Member States. The possibility of blocking coalitions provides incentives for business to oppose the proposals actively.
- When the choice of policy instrument leads to the perception that there are large numbers of 'losers' – in this case business and consumers – while there are few identifiable winners.

Modes of Industrial Influence

The carbon/energy tax story makes it clear that there are still circumstances in which it will be in the interest of industry to adopt a highly negative approach to proposed environmental measures. In this case, political lobbying activity of the simplest and most traditional kind offered potential pay-offs which were well in excess of either the direct costs or any loss of public image. The central objective of this strategy was not to adapt to or anticipate the policy agenda – it was to modify it radically.

However, the new business desire to demonstrate a pro-active approach to environmental policy-making was evident. Very few firms or sectors attempted to use the strategy, employed extensively during the debate on acid rain, of exploiting ambiguities in scientific evidence and denying that there was an environmental problem. Instead, business broadly accepted Community policy goals and proposed alternative measures which the Community and national governments might adopt. As well as proposing the use of traditional command-and-control instruments, industry also proposed setting voluntary sectoral agreements. The latter instrument may accord with the Community's new strategy for shared responsibility, but the first does not.

Postscript

The original carbon/energy tax proposal was abandoned in late 1994. The UK and Spain had been strongly opposed, while Greece, Ireland and Portugal had been seeking concessions, such as a delayed introduction of the tax. With a unanimous decision required, the German Presidency of the Council of Ministers was unable to force agreement. German authority was weakened because it was the only state not to have set a specific CO_2 target for the year 2000 (CEC, 1994).

In March 1995, the Commission launched a new proposal, maintaining the same tax structure, but allowing Member States to introduce the tax at their own discretion and to decide the overall level of the tax. This allows the possibility of full harmonization at a future date. Nevertheless, it seems unlikely that this new measure will be agreed easily.

In spite of the huge obstacles which the proposal has faced, there is a remarkable sense of inevitability among industrial interest groups as well as Commission officials that some kind of fiscal measure will eventually be agreed to further climate policy. However, any measure which might be agreed would be substantially different from the current proposal. It is also unlikely that it would contribute to a stabilization of CO_2 emissions within the Community by the year 2000, a prospect which is, in any event, now looking increasingly remote (CEC, 1994).

REFERENCES

Commission of the European Communities (1986) 'Council Resolution concerning new Community energy policy objectives for 1995 and the convergence of the policies of the Member States', *Official Journal of the European Communities*, C241, CEC, Brussels

Commission of the European Communities (1988) *Communication to the Council: The Greenhouse Effect and the Community* COM(88), 656 final, CEC, Brussels

Commission of the European Communities (1990) 'Energy for a New Century: The European Perspective', *Energy in Europe*, July, Special Issue, CEC, Brussels

Commission of the European Communities (1991) *Communication to the Council: A Community Strategy to Limit Carbon Dioxide Emissions and to Improve Energy Efficiency*, SEC(91) 1744, CEC, Brussels

Commission of the European Communities (1992a) *Communication to the Council: A Community Strategy to Limit Carbon Dioxide Emissions and to Improve Energy Efficiency*, COM(92), 246 final, 1 June, CEC, Brussels

Commission of the European Communities, (1992b) *Proposal for a Council Directive introducing a tax on carbon dioxide emissions and energy*, COM(92), 226 final, 30 June, CEC, Brussels,

Commission of the European Communities (1992c) 'The Climate Challenge: Economic Aspects of the Community's Strategy for Limiting CO_2 Emissions', *European Economy*, no 51, May, CEC, Brussels

Commission of the European Communities (1993a) 'Resolution of the Council on a Community programme of policy and action in relation to the environment and sustainable development', *Official Journal of the European Communities*, 17 May, no C138, CEC, Brussels, (sometimes known as Towards Sustainability or the Fifth Environmental Action Programme)

Commission of the European Communities (1993b) 'Council Decision 93/389/EEC for a monitoring mechanism of Community CO2 and other greenhouse gas emissions', *Official Journal of the European Communities*, 9 July, no L 167, CEC, Brussels

Commission of the European Communities (1993c) 'Council Decision 93/500/EEC concerning the promotion of renewable energy sources in the Community (Altener Programme)', *Official Journal of the European Communities*, no L 235, 18 September, CEC, Brussels

Commission of the European Communities (1993d) 'Council Directive 93/76/EEC to limit carbon dioxide emissions by improving energy efficiency (SAVE)', *Official Journal of the European Communities*, no L 237, 22 September, CEC, Brussels

Commission of the European Communities (1994) *First evaluation of existing national programmes under the monitoring mechanism of Community CO$_2$ and other greenhouse gas emissions*, COM (94), 67 final, 10 March, CEC, Brussels,

Environmental Data Services (1993) 'EC still divided over carbon/energy tax', *The ENDS Report*, no 225, October, pp 35–36, London

Enquete Kommission, (1988) *Protecting the Earth's Atmosphere*, Bundestag: Bonn

Forum Europe, (1992) *Carbon Tax Survey*, Forum Europe, Brussels

Grubb, M (ed) (1992) *Climate Change in the European Community*, Royal Institute of International Affairs, London

Haigh, N (1993) *Manual of Environmental Policy: The EC and Britain*, Longman, London

Haigh, N and Baldock, D (1989) *Environmental Policy and 1992*, Institute for European Environmental Policy, London

Netherlands Ministry of Economic Affairs (1992) *Long-term Agreements on Energy Efficiency in Industry: The Approach of the Netherlands*, Netherlands Ministry of Economic Affairs, The Hague

Netherlands Second Chamber of the States General (1989) *National Environmental Policy Plan*, SDU, 's-Gravenhage

Schmidheiny, S (1992) *Changing Course: A Global Business Perspective on Development and the Environment*, MIT, Cambridge

Stavins, R N and Whitehead, B W (1992) 'Dealing with Pollution: Market-Based Incentives for Environmental Protection', *Environment*, vol 34, no 7, September, Heldref, Washington DC

UK Department of the Environment (1994) *Climate Change: The UK Programme*, Cm 2427, January HMSO, London

UK Department of Trade and Industry (1992) *Energy Related Carbon Emission in Future Scenarios for the UK*, Energy Paper no 59, HMSO, London

16

Green Jobs? The Employment Implications of Environmental Policy

Michael Jacobs

SUSTAINABLE DEVELOPMENT AND THE 'DOUBLE DIVIDEND'

Jobs Versus Environment?

In the past, economic development and environmental protection were considered mutually antagonistic goals. Promotion of one would inevitably mean damage to the other. In recent years the concept of 'sustainable development' has attempted to overcome this apparent conflict: it is now widely accepted that by integrating environmental concerns into economic policy, business and industrial activities can be 'greened'.

But how far this is possible remains open to much dispute. In particular, the relationship between environmental policy and employment has been a source of considerable concern. Do environmental policies not tend to destroy jobs? In an era of mass unemployment, the belief that they do will inevitably undermine support for environmental protection.

This report is an examination of the 'jobs versus environment' argument. It shows that environmental policies do not, in general, destroy jobs. On the contrary, many environmental measures are likely to be job-creating. Even more importantly, it shows that environmental improvement is likely to become an essential part of economic development over the next twenty years – to the extent that failure to enact environmental protection measures may lead to worse economic performance and, therefore, ultimately fewer jobs.

Sustainable Development and Economic Restructuring

It is important to understand the reason for this, because it throws light on the real meaning of 'sustainable development'. Sustainable development does not mean a static economy, a return to pre-industrial technology, or 'zero growth'. It means a restructuring of global and national economies in such a way as to gain increased economic well-being – including employment – while reducing the impact on the world's ecosystems and natural resources.

Structural change occurs anyway. This century alone has witnessed several profound shifts in the structure of national and international economies. The development of the internal combustion engine had a major effect on all forms of motive power, particularly in transport. Between the wars mass production of manufactured goods revolutionized their price and availability and the organization of the labour force. In the last thirty years the advanced economies have become 'post-industrial', as employment in the service sectors has displaced the previous dominance of manufacturing. Now the geographical focus of production is shifting to the Pacific Rim and possibly to Eastern Europe. In just the last two decades the microprocessor has transformed not just production processes but the patterns of everyday life. The electronic 'super-highway' promises further change still.

These processes of economic and social restructuring cannot be prevented, but their precise form is not inevitable. The claim of 'sustainable development' is that humankind can bend the direction of restructuring towards environmental efficiency. By appropriate intervention, the new investments in technologies and production systems and the new patterns of living to which they give rise can be steered towards a major reduction in environmental impact. Many of the required changes are already emerging – from energy-efficient and 'clean' technologies to greener consumer lifestyles. Sustainable development seeks to harness these movements so that they prevail more widely, influencing the shape and effect of economic and social change. This objective has sometimes been described as 'ecological restructuring'.

The Consequences for Employment

In this process, the nature and distribution of employment will inevitably alter – as it is already changing under the continuing influence of previous structural shifts. But there is no reason to suppose that raising environmental productivity will reduce the number of jobs available. On the contrary, the conclusion of this study is that a sustainable economy is likely to support higher employment than an unsustainable one. This is so for four reasons:

1. Environmental regulation tends to stimulate investment in environmental equipment and services, as firms are required to comply with higher standards. This investment creates jobs. Although there is also a negative impact on jobs from higher costs, almost all the available evidence suggests that the overall employment outcome is positive.
2. It is now clear that raising the efficiency with which the economy uses environmental resources – the objective of environmental-economic policy – is likely to be one of the keys to raising productivity and competitiveness in the economy in general. This is because environmental resources cost money; and as public pressure for protection mounts, the cost of damaging the environment will rise. Reducing environmental costs per unit of output - that is, raising environmental productivity – will then become a substantial component of raising productivity generally. Economies which do not do this will become less competitive in the global economy, and will lose jobs.
3. One of the major policy changes towards a sustainable economy is likely to

be a shift in the structure of taxation. At present nearly all countries impose heavy taxes on employment (in the UK, directly through employers' National Insurance contributions, and indirectly through income tax and VAT) while the use of energy and natural resources and the production of waste and pollution are hardly taxed at all. (In effect, given the damage they cause, they are subsidized.) Implementation of the so-called 'Eco-Tax Reform', in which the burden of taxation would gradually be reversed, would simultaneously create additional incentives to employment and disincentives to environmental damage. As this study shows, a substantial gain in employment can be expected.

4. The continuing need for work on environmental protection and enhancement offers considerable potential – subject to budgetary constraints – for job creation through public spending.

The Importance of Policy

These conclusions demonstrate that the relationship between economic growth, employment and the environment is much more complex than is generally believed. Both environmental damage and employment can be decoupled from growth. By raising environmental productivity, environmental impact can be reduced even while output rises. The level of employment, meanwhile, is affected by the *structure* of production at least as much as by its rate of growth. Maximum growth does not necessarily generate maximum employment. Most important of all, the evidence suggests that those patterns of production which generate environmental improvements tend also to be job creating. There need be no trade-off between jobs and the environment.

This is a heartening result, but it comes with two crucial caveats. First, none of this will happen by itself. There are tendencies in the global economy which will push towards environmental efficiency; but there are equally pressures in the opposite direction. Many environmental investments will be profitable, but only in time-scales which the free market, tending as it does to the short-term, will not support. The current structure of taxation and regulation inhibit many environmental investments. Research and development and innovation are frequently hindered by institutional factors. Positive environmental policy – carefully designed, as we discuss below – is therefore vital.

Second, the net effect of job creation should not disguise the fact that some job losses are likely to be experienced by particular firms, people and regions. In theory there need be no reason why gains and losses should not occur in the same sectors and occupations. In practice, however, many of the most sensitive sectors are 'older' manufacturing industries located in traditional industrial areas. By contrast many of the firms in environmental sectors are new, and are therefore located in newer industrial locations. For this reason there may well prove to be a geographic mismatch between job creation and potential loss. Such regional effects can generate both hardship and, consequently, political opposition. It is therefore very important that measures are taken to mitigate them.

The appropriate policy framework is therefore crucial. But if this can be put in place, this report shows that the 'double dividend' of environmental protection and job creation is achievable.

ANALYSIS OF THE EMPLOYMENT EFFECTS OF ENVIRONMENTAL POLICY

Types of Environmental Policy and Employment Effects

This report discusses three principal types of government environmental policy:

- *Regulatory measures.* This term covers nearly all of what is generally known as 'environmental policy': measures designed to reduce the environmental impact of firms and households, whether by law, financial incentive (so-called 'economic instruments') or encouragement.
- *'Green public spending'.* This goes both on infrastructure (eg transport, sewage treatment) and specific 'job creation' programmes in the environmental field.
- *'Eco-tax reform'.* A shift in taxation away from labour, VAT and savings (and possibly income) towards energy, resources, waste and pollution.

A fourth type of policy is also discussed:

- Financial and other support given by government to 'environmental' research and development.

In examining regulatory measures, we make an important distinction between two different kinds of effect. In the short term, firms can be expected to respond to environmental policies by installing 'add-on' technologies, such as pollution-control equipment. The effects on employment of such responses we call 'adjustment effects'. In the longer term, in some sectors, firms can be expected to introduce new, 'cleaner' production systems altogether. Such systems will have a different impact on employment: we call these 'adaptation effects'. Each of these types of effect is examined.

Regulatory Measures: Adjustment Effects

Over the relatively short term, regulatory measures aimed at protecting the environment have two principal effects. They increase the costs faced by the firms which have been regulated (what we call here the 'regulated sector'); and they create demand (in the 'environmental sector') for the environmental equipment and services which enable the regulated firms to comply with the new standards.

These two effects have contradictory implications for employment. Higher costs tend to reduce jobs in the regulated sector. Many of the claims made about the closure of factories, the relocation of firms to countries with lower standards and other job-destroying effects of environmental policies are exaggerated; but it remains true that employment in some sectors is sensitive to more stringent environmental policy.

On the other hand, such policy creates jobs in the environmental sector. This sector is now very large, with an estimated global market of more than $133bn, growing at a rate of 5 per cent. It is estimated that 116,000 people are employed in the UK (in Europe as a whole, 962,000) as a result of European environmental policy. Importantly, there appears to be a significant relationship between the stringency of a country's environmental standards and the strength of its environmental sector. Evidence from (among others) Germany, Japan, the USA and Sweden suggests that domestic regulation provides firms with a 'first mover advantage' in environmental industries, and therefore higher employment.

The net consequence for employment of these two contradictory effects is an empirical matter. A number of macroeconomic modelling studies have investigated this. Almost all of them suggest that the net impact on jobs is positive, though small. One recent simulation for the UK economy, however, suggests a more significant macroeconomic effect. A major environmental programme (including a carbon tax, water quality improvements and a fourfold rise in pollution expenditures) is projected to create an additional 682,000 jobs in a 15-year period.

Regulatory Measures: Adaptation Effects

In the longer term firms can be expected to adapt to regulatory measures by installing cleaner technologies and production systems. Because they save input and waste costs, these are likely to be more productive than those they replace, that is, a given unit of output will cost less to produce.

As clean systems replace 'add on' adjustment-effect technologies, employment in the environmental sector will tend to fall. The new systems will have to be manufactured and serviced, but if (as is likely) they are introduced at the time when new investments would anyway have been made, these jobs will not be additional. Indeed, in so far as clean systems replace add-on equipment, the environmental sector will tend to disappear: environmental activities will not be separate and identifiable, but will be incorporated into 'ordinary' spending and operations.

In the regulated sector, clean systems should raise productivity, and therefore tend to increase jobs. But if they also increase labour productivity, this effect may be cancelled out. In this sense clean systems may contribute to the phenomenon of 'jobless growth': it is a matter of dispute among economists as to whether labour displaced from one sector can always be reabsorbed elsewhere in the economy. It is possible that the global economy could experience a new economic upturn as part of a 'long wave' – perhaps built partly on environmental improvements. But this is speculative.

The key to securing jobs from clean technologies and production systems will be innovation. Environmental sector firms able to develop and supply the new systems will benefit – in foreign as well as domestic markets. Moreover, because such systems are more productive, regulated sector firms *installing* them will also gain. Since the evidence suggests that domestic regulation stimulates domestic innovation, environmental regulation may turn out to be an important source of national competitive advantage. By the same token, countries which do not raise environmental performance may lose out. It may become necessary to introduce environmental policy simply in order to *retain* jobs in the face of rising standards – and therefore potential competitive advantage – elsewhere.

Green Public Expenditure

Public spending on environmental projects can be of two broad types:

- *Infrastructure.* For example, energy conservation programmes, solid-waste treatment and recycling plants, public transport.
- *Environmental enhancement and clean-up activities.* For example, afforestation, river and beach cleaning, coastal protection, nature conservation and enhancement.

Both types of spending already support many permanent full-time jobs, in local authorities, public and voluntary agencies (an estimated 200,000 in the European Union as a whole). 'Green job creation' schemes could create additional short-term employment. The net cost per job-year of enhancement and clean-up programmes is calculated as approximately £15,000 (taking into account the £9,000 which each unemployed person already costs the state in benefits and lost taxes). Such schemes create small multiplier effects and therefore contribute to wider employment benefit, but in themselves tend not to provide much training and therefore do little to reduce structural unemployment. Infrastructure spending has a wider impact on economic efficiency, but is considerably more expensive, and the jobs cannot be so easily targeted on the unemployed.

One area of 'green public spending' with considerable employment potential is energy conservation. This creates jobs not only in the manufacture and installation of insulation and other materials, but through the 'respending' effect of the savings made on energy bills. In the UK it is estimated that 500,000 job-years could be created over a period of ten years given a programme investment of £15.5bn, at a net cost per job-year of £23,000.

Eco-Tax Reform

'Eco-tax reform' would shift the burden of taxation away from economic 'goods', such as labour, savings and VAT, towards environmental 'bads', such as energy use, pollution and waste. The rationale for such a shift is that the present tax system penalizes labour (in the UK, directly through employers' National Insurance contributions; indirectly through income tax and VAT) while low or no taxation is imposed on environmental damage. The tax system therefore provides perverse incentives: against employment and for pollution.

The eco-tax reform has been simulated by a number of macroeconomic modelling studies, for the UK and other European countries. These model the introduction of an energy or carbon/energy tax, and/or an increase in road fuel tax. This is offset either by a reduction in employers' social security contributions or by a reduction in VAT. The results suggest that a revenue neutral tax shift of this kind would not only reduce environmental damage (by raising its price) but would also generate significantly higher employment.

The employment effect is maximized when the offsetting tax reduction is of employers' social security contributions targeted on employees at the minimum wage. A general reduction in labour costs generates a smaller effect, as does a reduction in VAT. If the revenues are recycled by reducing income tax, employment is not much changed. Other macroeconomic effects (such as on competitiveness and inflation) are relatively small, though there are significant changes in the distribution of activity between sectors. In particular, the economy is made considerably more labour intensive. The simulations do not model technological change, however, so if the effect of higher energy prices is to stimulate the adoption of more energy-efficient technologies, the employment effects may be different.

POLICY RECOMMENDATIONS

The Regulatory Framework

The employment benefits of regulatory measures can be maximized by careful design of the measures themselves and by the creation of beneficial economic conditions.

- Certain factors require a balancing of negative and positive influences on employment. Thus, more stringent environmental standards can stimulate higher levels of demand for environmental products, but they can also raise costs for complying firms. A gradual timetable for the implementation of new measures minimizes costs, but does less to bring forward new investment. An optimal policy will maximize the net employment impact.
- The type of regulatory measures can also affect costs. Measures which allow some flexibility in response are likely to be less costly than those which do not: thus performance standards and some kinds of financial incentive may be cheaper than technology standards.
- The certainty of the regulatory framework over, say, a ten-year period is important. If firms know the kinds of regulatory constraints they will be operating in, they are more likely to invest to meet them. This is particularly true if there is a clear intention on the part of government to raise standards over time.
- Measures introduced in one country alone may reduce competitiveness, though the effect is likely to be outweighed by other factors. In internationally traded sectors where environmental costs constitute a significant proportion of total costs, measures applying internationally will be preferable.
- Particularly for small- and medium-sized enterprises, financial and other assistance, such as information, may play a significant role in reducing the costs of compliance.
- Low interest rates and high demand (high profitability) are more likely to encourage investment and enable firms to absorb additional costs without employment effects.
- Innovation in clean technologies and production systems will be assisted by an innovatory and long-term investment culture in firms and investment institutions. This may require changes to institutional structures and tax regimes. The availability of venture capital for small- and medium-sized firms may be particularly important.

Mitigating Distributional Impacts

Environmental measures may cause job loss in certain sectors and regions, even though job gains elsewhere may be greater. Such distributional impacts can be mitigated by:

*   Employment audits of key measures.
*   Regional economic development assistance.
*   Specific support for industries which are likely to suffer under environmental measures (eg for diversification).
*   Education and (re)training measures.
*   Providing incentives for investment in the environmental sector, where jobs will be created, to be directed towards regions experiencing job loss.

Government Support for Environmental Innovation

Technical innovation in response to environmental policy may lead to national competitive advantage. There is therefore a strong case for government support for environmental Research and Development. The results of R&D are both uncertain and to some extent a public good, so private companies tend to under-investment. Government programmes may also be able to help stimulate innovatory 'cultures' in the management of firms.

Support for R&D is appropriate not only in the field of clean technologies (where the risks involved are significant, and many of the systems completely new) but also for more efficient end-of-pipe technologies. These are also possible sources of competitive advantage.

A number of countries have R&D programmes of these kinds. Japan has developed a 100-year plan for environmental sustainability entitled New Earth 21, with present appropriations of 5 billion yen for clean technologies and 12 billion yen for energy conservation. The US has recently initiated a new support programme for technologies with low environmental impact (with the specific goal of creating high-skill employment). The Dutch National Environmental Policy Plan allocated £43m over four years to environmental R&D. The European Union Framework Programme provided approximately Ecu580m (£450m) for environmental and energy research in 1990–94, while the EUREKA programme has received about £500m from 20 European countries for 32 environmental research projects. The UK's two programmes, the Environmental Technology Innovation Scheme (ETIS) and the DEMOS fund for demonstration projects, have recently been disbanded.

Public Expenditure

There is a strong case on environmental, employment and wider economic efficiency grounds for public expenditures on environmental infrastructure such as public transport. Energy conservation measures offer substantial employment gains and can to a considerable extent pay for themselves through lower bills.

Short-term job creation programmes in environmental clean-up and enhancement can be relatively inexpensive per job-year created. The wider economic effects are not very large, but the environmental benefits can be substantial. Employment in this area does not have to be short-term.

Tax Reform

Strong consideration should be given to a gradual tax reform package in which a carbon/energy tax (and/or a road fuel tax or other forms of environmental taxation) would be offset by a reduction in employers' National Insurance contributions (and/or VAT). Macroeconomic modelling evidence suggests that such a package would increase employment while reducing environmental damage. A reduction targeted at low-paid workers would have a larger employment effect.

CONCLUSIONS: A NEW MACRO-ENVIRONMENTAL ECONOMICS?

Uncertainty and the Scale of Effects

Environmental policies are not the answer to unemployment. The effects on employment discussed in this report are, in most cases, *tendencies* resulting from the environmental measures: whether employment in the economy actually rises or falls depends on wider economic conditions and policies. With the exception of tax reform, the net employment effects of environmental policies are likely to be relatively small; certainly too small to outweigh the impacts of wider economic measures.

Moreover, the effect of future environmental policies on employment cannot be predicted with any certainty. The nature of those policies must be specified; the conditions in which they are introduced will vary; sectoral studies cannot estimate overall effects; macroeconomic models are inexact and cannot model unpredictable change. Nevertheless, nearly all the evidence that it is possible to collect suggests that, in the short- to medium-term at least, environmental policies will have a positive rather than a negative effect on jobs. There will be job loss in certain sectors, and if this is geographically concentrated in older industrial areas it may be particularly damaging and will need to be specifically mitigated. But overall we can expect more jobs to be gained. The old argument that environmental policy destroys jobs can finally be laid to rest.

Macroenvironmental Economics

Having looked at the three main types of environmental economic policy we can see why this should be so. It is widely recognized that the UK economy needs a higher level of investment to improve competitiveness and expand capacity. In some industrialized economies high savings ratios and long-term investment cultures support much higher levels of investment than prevail in Britain. Where 'endogenous' investment is not forthcoming, the Government can engage in public investment to make up the gap. This is still one route to higher employment – as discussed in this report, it offers some possibilities for combining employment with environmental goals, particularly in fields such as transport and energy conservation.

However, we can now see that there is another way in which the Government can stimulate investment: it can regulate. Carefully judged in extent, form and timing, regulatory measures can do precisely the opposite of what they are commonly supposed to do; they can create jobs and raise output. They can do this by forcing or encouraging firms to invest in new equipment and technology where they would not have done otherwise. As we have shown in this report, regulation is thus a macroeconomic instrument as well as a microeconomic one.

The eco-tax reform proposal adds another twist to this new macroenvironmental economics. At the same time that higher environmental prices stimulate investment, the reduction in social security contributions can make labour cheaper and thus add to job creation. Indeed, reducing labour taxes in this way appears to have the potential to bridge a gap in current thinking about employment policy and the labour market. On one side are those who argue that unemployment will be reduced only if wages can be made more flexible, so that workers can 'price themselves into jobs'. On the other side are those who believe that lower wages and increased job insecurity will serve only to reduce productivity and to add to social welfare costs. By focusing on labour taxes rather than wages, the eco-tax reform would cut labour costs, thereby satisfying the demand for greater flexibility, while not cutting wages, and so leaving workers' conditions unchanged.

In the long term, when integrally cleaner production systems begin to be introduced, the effect on jobs is much harder to predict. It will depend in part on the ability of the economy to absorb workers displaced from sectors where labour productivity has risen faster than output. But in this time-scale the issue is not about jobs in comparison with the present. Over the next 20 years, industrialized economies will anyway undergo substantial restructuring. The available paths are at least as likely to involve reductions in employment as the path of 'clean production'. There will be job loss and job gain. The argument for a macroenvironmental economics is that the employment prospects are at least as good on an 'environmental' path, and the environmental consequences are infinitely better.

Indeed we may have little choice in the matter. If other countries go down the environmental route, the demands of international competitiveness may force us to do the same. It would be better to prepare now than wait – as in some other fields – until we are left behind.

17

Business, the Environment and Local Government

Roger Levett

INTRODUCTION

Every company is 'local' to somewhere, and what it can or cannot do about the environment will depend on local circumstances. These include the influence of local authorities, Training and Enterprise Councils (TECs) and other public agencies.

This chapter falls into two parts. The first describes what these public agencies active in local economic development *can* do and *are* doing to make the local economy more sustainable. The message of this part is positive: 'greening the local economy' is not impossible or self-contradictory: there *are* methods and approaches which have been shown to bring real benefits for both environment and economy, and which other local authorities can copy.

The first part is based on a survey of UK local authority practice carried out by CAG Consultants for the Local Government Management Board (LGMB) and published as *Greening Economic Development* (LGMB, 1993a), updated and amplified from the author's subsequent research and consultancy work in the field (including Commission of the European Communities, 1994, International Centre for Local Environmental Initiatives, 1994). However it makes no claim to be comprehensive or representative, but rather to highlight some issues the author thinks important.

The second part of the chapter tempers the optimism of the first with a discussion of the *limits* to local authority action, and in turn the limits to the extent that businesses can sensibly be expected to take the sustainability agenda on, and the implications and lessons for policy making at national as well as local level.

The overall message of the chapter is one that is increasingly familiar throughout the sustainability movement: of creative action at local level making great strides, but sooner or later hitting limits that only central government can remove.

This chapter will break new ground in sustainability literature by *not* starting with the customary quotation, obeisance and exegesis of the Brundtland definition of sustainable development. Instead it will simply take as its starting point the notion that human activities are threatening the environment's ability to keep on providing the resources and 'environmental services' – including climate maintenance, water purification and waste decomposition – which we need for survival and basic welfare.

Breathing apart, virtually all the human activities which affect the environment are 'economic': they include extracting raw materials, processing them into products, using and consuming those products, and getting rid of the resulting wastes. The *way* that these threaten future environmental provision is by overloading the natural systems which provide resources and carry out services or, as ecologists put it, exceeding the 'carrying capacity' of the environment. It is this quality of breaking through the resilience and ability of natural systems to 'bounce back' – as it were, snapping the rubber band instead of stretching it – which distinguishes environmental *sustainability* questions from the wider category of environmental *protection* issues.

Carrying capacities arise at all spatial levels, from the ability of a stream to provide for the biochemical oxygen demand of an effluent put into it, or a woodland's ability to keep providing a yield of timber year on year, to the combined ability of all the world's forests, farmland and sea plants to mop up extra carbon dioxide added to the atmosphere by power stations, transport, industry, heating, lighting and other uses of fossil fuels.

The idea is gaining acceptance that each geographic region, river catchment and human settlement needs to be thought of as an ecosystem with its own characteristic set of carrying capacity limits. Some continental cities such as Gothenburg and Freiburg are starting to put this idea into practice: trying to measure resource flows and environmental change, to deduce carrying capacity limits from these, and to make compliance with these limits the objectives of environmental policies and programmes. This 'ecosystems' approach is advocated in Brugmann, 1992, Storksdieck & Otto-Zimmermann, 1994, and CEC, 1994.

It is proving very difficult and expensive to do this even for local environmental carrying capacities. It is harder still at regional and global level because the complexities and uncertainties increase. Indeed there is still no *proof* that global warming is really happening, let alone where the environment's carrying capacity for CO_2 and other 'greenhouse' gases lies. We are therefore a long way from the ideal of being able to say, for each area, what the maximum sustainable levels of different environmental pressures are, and therefore what levels of each kind of environmental impact businesses can be permitted. For the moment, the only prudent course is to follow some general rules of thumb aimed at reducing the kinds of impact which seem likely to have serious consequences. These could be summarized as:

- reduce energy and resource consumption and waste production across the board;
- switch from non-renewable resources to renewable ones being cropped within their replenishment capacity;
- convert 'one shot' resource use into circular flows through techniques such as refilling, reuse, recycling and recovery.

These aims are included in a number of LGMB publications endorsed by all the local authority associations (including LGMB, 1993a, LGMB, 1993b) and reflected in many local authority environmental strategies.

This chapter's focus is action by local authorities and other local public agencies in the UK to move economic activity in these directions. This is of course only a subset of environmental actions by business, sustainable development actions by local authorities, and local action for economic development. Indeed it is the area where all three of these fields overlap.

LOCAL AUTHORITY ACTION

Helping Businesses Improve Environmental Performance

Local authority economic development activity generally starts from orthodox assumptions about the blanket desirability of business activity, economic growth, conventional employment and so on. Economic development officers and the committees they report to tend to be suspicious of environmentalists and goals which they believe can oppose economic development. (The first of a number of delicious paradoxes which this chapter will uncover is that economic development officers and environmental officers often see themselves in exactly the same way, as outsiders preaching and promoting values which the authority only intermittently and unreliably supports.)

The palest green arguments have therefore been the most acceptable. The simplest, best and most frequently used of these is that if the local authority helps businesses reduce resource use, pollution and wastes, everyone wins both environmentally and commercially. Local people get a cleaner environment. Pressure is taken off transport and waste disposal infrastructure and thus off local government as provider and regulator. The businesses themselves save money, some of which at least will be spent or invested locally. They also increase their competitiveness and reduce their vulnerability to environmental regulation and hikes in resource and waste disposal costs, both now and in the future. They are therefore more likely to continue to provide jobs and prosperity for the area.

On this argument, helping local businesses improve their environmental performance is just like helping them obtain suitable premises, train their staff, market their products or manage their finances effectively – something which a prudent local authority will do to make sure those businesses remain successful and can continue to make their contribution to the area.

Coventry City Council's programme of environmental advice to industry is a good example. Specialist advisers (funded first under the Urban Programme, then by the European Social Fund) advise small and medium sized companies on issues such as energy conservation, pollution, waste reduction and recycling. Direct savings include:

- A small engineering works was spending £18,000 disposing of contaminated water. The advice given enabled them to eliminate the contamination and the consequent cost.
- A small glazing installer saved £3,500 p.a. as a result of advice given on recycling glass waste.
- A vehicle components coatings company had been ordering resins in 45-gallon drums. There were expensive to dispose of. As a result of advice they switched to bulk containers which were reusable, so saving costs and materials.

Direct visits to companies have proved very valuable. Businesses have been able to identify concrete issues on their premises more easily than at seminars, and nothing turns companies on to environmental management better than direct cost savings!

Other Coventry initiatives have included helping the local technical college develop an accredited training course in environmental advice, and working in partnership with other local authorities to help the Rover Group and several of its suppliers to pilot the BS7750 environmental management standard cooperatively.

Coventry is unusually advanced and committed among UK local authorities. Approaches used more commonly tend to focus on provision of information and encouragement rather than casework. These have included the following:

- Both the Environment Council and the Centre for Environment and Business in Scotland produce sets of one-page summaries of important environmental issues, available to companies on subscription. They are intended to make often arcane matters intelligible to non-technical readers and to bring the cost and time requirements within the reach of busy managers of smaller businesses.
- Several TECs (including recently West London) and Local Enterprise Companies (LECs) (including Grampian) have produced simple guidance for businesses on improving environmental performance.
- Islington Council produced *Greening your business: a self-help manual* with case studies of small businesses evaluating and improving their environmental performance.
- There are many green business award schemes, sometimes linked to other business awards and sometimes to other environmental awards, intended to stimulate entrants to think about their performance, and then to disseminate best practice.
- Local authorities including Oxfordshire have organized training for staff involved in 'front line' advice and support for small businesses so they can identify and help with environmental problems.
- Any number of conferences, seminars, training programmes and other special events have been offered to smaller businesses.
- Many authorities have catalysed or supported the launch of regional green business clubs, networks, forums and so on.

All these approaches have had some success in spreading the message. But all have come up against some common barriers, discussed later in this chapter.

Development of Green Business Opportunities

If improving resource efficiency is good for *all* businesses, the technologies, products and services which will help them do so will be commercial opportunities for *some* businesses. Many economic development strategies now include a reference to encouraging the environmental sector among the standard motherhood statements about creating a high output, high value-added economy and a highly trained and motivated workforce, building on traditional strengths while responding energetically to new opportunities etc etc without which no respectable strategy is complete. But few strategies include actions in support of this aim.

This may partly be because sectoral strategies are out of fashion and few authorities now have the resources to mount one. It is also because there is really no such thing as 'the environmental sector' in the sense that there is, for example, a footware sector or a publishing sector. Rather there is a larger or smaller environmental strand to the activities of a wide range of businesses in many *other* industry sectors such as civil and chemical engineering, manufacturing, distribution, property development. (For this reason statistics about the economic importance of 'the environmental sector' should be taken with a large pinch of salt.) In each of these there are some companies which have chosen to be specialists or leaders in environmental approaches. British Polythene and Davidsons among packaging manufacturers, Universal among office suppliers, Shanks and McEwan among waste management companies, B&Q among DIY outlets and March among industrial technology consultancies are some examples. But each of these has more in common with other firms in its own industry than they have with one another.

One possible local authority response to this nebulousness would be to discriminate in favour of firms at the environmentally better end of any industry. Possible proxies for good environmental performance include possession of a formal environmental policy (only meaningful when combined with some form of management system to ensure that it is implemented and that its success or otherwise is independently assessed and publicly reported), employment of specialist environmental managers, commitments to 'clean technology' approaches and low emissions. Many local authorities are beginning to apply requirements of this sort in their purchasing and tendering, as part of their own environmental management systems. Indeed the Government-sponsored local authority adaptation of the EU Eco-Management and Audit Scheme requires that 'management shall ensure that contractors working on the local authority's behalf apply environmental standards equivalent to the local authority's own' (HMSO, 1993). The same criteria could be used as a 'filter' for economic development assistance.

A different approach is to concentrate on developing particular areas of economic activity with environmental benefits. An early example was the Greater London Council (GLC)'s support for the London Energy and Employment Network (LEEN) which, as its name suggests, was concerned with developing business opportunities in energy conservation. This fizzled out through a combination of post-GLC funding problems and an initially over-ambitious and not sufficiently business-focused approach, although Optima Energy, a consultancy which can trace its origins back to LEEN, has continued to do important work in the field.

Lothian and Edinburgh Environmental Partnership (LEEP) is a leading current example. It is a nonprofit company, largely core funded by Edinburgh City Council and also supported by the Regional Council, the University and Friends of the Earth Scotland, all of whom are represented on its board. It was set up in 1990 specifically to develop business opportunities in three areas chosen for their importance for sustainability: energy efficiency, recycling/waste reduction and sustainable transport. Its aim is to act as a catalyst: to provide advice, development and planning effort or in some cases funding to enable businesses to get started.

Some of LEEP's most successful interventions have been among the smallest.

A few hours of staff advice and a £200 grant for a study visit to a similar business in Milton Keynes enabled an unemployed Edinburgh woman to set up a nappy laundry service which provides parents with an environmentally friendlier alternative to disposables, contracting spare capacity in an energy-efficient hospital laundry to do the washing. Similar small scale support helped launch Edinburgh's first pedal cycle courier company.

At the other extreme of effort lies the 'billsavers' project currently under development with EU LIFE funding. The basic idea is to finance low-income households to replace obsolete domestic appliances with more energy-efficient new ones, and pay back the costs out of the energy savings. If it succeeds it will be the first domestic application of an 'energy services company' approach in the UK.

The project has the active support of energy utilities, appliance manufacturers, technical consultants, the City Council and tenants' organizations. But without LEEP none of these would have felt the project was a high enough priority to put in the research, coordination, negotiation and promotional effort necessary to bring them all together, or to do the groundwork to establish technical and financial feasibility and develop appropriate and effective methods of working. This catalytic role was LEEP's distinctive contribution.

LEEP 'adds value' by making possible businesses which would otherwise not get started. It must therefore aim to operate in a 'twilight zone' between those business opportunities which are already sufficiently commercially attractive and well understood to get started *without* any special help, and those which are unlikely ever to develop into viable businesses and so do not *warrant* special help.

Inevitably this means LEEP will sometimes devote considerable effort to developing projects which do not work. LEEP established, for example, that the intuitively elegant and attractive idea of combining *collection* of paper for recycling with *delivery* of new recycled stationery to small businesses does not work. The reason? Most companies buy their stationery in occasional big bulk orders with occasional panic afterthoughts requiring instant response. But they want their recyclables taken away on a frequent but regular and reliable routine. The three different schedules just don't match.

Similarly there seemed to be a great deal going for another LEEP project, a computer matching service for commuter car sharers. Edinburgh has a great deal of car commuting concentrated on a few standard radial routes to a few main city centre destinations; many office workers still keep a strict 'nine to five' routine; and there is widespread public concern at rising congestion and air pollution. But despite sponsorship and encouragement from several large city centre employers and highly committed promotional support from the main local evening paper, very few prospective sharers joined. The project concluded that most people who wished to share their cars had already found partners through word of mouth. The majority did not want to share because they valued their independence, flexibility and privacy. Difficulty finding partners to share with was not the problem, so making it easier was not the solution.

These dead ends at least save others making the same mistakes. The clear lesson of the car sharing project is that serious shifts to car sharing will require positive incentives such as preferential parking or special lanes for multiply-occupied vehicles, as in the US. It can also be argued that a stream of failures provides reassurance that LEEP is really doing its job of pushing back the frontiers of what is possible. However this is thin consolation for staff having to admit defeat after weeks or months of committed effort on projects of the sort just dismissed in a paragraph each.

Businesses Based on Delivering Local Environmental Policies

Another approach is for a local authority to help develop businesses to deliver its own environmental agenda. Sheffield went into partnership with a Finnish district heating company to develop a refuse-based district heating scheme; a consortium of London boroughs have done likewise to build the SELCHP (South East London Combined Heat and Power) plant.

In 1983 Glasgow City Council helped establish Heatwise as a separate business to undertake draughtproofing and insulation work to help tackle the city's enormous problems of cold, damp housing, illness and fuel debt caused by a combination of poor thermal performance, low incomes and the cold damp climate.

The hope was that the extra flexibility of an organization outside the council would give both efficient service delivery and the opportunity to use the council's own contributions to 'lever' funding from a variety of government schemes. The project was modelled on Keeping Newcastle Warm, the first of the Community Insulation Projects which exploited the potential to link the Department of Energy's grants to establish insulation projects, the DoE's Homes Insulation Scheme and DHSS Single Payments to pay for insulation and draughtproofing materials, and the Manpower Services Commission's Community Programme which paid the wages of long-term unemployed people for up to a year of work and training on the projects, with tight but workable allowances for supervision and equipment.

By 1993 Heatwise had become the Wise Group, a business empire of six companies employing over 600 people at any one time, providing landscaping, physical property improvements, urban forestry and recycling, as well as energy efficiency, with offshoots in Motherwell outside Glasgow and Newham in East London.

The success was achieved through consistently following the original formula of delivering the local environmental services required by the council reliably, competitively and to high quality standards, in a format carefully designed to meet the policy aims and criteria of a range of other public funders. Each component of the funding package is negotiated on the basis of the 'leverage' it will achieve through all the others. The various funding bodies are like a ring of Boy Scouts, each sitting on the lap of the one behind: they all get comfort for as long as they all sit still.

A weakness of this arrangement is that whenever one Boy Scout gets up and walks away, the whole ring falls down unless the gap is quickly filled. Over the last 10 years the turnover of Government funding schemes has resembled a game of musical chairs – or, from the point of view of the recipients, hide and seek. Or blind man's buff. None of the original Government schemes mentioned above still exists. Indeed, of the four government organizations mentioned, only the DoE has not been abolished or transformed.

The Wise Group has only survived, let alone prospered, by devoting large amounts of very high quality management attention to remaking the funding coalition every time the rules changed. For example when the Government replaced the Community Programme with Employment Training (ET), one of the (many) ways the new scheme was meaner was that it paid trainees 'benefit plus' – a small flat rate cash addition to whatever benefits they had previously been claiming – instead of the 'rate for the job'. This was unacceptable to the trade unions and Glasgow City Council, a staunch Labour authority, said it could not use Wise Group trainees if they were on ET 'benefit plus' rates.

After months of negotiation a deal was done: the Wise Group would use European Social Fund (ESF) money to top up the ET payments from 'benefit plus' to 'rate for the job' levels. The unions were happy because the trainees would be getting the rate for the job; the City Council was happy because the unions were happy, the ESF administrators were happy because the ET funding made their money go further, and the MSC (being renamed Training Agency) was relieved to have secured a substantial and reliable block of take-up for an unpopular and problematic new scheme.

Lessons

Several lessons can be drawn from projects of the sort mentioned above:

- *Strong local government helps.* Coventry, Edinburgh, Glasgow and Sheffield are all large authorities with (historically at least) considerable staff and financial resources, and consistent and settled political leadership. Coventry and Sheffield are unitary authorities; Edinburgh and Glasgow so large and powerful as to function in many ways more like partners than subordinates to their respective regions. These are the sorts of authorities with the muscle to give bold new ideas substantial support, and the confidence to give them enough time to come right.
- *Business does not always know what is best for business.* A second delicious paradox is that in greening economic development, as indeed in economic development more generally, public agencies and public employees can often help businesses perform better. (In normal times this point would be too obvious to be worth making, but we do not live in normal times.)
- *Progress takes time.* All the main examples took time to hit their stride. They also all built on a long history of earlier experiments and projects. Coventry established its Pollution Prevention Panel – a forum for business and city council representatives to discuss and work cooperatively towards solutions to business environmental problems – as long ago as 1970. This made collaboration with the council on environmental issues part of the normal fabric of business life in the city for a quarter of a century. The habits, methods, contacts and expectations which this long experience built up have been crucial for making the more recent initiatives discussed above possible.

    There is a complex genealogy of influences, examples and people in this field. The Wise Group grew, over ten years, from Heatwise, which was modelled on Keeping Newcastle Warm. LEEP started as an attempt to salvage something worthwhile from the remains of two less successful intermediate Edinburgh initiatives. One of these, Heatcare, had been based on (and helped start) by Heatwise. The other, the Energy Centre, was the brainchild of the Lothian Energy Group, a predominantly academic grouping. Key figures in Keeping Newcastle Warm went on to develop Neighbourhood Energy Action and then to Business in the Community and the Combined Heat and Power Association.

In a different part of the family tree, several people who helped develop the Recycling Cities programme as members of FoE's Projects Unit are now working on Global Action Plan, a programme of support for environmental action by individuals and households. Others are involved in Projects in Partnership, an attempt to break down the behavioural and cultural barriers to better energy efficiency behaviour through cooperation with relevant industry interests.

The Recycling Cities programme also led to the creation of the National Recycling Forum, a coalition of business, local government and voluntary interests which has sponsored research and information exchange in waste minimization as well as reuse, and many of whose policy recommendations have been taken up in the Government's draft waste strategy for England and Wales.

- *The private sector has no monopoly of entrepreneurship, innovation or creativity.* In all the main examples quoted, the inspiration and the leading figures came from the voluntary or public sector, and were motivated mainly by public good rather than commercial considerations.

LIMITS TO LOCAL ACTION TO GREEN ECONOMIC DEVELOPMENT

The success stories in the last section might prompt the question: if environment is good for businesses, and local authorities can promote green business, why isn't the economy getting more sustainable, and why are the genuine success stories so few that the same examples crop up over and over again? This second part discusses some of the reasons. It moves from current limitations on local government action to limits on the scope for businesses themselves to promote sustainability, and back to a new understanding of the role for central and local government action.

Resource pressures on local government

The first barrier to greening the local economy is very simple: the resource pressures on local government. Economic development and proactive environmental policy are both 'discretionary' functions, where local authorities have *powers* but not *duties*. Cutting them does not lay the council open to legal liabilities like (for example) failing to keep roads or buildings safe or collect the rubbish, or produce immediate obvious suffering to local people like (for example) closing old people's homes and sacking teachers. Financial stringency may initially encourage efficiency, but beyond a certain point it simply forces authorities to sacrifice coherent forward-looking strategy to short term crisis management.

Resource limits have a specific effect on initiatives to integrate environment and development. Where environmental aims stimulate *new* economic development activities, these obviously cost money. Where environmental aims change the way existing activities are done, this requires at least a reallocation of officer time and attention. The only way that environmental aims can be built into economic development activities *without* resource costs is if the environment is used as an extra barrier to activity, for example through exclusion or discouragement of particular businesses or activities on environmental grounds.

Proactive use of environment requires extra resources. Shortage of resources forces authorities to the other extreme – in other words into a 'development versus environment' stance. The apparent opposition of environment and economy in many local policies is largely an artefact of central government restrictions on local expenditure and action. And where the argument is forced into these terms, environment rarely wins.

Consider a recent example from an English city authority with a large commercial property portfolio. Most of the property is let to smaller local businesses, and in an environmental management exercise the council's role as landlord was identified as an important potential environmental effect. Officers were highly creative in identifying ways that lettings policy and lease conditions could be used to influence the environmental performance of these tenants, for example by requiring minor repairs and refurbishments to be done to high energy efficiency standards, avoiding use of tropical hardwoods or lead paints, providing cycle as well as car parking, and so on.

Many of these suggestions would have cost tenants money, at least in the short term. All would have constrained their behaviour and required them to give management time and attention to matters not normally raised by property leases. This would make renting from the council less attractive than renting comparable properties from private sector landlords without environmental complications. The council would have to reduce its rents to compensate. But the Valuers Department's main aim was to manage the portfolio so as to maximize rental income to the city. Officers were ready and willing to promote better environmental performance through lettings – but only if at political level members accepted the cost. This was not politically realistic at a time when the authority was having to make painful and unpopular service cuts.

Management Pressures on Local Government

In addition to financial restrictions, local government has been subjected to an extraordinary succession of management upheavals in the 1980s and 1990s. At corporate level these have included compulsory competitive tendering (first blue collar, now white collar), the attempted replacement of domestic rates with the Poll Tax, the ensuing shambles and return to Council Tax, business rates changes, the Citizens' Charter and the development of performance indicators and (unfortunately neither last nor least) Local Government Review. In addition there have been continual, and often arbitrary and unpredictable, changes in the rules and requirements *within* many service areas including housing, education and social services.

Each time councils are faced with a new threat, they naturally pull their best and brightest people in to work on the response. The best and brightest often tend to be working in challenging new areas such as environment or economic development. These are therefore most likely to be raided for staff when each threat arrives, particularly since it can be argued that proactive longer-term work in areas such as these should in any case be put 'on hold' pending resolution of the latest set of uncertainties.

Local Government Review (LGR) has been particularly effective at retarding the best work on environment and economy. Abolition is the greatest threat any authority can face, and calls for the best efforts at resistance. The protractedness and complication of the process has ensured that the people seconded to work on it were tied up for long periods. The extended period of uncertainty has made strategic planning difficult for many authorities for years. Finally, by setting the different tiers of local government against each other it has made particularly difficult the sorts of collaboration and partnership which are at the leading edge of both environmental and economic development work.

The effect of these management initiatives is thus a bit like flu: the patient loses the ability to do anything more dynamic than doze in bed while all available energy is devoted to containing and repelling the threat. Our next delicious paradox is therefore that the more exciting and dynamic *management* change becomes, the more static, unambitious and unimaginative an organization's *policies* and *activities* are likely to be. It is no accident that much of the boldest and most creative work has been done by big, stable authorities: those best able to defend themselves against disruptions.

It is also a tribute to the vision and determination of members and officers that *anything* creative and innovative has been done. However it illustrates a further delicious paradox: that the continual pressure on local government has forced local authorities to become remarkably resilient, entrepreneurial and resourceful, at both member and officer level.

Additionality Versus Substitution

Another problem is that of 'additionality' versus 'substitution'. This is not peculiar to green economic development: all public intervention in a market economy runs the risk of simply *moving* activity rather than *adding* to it. Enterprise Zones, City Challenge projects and suchlike have been criticized for increasing business activity in their targeted areas by tempting businesses to move in from the surrounding areas.

In the late 1980s, smart companies considering major developments would express interest in one potential site in (say) Merseyside, one in the South Wales coalfields, one in Strathclyde and one in Derry (or Kerry), and make sure that the regional economic development agencies in each knew of the others. Top executives could then spend a happy week or two being treated to lavish tours of each region, during which they would invite each set of hosts to better the package of support and inducements offered by the previous ones. Sometimes a second or even third round of visits would be needed to complete the auction.

Regional development agencies became a bit more circumspect after some of the plum investments wooed so assiduously turned out to be lemons, and others shamelessly moved on to the next waiting country after only a couple of years hoovering up tax breaks, training subsidies and marketing support. However the system has been given a new lease of life by the breaking up of the former Scottish Development Agency into eight Local Enterprise Companies henceforth able to compete with each other within Scotland, so that the shrewd potential inward investor can now enjoy a whole week of golf afternoons and whisky evenings back to back with only a short drive and a perfunctory site inspection separating each from the next.

Much inward investment promotion may thus be a futile 'zero sum game' in which one area only gains benefits by depriving others of them, and the only winners are commercial interests cunning enough to play one public agency off against another. The problem is particularly obvious for some kinds of environmental business development. For example, collecting newspapers for recycling is one of the most obvious, tangible and satisfying environmental activities available to ordinary people. Through the 1970s and 1980s, whenever market fluctuations created a little extra demand for newspapers, voluntary groups and local authorities rushed to establish new collections. Each time, the new collections soon oversaturated the market. Merchants responded, as elementary market theory would predict, by driving prices down.

Unfortunately the collectors did not, as elementary market theory says they should, pull out when the price fell below covering their costs. Instead they appealed for subsidies to enable them to continue the great crusade of saving paper. Some councils obliged, mindful of the great public enthusiasm for recycling and the unpopularity of allowing recycling schemes to fail. The result was to allow the merchants to push prices still lower. This drove *un*subsidized paper collections – including some long established ones – out of business. It also increased merchant profits: the merchants knew there was no point in reducing the prices at which they sold to the mills because the mills were already taking all the paper they could handle.

Only when enough collectors had given up could prices stabilize – until the next blip started the whole process off again. Throughout the cycle, quantities of paper *recycled* only changed marginally, although quantities *collected* changed dramatically. The difference was stockpiled, landfilled or exported.

The same problem can work across national boundaries. The German packaging ordinances require manufacturers to recover certain minimum percentages of packaging for recycling. They are widely believed to have resulted in the dumping in other countries of materials for which there was no reprocessing capacity or demand in Germany. Visiting a municipal recycling depot in Munich in 1992 the author was at first puzzled that it seemed to be selling high grade waste paper to merchants at a lower price than the low grade paper. A more careful phrasing of the question revealed that the figures being quoted were not prices merchants paid for the materials, but what the *council* paid to the merchants to take the materials off their hands. This paper may well have been shipped to the UK and offered to mills at a price which drove British collections out of business.

The lesson for greening local economic development is to concentrate on areas of definite additionality, or where more sustainable alternatives substitute for non-environmental. Within the field of recycling, wise authorities (and businesses) have concentrated on recycling of (for example) higher-grade office paper or aluminium cans, where industry demand is far greater than supply. Other areas of green business development which are relatively immune to additionality problems include the building of cycle ways and improving energy efficiency in local buildings. In many authorities these are not seen as economic development activities.

Behavioural Limits to Business Interest

The businesses and managers who most need environmental advice and information are precisely those who are least likely to go out of their way to get it. Voluntary measures only reach those who volunteer. Before volunteering for green business activities, businesspeople have at least to believe there is an issue, and it is this first step which most smaller British companies have yet to take.

The environmental auditing roadshow presented by Scottish Enterprise in 1991 provides a cautionary example. Great trouble was taken to construct a high quality programme of expert presentations on practical topics and to market it thoroughly. At each of eight venues throughout Scotland, attendance ranged from the 20s to the 40s. In pure 'head count' terms this was not at all bad. However about one-third of those attending were staff from local authorities, enterprise trusts and other public and advisory bodies. Another quarter were environmental management specialists from larger companies with more advanced environmental policies, who generally knew the material anyway. A further quarter or so were consultants, academics and professionals hoping to pick up business. Only perhaps one-sixth of those attending were the small entrepreneurs and environmentally less aware managers on whose behalf the whole exercise had been mounted.

Many conferences and training programmes have similar experiences. The many successful commercial training courses on environment and business topics are largely attended by specialists from large companies who already know *enough* to know what *more* they need to know, and can afford the time and money to go and get it. They are doing very little to spread the word to the small companies who most need to be started on the path. Similarly a large proportion of subscribers to information services, users of self-help guides, pillars of green business clubs and such like are the already-converted.

The reason is not at all mysterious. It is the same reason why the Energy Efficiency Office is still, 13 years after its launch, plaintively pointing out that most businesses could cheaply and easily save 20 per cent of their energy bills, and why most companies are still not doing it. Any company has to concentrate limited money and management attention on the small number of possible activities which are most important for the future of the business, and most businesses will have more urgent priorities than the environment.

Managers of a successful, prospering business will give more attention to developing new products and markets, and managing expansion, than to making small savings on energy or wastes, particularly where expansion is expected to reduce their proportionate importance to the company. Managers of an unsuccessful, faltering business will generally have far more pressing worries and demands on their time than small scale resource and environmental impacts, and will be uninterested in investments which will only pay back over a future the company may not have.

This is the same 'heads I win/tails you lose' logic which makes VAT on domestic fuel ineffectual as an environmental tax. Householders wealthy enough to respond by investing in energy efficiency improvements generally feel they have better things to do with their leisure than fuss about saving a few extra pounds on their fuel bills. Conversely the many people for whom any increase in fuel costs poses a serious problem cannot afford to do anything about it – other than putting up with a colder house.

Limits to Commercial Viability of Sustainability Action

Behind these behavioural barriers to business interest in sustainability lies a more intractable problem. Granted that there are enormous opportunities for 'no regrets' actions which both save money and improve the environment. But there are limits beyond which further environmental improvements result in commercial costs.

Sainsbury's, the supermarket chain, provides a good example of both opportunities and limits. Over many years they have worked towards outstanding standards of energy efficiency in their stores, through applying the best individual technologies in refrigeration, lighting and so on, then progressively integrating the different energy uses and using sophisticated monitoring and control technologies. They also stock environmentally preferable alternatives to a number of products, host recycling banks in their car parks and encourage shoppers to reuse their carrier bags by giving a penny refund on each bag reused. But at the same time Sainsbury's have also energetically promoted and developed out-of-town superstores which have increased the car dependence and energy intensity of shopping and the relative disadvantage of shoppers without cars.

The John Lewis Partnership offers a further example. They argued strongly against a proposed new retail park outside Bristol on the grounds that it would undermine the viability of the central shopping area which is accessible by public transport from all over the city. But when the new development was eventually approved, John Lewis announced they would close their city centre store and move out to the new site.

Even The Body Shop, one of the most environmentally committed companies in the UK, has moved to a site on the outskirts of its home town to which most staff commute by car. In Sweden Volvo's top management recognize that some time in the next few decades environmental and social pressures will greatly reduce the market for the sorts of cars they make. They are devoting considerable resources to developing buses, trams and such like so they will be ready when this happens. But meanwhile they continue to make and promote heavy resource-wasteful cars.

It would be naive to accuse any of the companies just discussed of hypocrisy or even inconsistency. Their pro-environmental actions are directed to exactly the same end as their anti-environmental ones: commercial security and success. It is commercially rational for Sainsbury's to devote great attention to energy efficiency because it can achieve significant savings in an important area of corporate costs. The unusually long paybacks Sainsbury's accept reflect their strong cash flow and confidence in the future. Stocking green products is rational because enough customers are prepared to pay the extra, and having bottle banks on site gains more goodwill than it costs in parking space.

However Sainsbury's continue to sell cheaper un-green alternatives because most customers still want them, and like the other supermarket chains they calculate that the cost and trouble of providing facilities for return of bottles for refilling would be greater than the customer goodwill they would gain. The environmental superiority of refilling will be quite irrelevant to this decision until it is reflected to a significant degree in customer preferences and demands, whereupon Sainsbury's will doubtless oblige – closely followed by Safeway, Tesco, Asda and the others at the point where their respective market shares are threatened.

Similarly, out-of-town developments are rational because the combination of availability of large parcels of cheap clean land, ease of centralized distribution through the motorway network, heavy investments in local roads infrastructure, and tendency for wealthier potential customers to have cars and live on the outskirts of towns, makes them more profitable than city centre stores. If Sainsbury's and John Lewis did not exploit such sites others would. Similarly if Volvo stopped building their sort of car while there was still a market for it, others would simply take over the market.

The Need to Manage Markets to Promote Sustainability

It would be unrealistic to expect any of these companies to behave differently. They are only doing what any company must do if it wishes to stay in business: make the most commercially advantageous decisions possible given current and anticipated market conditions. The great strength of the market system – its impersonal, mechanical, value-free way of allocating resources – is also its great weakness: its inability to recognise or reflect any values or aims which are not embodied in price relationships. 'Free market' is a peculiarly misleading description for an institution which so rigidly prescribes the factors which can permissibly affect decisions and their relative weightings, and punishes those who allow wider considerations to affect their judgements with business failure.

This throws a surprising new light on the Government's repeated insistence on the leading role of voluntary action by companies in working towards sustainable development. This is normally seen as a compliment and a liberation to business. In fact it is an unfair burden: companies can only live up to the expectations being placed on them by damaging their own commercial positions.

The inevitable failure of voluntary business action to deliver serious moves towards sustainability might, in the current political climate, be taken as proof of the impracticality of sustainability. But this is two-edged. A government with different preconceptions – or public opinion after a serious environmental crisis – might conclude that the fault is with the free market for being unsustainable, rather than with sustainability for being incompatible with market forces.

A further delicious paradox is therefore that people wishing to safeguard the credibility and popularity of the market system in the longer term might be wise to press governments to intervene to create market conditions in which businesses can go a lot further towards sustainable behaviour than at present, instead of merely repeating complimentary but impracticable exhortations to the business community.

Land Use Planning

One area in which the Government has appeared to move towards intervention is the land use planning system. This is one of the few parts of the UK's machinery of government which explicitly and unashamedly restricts private freedoms for the sake of the public good, and uses open and participatory processes to decide what the public good *is*. The fact that after years of neglect, attrition and hostility the Government has since the early 1990s been building the system up and encouraging it to be more proactive marks an extremely significant change of heart.

Between 1992 and 1994 the publication of a new series of Planning Policy Guidance Notes (PPGs) signalled a quiet revolution. The first of the new set, PPG12, explicitly sanctioned and encouraged local planning authorities to use the planning system to promote sustainable development, and called for environmental appraisal of all plans. The subsequent PPGs have consolidated this message and applied it to more detailed aspects of the system. Highlights include PPG13 which calls for integration of land use and transport planning to reduce the need for travel and encourage the use of non-car modes, and PPG6 which encourages planners to oppose urban fringe and out-of-town retail developments which would threaten existing centres.

However the Government's newly discovered enthusiasm for the planning system as a motor of sustainability carries similar pitfalls to its encouragement of voluntary action by businesses. Even if local authorities exploit the new guidance to the full, the practical impacts will be limited. The planning system is still restricted to matters of 'land use' (although defined a bit more broadly than before), it can only respond to developer initiatives, and it only influences the 1–2 per cent of the built environment that is developed or redeveloped each year. It has also been pointed out that PPG6, perhaps the most provocative of the bunch, did not come out until out-of-town retailing was approaching saturation – a case of shutting the stable door after the horse had been taken away to the knackers.

More seriously, local authorities will not *dare* exploit the PPGs to the full because of the risk of driving business away. The PPGs provide councils with some new sticks, but without corresponding carrots. For example if we want businesses to locate on urban derelict sites, and near good public transport connections, we have to make the derelict sites cheap and easy to develop, and the public transport reliable, convenient and attractive. Banning development on greenfield sites *without* these compensatory measures will simply make investors look elsewhere. Like the resource limitations already discussed, this creates a spurious opposition between economic and environmental interests instead of helping integrate them. And by raising expectations which broader circumstances will stop councils from satisfying, the 'new planning' risks undermining rather than consolidating the role of local government.

Central Government Action is Essential

All the frustrations and limitations discussed point to one simple message: there is no substitute for active management of the economy by government to make more sustainable behaviour commercially viable. Many of the local actions described should be seen as pathfinders for central government action rather than alibis for central government inaction. For example the LEEP 'billsavers' project mentioned above shines forth as a good deed of demand management in a wicked world of energy sales – but far more environmental impact could be achieved less laboriously through government building a 'least cost planning' approach into energy utility regulation; and far more social equity improvement could be achieved through reforming energy tariff structures to charge lower unit prices to small energy users rather than higher ones as at present (see Levett, 1994)

Likewise, ecological tax reform – shifting of taxation off labour and value added and onto use of natural resources and wastage (which can be thought of as 'value subtracted') – could, if properly designed and combined with other measures, achieve a great deal more to motivate companies to reduce resource consumption than just advice and exhortation.

Local action is often currently a manifestation of the 'residuarity principle', that counterpart of the better-known 'subsidiarity principle' which says that where the most appropriate level of government is unwilling or unable to act on some crucial issue, other levels have the right to have a go, however limited their effectiveness may be.

Another delicious paradox is that the government's unwillingness to make big, simple, consistent interventions such as ecological tax reform is leading it to reinvent the sort of thicket of arbitrary, cross-cutting localized measures – a bit of fuel levy here, some VAT exemptions there, some landfill tax, recycling credits changing hands at different rates between different types of waste authority, sometimes extended to voluntary groups, sometimes not, a succession of bidding rounds for renewable energy subsidies, each on different terms – which it has consistently been trying to eliminate from the economy in the name of the 'level playing field'.

The Future: Redefining Economic Success

The necessity of central government action does not imply a lack of need for local action. In fact the opposite is true: central government action to green the economy would greatly increase the benefits of, and the scope for, many of the kinds of local action described.

Indeed a general move towards sustainability would open up a much more profound role for local action on economic development. This chapter started with very light green arguments about environmental improvement and business. The hue has been steadily deepening, but the discussion has so far stayed largely within standard assumptions about the blanket desirability of economic activity.

These assumptions are now increasingly being challenged in local consultative processes, being initiated by local authorities under the Local Agenda 21 banner, to decide on the meaning of sustainable development for an area and on action to be taken towards it. *Local Agenda 21: Principles and Process* (LGMB, 1994) includes the following ringing declarations:

> *Human wellbeing has social, cultural, moral and spiritual dimensions as well as material. Development worthy of the name must seek to support all of these, not some at the expense of others ... Development and economic growth are quite different things. It is possible to have either without the other ... We need broader indicators than economic growth to measure development by.*

The middle of these in particular was only approved by representatives of the local authority associations in mid 1994 after protracted discussion and with some trepidation. Yet by late 1995 this is already coming to seem part of the standard litany of local government environmentalism. In some local authorities, economic development strategies are being generated through, or heavily influenced by, Local Agenda 21 processes, and are building in concerns for equity and non-economic quality of life as well as for environmental sustainability.

Some propose to measure the success of the local economy in terms of providing opportunities for the greatest possible range of people to participate with dignity and fulfilment in local economic life and to have their basic needs satisfied. On a yardstick like this, a local economy with low incomes, employment levels, car ownership and so on but where everyone interested can work on a back-lot communal organic vegetable garden, or swap services with neighbours through a Local Exchange and Trading Scheme (LETS), and get to the shops on foot and the hospital by bus, may be regarded as a great deal more successful than one where well-educated white males can drive along urban motorways to lucrative financial services jobs in hi-tech offices while everyone else relies on trickle-down (which the Government's own research admits doesn't).

There are clearly limits to how far such approaches are realistic and deliverable in an economy geared to very different aims. But it is only at local level that a new value-based view of the economy and of desirable directions for economic development can be articulated.

CONCLUSION

Local authorities and other local agencies are already playing a significant role in greening the local economy – and demonstrating that the public sector has a positive and constructive role to play in the economy.

There are limits to how far businesses can go – and therefore to how far public sector action can push them. Government action is essential to move the barriers. Both the Government's enthusiasms for voluntary action by businesses and the renewal of the planning system are welcome, but could turn out to be poisoned chalices without corresponding action by the Government itself.

REFERENCES

Brugmann, J (1992) *Managing Human Ecosystems: Principles for Ecological Municipal Management* ICLEI, Toronto.

Commission of the European Communities (1994) *European Sustainable Cities: first report of the EU Expert Group on the Urban Environment Sustainable Cities Project*, Brussels

HMSO (1993) *A guide to the Eco-Management and Audit scheme for UK Local Government*, London

International Centre for Local Environmental Initiatives (1994) *Guide to Environmental Management for Local Authorities in Central and Eastern Europe: Volume 9: Environmental Issues in Land Use Planning and Economic Development Planning*, Freiburg

Levett, R (1994) 'Sustainable Pricing Structures' in *Town and Country Planning*, October 1994

Local Government Management Board (1993a) *Greening Economic Development*, LGMB, Luton

Local Government Management Board (1993b) *A Framework for Local Sustainability*, LGMB, Luton

Local Government Management Board (1994) *Local Agenda 21 Principles and Process, A Step by Step Guide*, LGMB, Luton

Storksdieck, M and K Otto-Zimmermann (1994) *Local Environmental Budgeting*, ICLEI, Freiburg

Publication Details

PART I
PERSPECTIVES ON BUSINESS AND THE ENVIRONMENT

'A Teasing Irony' by Paul Hawken – chapter 1, *The Ecology of Commerce: How Business Can Save the Planet*, Weidenfeld and Nicolson, 1994.

'Shaping the Post-Modern Economy: Can Business Play a Creative Part?' by James Robertson – chapter 9, *Managing the Unknown by Creating New Futures*, ed Boot, Lawrence and Morris, McGraw-Hill, 1994.

PART II
BUSINESS STRATEGY AND THE ENVIRONMENT

'America's Green Strategy' by Michael Porter – *Scientific American*, April 1991.

'It's Not Easy Being Green' by Noah Walley and Bradley Whitehead – *Harvard Business Review*, Volume 72, Number 3, May–June 1994.

'The Challenge of Going Green' by various commentators – *Harvard Business Review*, Volume 72, Number 3, July–Aug 1994.

'Green and Competitive: Ending the Stalemate' by Michael Porter and Claas van der Linde – *Harvard Business Review*, Volume 73, Number 5, Sept–Oct 1995.

'Strategic Management for a Small Planet' by W Edward Stead and Jean Garner Stead – chapter 9, *Strategic Management and Sustainability: Strategic Decision Making and the Environment*, Sage Publications, 1992.

'Corporate Strategy and the Environment' by Colin Hutchinson – *Long Range Planning*, Volume 25, Number 4, 1992.

PART III
RESEARCH, DEVELOPMENT AND TECHNOLOGY

'Introduction to clean technology' by Roland Clift and Anita Longley – chapter 6, *Clean Technology and the Environment*, Blackie, 1995. NB This chapter has been slightly edited for inclusion in the Reader.

A Clean Break? The Role of Corporate R&D in Creating Sustainable Technology Regimes by I Miles and K Green – unpublished.

'Beyond the Technical Fix' by David Fleming – specially written for Reader.

PART IV
TECHNIQUES FOR ENVIRONMENTAL IMPROVEMENT

'Corporate Reporting for Sustainable Development' by Rob Gray – *Environmental Values*, Volume 3, Number 1, Spring 1994, The White Horse Press.

'Industrial Ecology: A Practical Framework for Environmental Management' by Rolf Marstrander – chapter 12, *Environmental Management Handbook*, ed, Pitman Publishing, 1994.

'Breaking the Link Between Quality and the Environment: Auditing for Sustainability and Life-Cycle Assessment' by Richard Welford – *Business Strategy and the Environment*, Volume 2, Part 4, Winter 1993, ERP Environment.

PART V
BUSINESS AND THE ECONOMY

'Business and the Genesis of the EC Carbon Tax Proposal' by Dr Anthony Ikwue and Jim Skea – *Business Strategy and the Environment*, Volume 3, Part 2, Summer, 1994, ERP Environment.

'Green Jobs? The Employment Implications of Environmental Policy' by Michael Jacobs – chapter 1, *Green Jobs? The Employment Implications of Environmental Policy*, World Wildlife Fund, 1994.

'Business, The Environment and Local Government' by Roger Levett – specially written for Reader.

Further Reading

BOOKS ON BUSINESS AND THE ENVIRONMENT

There have been many books published on business and the environment in the last ten years. That trend is likely to continue as interest continues to develop and as we develop more and more sophisticated methods of dealing with environmental issues. A characteristic of this growth in publications is that more recent books have become more detailed in their analysis of corporate environmental management but also more critical of some aspects of the contemporary approach to environmental issues. Many of the books listed below provide the reader with a good grounding in those contemporary approaches whilst others challenge the reader to think more widely about how we are to reach the ultimate goal of sustainable development. Earlier books tend to be about adapting business practices to include environmental concerns whereas many more recent books have begun to challenge the very way we do business.

Costing the Earth
(Frances Cairncross, The Economist Books, 1991)

This book has become one of the best known books on the relationship between businesses and the protection of the environment. Its more journalistic treatment of issues makes it a very interesting read. The book argues that the right government policies, harnessed to the inventive powers of companies, can unite the goals of the ecologist with the needs of industry and the targets of politicians. The author promotes the use of the market mechanism and economic forces in order to achieve environmental improvement and implicitly argues that businesses can and will take the lead in forming a new environmental agenda.

Changing Course: A Global Business Perspective on Development and the Environment
(Stephan Schmidheiny, The MIT Press, 1992)

This has become one of the most cited texts in the area of business and the environment and has laid the foundations of much of the work which has followed. Espousing the concept of eco-efficiency, it has been influential in defining corporate environmental strategies and practices. Criticised by many, more radical environmentalists, the book nevertheless provides a large number of cases and examples of how businesses are responding to the environmental challenge. It emphasises the need to adapt market forces to bring about changes in production, investment and trade which combine the objectives of economic growth and environmental protection.

Environmental Strategies for Industry: International Perspectives on Research Needs and Policy Implications
(Kurt Fischer and Johan Schot, Island Press, 1993)

This book provides case studies and discussion of business strategies that explore industry's response to environmental concerns. It analyses the process of 'greening' in industry and includes chapters on organizational theory, cleaner technology, waste reduction, pollution prevention, technology and product stewardship. It ends by identifying a range of research needs that are still pertinent today.

Accounting for the Environment
(Rob Gray, Paul Chapman Publishing, 1993)

The wide coverage of topics in this book is a little obscured by the title and it does offer a good overview of issues related to business and the environment. However, its main focus is on seeking to answer the question 'what can/should accountants do in response to the developing environmental agenda?' The book lays out the best accounting and reporting practices with regard to the environment and provides ideas for experimentation and future development.

Managing the Environment
(John Beaumont, Lene Pedersen and Brian Whitaker, Butterworth-Heinemann, 1993)

This book offers an interdisciplinary and multi-functional management approach to the environmental issues affecting business practice. It considers the impact of environmental issues on various management functions including accounting and finance, marketing, production and operations, information systems and organizational behaviour and culture. A number of case studies form an important part of the book.

Environmental Management and Business Strategy
(Richard Welford and Andrew Gouldson, Pitman Publishing, 1993)

This is a solid introductory text book for those interested in how to improve the environmental performance of businesses. It includes chapters on the legislative framework, environmental impact assessment, environmental reviews and audits, environmental management systems, green marketing, eco-labelling, SMEs and regional development strategies. It equips readers with a knowledge of the issues surrounding environmental management and an understanding of the tools for environmental improvement.

Cases in Environmental Management and Business Strategy
(Richard Welford, Pitman Publishing, 1994)

This is a companion text to the book by Welford and Gouldson. After a review of the essential elements of environmental management it illustrates approaches to environmental improvement through a number of in-depth case studies. The cases include VW–Audi, IBM UK, British Telecom, The Body Shop International, the food retailing industry and the Avonmore–Avoca Regional Environmental

Management System. Coverage includes environmental management systems, life cycle assessment, environmental auditing, green marketing and the SME sector.

Green, Inc: A Guide to Business and the Environment
(Frances Cairncross, Earthscan, 1995)

Following on from her previous book *Costing the Earth*, Frances Cairncross argues that economic growth does not have to be at the expense of environmental protection. It is argued that governments, business and the environmental movement should grasp the opportunities available for making the environment a profit opportunity. Written in a clear and forceful style, Cairncross offers a checklist for action, which is of considerable practical value for practitioners.

Environmental Strategy and Sustainable Development
(Richard Welford, Routledge, 1995)

This is one of the very few books which tackles the relationship between business and sustainable development, arguing that traditional approaches to environmental management cannot, on their own, deliver sustainability. At the core of the book a distinction is made between environmental auditing, ecological auditing and auditing for sustainability. It is argued that a more sustainable company is an ethical company which places greater emphasis on issues such as equity, futurity and education. It suggests that green marketing must represent a radical departure from traditional marketing and that economic development strategies must look towards modern forms of bioregionalism.

Environmental Management Systems
(David Hunt and Catherine Johnson, McGraw-Hill, 1995)

This text takes an in-depth look at mainstream environmental management systems. It covers the requirements of BS7750, ISO14001 and the European Union eco-management and audit scheme. It provides detailed guidance for the implementation of an EMS covering such topics as carrying out a preparatory review, evaluating environmental effects, setting sound objectives, and establishing control and monitoring systems. It describes a framework that facilitates meeting regulatory requirements, improving environmental performance, minimising waste and saving costs.

Environmentally Sustainable Business: A Local and Regional Perspective
(Peter Roberts, Paul Chapman Publishing, 1995)

This book differs from many others because it provides us with a new perspective based around spatial factors, stressing local and regional issues which have often been somewhat neglected. The author combines his considerable expertise relating to regional and local planning and development with a very clear consideration of the challenge of integrating business operations with care for the environment. He shows that geography matters because it exerts a considerable influence upon the evolution of economic activities. The text is supported by case studies and other illustrative material and together they explore ways of improving the environmental performance and management of business and the role that such activities can play in local and regional development.

Corporate Environmental Management: Systems and Strategies
(Richard Welford, Earthscan, 1996)

This definitive text deals with the tools of environmental management and provides description, analysis and a critique of the mainstream approaches to corporate environmental management. Chapters cover environmental management systems, systems standards, environmental policies and Charters, environmental auditing, life cycle assessment, environmental reporting, the measurement of environmental performance, local environmental initiatives and auditing for sustainability. It stresses the systems based approach to achieving environmental improvement but also examines the limitations of that approach. It is perhaps the most detailed analysis of corporate environmental strategies to date.

JOURNALS

There is an increasing number of journals which now deal exclusively or partially with issues associated with business and the environment. This reflects the rapidly increasing interest in these issues. The advantage of journal articles is that they often provide a much more in-depth analysis of particular management tools and cases than is possible in more general books. Many mainstream management journals include articles about corporate environmental management but the leading journals with a particular remit to examine environmental issues are listed here.

Business Strategy and the Environment
(Editor: Richard Welford)
ERP Environment in association with John Wiley & Sons

This is the leading academic journal dealing with business and the environment. Published four times a year, it has in-depth articles on a range of issues. It has a rigorous review procedure providing readers with expert analysis and commentary on contemporary issues. It is particularly useful to researchers and academics but is still accessible to practitioners working in this field. It has a strong international flavour and carries traditional articles, shorter 'briefing' papers, policy and practice reviews, book reviews and the newsletter of the Greening of Industry Network.

Eco-Management and Auditing
(Editor: Richard Welford)
ERP Environment in association with John Wiley & Sons

This is a practitioner-based journal but all papers go through a review procedure. It publishes shorter articles of a practical nature covering issues such as environmental management systems, environmental reporting, accounting and the environment, environmental auditing, waste management and cleaner technology. Published three times a year, it often contains practical case studies, industry analysis and country specific profiles.

Sustainable Development
(Editor: Adil Khan)
ERP Environment in association with John Wiley & Sons

This is a wide ranging international journal dealing with all aspects of sustainable development. However, it regularly has contributions with a business focus. Published three times a year, it also has interesting papers on defining sustainable development, issues relating to developing countries and a strong focus on issues related to Local Agenda 21. It has a strong link with the International Sustainable Development Research Network (ISDRN) and publishes the annual conference report of the ISDRN conference.

Business and Environment Abstracts
(Editors: Michael Brophy and Richard Starkey)
ERP Environment in association with John Wiley & Sons

This is an invaluable resource for researchers and anyone trying to keep up with the rapidly expanding literature in the field of business and the environment. It is published twice a year and is made up of general review articles and abstracts of articles recently published.

Greener Management International
(Editor: Grant Ledgerwood)
Greenleaf Publishing

This is a journal of corporate environmental strategy and practice which aims to offer articles for both researchers and practitioners. Its coverage includes operations management, logistics, environmental management systems, environmental auditing, life cycle assessment, corporate communications and industry profiles. Four issues a year provide a regular and useful review of recent events, articles and reviews.

Total Quality Environmental Management
(Editors: Chris FitzGerald and John Willig)
John Wiley and Sons

Four issues of this journal are published every year, targeted at environmental managers, engineers, quality directors and other environmental professionals. It publishes practical articles on a range of issues including environmental management systems, environmental auditing and reporting, waste minimization and industry profiles.

Journal of Cleaner Production
(Editor: Don Huisingh)
Butterworth-Heinemann

This journal provides an interdisciplinary, international forum for the exchange of information on the technologies, concepts and policies designed to help to ensure a safer environment. It aims to encourage industrial innovation and the implementation of new cleaner technologies. Four issues a year provide original research papers, shorter papers, notes and comments, reviews and literature surveys.

Pollution Prevention Review

(Editor: Ann Graham)
Executive Enterprises Publications

The aim of this quarterly journal is to provide pollution prevention specialists, researchers and concerned managers in industry with relatively short, practical articles and case studies. The journal has an American bias which provides readers with updates on legislation, policy, reviews and details of other resources.

Index